Applied Time Series Modelling and Forecasting

Applied Time Series Modelling and Forecasting

Richard Harris and Robert Sollis

Durham University

WILEY

Telephone (+44) 1243 779777

Email (for orders and customer service enquiries): cs-books@wiley.co.uk
Visit our Home Page on www.wileyeurope.com or www.wiley.com

Reprinted 2005

Other Wiley Editorial Offices

John Wiley & Sons Inc., 111 River Street, Hoboken, NJ 07030, USA

Jossey-Bass, 989 Market Street, San Francisco, CA 94103-1741, USA

Wiley-VCH Verlag GmbH, Boschstr. 12, D-69469 Weinheim, Germany

John Wiley & Sons Australia Ltd, 33 Park Road, Milton, Queensland 4064, Australia

John Wiley & Sons (Asia) Pte Ltd, 2 Clementi Loop #02-01, Jin Xing Distripark, Singapore 129809

John Wiley & Sons Canada Ltd, 22 Worcester Road, Etobicoke, Ontario, Canada M9W 1L1

Wiley also publishes its books in a variety of electronic formats. Some content that appears in print may not be available in electronic books.

Library of Congress Cataloging-in-Publication Data

A catalogue record for this book is available from the Library of Congress

British Library Cataloguing in Publication Data

A catalogue record for this book is available from the British Library

ISBN 10: 0-470-84443-4 (PB)   ISBN 13: 978-0-470-84443-4 (PB)

Project management by Originator, Gt Yarmouth, Norfolk (typeset in 10/12pt Times)

Contents

Preface

This book is intended for students and others working in the field of economics who want a relatively non-technical introduction to applied time series econometrics and forecasting involving non-stationary data. The emphasis is on the why and how, and as much as possible we confine technical material to boxes or point to the relevant sources that provide more details. It is based on an earlier book by one of the present authors entitled *Using Cointegration Analysis in Econometric Modelling* (see Harris, 1995), but as well as updating the material covered in the earlier book, there are two major additions involving panel tests for unit roots and cointegration, and the modelling and forecasting of financial time series.

We have tried to incorporate into this book as many of the latest techniques in the area as possible and to provide as many examples as necessary to illustrate them. To help the reader, one of the major data sets used is supplied in the Statistical Appendix, which also includes many of the key tables of critical values used for various tests involving unit roots and cointegration. There is also a website for the book (http://www.wiley.co.uk/harris) from which can be retrieved various other data sets we have used, as well as econometric code for implementing some of the more recent procedures covered in the book.

We have no doubt made some mistakes in interpreting the literature, and we would like to thank in advance those readers who might wish to point them out to us. We would also like to acknowledge the help we have received from those who have supplied us with their econometric programming code, data, and guidance on the procedures they have published in articles and books. Particular thanks are due to Peter Pedroni (for his generous offer of time in amending and providing software programmes for Chapter 7), and Robert Shiller for allowing us to use his Standard & Poor's (S&P) Composite data in Chapter 8. We would also like to thank Jean-Phillipe Peters for help with the *G@RCH 2.3* programme, also used in Chapter 8. Others who generously provided software include Jorg Breitung, David Harvey, Robert Kunst and

Johan Lyhagen. Of course, nobody but ourselves take responsibility for the contents of this book.

We also thank Steve Hardman at Wiley, for his willingness to support this project and his patience with seeing it to fruition. Finally, permission from the various authors and copyright holders to reproduce the Statistical Tables is gratefully acknowledged.

1
Introduction and Overview

Since the mid-1980's applied economists attempting to estimate time series econometric models have been aware of certain difficulties that arise when unit roots are present in the data. To ignore this fact and to proceed to estimate a regression model containing non-stationary variables at best ignores important information about the underlying (statistical and economic) processes generating the data, and at worst leads to nonsensical (or spurious) results. For this reason, it is incumbent on the applied researcher to test for the presence of unit roots and if they are present (and the evidence suggests that they generally are) to use appropriate modelling procedures. De-trending is not appropriate (Chapter 2) and simply differencing the data[1] to remove the non-stationary (stochastic) trend is only part of the answer. While the use of differenced variables will avoid the spurious regression problem, it will also remove any long-run information. In modelling time series data we need to retain this long-run information, but to ensure that it reflects the co-movement of variables due to the underlying equilibrating tendencies of economic forces, rather than those due to common, but unrelated, time trends in the data.

Modelling the long run when the variables are non-stationary is an expanding area of econometrics (both theoretical and applied). It is still fairly new in that while it is possible to find antecedents in the literature dating back to, for example, the seminal work of Sargan (1964) on early forms of the error-correction model, it was really only in 1986 (following the March special issue of the *Oxford Bulletin of Economics and Statistics*) that cointegration became a familiar term in the literature.[2] It is also a continually expanding area, as witnessed by the number of articles that have been published since the mid-1980s. There have been and continue to be major new developments.

[1] That is, converting x_t to Δx_t, where $\Delta x_t = x_t - x_{t-1}$, will remove the non-stationary trend from the variable (and if it does not, because the trend is increasing over time, then x_t will need to be differenced twice, etc.).

[2] Work on testing for unit roots developed a little earlier (e.g., the PhD work of Dickey, 1976 and Fuller, 1976).

The purpose of this book is to present to the reader those techniques that have generally gained most acceptance (including the latest developments surrounding such techniques) and to present them in as non-technical a way as possible while still retaining an understanding of what they are designed to do. Those who want a more rigorous treatment to supplement the current text are referred to Banerjee, Dolado, Galbraith and Hendry (1993) and Johansen (1995a) in the first instance and then of course to the appropriate journals. It is useful to begin by covering some introductory concepts, leaving a full treatment of the standard econometric techniques relating to time series data to other texts (see, for example, Hendry, 1995). This is followed by an overview of the remainder of the book, providing a route map through the topics covered starting with a simple discussion of long-run and short-run models (Chapter 2) and then proceeding through to estimating these models using multivariate techniques (Chapters 5 and 6). We then cover panel data tests for unit roots and cointegration (Chapter 7) before concluding with an in-depth look at modelling and forecasting financial time series (Chapter 8).

SOME INITIAL CONCEPTS

This section will review some of the most important concepts and ideas in time series modelling, providing a reference point for later on in the book. A fuller treatment is available in a standard text such as Harvey (1990). We begin with the idea of a data-generating process (hereafter d.g.p.), in terms of autoregressive and moving-average representations of dynamic processes. This will also necessitate some discussion of the properties of the error term in a regression model and statistical inferences based on the assumption that such residuals are 'white noise'.

Data-generating Processes

As economists, we only have limited knowledge about the economic processes that determine the observed data. Thus, while models involving such data are formulated by economic theory and then tested using econometric techniques, it has to be recognized that theory in itself is not enough. For instance, theory may provide little evidence about the processes of adjustment, which variables are exogenous and indeed which are irrelevant or constant for the particular model under investigation (Hendry, Pagan and Sargan, 1984). A contrasting approach is based on statistical theory, which involves trying to characterize the statistical processes whereby the data were generated.

We begin with a very simple stationary univariate model observed over the sequence of time $t = 1, \ldots, T$:

$$\left.\begin{aligned} y_t &= \rho y_{t-1} + u_t \qquad |\rho| < 1 \\ \text{or} \quad (1 - \rho L)y_t &= u_t \end{aligned}\right\} \tag{1.1}$$

where L is the lag operator such that $Ly_t = y_{t-1}$. This statistical model states that the variable y_t is generated by its own past together with a disturbance (or residual) term u_t. The latter represents the influence of all other variables excluded from the model, which are presumed to be random (or unpredictable) such that u_t has the following statistical properties: its expected value (or mean) is zero $[E(u_t) = 0]$ fluctuations around this mean value are not growing or declining over time (i.e., it has constant variance denoted $E(u_t^2) = \sigma^2$); and it is uncorrelated with its own past $[E(u_t u_{t-i}) = 0]$. Having u_t in (1.1) allows y_t to also be treated as a random (stochastic) variable.[3]

This model can be described as a d.g.p., if the observed realization of y_t over time is simply one of an infinite number of possible outcomes, each dependent on drawing a sequence of random numbers u_t from an appropriate (e.g., standard normal) distribution.[4] Despite the fact that in practice only a single sequence of y_t is observed, in theory any number of realizations is possible over the same time period. Statistical inferences with respect to this model are now possible based on its underlying probability distribution.

The model given by equation (1.1) is described as a first-order autoregressive (AR) model or more simply an AR(1) model. It is straightforward to derive the statistical properties of a series generated by this model. First, note that (1.1) can be rearranged as:

$$y_t = [1/(1 - \rho L)]u_t \tag{1.2}$$

It can be shown that $1/(1 - \rho L) = (1 + \rho L + \rho^2 L^2 + \rho^3 L^3 \ldots)$, and therefore the AR(1) model (1.1) can be converted to an infinite order moving average of the lagged disturbance terms:[5]

$$y_t = u_t + \rho u_{t-1} + \rho^2 u_{t-2} + \cdots \tag{1.3}$$

Taking expectations gives $E(y_t) = 0$ (since $E(u_t) = 0$ for all t), thus the mean of y_t, when the d.g.p. is (1.1), is zero. The formula for the variance of y_t is $\text{var}(y_t) = E[\{y_t - E(y_t)\}]^2$. Since in this case the mean of y_t is zero, the formula for the variance simplifies to $E(y_t^2)$. Using this gives:

$$\begin{aligned} E(y_t^2) &= E(\rho y_{t-1} + u_t)^2 \\ &= E(\rho^2 y_{t-1}^2) + E(u_t^2) + 2\rho E(y_{t-1} u_t) \\ &= \rho^2 E(y_{t-1}^2) + \sigma^2 \end{aligned} \tag{1.4}$$

[3] In contrast, y_t would be a deterministic (or fixed) process if it were characterized as $y_t = \rho y_{t-1}$, which, given an initial starting value of y_0, results in y_t being known with complete certainty each time period. Note also that deterministic variables (such as an intercept of time trend) can also be introduced into (1.1).

[4] The standard normal distribution is of course appropriate in the sense that it has a zero mean and constant variance and each observation in uncorrelated with any other.

[5] This property is known as *invertibility*.

Repeatedly substituting for $E(y_{t-1}^2)$ on the right-hand side of (1.4) leads to a geometric series that converges to $E(y_t^2) = \sigma^2/(1 - \rho^2)$.

The autocovariance of a time series is a measure of dependence between observations. It is straightforward to derive the autocovariance for an AR(1) process. Generally, the autocovariance is $\gamma_k = E[(y_t - \mu)(y_{t-k} - \mu)]$ for $k \neq 0$, where μ represents the mean of y_t. When y_t is generated by (1.1), since $E(y_t) = 0$, the autocovariance formula simplifies to $E(y_t y_{t-k})$. Using this formula, it can be shown that the kth autocovariance is given by:

$$\gamma_k = \rho^k \gamma_0 \qquad k = 1, 2 \ldots \tag{1.5}$$

The autocorrelation coefficient for a time series is a standardized measure of the autocovariance restricted to lie between -1 and 1. The kth autocorrelation is given by:

$$\frac{E[(y_t - \mu)(y_{t-k} - \mu)]}{E[(y_t - \mu)^2]} = \frac{\gamma_k}{\gamma_0} \tag{1.6}$$

Thus the kth autocorrelation when y_t is generated by (1.1) is given by ρ^k. Note that the autocovariances and autocorrelation coefficients discussed above are population parameters. In practice, the sample equivalents of these amounts are employed. In particular they are used when specifying time series models for a particular data set and evaluating how appropriate those models are, as in the Box–Jenkins procedure for time series analysis (Box and Jenkins, 1970). These authors were the first to develop a structured approach to time series modelling and forecasting. The Box–Jenkins approach recognizes the importance of using information on the autocovariances and autocorrelations of the series to help identify the correct time series model to estimate, and when evaluating the fitted disturbances from this model.

Another simple model that is popular in time series econometrics is the AR(1) model with a constant:

$$y_t = \delta + \rho y_{t-1} + u_t \qquad |\rho| < 1 \tag{1.7}$$

Adding a constant to (1.1) allows y_t to have a non-zero mean. Specifically, the mean of y_t when (1.7) is the d.g.p. is given by $E(y_t) = \delta/(1 - \rho)$. To see this note that (1.7) can be written as:

$$(1 - \rho L)y_t = \delta + u_t \tag{1.8}$$

so that

$$\begin{aligned} y_t &= [1/(1 - \rho L)](\delta + u_t) \\ &= (1 + \rho + \rho^2 + \cdots)\delta + (u_t + \rho u_{t-1} + \rho^2 u_{t-2} + \cdots) \end{aligned} \tag{1.9}$$

Since we are assuming that $E(u_t) = 0$, the expected value of (1.9) simplifies to:

$$E(y_t) = (1 + \rho + \rho^2 + \cdots)\delta \tag{1.10}$$

which is a geometric series that converges to $E(y_t) = \delta/(1 - \rho)$. To calculate the variance of y_t when the d.g.p. is (1.7), it is easiest to work with the de-meaned series $x_t = y_t - \mu$. We can then rewrite (1.7) as:

$$x_t = \rho x_{t-1} + u_t \tag{1.11}$$

It follows that $\text{var}(y_t) = E(x_t^2)$, and that $E(x_t^2) = \sigma^2/(1 - \rho^2)$. Therefore y_t generated by the AR(1) model with a constant has a mean of $E(y_t) = \delta/(1 - \rho)$ and a variance of $\text{var}(y_t) = \sigma^2/(1 - \rho^2)$.

The simple time series model (1.1) can be extended to let y_t depend on past values up to a lag length of p:

$$\left.\begin{array}{ll} & y_t = \rho_1 y_{t-1} + \rho_2 y_{t-2} + \cdots + \rho_p y_{t-p} + u_t \\ \text{or} & \text{A(L)}y_t = u_t \end{array}\right\} \tag{1.12}$$

where A(L) is the polynomial lag operator $1 - \rho_1 L - \rho_2 L^2 - \cdots - \rho_p L^p$. The d.g.p. in (1.12) is described as a pth-order AR model.[6] The mean, variance and covariance of AR(p) processes when $p > 1$ can also be computed algebraically. For example, for the AR(2) model with a constant:

$$y_t = \delta + \rho_1 y_{t-1} + \rho_2 y_{t-2} + u_t \tag{1.13}$$

assuming $\rho_1 + \rho_2 < 1$ and that u_t is defined as before, the mean of y_t is $E(y_t) = \delta/(1 - \rho_1 - \rho_2)$ and the variance of y_t is:[7]

$$\text{var}(y_t) = \frac{(1 - \rho_2)\sigma^2}{(1 + \rho_2)(1 - \rho_1 - \rho_2)(1 + \rho_1 - \rho_2)} \tag{1.14}$$

An alternative to the AR model is to specify the dependence of y_t on its own past as a moving average (MA) process, such as the following first-order MA model:

$$y_t = u_t + \theta u_{t-1} \qquad |\theta| < 1 \tag{1.15}$$

or a model with past values up to a lag length of q:

$$\left.\begin{array}{ll} & y_t = u_t + \theta_1 u_{t-1} + \cdots + \theta_q u_{t-q} \\ \text{or} & y_t = B(L)u_t \end{array}\right\} \tag{1.16}$$

where $B(L)$ is the polynomial lag operator $1 + \theta_1 L + \theta_2 L^2 + \cdots + \theta_q L^q$. In practice, lower order MA models have been found to be more useful in econometrics than higher order MA models, and it is straightforward to derive the statistical properties of such models. For example, for the first-order MA model (the MA(1) model) given by (1.15), the mean of y_t is simply $E(y_t) = 0$, while the variance of y_t is $\text{var}(y_t) = (1 + \theta^2)\sigma^2$. It turns out that,

[6] Hence, (1.1) was a first-order AR process.

[7] The importance of the assumption $\rho_1 + \rho_2 < 1$ will become clear in the next chapter.

for the MA(1) model, the first autocovariance is $\gamma_1 = \theta\sigma^2$, but that higher autocovariances are all equal to zero. Similarly, the first autocorrelation coefficient is $\rho_1 = \theta/(1+\theta^2)$, but higher autocorrelation coefficients are all equal to zero.

Finally, it is possible to specify a mixed autoregressive moving average (ARMA) model:

$$A(L)y_t = B(L)u_t \tag{1.17}$$

which is the most flexible d.g.p. for a univariate series. Consider, for example, the ARMA(1, 1) model:

$$y_t = \rho_1 y_{t-1} + u_t + \theta_1 u_{t-1} \qquad |\rho_1| < 1,\ |\theta_1| < 1 \tag{1.18}$$

As with the AR(1) model, note that the ARMA(1, 1) model can be rewritten as an infinite order MA process:

$$\begin{aligned} y_t &= (1+\theta_1 L)(1-\rho_1 L)^{-1} u_t \\ &= \sum_{j=0}^{\infty} \omega_j u_{t-j} \end{aligned} \tag{1.19}$$

Since we are assuming that $E(u_t) = 0$, it follows that $E(y_t) = 0$. The variance of y_t is given by:

$$\begin{aligned} E(y_t^2) &= E[(\rho_1 y_{t-1} + u_t + \theta_1 u_{t-1})^2] \\ &= E(\rho_1^2 y_{t-1}^2 + 2\rho_1\theta_1 y_{t-1}u_{t-1} + u_t^2 + \theta_1^2 u_{t-1}^2) \end{aligned} \tag{1.20}$$

Using the autocovariance notation, the variance of y_t can be written:

$$\gamma_0 = \rho_1^2\gamma_0 + 2\rho_1\theta_1\sigma^2 + \sigma^2 + \theta_1^2\sigma^2 \tag{1.21}$$

which can be rearranged as:

$$\gamma_0 = \left(\frac{1+\theta_1^2+2\rho_1\theta_1}{1-\rho_1^2}\right)\sigma^2 \tag{1.22}$$

The higher autocovariances can be obtained in a similar way, and it can be shown that:

$$\begin{aligned} \gamma_1 &= \rho_1\gamma_0 + \theta_1\sigma^2 \\ &= \left(\frac{(1+\rho_1\theta_1)(\rho_1+\theta_1)}{(1-\rho_1^2)}\right)\sigma^2 \end{aligned} \tag{1.23}$$

$$\gamma_2 = \rho_1\gamma_1 \tag{1.24}$$

and $\gamma_k = \rho_1\gamma_{k-1}$ for $k \geq 2$. The autocorrelation coefficients are given by:

$$\rho_1 = \frac{\gamma_1}{\gamma_0} = \frac{(1+\rho_1\theta_1)(\rho_1+\theta_1)}{(1+\theta_1^2+2\rho_1\theta_1)} \tag{1.25}$$

and $\rho_k = \rho_1\rho_{k-1}$ for $k \geq 2$.

So far the d.g.p. underlying the univariate time series y_t contains no economic information. That is, while it is valid to model y_t as a statistical process (cf. the Box–Jenkins approach), this is of little use if we are looking to establish (causal) linkages between variables. Thus, (1.1) can be generalized to include other variables (both stochastic, such as x_t, and deterministic, such as an intercept), for example:

$$y_t = \alpha_0 + \gamma_0 x_t + \alpha_1 y_{t-1} + u_t \tag{1.26}$$

Since x_t is stochastic, let its underlying d.g.p. be given by:

$$x_t = \xi x_{t-1} + \varepsilon_t \qquad |\xi| < 1 \quad \text{and} \quad \varepsilon_t \sim \text{IN}(0, \sigma_\varepsilon^2) \qquad (1.27)^8$$

If u_t and ε_t are not correlated, we can state that $E(u_t\varepsilon_s) = 0$ for all t and s, and then it is possible to treat x_t *as if* it were fixed for the purposes of estimating (1.26). That is, x_t is independent of u_t (denoted $E(x_t u_t) = 0$) and we can treat it as (strongly) exogenous in terms of (1.26) with x_t being said to Granger-cause y_t. Equation (1.26) is called a conditional model in that y_t is conditional on x_t (with x_t determined by the marginal model given in (1.27)). Therefore, for strong exogeneity to exist x_t must not be Granger-caused by y_t, and this leads on to the concept of weak exogeneity.

Note, if (1.27) is reformulated as:

$$x_t = \xi_1 x_{t-1} + \xi_2 y_{t-1} + \varepsilon_t \tag{1.28}$$

then $E(x_t u_t) = 0$ is retained, but since past values of y_t now determine x_t the latter can only be considered *weakly* exogenous in the conditional model (1.26).[9]

Lastly, weak exogeneity is a necessary condition for super-exogeneity, but the latter also requires that the conditional model is structurally invariant; that is, changes in the distribution of the marginal model for x_t (equation (1.27) or (1.28)) do not affect the parameters in (1.26). In particular, if there are regime shifts in x_t then these must be invariant to (α_i, γ_0) in (1.26).

All three concepts of exogeneity will be tested later, but it is useful at this point to provide a brief example of testing for super-exogeneity in order to make the concept clearer.[10] Assuming that known institutional (e.g., policy)

[8] Note that $\varepsilon_t \sim \text{IN}(0, \sigma_\varepsilon^2)$ states that the residual term is independently and normally distributed with zero mean and constant variance σ_ε^2. The fact that σ_ε^2 is multiplied by a (not shown) value of 1 means that ε_t is not autocorrelated with its own past.

[9] That is, x_t still causes y_t, but not in the Granger sense, because of the lagged values of y_t determining x_t. For a review of these concepts of weak and strong exogeneity, together with their full properties, see Engle, Hendry and Richard (1983).

[10] This example is based on Hendry (1995, p. 537). Further discussion of super-exogeneity can be found in Engle and Hendry (1993), Hendry (1995, p. 172) and Favero (2001, p. 146).

and historical shifts (shocks) can be identified that affected x_t, it should be possible to construct a dummy variable (e.g., POL_t) that augments (1.28):

$$x_t = \xi_1 x_{t-1} + \xi_2 y_{t-1} + \xi_3 \text{POL}_t + \varepsilon_t \tag{1.28*}$$

Assuming that the estimate of $\hat{\xi}_3$ is (highly) significant in determining x_t, then super-exogeneity can be tested by including POL_t in the conditional model (1.26), and if this dummy is significant then super-exogeneity is rejected.[11]

The importance of these three concepts of exogeneity are discussed in Favero (2001, p. 146): (i) if we are primarily interested in inference on the (α_i, γ_0) parameters in (1.26), then if x_t is weakly exogenous we only need to estimate (1.26) and not also (1.28); (ii) if we wish to dynamically simulate y_t and x_t is strongly exogenous, again we only need to estimate (1.26) and not also (1.28); and (iii) if the objective of modelling y_t is for econometric policy evaluation, we only need to estimate the conditional model (1.26) if x_t has the property of being super-exogenous. The latter is a necessary condition to avoid the Lucas Critique (see Lucas, 1976). For example, suppose y_t is a policy variable of government (e.g., the money supply) and x_t is the instrument used to set its outcome (e.g., the interest rate), then x_t must be super-exogenous to avoid the Lucas Critique. Otherwise, setting x_t would change the policy model (the parameters of 1.26), and the policy outcome would not be what the model (1.26) had predicted.[12]

As with the univariate case, the d.g.p. denoted by (1.26) can be generalized to obtain what is known as an autoregressive distributed lag (ADL) model:

$$A(L)y_t = B(L)x_t + u_t \tag{1.29}$$

where the polynomial lag operators $A(L)$ and $B(L)$ have already been defined.[13] Extending to the multivariate case is straightforward, replacing y_t and x_t by vectors of variables, $\mathbf{y}_t$ and $\mathbf{x}_t$.

The great strength of using an equation like (1.29) as the basis for econometric modelling is that it provides a good first approximation to the (unknown) d.g.p. Recall the above arguments that theory usually has little

[11] That is, its exclusion from (1.26) would alter the estimates of (α_i, γ_0). Note also that the residuals $\hat{\varepsilon}_t$ from (1.28*) should not be a significant determinant of y_t in equation (1.26).

[12] For example, suppose the government uses the immediate history of y_t to determine what it wishes current y_t to be; hence, it alters x_t to achieve this policy outcome. However, economic agents also 'know' the model (the policy rule) underlying (1.26) and (1.28*). Thus when POL_t changes, agents alter their behaviour (the parameters of 1.26 change) since they have anticipated the intended impact of government policy. Econometric models that fail to separate out the expectations formulation by economic agents from the behavioural relationships in the model itself will be subject to Lucas's critique.

[13] While we could further extend this to allow for an MA error process, it can be shown that a relatively simple form of the MA error process can be approximated by sufficiently large values of p and q in (1.29).

to say about the form of the (dynamic) adjustment process (which (1.29) is flexible enough to capture), nor about which variables are exogenous (this model can also be used as a basis for testing for exogeneity). In fact, Hendry et al. (1984) argue that the process of econometric modelling is an attempt to match the unknown d.g.p. with a validly specified econometric model, and thus '... economic theory restrictions on the analysis are essential; and while the data are the result of economic behaviour, the actual statistical properties of the observables corresponding to y and z are also obviously relevant to correctly analysing their empirical relationship. In a nutshell, measurement without theory is as valueless as the converse is non-operational.' In practical terms, and according to the Hendry-type approach, the test of model adequacy is whether the model is *congruent* with the data evidence, which in a single equation model is defined in terms of the statistical properties of the model (e.g., a 'white noise' error term and parameters that are constant over time) and whether the model is consistent with the theory from which it is derived and with the data it admits. Finally, congruency requires the model to encompass rival models.[14]

Role of the Error Term u_t and Statistical Inference

As stated above, the error term u_t represents the influence of all other variables excluded from the model that are presumed to be random (or unpredictable) such that u_t has the following statistical properties: its mean is zero $[E(u_t) = 0]$; it has constant variance $[E(u_t^2) = \sigma^2]$; and it is uncorrelated with its own past $[E(u_t u_{t-i}) = 0]$. To this we can add that the determining variable(s) in the model, assuming they are stochastic, must be independent of the error term $[E(x_t u_t) = 0]$.[15] If these assumptions hold, then it is shown in standard texts like Johnston (1984) that estimators like the ordinary least squares (OLS) estimator will lead to unbiased estimates of the parameter coefficients of the model (indeed, OLS is the best linear unbiased estimator). If it is further assumed that u_t is drawn from the (multivariate) normal distribution, then this sufficies to establish inference procedures for testing hypotheses involving the parameters of the model, based on χ^2, t- and F-tests and their associated probability distributions.

Thus, testing to ensure that $u_t \sim \text{IN}(0, \sigma_u^2)$ (i.e., an independently distributed random 'white noise' process drawn from the normal distribution) is an essential part of the modelling process. Its failure leads to invalid inference

[14] A good discussion of congruency and modelling procedures is given in Doornik and Hendry (2001).

[15] Although not considered above, clearly this condition is not met in (1.1) and similar dynamic models, where y_{t-1} is a predetermined explanatory variable, since $E(y_t u_{t-i}) \neq 0$ for $i \geq 1$. However, it is possible to show by applying the Mann–Wald theorem (Johnston, 1984, p. 362) that with a sufficiently large sample size this will not lead to bias when estimating the parameter coefficients of the regression model.

procedures unless alternative estimators (e.g., generalized least squares—GLS—or systems estimators) and/or alternative probability distributions (such as the Dickey–Fuller distribution) are invoked.

FORECASTING

In applied economics, particularly applied macroeconomics and financial econometrics, often the main reason for estimating an econometric model is so that the estimated model can be used to compute forecasts of the series. While any type of econometric model can be used to compute forecasts (e.g., multivariate regression model, ADL model), it is univariate time series models such as the AR and ARMA models that have proved to be the most popular. The forecasting theory for univariate time series models has long been established (see in particular the work of Box and Jenkins, 1970) and univariate Box–Jenkins methods have continued to be popular with econometricians. Granger and Newbold (1986) set out a number of reasons why univariate forecasting methods in particular deserve consideration. Perhaps the most pertinent of these is the first reason they give:

> They are quick and inexpensive to apply, and may well produce forecasts of sufficient quality for the purposes at hand. The cost of making particular forecasting errors should always be balanced against the cost of *producing* forecasts, for it is hardly worth expanding large resources to obtain a relatively small increase in forecast accuracy if the payoff, in terms of improved decision making is likely to be only marginally beneficial (p. 151).

This is an important point, not just for forecasting but for econometrics as a whole. There are usually a number of alternative models or techniques in econometrics that could be employed to undertake any one task, ranging from the simple to the very complex—and the complex techniques are typically more costly to use than the simple. Granger and Newbold (1986) sensibly argue that only when the benefits of the complex techniques outweigh the additional costs of using them should they be the preferred choice. It is often the case that forecasts made from simple linear univariate models such as AR models are more accurate, or are only marginally less accurate than forecasts from more complex alternatives.

In this section we will briefly review how to compute optimal forecasts from some of the models discussed so far, beginning with the most simple univariate time series model—the AR(1) model. Let the h-steps ahead forecast of a time series y_{T+h} be represented by $\hat{y}_{T+h}$, where T is the sample size (thus we assume forecasts of the series are from the end of the sample onward). The forecast error $e_{T+h} = y_{T+h} - \hat{y}_{T+h}$ plays a vital role in the literature on forecasting. Note in particular that the optimal forecast of y_{T+h} is the forecast that minimizes the expected value of the squared forecast error $E[e^2_{T+h}]$. It can be proved that the h-steps ahead forecast that minimizes the expected value of the squared forecast error is simply the conditional expectation of y_{T+h}:[16]

$$\hat{y}_{T+h} = E(y_{T+h} \mid y_T, y_{T-1}, \ldots, y_1) \tag{1.30}$$

which can be written more concisely as:

$$\hat{y}_{T+h} = E(y_{T+h} \mid \Omega_T) \tag{1.31}$$

where Ω_T represents the information set at time T. The forecast function will include unknown population parameters, and in practice these parameters are replaced with their estimated values.

If we assume that the d.g.p. is the AR(1) model given by equation (1.1), the optimal h-steps ahead forecast is given by:

$$\begin{aligned}\hat{y}_{T+h} &= E(\rho y_{T+h-1} + u_{T+h} \mid \Omega_T) \\ &= \rho y_{T+h-1}\end{aligned} \tag{1.32}$$

where Ω_T is the relevant information set at time T. So in the case of a 1-step ahead forecast ($h = 1$), the optimal forecast is simply ρy_T. Forecasts greater than 1-step ahead are computed recursively. So, for example, in the case of 2-steps ahead forecasts, the optimal forecast is:

$$\begin{aligned}\hat{y}_{T+2} &= E(\rho y_{T+1} + u_{T+2} \mid \Omega_T) \\ &= E(\rho\rho y_T + u_{T+2} \mid \Omega_T) \\ &= \rho^2 y_T\end{aligned} \tag{1.33}$$

and for 3-steps ahead forecasts $\hat{y}_{T+3} = \rho^3 y_T$. It follows that the forecasting function for the optimal h-steps ahead forecast (1.32) can be rewritten:

$$\hat{y}_{T+h} = \rho^h y_T \tag{1.34}$$

Clearly, assuming $|\rho| < 1$, as $h \to \infty$ the forecast of y_{T+h} converges to zero. In fact, for this d.g.p., as $h \to \infty$ the h-steps ahead forecast of y_{T+h} converges to the mean of y_t, which in this case is zero. If the d.g.p. is the AR(1) model with a constant:

$$y_t = \delta + \rho y_{t-1} + u_t \tag{1.35}$$

where $|\rho| < 1$ and $u_t \sim \text{IID}(0, 1)$, then y_t has a non-zero mean equal to $\delta/(1 - \rho)$. The 1-step ahead forecast is given by:

$$\begin{aligned}\hat{y}_{T+1} &= E(\delta + \rho y_T + u_{T+1} \mid \Omega_T) \\ &= \delta + \rho y_T\end{aligned} \tag{1.36}$$

[16] The conditional expectation of y_{T+h} is the expected value of y_{T+h} conditioning on all information known about y at time T.

and the h-step ahead forecast is given by:

$$\hat{y}_{T+h} = (\rho^{h-1} + \rho^{h-2} + \cdots + \rho + 1)\delta + \rho^h y_T \tag{1.37}$$

Again, for this d.g.p., as $h \to \infty$ the forecast converges to the mean of y_t. This can be seen more clearly by noting that (1.37) is a geometric series, and as $h \to \infty$ it converges to:

$$\hat{y}_{T+h} = \frac{\delta}{(1-\rho)} \tag{1.38}$$

Both the forecast functions and properties of the forecasts depend on the exact d.g.p. assumed for y_t. For example, if the d.g.p. is the first-order MA model given by equation (1.15) the 1-step ahead forecast is given by:

$$\begin{aligned} \hat{y}_{T+1} &= E(u_{T+1} + \theta u_T \mid \Omega_T) \\ &= \theta u_T \end{aligned} \tag{1.39}$$

The optimal forecast of the first-order MA process when the forecast horizon is greater than 1-step ahead is just the mean of the series, which in this case is zero:

$$\begin{aligned} \hat{y}_{T+h} &= E(u_{T+h} + \theta u_{T+h-1} \mid \Omega_T) \qquad h > 1 \\ &= 0 \end{aligned} \tag{1.40}$$

For the ARMA(1, 1) model (1.18) the 1-step ahead forecast is given by:

$$\begin{aligned} \hat{y}_{T+1} &= E(\rho_1 y_T + u_{T+1} + \theta_1 u_T \mid \Omega_T) \\ &= \rho_1 y_T + \theta_1 u_T \end{aligned} \tag{1.41}$$

As with the AR model, when the forecast horizon is greater than 1-step ahead, forecasts from an ARMA model are computed recursively. For example, the 2-steps ahead forecast from an ARMA(1, 1) model is given by:

$$\begin{aligned} \hat{y}_{T+2} &= E(\rho_1 y_{T+1} + u_{T+2} + \theta_1 u_{T+1} \mid \Omega_T) \\ &= E[\rho_1(\rho_1 y_T + \theta_1 u_T) + u_{T+2} + \theta_1 u_{T+1} \mid \Omega_T] \\ &= \rho_1^2 y_T + \rho_1 \theta_1 u_T \end{aligned} \tag{1.42}$$

(note that $E(u_{T+2} \mid \Omega_T) = 0$ and $E(\theta_1 u_{T+1} \mid \Omega_T) = 0$), and the h-steps ahead forecast is given by:

$$\hat{y}_{T+h} = \rho_1^h y_T + \rho_1^{h-1}\theta_1 u_T \tag{1.43}$$

Assuming $|\rho_1| < 1$, as $h \to \infty$ again the forecast converges to the mean of the series—zero.

The forecasts referred to above are *point forecasts*; however, since the forecast itself (and forecast error) is a random variable, it is often helpful to compute *interval forecasts*. For the AR(1) model given by equation (1.1) the h-steps ahead forecast error is:

$$\begin{aligned} e_{T+h} &= y_{T+h} - \hat{y}_{T+h} \\ &= \rho y_{T+h-1} + u_{T+h} - \rho^h y_T \end{aligned} \tag{1.44}$$

which after repeated substitution can be rewritten as:

$$e_{T+h} = \rho^h y_T + u_{T+h} + \rho u_{T+h-1} + \cdots + \rho^{h-1} u_{T+1} - \rho^h y_T \tag{1.45}$$

Since it has a mean of zero, the variance of the h-steps ahead forecast error is:

$$E(e_{T+h}^2) = (1 + \rho^2 + \rho^4 + \cdots + \rho^{2h-2})\sigma^2 \tag{1.46}$$

and thus, for a 1-step ahead forecast from the first-order AR model, the variance of the forecast error is simply equal to the variance of the disturbance term u_t. Assuming that the forecast errors are normally distributed we can obtain a 95% confidence interval for the 1-step ahead forecast by computing $\hat{y}_{T+1} \pm 1.96\hat{\sigma}$, where $\hat{\sigma}$ is the estimated value of σ obtained when estimating the parameters of the fitted model. For the h-steps ahead forecast the 95% confidence interval is:

$$\hat{y}_{T+1} \pm 1.96\hat{\sigma}\sqrt{(1 + \rho^2 + \rho^4 + \cdots + \rho^{2h-2})} \tag{1.47}$$

If y_t is generated by the ARMA model (1.17) then computing forecast confidence intervals is more involved. The relevant theory is given in Box 1.1.

As already mentioned, we can compute forecasts from any type of econometric model. Consider a multivariate regression model:

$$y_t = \mathbf{x}_t'\boldsymbol{\beta} + \varepsilon_t \tag{1.48}$$

where $\mathbf{x}_t' = (x_{1t}, x_{2t}, \ldots, x_{kt})$ are explanatory variables and $\boldsymbol{\beta}$ is a vector of parameters of dimension $(k \times 1)$. Subject to the standard assumptions of the classical linear regression model, it can be shown the optimal forecast of y_{T+h} is given by the conditional expectation of y_{T+h}:[17]

$$\hat{y}_{T+h} = \mathbf{x}_{T+h}'\boldsymbol{\beta} \tag{1.49}$$

In practice $\boldsymbol{\beta}$ is replaced by the OLS estimator $\hat{\boldsymbol{\beta}} = (\mathbf{X}'\mathbf{X})^{-1}\mathbf{X}'\mathbf{y}$ where $\mathbf{y} = (y_1, y_2, \ldots, y_T)'$, $\mathbf{X}' = (\mathbf{x}_1', \mathbf{x}_2', \ldots, \mathbf{x}_T')$. Obviously, to compute this forecast requires knowledge of the values of the explanatory variables at time $T + h$. Assuming these values are known, then (1.49) is the appropriate forecasting function. However, if these values are not known, then the appropriate forecasting function is:

$$\hat{y}_{T+h} = \hat{\mathbf{x}}_{T+h}'\hat{\boldsymbol{\beta}} \tag{1.50}$$

[17] See Granger and Newbold (1986, ch. 6, sect. 6.2).

Box 1.1 Interval forecasts for ARMA model

First, note that the ARMA model:

$$A(L)y_t = B(L)u_t \tag{1.1.1}$$

can be rewritten as an infinite-order MA model:

$$\begin{aligned} y_t &= A^{-1}(L)B(L)u_t \\ &= \omega(L)u_t \\ &= \sum_{j=0}^{\infty} \omega_j u_{t-j} \end{aligned} \tag{1.1.2}$$

It follows that y_{T+h} is given by:

$$y_{T+h} = \omega_0 u_{T+h} + \omega_1 u_{T+h-1} + \cdots + \omega_{h-1} u_{T+1} + \sum_{j=0}^{\infty} \omega_{h+j} u_{T-j} \tag{1.1.3}$$

A candidate forecast of y_{T+h} can be written:

$$\hat{y}_{T+h} = \sum_{j=0}^{\infty} \omega_{h+j}^{*} u_{T-j} \tag{1.1.4}$$

in which case the forecast error is:

$$\begin{aligned} e_{T+h} &= y_{T+h} - \hat{y}_{T+h} \\ &= \omega_0 u_{T+h} + \omega_1 u_{T+h-1} + \cdots + \omega_{h-1} u_{T+1} + \sum_{j=0}^{\infty} (\omega_{h+j} - \omega_{h+j}^{*}) u_{T-j} \end{aligned} \tag{1.1.5}$$

It follows that the expected value of the squared forecast error is:

$$E(e_{T+h}^2) = (\omega_0^2 + \omega_1^2 + \cdots + \omega_{h-1}^2)\sigma^2 + \sum_{j=0}^{\infty} (\omega_{h+j} - \omega_{h+j}^{*})^2 \sigma^2 \tag{1.1.6}$$

which is minimized if $\omega_{h+j}^{*} = \omega_{h+j}$. Thus the optimal forecast of y_{T+h} is given by (1.1.4) where $\omega_{h+j}^{*} = \omega_{h+j}$. The variance of the forecast error associated with the optimal forecast is:

$$E(e_{T+h}^2) = (\omega_0^2 + \omega_1^2 + \cdots + \omega_{h-1}^2)\sigma^2 \tag{1.1.7}$$

and so the 95% forecast confidence interval is computed using the formula:

$$\hat{y}_{T+h} \pm 1.96\hat{\sigma}\sqrt{\sum_{j=0}^{h-1} \omega_j^2} \tag{1.1.8}$$

where $\hat{\mathbf{x}}'_{T+h}$ are h-step ahead forecasts of the explanatory variables, which could be obtained via univariate methods.

OUTLINE OF THE BOOK

The next chapter deals with short- and long-run models. Inherent in the distinction is the notion of equilibrium; that is, the long run is a state of equilibrium where there is no inherent tendency to change since economic forces are in balance, while the short run depicts the disequilibrium state. Long-run models are often termed 'static models', but there is no necessity to actually achieve equilibrium at any point in time, even as $t \to \infty$. All that is required is that economic forces move the system toward the equilibrium defined by the long-run relationship posited. Put another way, the static equilibrium needs to be reinterpreted empirically since most economic variables grow over time. Thus, what matters is the idea of a steady-state relationship between variables that are evolving over time. This is the way the term 'equilibrium' is used in this book.

When considering long-run relationships, it becomes necessary to consider the underlying properties of the processes that generate time series variables. That is, we must distinguish between stationary and non-stationary variables, since failure to do so can lead to a problem of spurious regression whereby the results suggest that there are statistically significant long-run relationships between the variables in the regression model—when in fact all that is being obtained is evidence of contemporaneous correlations rather than meaningful causal relations. Simple examples of stationary and non-stationary processes are provided, and it is shown that whether a variable is stationary depends on whether it has a unit root. Comparing stationary and non-stationary variables is also related to the different types of time trends that can be found in variables. Non-stationary variables are shown to contain stochastic (i.e., random) trends, while stationary variables contain deterministic (i.e., fixed) trends. Since random trends in the data can lead to spurious correlations, an example of a spurious regression is given together with some explanations of why this occurs.

This leads naturally to the question of when it is possible to infer a causal long-run relationship(s) between non-stationary time series. The simple answer is: when the variables are cointegrated. The Engle and Granger (1987) definition of cointegration is explained, alongside the economic interpretation of cointegration that states that if two (or more) series are linked to form an equilibrium relationship spanning the long run, then even though the series themselves may contain stochastic trends (i.e., be non-stationary), they will nevertheless move closely together over time and the difference between them is constant (i.e., stationary). Thus the concept of cointegration mimics the existence of a long-run equilibrium to which an economic system converges over time. The absence of cointegration leads back to the problem of spurious regression.

Finally, Chapter 2 discusses short-run (dynamic) models. Simple examples of dynamic models are presented and linked to their long-run steady-state (equilibrium) solutions. It is pointed out that estimating a dynamic equation in the levels of the variables is problematic and differencing the variables is not a solution, since this then removes any information about the long run. The more suitable approach is to convert the dynamic model into an error correction (sometimes called an equilibrium correction) model (ECM), and it is shown that this contains information on both the short-run and long-run properties of the model, with disequilibrium as a process of adjustment to the long-run model. The relationship between ECMs and the concept of cointegration is also explored, to show that if two variables y_t and x_t are cointegrated, then there must exist an ECM (and, conversely, that an ECM generates cointegrated series).

Having discussed the importance of unit roots, the next task (Chapter 3) is to test for their presence in time series data. This begins with a discussion of the Dickey–Fuller (DF) test for a unit root, showing that a t-test of the null hypothesis of non-stationarity is not based on the standard t-distribution, but the non-standard DF distribution. Assumptions about what is the most appropriate d.g.p. for the variable being tested are found to be important when performing the test; that is, should an intercept and trend (i.e., deterministic components) be included in the test equation? Not only does inclusion and exclusion lead to different critical values for the DF test, but they are also important to ensure that the test for a unit root nests both the null hypothesis and the alternative hypothesis. To do this it is necessary to have as many deterministic regressors in the equation used for testing as there are deterministic components in the assumed underlying d.g.p. In order to test what will probably be in practice the most common form of the null hypothesis (that the d.g.p. contains a stochastic trend against the alternative of being trend-stationary), it is necessary to allow both an intercept and a time trend t to enter the regression model used to test for a unit root.

To overcome the problems associated with which (if any) deterministic components should enter the DF test (including problems associated with test power), the sequential testing procedure put forward by Perron (1988) is discussed. Then the DF test is extended to allow for situations when more complicated time series processes underlie the d.g.p. This results in the augmented Dickey–Fuller (ADF) test, which entails adding lagged terms of the dependent variable to the test equation. A question that often arises in applied work is how many extra lagged terms should be added, and there is some discussion of this problem. This in turn leads to a consideration of the power and size properties of the ADF test (i.e., the tendency to under-reject the null when it is false and over-reject the null when it is true, respectively). In finite samples it can be shown that any trend-stationary process can be approximated arbitrarily well by a unit root process and, similarly, any unit root process can be approximated by a trend-stationary process, especially for smaller sample sizes. That is, some unit root processes display finite sample behaviour closer to (stationary) 'white noise' than to a (non-stationary) random walk (while some trend-stationary processes behave more like random walks in finite samples). This implies that a unit root test '... with high power against *any* stationary alternative *necessarily* will have correspondingly high probability of false rejection of the unit root null when applied to near stationary processes' (Blough, 1992, p. 298). This follows from the closeness of the finite sample distribution of any statistic under a particular trend-stationary process and the finite sample distribution of the statistic under a difference-stationary process that approximates the trend-stationary process. Thus, Blough (1992, p. 299) states that there is a trade-off between size and power in that unit root tests must have either high probability of falsely rejecting the null of non-stationarity when the true d.g.p. is a nearly stationary process (poor size properties) or low power against any stationary alternative. This problem of the size and power properties of unit root tests means that any results obtained must be treated with some caution, although we consider some recent improvements that in principle have good size and power properties (cf. Ng and Perron, 2002). We also cover recent developments such as asymmetric tests for unit roots (panel tests are covered in Chapter 7).

There are further 'problems' associated with testing for non-stationarity. A structural break in a series will have serious consequences for the power of the test, if it is ignored. Taking into account the possibility that the intercept and/or slope of the underlying d.g.p. has changed (at an unknown date or dates) can be handled using the testing methods outlined in Perron (1994). Examples are provided and discussed. Finally Chapter 3 discusses testing for seasonal unit roots (including when there are structural breaks) and periodic integration. First of all, it is suggested that where possible seasonally *un*adjusted data should be used when testing for unit roots, since the filters used to adjust for seasonal patterns often distort the underlying properties of the data. In particular, there is a tendency of the DF test to be biased toward rejecting the null hypothesis of non-stationarity substantially less often than it should when seasonally adjusted series are tested. However, using unadjusted data that exhibit strong seasonal patterns opens up the possibility that these series may contain seasonal unit roots (i.e., the seasonal processes themselves are non-stationary). Tests for seasonal unit roots are discussed based on the Hylleberg, Engle, Granger and Yoo (1990) approach, and an example is presented using UK data on consumption, income and wealth. Structural breaks and their impact on seasonal unit root-testing is covered next, and the chapter concludes with a discussion of the situation where observations on a variable y_t can be described by a different model for each quarter, with the result being a periodic autoregressive model.

After testing for unit roots in the data and assuming they are present, the next task is to estimate the long-run relationship(s). Chapter 4 deals with cointegration in single equations, while Chapter 5 considers the possibility of more than one cointegration relationship. The most common single equation approach to testing for cointegration is the Engle–Granger (EG) approach.

This amounts to estimating the static OLS regression model in order to obtain an estimate of the cointegration vector (i.e., the estimate of $\boldsymbol{\beta}$ that establishes a long-run *stationary* relationship between the non-stationary variables in the model). Such a simple and popular approach, which of course ignores any short-run dynamic effects and the issue of endogeneity, is justified on the grounds of the 'superconsistency' of the OLS estimator. The latter states that the OLS estimator of $\boldsymbol{\beta}$ with non-stationary $I(1)$ variables converges to its true value at a much faster rate than the usual OLS estimator with stationary $I(0)$ variables, assuming cointegration (Stock, 1987). The most common form of testing for cointegration is based on an ADF unit root test of the residuals from the OLS regression. The need to use the correct critical values for testing the null hypothesis of no cointegration is discussed along with its dependence on the presence or otherwise of $I(2)$ variables in the regression. A first potential problem with the test procedure is also discussed (namely, the common factor restriction imposed on the long-run model by the ADF test for cointegration). We also consider testing for cointegration using the EG approach with a structural break, using the procedure developed in Gregory and Hansen (1996).

Despite the popularity of the EG approach, there are other serious problems such as small sample bias and the inability to test statistical hypotheses; hence, the advent of alternative testing procedures. Testing whether the speed-of-adjustment coefficient is significant in an error correction model is one alternative, and this is comparable to estimating a dynamic ADL model and testing whether the model converges to a steady-state solution. The major advantage of the ADL approach is that it generally provides unbiased estimates of the long-run model and valid t-statistics (even, on the basis of Monte Carlo evidence, when some of the regressors in the model are endogenous). The fully modified estimator is also discussed, but yields few advantages over the standard OLS estimator.

However, there still remain several disadvantages with a single equation approach. The major problem is that when there are more than two variables in the model, there can be more than one cointegration relationship among these variables. If there is, then adopting a single equation approach is inefficient in the sense that we can only obtain a linear combination of these vectors. However, the drawbacks of the single equation model extend beyond its inability to validly estimate all the long-run relationships between the variables; even if there is only one cointegration relationship, estimating a single equation is potentially inefficient (i.e., it does not lead to the smallest variance against alternative approaches). It is shown that this results from the fact that, unless all the right-hand-side variables in the cointegration vector are weakly exogenous, information is lost by not estimating a system that allows each endogenous variable to appear on the left-hand side of the estimated equations in the multivariate model. Thus, it is only really applicable to use the single equation approach when there is a single unique cointegration vector and when all the right-hand-side variables are weakly exogenous. Before proceeding to the multivariate approach, Chapter 4 considers the short-run (EG) model based on a single equation and in particular gives an example of Hendry's general-to-specific modelling approach using the *PcGive* software package. The chapter then considers testing for seasonal cointegration and periodic cointegration, using single equation techniques and concludes with asymmetric testing for cointegration.

Chapter 5 is given over entirely to the Johansen procedure. Starting with a *vector* error correction model (VECM), it is shown that this contains information on both the short- and long-run adjustment to changes in the variables in the model. In particular, the problem faced is to decompose the long-run relationships into those that are stationary (and thus comprise the cointegration vectors) and those that are non-stationary (and thus comprise the 'common trends'). To do this, Johansen specifies a method based on reduced rank regressions, which is discussed in Box 5.1 used throughout the book to present the more difficult material. Before using Johansen's approach, it is important to consider whether the multivariate model contains $I(0)$ and $I(1)$ variables alone, in which case the modelling procedure is much simpler, or whether $I(2)$ variables are also present (i.e., variables that need to be differenced twice to achieve stationarity). If the latter, then the situation becomes far more complicated and Johansen has developed a procedure to handle the $I(2)$ model, although (at the time of writing) this is not fully available in *PcGive*. Instead, current practice is to test for the presence of $I(2)$ variables, and if they are present to seek to replace them through some form of differencing (e.g., if money supply and prices are $I(2)$, we could reformulate the model to consider real money $m_t - p_t$).

Since the Johansen approach requires a correctly specified VECM, it is necessary to ensure that the residuals in the model have the appropriate, standard Gaussian properties of being independently drawn from a normal distribution. This, *inter alia*, involves setting the appropriate lag length in the model and including (usually dummy) variables that only affect the short-run behaviour of the model. It is pointed out that residual mis-specification can arise as a consequence of omitting these important conditioning variables, and increasing the lag-length is often not the solution (as it usually is, for example, when autocorrellation is present). The procedures for testing the properties of the residuals are discussed and illustrated through examples. We then consider the method of testing for 'reduced rank' (i.e., testing how many cointegration vectors are present in the model). This involves a discussion of Johansen's trace and maximal eigenvalue tests and consideration of the small sample reliability of these statistics (at the same time an example of a likely $I(2)$ system is considered and the testing procedure for $I(2)$ variables is discussed). At this stage a major issue is confronted that presents considerable difficulty in applied work (namely, that the reduced rank regression procedure provides information on how many unique cointegration vectors *span* the cointegration space, while any linear combination of the stationary vectors is itself also a stationary vector and thus the estimates produced for any particular vector in $\boldsymbol{\beta}$ are not necessarily unique). To overcome this 'problem' will involve testing the validity of linear restrictions on $\boldsymbol{\beta}$. Before this, it is necessary to turn to the question of whether an intercept and trend should enter the short- and/or long-run model. Various models are presented and discussed along with the testing procedure for deciding which should be used in empirical work. An example of the use of the so-called Pantula principle is provided.

Weak exogeneity is considered next. This amounts to testing whether rows of the speed-of-adjustment matrix α are zero, and if such hypotheses are accepted the VECM can be respecified by conditioning on the weakly exogenous variables. The reasons for doing this, as well as a discussion of conditional and marginal models, are presented, while the concept of 'weak exogeneity' and how it is defined in various contexts is also discussed. The actual procedures that are used to perform tests of the null hypothesis that elements of α are zero are discussed together with examples that use *PcGive*. This then leads on to testing hypotheses about the cointegration relations involving $\boldsymbol{\beta}$, which involves imposing restrictions motivated by economic arguments (e.g., that some of the β_{ij} are zero or that homogeneity restrictions are needed such as $\beta_{ij} = -\beta_{2j}$) and then testing whether the columns of $\boldsymbol{\beta}$ are identified. The form of the linear restrictions is discussed in some detail, along with various examples.

Lastly, the discussion moves on to testing for unique cointegration vectors (and hence structural long-run relationships). This involves testing that the restrictions placed on each of the cointegration vectors (the columns of $\boldsymbol{\beta}$) in fact lead to an identified system (i.e., a model where any one cointegration vector cannot be represented by a linear combination of the other vectors). Johansen's method for identification is carefully discussed and illustrated by several examples. The importance of this approach is stressed, since the unrestricted estimates of $\boldsymbol{\beta}$ are often hard to interpret in terms of their economic information.

One point that is worth emphasizing on testing for cointegration, and which should be fairly obvious from the above overview of the book thus far, is that an applied economist should really begin his or her analysis by using a multivariate framework and not by using a single equation approach. The exception will obviously be when only two variables are involved. The main reason for taking a systems approach from the outset is that to do otherwise restricts the practitioner to considering only one cointegration relationship when there may in fact be more, and even if he or she is only interested in one vector, it is probable that he or she will not get consistent and efficient estimates without allowing for the possibility of other cointegration vectors. Of course, where tests for weak exogeneity permit, moving down to the single equation approach can be justified after using the Johansen procedure.

Chapter 6 considers modelling the short-run multivariate system and concludes with a short discussion on structural macroeconomic modelling. First of all, it is stressed that obtaining long-run estimates of the cointegration relationships is only a first step to estimating the complete model. The short-run structure of the model is also important in terms of the information it conveys on the short-run adjustment behaviour of economic variables, and this is likely to be at least as interesting from a policy viewpoint as estimates of the long run. Another important aspect of modelling both the short- and long-run structures of the system is that we can attempt to model the contemporaneous interactions between variables (i.e., we can estimate a simultaneous system, and this then provides an additional layer of valuable information). Based on the example of a small monetary model for the UK developed in Hendry and Mizon (1993) and Hendry and Doornik (1994), the following steps are illustrated: (i) use the Johansen approach to obtain the long-run cointegration relationships between the variables in the system; (ii) estimate the short-run vector autoregression (VAR) in error correction form (hence VECM) with the cointegration relationships explicitly included and obtain a parsimonious representation of the system; (iii) condition on any (weakly) exogenous variables thus obtaining a conditional parsimonious VAR (PVAR) model; and (iv) model any simultaneous effects between the variables in the (conditional) model, and test to ensure that the resulting restricted model parsimoniously encompasses the PVAR.

Chapter 7 considers testing for unit roots and cointegration with panel data (i.e., cross sectional time series data with $i = 1, \dots, N$ 'individuals' in each time period and with $t = 1, \dots, T$ observations for each individual over time). This offers the potential to increase the power of tests for integration and cointegration, since adding the cross section dimension to the time series dimension means that non-stationarity from the time series can be dealt with *and* combined with the increased data and power that the cross section brings. The latter acts as repeated draws from the same distribution, and thus while it is known that the standard DF-type tests lack power in distinguishing the unit root null from stationary alternatives, using the cross sectional dimension of panel data increases the power of unit root (and cointegration) tests that are based on a single draw from the population under consideration. The chapter considers in detail the various panel unit root tests that have been developed by, *inter alia*, Levin and Lin (1992, 1993); Im, Pesaran and Shin (1995, 1997); Harris and Tzavalis (1999); Maddala and Wu (1999); and Breitung (2000). All of these take non-stationarity as the null hypothesis and involve differing alternatives (depending on differing assumptions about the homogeneity of the cross sections in the panel) that all involve stationarity. The size and power of these tests is discussed and examples are given from estimating a well-known data set. Similarly, we consider the tests for cointegration and methods for estimation of the cointegration vector that have been developed in the literature. Cointegration tests using a single equation approach developed by Pedroni (1995, 1999) and Kao (1999) are discussed, where the null hypothesis is that there is no cointegration, while we also consider the approach taken by McKoskey and Kao (1998), who developed a residual-based test for the null of cointegration rather than the null of no cointegration in panels. The Larsson, Lyhagen and Lothgren (2001) use of a multi-equation framework to construct a panel test for cointegration rank in heterogeneous panels is considered, which is based on the average of the individual rank trace statistics developed by Johansen (1995a).

In terms of estimating cointegration vectors using panel data sets, we look at the various estimators available which include within- and between-group fully modified (FMOLS) and dynamic (DOLS) estimators. In particular the estimators devised by Kao and Chiang (2000) and Pedroni (2000, 2001) are presented. In addition, some progress has recently been made toward developing a multivariate approach to panel cointegration estimation, with Breitung (2002) having developed a two-step procedure that is based on estimating a VECM. All of these estimators are compared using appropriate empirical examples.

Chapter 8 focuses on conditional heteroscedasticity models and forecasting. It can be viewed as a stand-alone chapter of particular relevance to those studying on courses in financial econometrics, although the reader will benefit from having read previous chapters, as when we mention unit roots and cointegration in Chapter 8 we do so assuming a good knowledge of the concepts. Conditional heteroscedasticity models such as the autoregressive conditional heteroscedastic (ARCH) model introduced by Engle (1982) and the generalized version of this model (GARCH), introduced by Bollerslev (1986), have become extremely popular in financial econometrics. For economists studying at final year undergraduate or postgraduate level, hoping to pursue careers in financial economics, an understanding of ARCH and GARCH models is important given their widespread use. We begin the chapter assuming no previous knowledge of conditional heteroscedasticity models and spend some time introducing concepts. We work through the standard ARCH and GARCH models and go on to discuss multivariate versions of these models. The estimation of ARCH and GARCH models is then considered before moving on to demonstrate the models with an empirical application to US stock market data. Beginning with conventional ARCH and GARCH models we then continue with the same data set to illustrate the main extensions of these models, including the ARCH-M model in which the conditional variance appears as a regressor in the conditional mean. A common feature of financial time series is that negative shocks tend to increase volatility by more than positive shocks of the same absolute magnitude—this characteristic has been labelled the 'asymmetry effect' or 'leverage effect'.[18] A number of GARCH specifications have been proposed to capture this effect, and we consider the most popular. After briefly introducing integrated and fractionally integrated GARCH models, we move on to discuss the impact of conditional heteroscedasticity on conventional unit root and cointegration tests. In empirical analyses it is common practice to apply conventional unit root and cointegration tests ignoring the presence of conditional heteroscedasticity,

[18] The title 'leverage effect' is used because it is thought that the operating leverage of companies is responsible for the asymmetric behaviour of their share prices in response to 'good' and 'bad' news. See Nelson (1991), fn. 3.

since conventional unit root tests have been shown to be asymptotically robust to its presence. However, research has indicated that the finite sample properties of unit root tests can be adversely affected if ARCH or GARCH is present and is ignored. Furthermore, recently it has been shown that if the model used to compute a unit root test takes account of the ARCH effect and the parameters of this model are estimated simultaneously by maximum likelihood, the unit root test statistic does not have its conventional distribution. While research on these issues is still at a relatively early stage, we feel that they are important issues and are likely to be the subject of considerably more research in the future, hence we introduce the literature here.

The final part of this chapter considers some forecasting issues. We begin by discussing forecasting from ARCH or GARCH models and illustrate with a simple empirical application using the US stock market data previously employed. Forecasts are computed from ARCH and GARCH models and are evaluated using conventional measures of forecast accuracy such as mean squared error and graphical techniques. There have been a number of important developments in forecast evaluation, primarily published in the specialist econometrics and forecasting literature. In particular the development of tests of equal forecasting accuracy by Diebold and Mariano (1995), Harvey, Leybourne and Newbold (1997) and tests of forecast-encompassing of Chong and Hendry (1986), Harvey, Leybourne and Newbold (1998) and Clark and McCracken (2000, 2001). These tests allow the practitioner to test whether apparent differences in forecast accuracy are statistically significant and whether forecasts from one model contain information that is not present in the forecasts from a competing model. We illustrate the application of some of these tests using US stock market data (although they are applicable to forecasts from any kind of econometric model).

Important Terms and Concepts

Differencing and levels	d.g.p.	Congruency
ADL models	Strong, weak and super-exogeneity	'White noise' error term
Random (stochastic) variables	AR processes	MA processes
Polynomial lag operator	Forecasting	

2

Short- and Long-run Models

LONG-RUN MODELS

One particular example that will be used throughout the book is the UK demand-for-money function, especially since this model features extensively in the literature on cointegration. The static (or long-run) demand for money can either be derived from Keynesian theoretical models relating to the transactions demand theory (e.g., Baumol, 1952; Tobin, 1956; Laidler, 1984), or from the portfolio balance approach (e.g., Tobin, 1958), or from monetarist models based on the quantity theory of money (e.g., Friedman and Schwartz, 1982). Apart from deciding whether income or wealth (or both) should enter, a common empirical specification typically has demand for money positively determined by the price level P and income (and/or wealth) Y, and negatively related to its opportunity cost, the interest rate(s) R:

$$m^d = \beta_0 + \beta_1 p + \beta_2 y - \beta_3 R \tag{2.1}$$

where (here and elsewhere) variables in lower case are in logarithms. This model depicts an equilibrium relationship such that for given values of right-hand-side variables and their long-run impact on money demand (i.e., the β_i), there is no reason for money demand to be at any other value than m^d.

Although (2.1) is frequently used, it is often found in empirical work that $\beta_1 = 1$, and therefore price homogeneity is imposed so that the model becomes the demand for *real* money balances (i.e., p is subtracted from both sides of the equation). In addition, when interest rates are subject to regulation by policy-makers (i.e., they are a policy instrument), then they are no longer a good proxy for the actual costs of holding money, but rather tend to indicate the restrictiveness of monetary policy. In such instances, it is usual practice to supplement (or even replace) R in the model by including the inflation rate Δp as a proxy for the opportunity cost of $(m^d - p)$. Thus, an alternative empirical specification is:

$$m^d - p = \gamma_0 - \gamma_1 \Delta p + \gamma_2 y - \gamma_3 R \tag{2.2}$$

It is worth noting at this early stage that we have not made any assumptions about whether changes in any of the right-hand-side variables in (2.1) *cause* changes in the demand-for-money balances. In fact, this is a crucial issue in econometric modelling (including the issue of cointegration), and one that distinguishes whether we can estimate a model using a single equation approach (Chapter 4) or whether a system of equations needs to be estimated (Chapter 5). Since (2.1) depicts an equilibrium, then by definition the demand for money equates in the long run to its supply (with variables, such as interest rates, adjusting to bring about market-clearing).[1] If we were to assume that the money stock is under the control of policy-makers, then with $m^d \equiv m^s$ it is possible to rearrange (2.1) to obtain a new equation with, *inter alia*, the money supply determining prices (or interest rates, or income). Thus, if one or more of the right-hand-side variables in (2.1) are contemporaneously influenced by changes in money supply, we need to consider whether a system of equations should be estimated in order to determine all the endogenous variables in the model. That is, the variables in (2.1) may feature as part of several equilibrium relationships governing the joint evolution of the variables. More generally, if there are n variables in the equation, then there can exist up to $n - 1$ linearly independent combinations, each corresponding to a unique equilibrium relationship.

STATIONARY AND NON-STATIONARY TIME SERIES

In addition to the question of whether the model should be estimated using a single equation approach (e.g., ordinary least squares—OLS) or a systems estimator, it is necessary to consider the underlying properties of the processes that generate time series variables. That is, we can show that models containing non-stationary variables will often lead to a problem of spurious regression, whereby the results obtained suggest that there are statistically significant relationships between the variables in the regression model when in fact all that is obtained is evidence of contemporaneous correlations rather than meaningful causal relations.

Starting with a very simple data-generating process (d.g.p.), suppose that a variable y_t is generated by the following (first-order autoregressive (AR)) process:

$$y_t = \rho y_{t-1} + u_t \tag{2.3}$$

[1] There is no necessity to actually achieve equilibrium at any point in time, even as $t \to \infty$. All that is required is that economic forces are prevalent to move the system toward the equilibrium defined by the long-run relationship posited. Put another way, the static equilibrium presented in (2.1) needs to be reinterpreted empirically since most economic variables grow over time. Thus, of more importance is the idea of a steady state relationship between variables that are evolving over time. This is the way the term 'equilibrium' is used here. For a more detailed discussion of the definition of equilibrium used see Banerjee et al. (1993, ch. 1).

Box 2.1 Stationary and non-stationary variables

In (2.3), if $\rho = 1$, then y_t will be non-stationary and it is possible to re-arrange and accumulate y_t for different periods, starting with an initial value of y_{t-n}, to obtain:

$$y_t = y_{t-n} + \sum_{j=0}^{n-1} u_{t-j} \tag{2.1.1}$$

That is, the current value of y_t depends on its initial value and all disturbances accruing between $t - n + 1$ and t, while the variance of y_t is $t\sigma^2$ and this increases to become infinitely large as $t \to \infty$. In fact y_t does not converge to a mean value in any normal sense since if at some point $y_t = c$ then the expected time until y_t again returns to c is infinite (see Figure 2.1).

However, if $|\rho| < 1$, then y_t will be stationary and it is possible to rearrange and accumulate y_t for different periods, starting with an initial value of y_{t-n}, to obtain:

$$y_t = \rho^n y_{t-n} + \sum_{j=0}^{n-1} \rho^j u_{t-j} \tag{2.1.2}$$

Since $|\rho| < 1$, as $n \to \infty$ (2.1.2) reduces to y_t being determined solely by a finite moving average (MA) process of order n with most weight being placed on the first elements of the disturbance term (i.e., $u_t + \rho u_{t-1} + \rho^2 u_{t-2} \cdots$). Thus, when y_t is stationary, it has a constant mean and variance (and indeed covariance) that are independent of time. In this simple example, where y_t is determined by (2.3), y_t has a mean of 0 and a variance of $(\sigma^2/1 - p^2)$. Thus, it is possible to conclude that a stochastic process is (weakly) stationary if:

1 $E[y_t]$ = constant for all t;
2 $\mathrm{Var}[y_t]$ = constant for all t; and
3 $\mathrm{Covar}[y_t, y_{t+n}]$ = constant for all t.

Lastly, Figure 2.1 plots the non-stationary y_t together with a second variable $\Delta y_t (= y_t - y_{t-1})$, which is stationary since $\Delta y_t = u_t$ and u_t is stationary (given (1–3) above). In fact, the series y_t does not return to c because it is the sum of the past disturbance terms (i.e., it is the cumulative sum of the y_t series given in (2.1.1)).

Thus, current values of the variable y_t depend on the last period's value y_{t-1}, plus a disturbance term u_t, the latter encapsulating all other random (i.e., stochastic) influences. It is assumed that this disturbance term comprises T random numbers drawn from a normal distribution with mean equal to 0 and variance σ^2. (Note, in later examples of stationary and non-stationary

Box 2.2 Unit roots and stationarity

Consider the general nth order AR process (of which (2.3) is a special case):

$$y_t = \psi_1 y_{t-1} + \psi_2 y_{t-2} + \cdots + \psi_p y_{t-p} + u_t \tag{2.2.1}$$

To simplify the notation, all the y_{t-i} can be collected on the left-hand side in a single term:

$$\Psi(L)y_t = u_t \tag{2.2.2}$$

where $\Psi(L)$ is the polynominal lag operator $1 - \psi_1 L - \psi_2 L^2 - \cdots - \psi_p L^p$. By forming the characteristic $(1 - \psi_1 L - \psi_2 L^2 - \cdots - \psi_p L^p = 0)$ we see that if the roots of this equation are all greater than unity in absolute value (noting that some roots might be complex and thus their moduli must be greater than $|1|$),[2] then y_t is stationary. For the simple AR(1) case, if the root of $(1 - \psi_1 L = 0)$ is greater than unity in absolute value, then y_t will be stationary. Thus, the AR(1) model is stationary provided $|\psi_1| < 1$, since the root is simply $L = 1/\psi$.

In the case of an AR(3) process:

$$(1 - \psi_1 L - \psi_2 L^2 - \psi_3 L^3)y_t = u_t \tag{2.2.3}$$

and if a unit root exists, then it must be possible to factorize (2.2.3) into:

$$(1 + \alpha L + \beta L^2)(1 - L)y_t = u_t \tag{2.2.4}$$

where α and β depend on the ψ's. If there is only one unit root, then the roots of $(1 + \alpha L + \beta L^2 = 0)$ must both be greater than unity in absolute value. If this is so, then $(1 - L)y_t = \Delta y_t$ must be a stationary process although, because of the unit root, y_t is non-stationary. If there are two unit roots we can further factorize (2.2.4) into:

$$(1 - \gamma L)(1 - L)(1 - L)y_t = u_t \tag{2.2.5}$$

where γ depends on α and β. If $|\gamma| > 1$, then the second difference of y_t (i.e., $(1 - L)(1 - L)y_t = \Delta^2 y_t$) will be stationary. Thus, when two unit roots are present, twice-differencing a variable ensures that a stationary series is obtained. This principle applies when there are any number of unit roots.

Lastly, since a particular data series may be approximated by an

[2] Note that the roots of the characteristic equation can be complex (i.e., contain a real and imaginary part, $h \pm vi$, where h and v are two real numbers and i is an imaginary number) and the modulus is the absolute value of the complex root and is calculated as $\sqrt{(h^2 + v^2)}$.

unknown AR(p) process, involving up to p unit roots, it is useful to reformulate (2.2.1) as:

$$\Delta y_t = \psi^* y_{t-1} + \psi_1 \Delta y_{t-1} + \psi_2 \Delta y_{t-2} + \cdots + \psi_{p-1} \Delta y_{t-p} + u_t \qquad (2.2.6)$$

where $\psi^* = \psi_1 + \psi_2 + \cdots + \psi_p - 1$. In the AR(3) case, where there is at least one unit root, we can rewrite the left-hand side of (2.2.4) as $(1 + \alpha L + \beta L^2)\Delta y_t$ and rearrange to get:

$$\Delta y_t = -\alpha \Delta y_{t-1} - \beta \Delta y_{t-2} + u_t \qquad (2.2.7)$$

Comparing an AR(3) version of (2.2.6) with (2.2.7) indicates that $\psi^* = 0$ if there is a unit root (and consequently $\psi_1 + \psi_2 + \psi_3 = 1$). If $\psi^* < 0$, then $\psi_1 + \psi_2 + \psi_3 < 1$ and y_t must be stationary. In fact this result can be generalized to cover any AR(p) process, such that in any test for stationarity we need only consider the hypothesis that $\psi^* = 0$ against $\psi^* < 0$ based on (2.2.6).

variables, σ^2 will be set equal to 1.) The variable y_t will be stationary if $|\rho| < 1$. If $\rho = 1$ then y_t will be non-stationary.[3] A stationary series tends to return to its mean value and fluctuate around it within a more or less constant range (i.e., it has a finite variance), while a non-stationary series has a different mean at different points in time (and thus the concept of the mean is not really applicable) and its variance increases with the sample size (for more technical details see Box 2.1).

Figure 2.1 plots a non-stationary series based on a starting value of $y_0 = 0$. As can be seen, the variance of y_t is increasing with time and there is no tendency for the series to revert to any mean value. This contrasts both with $\Delta y_t (= y_t - y_{t-1})$, the stationary first difference of y_t that is also plotted in Figure 2.1, and with the stationary version of y_t appearing in Figure 2.2.[4] Stationary variables can be seen to fluctuate around their mean (equal to 0 here) and to have a finite variance. It is also apparent from Figure 2.1 that a non-stationary variable becomes stationary after it is differenced (although not necessarily just by *first*-differencing—it will be shown that the number of times a variable needs to be differenced in order to induce stationarity depends on the number of unit roots it contains).

The question of whether a variable is stationary depends on whether it has a unit root. To see this, rewrite (2.3) as:

$$(1 - \rho L) y_t = u_t \qquad (2.4)$$

where L is the lag operator (i.e., $Ly_t = y_{t-1}$, while $L^2 y_t = y_{t-2}$, etc.). By forming a characteristic equation (i.e., $(1 - \rho L) = 0$), we see that if the roots

[3] If $|\rho| > 1$, then y_t will be non-stationary and explosive (i.e., it will tend to either $\pm\infty$).
[4] Note that u_t was the same for all the series in Figures 2.1–2.3.

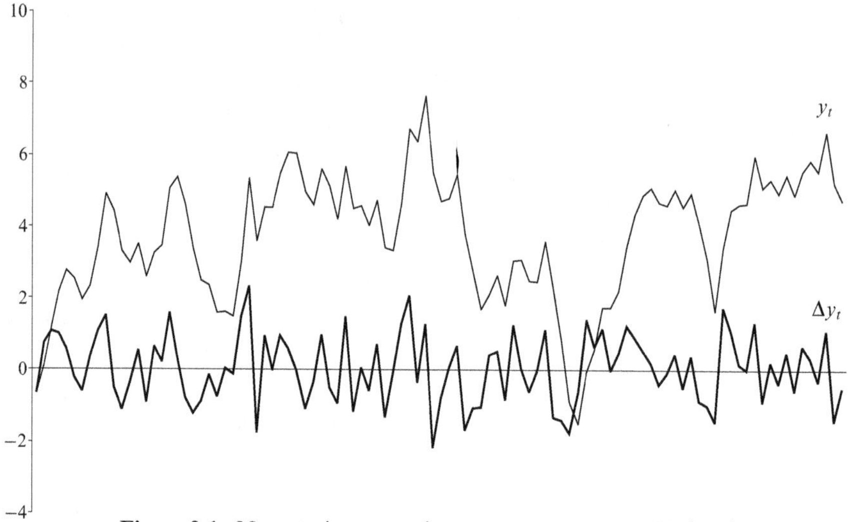

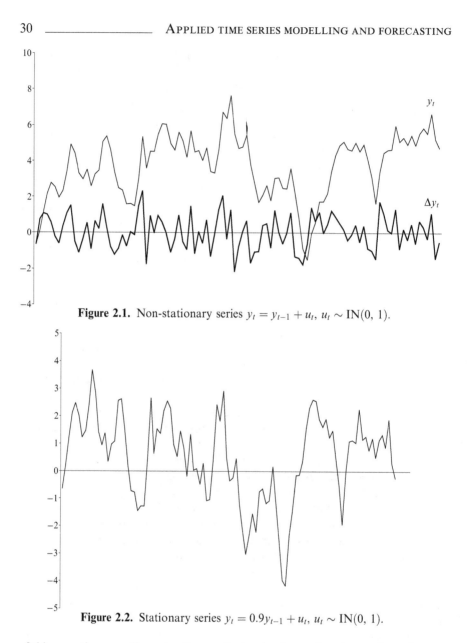

Figure 2.1. Non-stationary series $y_t = y_{t-1} + u_t$, $u_t \sim \text{IN}(0, 1)$.

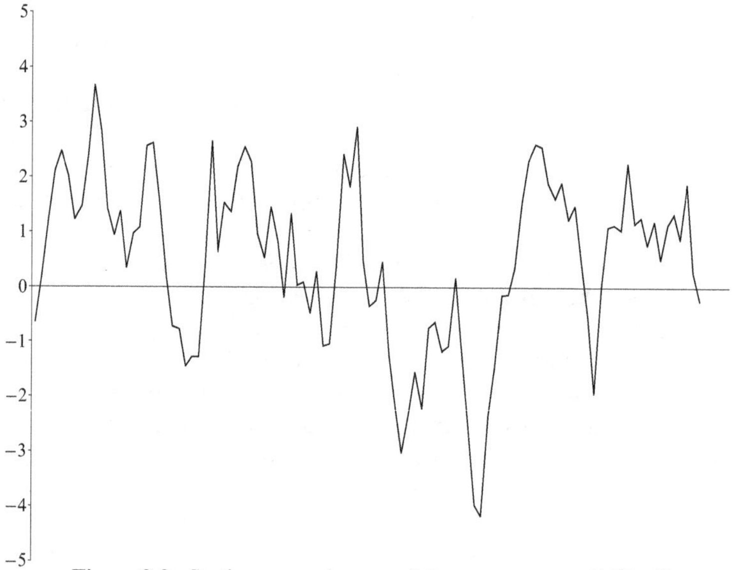

Figure 2.2. Stationary series $y_t = 0.9y_{t-1} + u_t$, $u_t \sim \text{IN}(0, 1)$.

of this equation are all greater than unity in absolute value then y_t is stationary. In our example, there is only one root ($L = 1/\rho$), thus stationarity requires that $|\rho| < 1$ (for more complicated examples, including more than one unit root, see Box 2.2).

Another way to consider stationarity is to look at the different types of time trends that can be found in variables. If we allow (2.3) to have a non-zero intercept:

$$y_t = \beta + \rho y_{t-1} + u_t \tag{2.5}$$

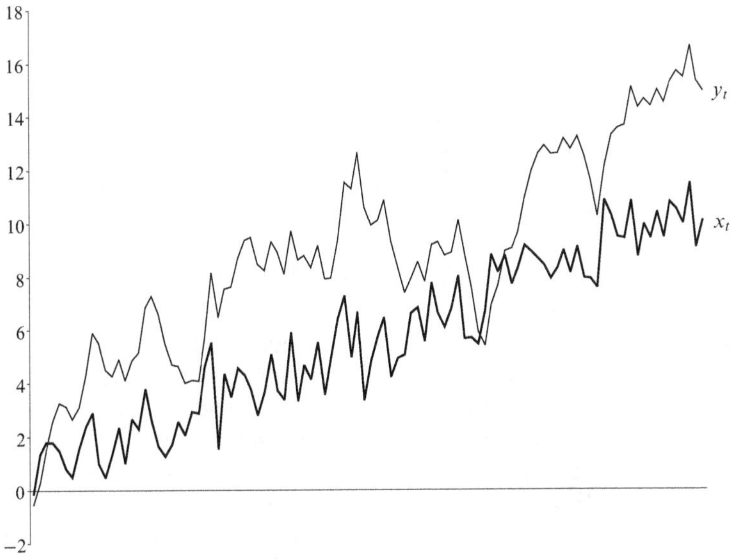

Figure 2.3. Non-stationary series with drift y_t and trend-stationary series x_t, where $y_t = y_{t-1} + 0.1 + u_t$, $x_t = 0.1t + u_t$ and $u_t \sim \text{IN}(0, 1)$.

and if $\rho = 1$, then by rearranging and accumulating y_t for different periods, starting with an initial value of y_0, the non-stationary series y_t can be rewritten as:

$$y_t = y_0 + \beta t + \sum_{j=1}^{t} u_j \tag{2.6}$$

(see also Box 2.1 and equation 2.1.1) where it can be seen that y_t does not return to a fixed deterministic trend $(y_0 + \beta t)$ because of the accumulation of the random error terms.[5] In fact, when $\rho = 1$, y_t will follow a stochastic trend (i.e., it will drift upward or downward depending on the sign of β, as shown in Figure 2.3). This can be seen by taking the first difference of y_t, giving $\Delta y_t = \beta + u_t$, with the expected (i.e., mean) value of Δy_t being equal to β, the growth rate of y_t (assuming the variable is in logs). Since the first difference of y_t is stationary (Δy_t fluctuates around its mean of β and has a finite variance), then y_t itself is referred to as difference-stationary since it is stationary after differencing.

In contrast, consider the following d.g.p.:

$$x_t = \alpha + \beta t + u_t \tag{2.7}$$

where $\alpha + \beta t$ is a deterministic trend and the disturbance u_t is the non-trend (stochastic) component. Since u_t is stationary [e.g., $u_t \sim \text{IN}(0, 1)$], x_t is said to be trend-stationary (i.e., it may trend, but deviations from the deterministic trend are stationary, see Figure 2.3). Note, that equations (2.6) and (2.7) have

[5] Note that the linear trend βt in (2.6) reflects the accumulation of the successive β intercepts when rearranging (2.5) for different periods.

the same form (they both exhibit a linear trend), except that the disturbance term in (2.6) is non-stationary.

Thus, considering the two types of trend, it has been possible to contrast difference-stationary and trend-stationary variables and, in passing, to note that the presence of a stochastic trend (which is non-stationary) as opposed to a deterministic trend (which is stationary) can make testing for unit roots complicated.

SPURIOUS REGRESSIONS

Trends in the data can lead to spurious correlations that imply relationships between the variables in a regression equation, when all that is present are correlated time trends. The time trend in a trend-stationary variable can either be removed by regressing the variable on time (with the residuals from such a regression forming a new variable which is trend-free and stationary) or nullified by including a deterministic time trend as one of the regressors in the model. In such circumstances, the standard regression model is operating with stationary series that have constant means and finite variances, and thus statistical inferences (based on t- and F-tests) are valid.

Regressing a non-stationary variable on a deterministic trend generally does not yield a stationary variable (instead the series needs to be differenced prior to processing). Thus, using standard regression techniques with non-stationary data can lead to the problem of spurious regressions involving invalid inferences based on t- and F-tests. For instance, consider the following d.g.p.:

$$y_t = y_{t-1} + u_t \qquad u_t \sim \text{IN}(0, 1) \tag{2.8}$$

$$x_t = x_{t-1} + v_t \qquad v_t \sim \text{IN}(0, 1) \tag{2.9}$$

That is, both x and y are uncorrelated non-stationary variables such that when the following regression model is estimated:

$$y_t = \beta_0 + \beta_1 x_t + \varepsilon_t \tag{2.10}$$

it should generally be possible to accept the null H_0: $\beta_1 = 0$ (while the coefficient of determination R^2 should also tend toward zero). However, because of the non-stationary nature of the data, implying that ε_t is also non-stationary, any tendency for both time series to be growing (e.g., see y_t in Figure 2.1) leads to correlation, which is picked up by the regression model, even though each is growing for very different reasons and at rates that are uncorrelated (i.e., δ_1 converges in probability to zero in the regression ($\Delta y_t = \delta_0 + \delta_1 \Delta x_t + \eta_t$)). Thus, correlation between non-stationary series does not imply the kind of causal relationship that might be inferred from stationary series.[6]

[6] In fact, this correlation occurs because x and y share a 'common trend'. Hence, relationships between non-stationary variables that seem to be significant, but are in fact spurious, are termed 'common trends' in the integration and cointegration literature.

Box 2.3 *An example of a spurious regression*

Figure 2.4 plots the UK money supply m_t for the period 1963q1–1989q2 together with a non-stationary random series with drift x_t, the latter defined as:

$$x_t = 0.1 + x_{t-1} + \varepsilon_t \qquad \varepsilon_t \sim \text{IN}(0, 1) \tag{2.3.1}$$

with $x_0 = 0$.

Although no formal testing has been undertaken yet, it is likely that m_t is non-stationary (although the possibility still exists that it is stationary around a deterministic trend). In any event, both series contain trends leading to the following spurious regression result:

$$m_t = \underset{(30.3)}{6.633} + \underset{(15.4)}{0.879}x_t + ut \tag{2.3.2}$$

where the t-value decidedly rejects the null of no association between the two series. The R^2 obtained was 0.70 and the Durbin–Watson statistic equalled 0.01. The residuals from the regression are also plotted, with u_t also seeming to be non-stationary (which should be the case if both m_t and x_t are non-stationary and there is no meaningful relationship between the two series).

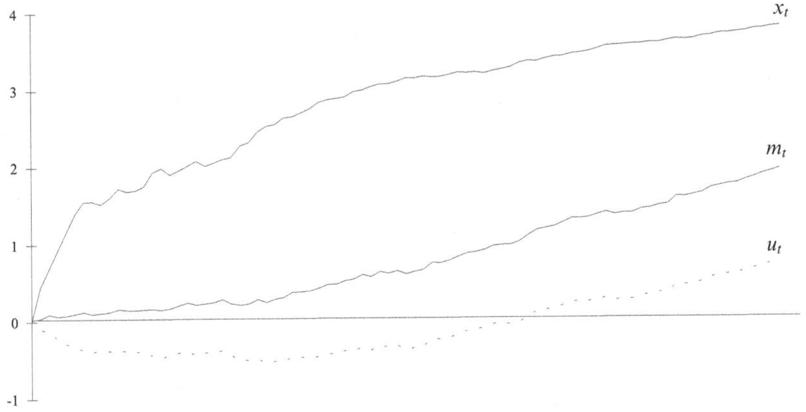

Figure 2.4. UK money supply m_t, 1963–1989, and non-stationary series with drift x_t, where $x_t = x_{t-1} + 0.1 + \varepsilon_t$ and $\varepsilon_t \sim \text{IN}(0, 1)$. Note that all variables are in logs and $u_t = m_t - 0.879x_t - 6.633$.

The problem of spurious correlation, resulting in a non-zero estimate of β_1, is compounded by the fact that t- and F-statistics do not have standard distributions generated by stationary series; with non-stationary series, there is a tendency to reject the null in both cases, and this tendency in fact increases with the sample size. In a Monte Carlo experiment reported in Banerjee, Dolado, Galbraith and Hendry (1993, pp. 73–75), equation (2.10) was estimated 10,000 times, with x and y as defined in (2.8 and 2.9), resulting in an estimated mean value for β_1 of -0.012 and an associated standard error of 0.006 (given a sample size of $T = 100$), thus rejecting the null that $E[\beta_1] = 0$. Based on the 10,000 replications, the probability of rejecting the null of no association at the conventional significance level of 0.05 was found to be 0.753 (i.e., in 75.3 per cent of the regressions values of $|t| > 1.96$ were obtained[7]). This was due to the fact that the mean t-statistic obtained from the experiment was -0.12 instead of zero, with an associated standard deviation of 7.3. The non-standard distribution of the t-statistic accounts for the very high rejection rate of the null. (See also Box 2.3.)

In summary, there is often a problem of falsely concluding that a relationship exists between two unrelated non-stationary series. This problem generally increases with the sample size and cannot be solved by attempting to de-trend the underlying series, as would be possible with trend-stationary data. This leads to the question of when it is possible to infer a causal long-run relationship(s) between non-stationary time series, based on estimating a standard regression such as (2.10).

COINTEGRATION

If a series must be differenced d times before it becomes stationary, then it contains d unit roots (see Box 2.2) and is said to be integrated of order d, denoted $I(d)$. Consider two time series y_t and x_t that are both $I(d)$. In general any linear combination of the two series will also be $I(d)$ (e.g., the residuals obtained from regressing y_t on x_t are $I(d)$). If, however, there exists a vector β such that the disturbance term from the regression ($u_t = y_t - \beta x_t$) is of a lower order of integration $I(d - b)$, where $b > 0$, then Engle and Granger (1987) define y_t and x_t as cointegrated of order (d, b). Thus, if y_t and x_t were both $I(1)$ and $u_t \sim I(0)$, then the two series would be cointegrated of order $CI(1, 1)$ (Box 2.4).

The economic interpretation of cointegration is that if two (or more) series are linked to form an equilibrium relationship spanning the long run, then even though the series themselves may contain stochastic trends (i.e., be non-stationary) they will nevertheless move closely together over time and the difference between them is constant (i.e., stationary). Thus the concept of cointegration mimics the existence of a long-run equilibrium to which an economic system converges over time, and u_t defined above can be interpreted as the disequilibrium error (i.e., the distance that the system is away from equilibrium at time t).

Figure 2.5 shows the UK money supply (based on the narrow measure M1 and aggregate price level for the period 1963q1–1989q2). Both series exhibit

[7] For stationary series, the probability of $|t| > 1.96$ is 5%.

Box 2.4 Orders of integration and cointegration

For series to be cointegrated, they must have comparable long-run properties. That is, supppose a series must be differenced d times before it becomes stationary; it is said to be integrated of order d, denoted $I(d)$. If a linear combination of any two time series y_t and x_t is formed and each is integrated of a different order, then the resulting series will be integrated at the highest of the two orders of integration. Thus if $y_t \sim I(1)$ and $x_t \sim I(0)$, then these two series cannot possibly be cointegrated as the $I(0)$ series has a constant mean while the $I(1)$ series tends to drift over time, and consequently the error $[u_t = (y_t - \alpha x_t) \sim I(1)]$ between them would not be a constant over time. Cointegration requires that if y_t and x_t are both $I(d)$, and if there exists a vector β such that the disturbance term from the regression $(u_t = y_t - \beta x_t)$ is of a lower order of integration $I(d-b)$, where $b > 0$, then y_t and x_t are cointegrated of order (d, b).

However, it is possible to have a mixture of different order series when there are three or more series in the model. As Wickens and Pagan (1989) point out, in this instance a subset of the higher order series must cointegrate to the order of the lower order series. So, if $y_t \sim I(1)$, $x_t \sim I(2)$ and $z_t \sim I(2)$, then as long as we can find a cointegration relationship between x_t and z_t such that $v_t(= x_t - \lambda z_t) \sim I(1)$, then v_t can potentially cointegrate with y_t to obtain $w_t(= v_t - \xi v_t) \sim I(0)$.

Lastly, and again if there are $n > 2$ variables in the model, there can be more than one cointegration vector. It is possible for up to $n - 1$ linearly independent cointegration vectors to exist, and this has implications for testing and estimating cointegration relationships (Chapter 4). Only when $n = 2$ is it possible to show that the cointegration vector is unique.

trends, although until formally tested (see Chapter 3) both could be stationary variables around a deterministic trend, rather than difference-stationary (the latter implying that they contain one or more unit roots). Assuming for now that m_t and p_t are non-stationary (and possibly $I(1)$), it can be seen that both series generally appear to move together over time, suggesting that there exists an equilibrium relationship (cf. the demand-for-money relationship discussed earlier). The outcome of regressing m_t on p_t (plus a constant) is to obtain the residual series e_t, which on visual inspection might be $I(0)$ stationary. This suggests that there possibly exists a cointegration vector (for the data used here $\beta = 1.1085$, with a t-value of 41.92) that defines a constant (equilibrium) relationship between money and prices.

Thus, following directly from the identification of cointegration with equilibrium, it is possible to make sense of regressions involving non-stationary variables. If these are cointegrated, then regression analysis imparts meaningful information about long-run relationships, whereas if cointegration is not established we return to the problem of spurious correlation.

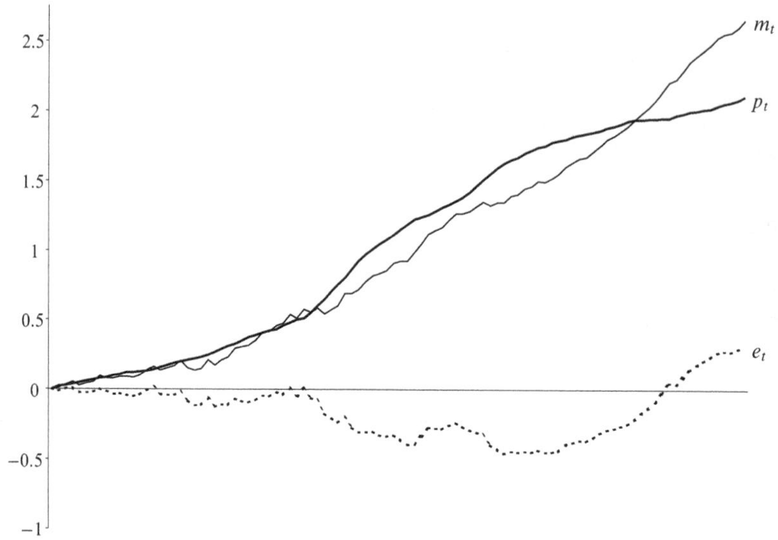

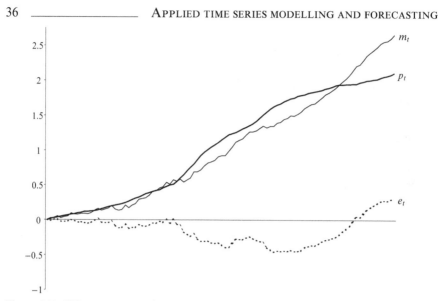

Figure 2.5. UK money supply m_t and price level p_t, 1963–1989, where $e_t = m_t - 1.1085p_t - 11.166$.

SHORT-RUN MODELS

Equation (2.1) sets out the equilibrium relationship governing the demand for money. However, even assuming that it is possible to *directly* estimate this long-run model (an issue discussed in some detail in Chapter 4), it is also of interest to consider the short-run evolution of the variables under consideration, especially since equilibrium (i.e., the steady state) may rarely be observed. This is important from a forecasting perspective, as is the economic information that can be obtained from considering the dynamics of adjustment.

The major reason that relationships are not always in equilibrium centres on the inability of economic agents to instantaneously adjust to new information.[8] There are often substantial costs of adjustment (both pecuniary and non-pecuniary) that result in the current value of the dependent variable Y being determined not only by the current value of some explanatory variable X but also by past values of X. In addition, as Y evolves through time in reaction to current and previous values of X, past (i.e., lagged) values of itself will also enter the short-run (dynamic) model. This inclusion of lagged values of the dependent variable as regressors is a means of simplifying the form of the dynamic model (which would otherwise tend to have a large number of highly correlated lagged values of X); by placing restrictions on how current

[8] Even if expectations were fully efficient and agents could anticipate and therefore react contemporaneously to changes in determinants, there are likely to be (non-linear) adjustment costs that make it uneconomic to move instantaneously to a new equilibrium.

Y_t adjusts to the lagged values of X_{t-i} ($i = 0, \ldots, q$), it is possible to reduce the number of such terms entering the estimated equation at the cost of some extra lagged terms involving Y_{t-i} ($i = 1, \ldots, p$).[9] A very simple dynamic model (with lags $p = q = 1$) of short-run adjustment is:

$$y_t = \alpha_0 + \gamma_0 x_t + \gamma_1 x_{t-1} + \alpha_1 y_{t-1} + u_t \tag{2.11}$$

where the white noise residual is $u_t \sim \text{IN}(0, \sigma^2)$. Clearly the parameter coefficient γ_0 denotes the short-run reaction of y_t to a change in x_t, and not the long-run effect that would occur if the model were in equilibrium. The latter is defined as:

$$y_t = \beta_0 + \beta_1 x_t \tag{2.12}$$

So, in the long run the elasticity between Y and X is $\beta_1 = (\gamma_0 + \gamma_1/1 - \alpha_1)$, assuming that $\alpha_1 < 1$ (which is necessary if the short-run model is to converge to a long-run solution).

The dynamic model represented by (2.11) is easily generalized to allow for more complicated, and often more realistic, adjustment processes (by increasing the lag lengths p and q). However, there are several potential problems with this form of the dynamic model. The first has already been mentioned and concerns the likely high level of correlation between current and lagged values of a variable, which will therefore result in problems of multicollinearity (high R^2, but imprecise parameter estimates and low t-values, even though the model may be correctly specified). Using the Hendry-type 'general-to-specific' approach, which would involve eliminating insignificant variables from the estimated model, might therefore result in mis-specification (especially if $\mathbf{X}$ is in fact a vector of variables). Also, some (if not all) of the variables in a dynamic model of this kind are likely to be non-stationary, since they enter in levels. As explained earlier, this leads to the potential problem of common trends and thus spurious regression, while t- and F-statistics do not have standard distributions and the usual statistical inference is invalid.[10] A solution might be to respecify the dynamic model in (first) differences. However, this then removes any information about the long-run from the model and consequently is unlikely to be useful for forecasting purposes.

A more suitable approach is to adopt the error correction model—sometimes called an equilibrium correction model—(ECM) formulation of the dynamic model. Rearranging and reparameterizing (2.11) gives:

$$\Delta y_t = \gamma_0 \Delta x_t - (1 - \alpha_1)[y_{t-1} - \beta_0 - \beta_1 x_{t-1}] + u_t \tag{2.13}$$

[9] For instance, if the effects of the X_{t-i} are restricted to decline in a geometric progression $(1 + \varphi + \varphi^2 + \varphi^3 \cdots)$ so that more distant lags have little impact on current Y, then we end up with the Koyck lag model: $y_t = \alpha_0(1 - \varphi) + \gamma_0 x_t + \varphi y_{t-1} + e_t$, which is equivalent to $y_t = \alpha_0 + \gamma_0(x_t + \varphi x_{t-1} + \varphi^2 x_{t-2} \cdots) + u_t$, where $e_t = u_t - \varphi u_{t-1}$.

[10] However, as will be discussed in Chapter 4, if the right-hand-side variables in the model are weakly exogenous, invalid inference and potential bias will not be a problem.

where $\beta_0 = \alpha_0/(1-\alpha_1)$. Equations (2.11) and (2.13) are equivalent, but the ECM has several distinct advantages. First, and assuming that X and Y are cointegrated, the ECM incorporates both short-run and long-run effects. This can be seen by the fact that the long-run equilibrium (2.12) is incorporated into the model. Thus, if at any time the equilibrium holds then $[y_{t-1} - \beta_0 - \beta_1 x_{t-1}] = 0$. During periods of disequilibrium, this term is non-zero and measures the distance the system is away from equilibrium during time t. Thus, an estimate of $(1-\alpha_1)$ will provide information on the speed of adjustment (i.e., how the variable y_t changes in response to disequilibrium).[11] For instance, suppose that y_t starts to increase less rapidly than is consistent with (2.12), perhaps because of a series of large negative random shocks (captured by u_t). The net result is that $[y_{t-1} - \beta_0 - \beta_1 x_{t-1}] < 0$, since y_{t-1} has moved below the steady-state growth path, but since $-(1-\alpha_1)$ is negative, the overall effect is to boost Δy_t thereby forcing y_t back toward its long-run growth path as determined by x_t (in equation (2.12)).

A second feature of the ECM is that all the terms in the model are stationary so standard regression techniques are valid, assuming cointegration and that we have estimates of β_0 and β_1. There is clearly a problem if they need to be estimated at the same time in the ECM. Often β_1 is set equal to one (and β_0 is set equal to zero) and justified on the basis that the theory imposes such a long-run elasticity. This can be tested by including x_{t-1} as an additional regressor, since it should have an estimated coefficient value of zero, if in fact $[\beta_0, \beta_1]' = [0, 1]'$. However, including the potentially non-stationary variable x_{t-1} is itself problematic, since the t-statistic of the coefficient of x_{t-1} does not have a standard normal distribution, thereby invalidating the usual testing procedure. The issues of testing for cointegration and estimating the ECM are considered in Chapter 4.

Third, as should be obvious from equations (2.12) and (2.13), the ECM is closely bound up with the concept of cointegration. In fact, Engle and Granger (1987) show that if y_t and x_t are cointegrated $CI(1, 1)$, then there must exist an ECM (and, conversely, that an ECM generates cointegrated series). The practical implication of Granger's representation theorem for dynamic modelling is that it provides the ECM with immunity from the spurious regression problem, providing that the terms in levels cointegrate.

The simple ECM depicted in (2.13) can be generalized to capture more complicated dynamic processes. Increasing the lag length p and/or q in (2.11) results in additional lagged first differences entering (2.13). In general, we can reformulate the ECM as:

$$A(L)\Delta y_t = B(L)\Delta x_t - (1-\pi)[y_{t-p} - \beta_0 - \beta_1 x_{t-p}] + u_t \qquad (2.14)$$

[11] Large values (tending to -1) of $-(1-\alpha_1)$ indicate that economic agents remove a large percentage (since the model is in logs) of the resulting disequilibrium each period. Small values (tending toward 0) suggest that adjustment to the long-run steady state is slow, perhaps because of large costs of adjustment (pecuniary and non-pecuniary).

where $A(L)$ is the polynomial lag operator $1 - \alpha_1 L - \alpha_2 L^2 - \cdots - \alpha_p L^p$, $B(L)$ is the polynomial lag operator $\gamma_0 + \gamma_1 L + \gamma_2 L^2 + \cdots + \gamma_q L^q$ and $\pi = (\alpha_1 + \alpha_2 + \cdots + \alpha_p)$. Lastly, it is also possible to specify the ECM in multivariate form, explicitly allowing for a set of cointegration vectors. This will be explored more fully in Chapter 5.

CONCLUSION

This chapter has considered short- and long-run models. Inherent in the distinction is the notion of equilibrium; that is, the long run is a state of equilibrium where economic forces are in balance and there is no tendency to change, while the short run depicts the disequilibrium state where adjustment to the equilibrium is occurring. When dealing with non-stationary data, equilibrium is synonymous with the concept of cointegration. Failure to establish cointegration often leads to spurious regressions that do not reflect long-run economic relationships, but rather reflect the 'common trends' contained in most non-stationary time series. Cointegration is also linked very closely to the use of short-run ECMs, thus providing a useful and meaningful link between the long- and short-run approach to econometric modelling.

Important Terms and Concepts

Static (long-run) models	Equilibrium	Stationary and non-stationary variables
Spurious regression	Unit roots	Difference-stationary
Trend-stationary	Monte Carlo experimentation	Cointegration
Dynamic (short-run) models	ECM	

3
Testing for Unit Roots

When discussing stationary and non-stationary time series, the need to test for the presence of unit roots in order to avoid the problem of spurious regression was stressed. If a variable contains a unit root, then it is non-stationary, and unless it combines with other non-stationary series to form a stationary cointegration relationship, then regressions involving the series can falsely imply the existence of a meaningful economic relationship.

In principle it is important to test the order of integration of each variable in a model, to establish whether it is non-stationary and how many times the variable needs to be differenced to result in a stationary series. Also, as will be seen, testing for stationarity for a single variable is very similar to testing whether a linear combination of variables cointegrate to form a stationary equilibrium relationship. Testing for the presence of unit roots is not straightforward. Some of the issues that arise are as follows:

- It is necessary to take account of the possibility that the underlying (but, of course, unknown) data-generating process (d.g.p.) may, *inter alia*, include a time trend (stochastic or deterministic).
- The d.g.p. may be more complicated than a simple autoregressive AR(1) process (e.g., (2.3)), and indeed may involve moving average (MA) terms.
- It is known that when dealing with finite samples (and especially small numbers of observations) the standard tests for unit roots are biased toward accepting the null hypothesis of non-stationarity when the true d.g.p. is in fact stationary, but close to having a unit root (i.e., there is a problem with the power of the test).
- There is concern that an undetected structural break in the series may lead to under-rejecting of the null.
- Quarterly data might also be tested for seasonal unit roots in addition to the usual test for unit roots at the zero frequency level. Observations on a

variable y_t can also be described by a different model for each quarter, with the result being a periodic AR model.[1]

THE DICKEY–FULLER TEST

There are several ways of testing for the presence of a unit root. The emphasis here will be on using the Dickey–Fuller (DF) approach (cf. Dickey and Fuller, 1979) to testing the null hypothesis that a series does contain a unit root (i.e., it is non-stationary) against the alternative of stationarity. There are other tests of this null (e.g., the Sargan–Bhargava (1983) cointegration regression Durbin–Watson (CRDW) test, based on the usual Durbin–Watson statistic, and the non-parametric tests developed by Phillips and Perron, based on the Phillips (1987) Z test, which involve transforming the test statistic to eliminate any autocorrelation in the model), but DF tests tend to be more popular either because of their simplicity or their more general nature. There are also more recent tests that take as the null the hypothesis that a series is stationary, against the alternative of non-stationarity (see, for example, Kahn and Ogaki, 1992 and Kwiatkowski, Phillips, Schmidt and Shin, 1992). These have not achieved widespread usage, and since the consequences of non-stationarity are so important, it is probably better to take a conservative approach with non-stationarity as the maintained hypothesis.[2]

The simplest form of the DF test amounts to estimating:

$$y_t = \rho_a y_{t-1} + u_t \tag{3.1a}$$

or

$$(1 - L)y_t = \Delta y_t = (\rho_a - 1)y_{t-1} + u_t \qquad u_t \sim \text{IID}(0, \sigma^2) \qquad (3.1\text{b})^3$$

Either variant of the test is applicable, with the null being H_0: $\rho_a = 1$ against the alternative H_1: $\rho_a < 1$. The advantage of (3.1b) is that this is equivalent to testing $(\rho_a - 1) = \rho_a^* = 0$ against $\rho_a^* < 0$; more importantly, though, it also simplifies matters to use this second form of the test when a more complicated AR(p) process is considered (cf. Box 2.2).[4] The standard approach to testing

[1] Note that fractional integration and unit roots are discussed in Chapter 8 (when discussing integrated generalized autoregressive conditional heteroscedastic (GARCH) models), since long memory processes are more applicable to financial data that are observed more often than say each quarter.

[2] It is sometimes useful to test using both alternatives of the null, to ensure that each corroborates the other, although the underlying distributions of, say, the DF test (of the null of non-stationarity) and the KPSS test (of the null of stationarity—see Kwiatkowski et al., 1992) have different d.g.p.s and are therefore strictly not comparable. Nonetheless, recently Carrion-i-Silvestre, Sanso-i-Rossello and Ortuno (2001) have computed joint statistics (called the joint confirmation hypothesis) of the probability of rejecting the null of a unit root using both tests.

[3] Note that we are not assuming that the residuals u_t are drawn from a normal distribution; rather they are drawn from the DF distribution.

[4] Note that if we reject $\rho^* = 0$ in favour of $\rho^* < 0$, then we can safely reject $\rho^* > 0$.

Table 3.1 Critical values for the DF test (source: Fuller, 1976).

Sample size	Critical values for τ level of significance			Critical values for τ_μ level of significance			Critical values for τ_τ level of significance		
	0.01	0.05	0.10	0.01	0.05	0.10	0.01	0.05	0.10
DF distribution									
25	−2.66	−1.95	−1.60	−3.75	−3.00	−2.63	−4.38	−3.60	−3.24
50	−2.62	−1.95	−1.61	−3.58	−2.93	−2.60	−4.15	−3.50	−3.18
100	−2.60	−1.95	−1.61	−3.51	−2.89	−2.58	−4.04	−3.45	−3.15
t-distribution									
∞	−2.33	−1.65	−1.28	−2.33	−1.65	−1.28	−2.33	−1.65	−1.28

such a hypothesis is to construct a *t*-test; however, under non-stationarity, the statistic computed does not follow a standard *t*-distribution, but rather a DF distribution. The latter has been computed using Monte Carlo techniques, which involves taking (3.1) as the underlying d.g.p., imposing the null hypothesis by fixing $\rho_a = 1$ and randomly drawing samples of the u_t from the normal distribution; this then generates thousands of samples of y_t, all of which are consistent with the d.g.p: $y_t = y_{t-1} + u_t$. Then for each of the y_t a regression based on (3.1) is undertaken, with ρ_a *now free to vary*, in order to compute (on the basis of thousands of replications) the percentage of times the model would reject the null hypothesis of a unit root when the null is true. These are the critical values for rejecting the null of a unit root at various significance levels (e.g., 10%, 5% and 1%) based on the DF distribution of $[(\rho_a - 1)/\text{SE}(\rho_a)]$.[5]

It is informative to compare the critical values for the DF and standard *t*-distributions. Assume that model (3.1b) has been estimated for some series y_t, resulting in a *t*-ratio of -1.82 attached to the coefficient of y_{t-1}. Looking at the first set of critical values in Table 3.1, it is clear that for different sample sizes it would be necessary to accept the null of non-stationarity at the 5% significance level using the values of the DF τ-distribution. However, using the comparable critical values for the standard *t*-distribution (the final row), the null could be rejected at this significance level. Thus, failure to use the DF τ-distribution would lead on average to over-rejection of the null.

[5] Note that the d.g.p. underlying the DF distribution is that given in (3.1), containing no constant or trend. Critical values are then obtained for three models used to test the null of a unit root: (i) a no constant/no trend regression (i.e., (3.1) in the text and the first block of values in Table 3.1); (ii) only a constant in the model ((3.2) and block 2 in Table 3.1); and (iii) both a constant and a trend ((3.3) and block 3 in Table 3.1). If the d.g.p. is altered to include a non-zero constant, the critical values obtained from (iii) are not affected; the DF distribution is invariant to the value of the constant in the d.g.p., and thus it is sufficient to use (3.1) as the underlying d.g.p. for calculating critical values (Fuller, 1976). This property of the DF distribution is known as similarity and leads to similar tests (i.e., tests for which the distribution of the test statistic under the null hypothesis is independent of nuisance parameters in the d.g.p.).

Testing for a unit root using (3.1) involves making the prior assumption that the underlying d.g.p. for y_t is a simple first-order AR process with a zero mean and no trend component (i.e., no deterministic variables). However, it also assumes that in the d.g.p. at time $t = 0$, y_t also equals zero, since in a model with no deterministic variables the mean of the series is determined by the initial observation under the hypothesis of a unit root. *So using regression equation (3.1) is only valid when the overall mean of the series is zero.* Alternatively, if the 'true' mean of the d.g.p. were known, it could be subtracted from each observation, and (3.1) could then be used to test for a unit root; but this is unlikely to happen in practice.[6] Thus, when the underlying d.g.p. is given by (3.1), but it is not known whether y_0 in the d.g.p. equals zero, then it is better to allow a constant μ_b to enter the regression model when testing for a unit root:

$$\Delta y_t = \mu_b + (\rho_b - 1)y_{t-1} + u_t \qquad u_t \sim \text{IID}(0, \sigma^2) \tag{3.2}$$

The appropriate critical values to be used in this case are given by the DF distribution relating to τ_μ, since the latter was generated assuming that the underlying d.g.p. is given by (3.1), but the model used for testing is (3.2).[7] Note that ρ_b and τ_μ are both invariant with respect to y_0 (i.e., whatever the unknown starting value of the series, the distribution of the test statistic τ_μ is not affected). This is an important property, since in its absence critical values would depend on some unknown value of y_0, and we would therefore need to know both the value of y_0 and its associated DF distribution before we could undertake any test for a unit root.

However, (3.2) cannot validly be used to test for a unit root when the underlying d.g.p. is also given by (3.2). In this instance, if the null hypothesis is true $\rho_b = 1$, and y_t will follow a stochastic trend (i.e., it will drift upward or downward depending on the sign of μ_b) (see the discussion of equations (2.5) and (2.6) in the last chapter). Under the alternative hypothesis that $\rho_b < 1$, then y_t is stationary around a constant mean of $\mu_b/(1 - \rho_b)$, *but it has no trend.* Thus, using (3.2) to test for a unit root does not nest both the null hypothesis and the alternative hypothesis. Put another way, suppose the true d.g.p. is a stationary process around a deterministic trend (e.g., $y_t = \alpha + \beta t + u_t$) and (3.2) is used to test whether this series has a unit root. Since the d.g.p. contains a trend component (albeit deterministic), the only way to fit this trend is for the regression equation to set $\rho_b = 1$, in which case μ_b becomes the coefficient β on the trend (cf. equations (2.6) and (2.7)). This would be equivalent to accepting the null that there is a stochastic (i.e., non-stationary) trend, when in fact the true d.g.p. has a deterministic (i.e., stationary) trend. What this example illustrates is that in order to test what will probably be in practice the most

[6] Nankervis and Savin (1985) have shown that using (3.1) with $y_0 \neq 0$ can lead to problems over rejection of the null when it is true (i.e., there are problems with the size of the test).

[7] See also footnote 5 for more details.

common form of the null hypothesis (that the d.g.p. contains a stochastic trend against the alternative of being trend-stationary), it is necessary to have as many deterministic regressors as there are deterministic components in the d.g.p., and thus we must allow a time trend t to enter the regression model used to test for a unit root:

$$\Delta y_t = \mu_c + \gamma_c t + (\rho_c - 1)y_{t-1} + u_t \qquad u_t \sim \text{IID}(0, \sigma^2) \tag{3.3}$$

The appropriate critical values are given by the DF distribution relating to τ_τ (see Table 3.1); it is interesting to note that $\tau_\tau < \tau_\mu < \tau$ and then to make comparisons with the standard t-values. Clearly, the inappropriate use of the latter would lead to under-rejection of the null hypothesis, and this problem becomes larger as more deterministic components are added to the regression model used for testing. Note also that ρ_c and τ_τ are both invariant with respect to y_0 and μ_c, so neither the starting value of the series nor the value of the drift term have any affect on the test statistic τ_τ.

It is possible that the underlying d.g.p. is given by (3.3), which would mean that y_t has both a stochastic and a deterministic trend. In this event, one would need a regression model that includes an additional term (such as t^2) in order to be able to test for a unit root, necessitating an additional block of critical values in Table 3.1. In practice, this is unlikely to be a problem since the hypothesis of a unit root with a deterministic trend is usually precluded a priori, because it implies an implausible, ever-increasing (or decreasing) rate of change (if y_t is in logarithmic form).[8]

Before discussing the testing procedure that should be adopted when using the DF test, it is worth noting that tests of the joint hypothesis that $\gamma_c = 0$ and $\rho_c = 1$ can also be undertaken, using the non-standard F-statistic Φ_3 reported in Dickey and Fuller (1981).[9] In (3.3), if the DF t-test of the null hypothesis H_0: $\rho_c = 1$ is not rejected, but the joint hypothesis H_0: $(\rho_c - 1) = \gamma_c = 0$ is, then this implies that the trend is significant under the null of a unit root and *asymptotic* normality of the t-statistic $[(\rho_c - 1)/\text{SE}(\rho_c)]$ follows. Thus, instead of using the critical values from the DF-type distribution, the standard t-statistic (for $n = \infty$) should be used to test H_0: $(\rho_c - 1) = 0$. This result follows from West (1988) and occurs when a stochastic trend is present in the regression, but it is *dominated* by a deterministic trend component. This form of dominance is also present when testing the joint hypothesis that $\mu_b = 0$ and $\rho_b = 1$, using (3.2) and the F-statistic Φ_1 (given in Dickey and Fuller, 1981).[10] If one fails to reject H_0: $\rho_b = 1$, but can reject the joint hypothesis

[8] Thus, if the null hypothesis H_0: $(\rho_c - 1) = 0$ is true, we should expect the trend not to be significant in (3.3), otherwise we would need the extra block of DF critical values. Note that if the deterministic trend is significant under a joint test and dominates the stochastic trend, then asymptotic normality of the t-statistic follows, as we now go onto discuss.

[9] Note that Φ_3 is invariant with respect to y_0 and μ_c.

[10] Note that Φ_1 is invariant with respect to y_0.

H_0: $(\rho_b - 1) = \mu_b = 0$, then the constant is significant under the null of a unit root and *asymptotic* normality of the *t*-statistic $[(\rho_c - 1)/\text{SE}(\rho_c)]$ follows. Note that rejection of either of the above joint hypotheses, using the appropriate *F*-test, results in both the d.g.p. and the regression model used to test for a unit root having the same form (unlike the tests outlined above involving the DF distribution). This is known as an exact test, while the tests based on the DF distribution are called similar tests.[11] However, there are two reasons to be cautious about conducting unit root tests using exact tests: first, asymptotic normality of the *t*-statistic *only* occurs when the non-zero constant (and trend) in the d.g.p. is (are) matched by a constant (and trend) in the model used for testing. So, for example, including a trend in the model when the d.g.p. does not have a trend means that we have to use the DF distribution to obtain valid critical values. Since it is unlikely that we will be sufficiently confident about the correct specification of the d.g.p., it is probably safer to use the DF distribution. Second, it has been suggested (Banerjee, Dolado, Galbraith and Hendry, 1993) that in *finite* samples, the DF distributions may be a better approximation than the normal distribution, even though asymptotically (i.e., $n \to \infty$) the latter is to be preferred.[12]

One last item of information that will help in deciding a possible testing strategy is that the inclusion of additional deterministic components in the regression model used for testing, beyond those included in the (unknown) d.g.p., results in an increased probability that the null hypothesis of non-stationarity will be accepted when in fact the true d.g.p. is stationary (i.e., the power of the test of the unit root hypothesis decreases against stationary alternatives).[13] This problem was mentioned when comparing the values in Table 3.1, since critical values for rejecting the null are ordered as follows: $\tau_\tau < \tau_\mu < \tau$. That is, adding a constant and then a trend to the model increases (in absolute value) the critical values, making it harder to reject the null hypothesis, even when it should be rejected.[14]

To summarize the issues so far discussed, *t*-tests of the null hypothesis of a unit root must use critical values from the DF distribution and not the stan-

[11] That is, a similar test having a DF distribution requires that the regression model used for testing contains more parameters than the d.g.p. (see Kiviet and Phillips, 1992).

[12] Recently, Ohtani (2002) has computed the appropriate exact critical values for DF tests where the constant or trend term are significantly different from zero and exact tests apply. He argues these should be used instead of assuming asymptotic normality.

[13] Note that this will also be a problem when we consider adding lagged values of the Δy_{t-i} as additional regressors when using the ADF test (see below).

[14] This needs, however, to be counterbalanced by the fact that (in finite samples) as we add deterministic regressors to the regression model, there is a downward bias away from zero in the estimate of ρ, and this bias increases as the number of deterministic regressors increases. However, even though this suggests that the asymptotic low power of the test and finite bias may help to cancel each other out, Monte Carlo simulation does tend to confirm that there still remains a problem in finite samples (e.g., Schwert, 1989).

Table 3.2 Perron's (1988) testing procedure using the DF test (unknown d.g.p.).

Step and model	Null hypothesis	Test statistic	Critical values*
(1) $\Delta y_t = \mu_c + \gamma_c t + (\rho_c - 1)y_{t-1} + u_t$	$(\rho_c - 1) = 0$	τ_τ	Fuller (table 8.5.2, block 3)
(2) $\Delta y_t = \mu_c + \gamma_c t + (\rho_c - 1)y_{t-1} + u_t$	$(\rho_c - 1) = \gamma_c = 0$	Φ_3	Dickey and Fuller (table VI)
(2a) $\Delta y_t = \mu_c + \gamma_c t + (\rho_c - 1)y_{t-1} + u_t$	$(\rho_c - 1) = 0$	t	Standard normal
(3) $\Delta y_t = \mu_b + (\rho_b - 1)y_{t-1} + u_t$	$(\rho_b - 1) = 0$	τ_μ	Fuller (table 8.5.2, block 2)
(4) $\Delta y_t = \mu_b + (\rho_b - 1)y_{t-1} + u_t$	$(\rho_b - 1) = \mu_b = 0$	Φ_1	Dickey and Fuller (table IV)
(4a) $\Delta y_t = \mu_b + (\rho_b - 1)y_{t-1} + u_t$	$(\rho_b - 1) = 0$	t	Standard normal
(5) $\Delta y_t = (\rho_a - 1)y_{t-1} + u_t$	$(\rho_a - 1) = 0$	τ	Fuller (table 8.5.2, block 1)

* Fuller (1976) and Dickey and Fuller (1981).

dard t-distribution. Similarly, F-tests of the joint hypothesis concerning the unit root and the significance of constant or trend terms must also use the critical values of the appropriate DF distribution (obtained from Dickey and Fuller, 1981). It is necessary to ensure that the regression model used for testing has more deterministic components than the hypothesized d.g.p., otherwise the test will not nest the null and alternative hypotheses. In general, since the underlying d.g.p. is unknown, this suggests using (3.3) for testing the unit root hypothesis. However, having unnecessary nuisance parameters (constant and trend terms) will lower the power of the test against stationary alternatives. Thus, Perron (1988) has put forward the sequential testing procedure outlined in Table 3.2, which starts with the use of (3.3) and then eliminates unnecessary nuisance parameters. If we fail to reject the null using the most general specification (perhaps because of the low power of the test), testing continues on down to more restricted specifications. The testing stops as soon as we are able to reject the null hypothesis of a unit root. Note, steps (2a) and (4a) are only undertaken if we are able to reject the joint hypotheses in (2) and (4), respectively. Even in these situations, tests based on the DF distributions may be preferable, in which case the results obtained from steps (2a) and (4a) should be treated with some caution.

There are several econometric packages available that will allow the user to go through this testing strategy fairly easily, and they usually provide the appropriate critical values.[15] However, all the tests can be carried out

[15] In most packages (such as *PcGive*) the critical values used are those obtained by MacKinnon (1991), who calculated response surfaces to allow appropriate critical values to be obtained for various sample sizes (and not just those listed in the DF tables).

running ordinary least squares (OLS) regressions and by referring to the DF tables referenced in Table 3.2 (also reproduced in the Statistical Appendix at the end of the book).

AUGMENTED DICKEY–FULLER TEST

If a simple AR(1) DF model is used when in fact y_t follows an AR(p) process, then the error term will be autocorrelated to compensate for the mis-specification of the dynamic structure of y_t. Autocorrelated errors will invalidate the use of the DF distributions, which are based on the assumption that u_t is 'white noise'. Thus, assuming y_t follows an pth order AR process:

$$\left.\begin{aligned} & y_t = \psi_1 y_{t-1} + \psi_2 y_{t-2} + \cdots + \psi_p y_{t-p} + u_t \\ \text{or} \quad & \Delta y_t = \psi^* y_{t-1} + \psi_1 \Delta y_{t-1} + \psi_2 \Delta y_{t-2} + \cdots \\ & \qquad + \psi_{p-1} \Delta y_{t-p+1} + u_t \qquad u_t \sim \text{IID}(0, \sigma^2) \end{aligned}\right\} \tag{3.4}$$

where $\psi^* = (\psi_1 + \psi_2 + \cdots + \psi_p) - 1$. If $\psi^* = 0$, against the alternative $\psi^* < 0$, then y_t contains a unit root. To test the null hypothesis, we again calculate the DF t-statistic $[\psi^*/\text{SE}(\psi^*)]$, which can be compared against the critical values in Table 3.1 (for τ). Note that this is only strictly valid in large samples, since in small samples percentage points of the augmented Dickey–Fuller (ADF) distribution are generally not the same as those applicable under the strong assumptions of the simple DF model (Banerjee et al., 1993, p. 106).

As with the simple DF test, the above model needs to be extended to allow for the possibility that the d.g.p. contains deterministic components (constant and trend). As the model is extended, the appropriate large sample critical values are those given in Table 3.1. The model needed to test for the null hypothesis of a stochastic trend (non-stationary) against the alternative of a deterministic trend (stationary) is as follows:

$$\Delta y_t = \psi^* y_{t-1} + \sum_{i=1}^{p-1} \psi_i \Delta y_{t-i} + \mu + \gamma t + u_t \qquad u_t \sim \text{IID}(0, \sigma^2) \tag{3.5}$$

The augmented model can be extended even further to allow for MA parts in the u_t.[16] It is generally believed that MA terms are present in many macro-economic time series after first-differencing (e.g., time average data, an index of stock prices with infrequent trading for a subset of the index, the presence of errors in the data, etc.).[17] Said and Dickey (1984) developed an approach in

[16] For example, $u_t = \varepsilon_t - \theta\varepsilon_{t-1}$, where $\varepsilon_t \sim \text{IID}(0, \sigma^2)$.

[17] When the MA terms have values close to -1, it is well known (Schwert, 1989) that this affects the size of the ADF test, with the model incorrectly over-rejecting the null of non-stationarity when it is true (i.e., more often than expected with respect to a type 1 error). Hence, as shown below, it is argued that the lag length in the ADF test needs to be sufficiently large to capture any MA processes.

which the orders of the AR and MA components in the error term are unknown, but can be approximated by an AR(k) process, where k is large enough to allow a good approximation to the unknown autoregressive moving average—ARMA(p, q)—process, so ensuring that u_t is approximately 'white noise'. In terms of the augmented model the Said–Dickey approach can be approximated by replacing the lag length of $(p - 1)$ with k, with the technical condition that k increases at a suitable rate as the sample size increases.[18]

Thus, the ADF test is comparable with the simple DF test, but it involves adding an unknown number of lagged first differences of the dependent variable to capture autocorrelated omitted variables that would otherwise, by default, enter the error term u_t (an alternative approach to adding lagged first differences of the dependent variable is to apply a non-parametric correction to take account of any possible autocorrelation; this is the Phillips and Perron approach and is discussed in Box 3.1). In this way, we can validly apply unit root tests when the underlying d.g.p. is quite general. However, it is also very important to select the appropriate lag length; too few lags may result in over-rejecting the null when it is true (i.e., adversely affecting the size of the test), while too many lags may reduce the power of the test (since unnecessary nuisance parameters reduce the effective number of observations available). Banerjee et al. (1993) favour a generous parameterization, since '... if too many lags are present ... the regression is free to set them to zero at the cost of some loss in efficiency, whereas too few lags implies some remaining autocorrelation ... and hence the inapplicability of even the asymptotic distributions in ...' (see Table 3.1 on p. 43).

Suggested solutions to the choice of p in (3.5) involve using a model selection procedure that tests to see if an additional lag is significant (e.g., if it increases the value of $\bar{R}^2$, which in a linear model is equivalent to using the Akaike information criterion—see, for example, Greene, 2000, p. 306). However, it was shown in Harris (1992a) that maximizing $\bar{R}^2$ to choose the value of p in the ADF test proved to be unsatisfactory; Monte Carlo experiments undertaken using various d.g.p.s (ARMA, AR and MA) suggested that there were problems with the size of this form of the ADF test. Rather, choosing a fairly generous value of p (using a formula suggested by Schwert, 1989 that allows the order of autoregression to grow with the sample size T) resulted in a test with size close to its nominal value (i.e., the model incorrectly rejected the null when it is true close to the 10%, 5% and 1% times expected on the basis of making a type 1 error). This is consistent with Banerjee et al. (1993), and thus Harris suggested that the lag length should normally be chosen on the basis of the formula reported in Schwert (1989, p. 151): that is $l_{12} = \text{int}\{12(T/100)^{1/4}\}$.

[18] This is an approximation to the Said–Dickey approach, since the latter does not include a model incorporating a deterministic trend, while the model with drift ($\mu \neq 0$) should necessitate that the first regressor in (3.5) becomes $(y_{t-1} - \bar{y})$, where $\bar{y}$ is the mean of y over the sample.

Box 3.1 Phillips–Perron-type tests for unit roots.

The ADF-type test includes additional higher order lagged terms to account for the fact that the underlying d.g.p. is more complicated than a simple AR(1) process. The extra terms, involving lags of the dependent variable. 'whiten' the error term in the regression equation used for testing, since autocorrelated errors (due to the mis-specification of the dynamic structure of y_t) will invalidate the used of the DF distributions.

An alternative approach is that suggested by Phillips (1987) and extended by Perron (1988) and Phillips and Perron (1988). Rather than taking account of the extra terms in the d.g.p. by adding them to the regression model, a non-parametric correction to the t-test statistic is undertaken to account for the autocorrelation that will be present (when the underlying d.g.p. is not AR(1)). Thus, DF-type equations (cf. (3.1)–(3.3)) are estimated in line with Perron's (1988) testing strategy and then the t-test statistic (of the null hypothesis of non-stationarity) is amended to take account of any bias due to autocorrelation in the error term of the DF-type regression model. This bias results when the variance of the 'true' population:

$$\sigma^2 = \lim_{T\to\infty} E(T^{-1}S_T^2)$$

differs from the variance of the residuals in the regression equation:

$$\sigma_u^2 = \lim_{T\to\infty} T^{-1}\sum_{t-1}^{T} E(u_t^2)$$

Consistent estimators of σ_u^2 and σ^2 are:

$$S_u^2 = T^1\sum_{t=1}^{T}(u_t^2) \qquad S_{Tl}^2 = T^{-1}\sum_{t=1}^{T}(u_t^2) + 2T^{-1}\sum_{t=1}^{l}\sum_{t=j+1}^{T} u_t u_{t-j} \qquad (3.1.1)$$

where l is the lag truncation parameter used to ensure that the autocorrelation of the residuals is fully captured. In practice, the estimate for S_{Tl}^2 is not guaranteed to be non-negative in finite samples, and therefore the formula is modified in practice to include a term that ensures non-negativity.[19] It can be seen from (3.1.1) that when there is no autocorrelation the last term in the formula defining S_{Tl}^2 is zero and $\sigma_u^2 = \sigma^2$.

Based on (3.1.1), an asymptotically valid test that $\rho_b = 1$ in (3.2), when the underlying d.g.p. is not necessarily an AR(1) process, is given by the Phillips Z-test:

$$Z(\tau_\mu) = (S_u/S_{Tl})\tau_\mu - \tfrac{1}{2}(S_{Tl}^2 - S_u^2)\left\{S_{Tl}\left[T^2\sum_{t=2}^{T}(y_{t-1} - y_{-1})^2\right]^{1/2}\right\}^{-1} \qquad (3.1.2)$$

[19] Specifically, an additional term $1 - j(l+1)^{-1}$ follows the second summation sign in the formula for S_{Tl}^2.

where τ_μ is the t-statistic associated with testing the null hypothesis $\rho_b = 1$ in (3.2). The critical values for this test statistic are the same as those for τ_μ (cf. Table 3.1), and $Z(\tau_\mu)$ reduces to the DF test statistic τ_μ when autocorrelation is not present (since $S_u = S_{Tl}$). Other Z-tests corresponding to tests involving trend and no constant or trend terms (and joint tests of hypotheses) are provided in table 1 of Perron (1988).

Monte Carlo work (most notably Schwert, 1989) suggests that the Phillips-type test has poor size properties (i.e., the tendency to over-reject the null when it is true) when the underlying d.g.p. has large negative MA components and MA terms are present in many macroeconomic time series. Banerjee et al. (1993) also state: '... one might suspect as well that the power of the Said–Dickey procedure would be higher for processes involving AR errors, because the test regression captures AR terms precisely' (p. 113). Note, however, that Perron and Ng (1996) improve the (size) performance of the Phillips-type test when there are negative MA terms through the addition of appropriate modification factors to the original test statistics. They refer to the new tests as modified Z-tests.

More recently, Ng and Perron (1995) argue in favour of a general-to-specific sequential t-test for the significance of the last lag that has the ability to yield higher values of p (when there are negative MA errors) rather than standard lag length selection criteria. Hence this reduces size distortions, but (as noted in Ng and Perron, 2002) this approach also tends to over-parameterize when MA errors are not important. Weber (2001) argues in favour of a specific-to-general approach whereby p is initially set at a low value, and then F-tests are conducted for eliminating longer lags from the model (i.e., the lag length in the ADF regression is set at the smallest p such that all longer lags up to $p^{\max}$—where the latter might be obtained using the Schwert formula—are jointly insignificant).[20] The problem for all these methods of setting p is linked to the type of information-based rule used when devising and implementing the lag selection criteria. Thus Ng and Perron (2002) have analysed these various information criterion (e.g., the Akaike criteria typically used) and have suggested a new modified criterion that has as a central feature the imposition of the null hypothesis of a unit root when selecting the lag length. They present evidence that their new procedure leads to substantial improvements in the size of the unit root test. We will implement this later (cf. Box 3.3) when discussing the size and power problems of unit root tests more generally.

[20] Weber shows that his specific-to-general approach works well when the true d.g.p. has few lags, although the Akaike information Criterion (AIC) works better when the lag length in the true model is longer. Note that he does not deal with the problem of MA terms with values close to -1, so does not directly consider the problem discussed by Schwert (1989), Banerjee et al. (1993) and Ng and Perron (2002).

Table 3.3 Augmented Dickey–Fuller and Phillips–Perron Z-tests of unit roots: UK money demand data (1963q1–1989q2), seasonally unadjusted.

Variable (and lag length*)	Test statistic (see Table 3.2 and Box 3.1)					
	τ_τ	$Z(\tau_\tau)$	τ_μ	$Z(\tau_\mu)$	τ	$Z(\tau)$
log Real MI	−0.21	1.48**	−0.48	2.24	0.88	0.05
(lag length)	(6)	(6)	(6)	(6)	(7)	(7)
log TDE	−1.35	−45.94***	0.29	−0.31	3.02	0.06
(lag length)	(11)	(11)	(11)	(11)	(11)	(11)
$\Delta \log P$	−2.13	−16.77	−2.16	−16.86***	−0.84	−3.87
(lag length)	(3)	(3)	(3)	(3)	(3)	(3)
R	−2.05	−8.60	−2.14	−9.11	−0.73	−1.26
(lag length)	(3)	(3)	(3)	(3)	(3)	(3)
Δ log Real MI	−2.67	−117.91***	−2.37	−115.63***	−2.22***	−113.76***
(lag length)	(7)	(7)	(6)	(6)	(6)	(6)
Δ log TDE	−2.78	−105.56***	−2.77**	−106.12***	−1.56	−136.77***
(lag depth)	(11)	(11)	(11)	(11)	(9)	(9)
$\Delta^2 \log P$	−7.26***	−147.45***	−7.26***	−147.96***	−7.29***	−148.39***
(lag length)	(2)	(2)	(2)	(2)	(2)	(2)
ΔR	−6.08***	−84.89***	−6.03***	−84.69***	−6.06***	−85.19***
(lag length)	(2)	(2)	(2)	(2)	(2)	(2)

* The lag length was set by AIC + 2 on every occasion (see text for details).
** Rejects the null hypothesis at the 5% level.
*** Rejects the null hypothesis at the 10% level.

The results from using the ADF and Phillips–Perron (PP) Z-tests when applied to UK money demand data are reported in Table 3.3 (plots of the actual series are provided in Figure 3.1). Tests applied to the actual series and each variable in first differences are reported, with the *TSP* (4.5) econometric software package providing the required test statistics.[21] Note, the τ-statistic based on (3.1) is not really applicable unless the overall mean of the series is zero (cf. Figure 3.1), although it is included in Table 3.3 for completeness. On the basis of the ADF test applied to each series in levels, the UK money demand data appears to comprise a set of $I(1)$ variables, since we fail to reject the null of non-stationarity. The PP tests generally confirm this, although the variable representing real output (log TDE) is found to be a trend-stationary series, while, inflation is apparently stationary when only a constant

[21] The COINT procedure in the *TSP* software package provides the various forms of the test statistics as used here; it also calculates for the user the value p that minimizes the AIC (which in a linear model is equivalent to maximizing $\bar{R}^2$). Note, however, that the actual information criterion used is AIC + 2, in order to avoid the problem of poor size properties of the test statistic when there are (large) negative MA terms in the d.g.p. Other packages typically report the ADF τ-statistic for various user specified lag lengths (e.g., *PcGive*).

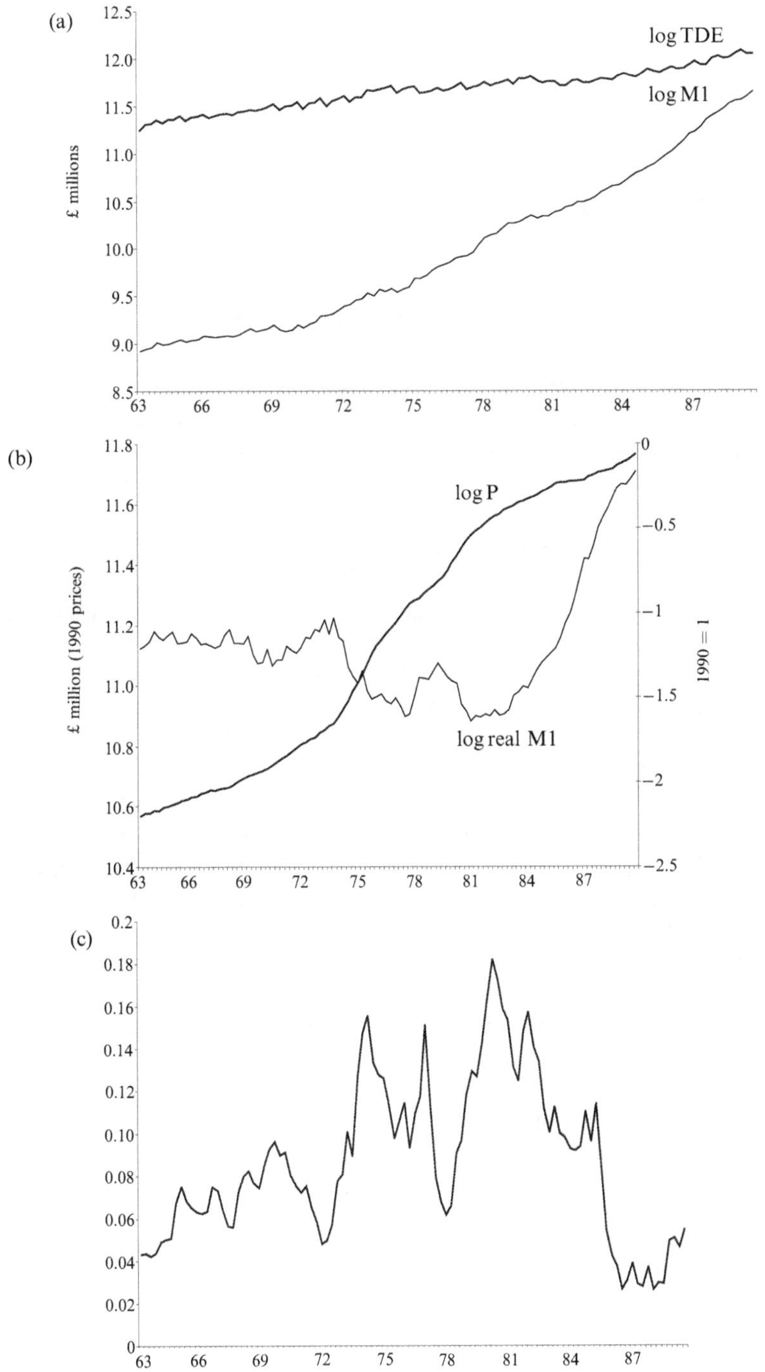

Figure 3.1. (a) log money supply and log real total domestic expenditure (1990 prices); (b) log real money supply and log prices; (c) interest rate.

is included in the test regression model.[22] When taking the first difference of each series ($\Delta y_t = y_t - y_{t-1}$), the results would tend to confirm the hypothesis that each series is $I(1)$, as differencing removes the unit root, although there is some evidence that the real money supply and real output may not be stationary after differencing (with reference to the ADF test), suggesting they may contain two unit roots (i.e., they are $I(2)$). As to whether each series is $I(1)$ or $I(2)$, this requires testing for more than one unit root (see Box 3.2).

POWER AND LEVEL OF UNIT ROOT TESTS

Choosing the correct form of the ADF model is problematic, and using different lag lengths often results in different outcomes with respect to rejecting the null hypothesis of non-stationarity.[23] These problems are compounded by the fact that there are several issues related to the size and power of unit root tests, especially concerning the small sample properties of these tests.

Blough (1992) was among the first to discuss the trade-off that exists between the size and power properties of unit root tests.[24] The usual requirements for a hypothesis test, based on standard statistical inferences, is that the size of the test should be close to its nominal value (see above) and should have high power (through consistently rejecting the null when it is false) against at least some alternatives. However, in finite samples it can be shown that '... any trend-stationary process can be approximated arbitrarily well by a unit root process (in the sense that the autocovariance structures will be arbitrarily close)' (Campbell and Perron, 1991, p. 157). Similarly, any unit root process can be approximated by a trend-stationary process, especially when the sample size is small. That is, some unit root processes display finite sample behaviour closer to (stationary) 'white noise' than to a (non-stationary) random walk (while some trend-stationary processes behave more like random walks in finite samples). This implies that a unit root test '... with high power against *any* stationary alternative *necessarily* will have correspondingly high probability of false rejection of the unit root null when applied to near stationary processes' (Blough, 1992, p. 298). This follows from the closeness of the finite sample distribution of any statistic under a particular trend-stationary process and the finite sample distribution of the statistic under a difference-stationary process that approximates the trend-stationary process. Thus, Blough (1992, p. 299) states that there is a trade-off between size and power

[22] This may result from the presence of negative MA terms in the d.g.p., which has been shown to affect the size of the PP test.

[23] As already noted, if there are large negative MA terms in the d.g.p., then setting too small a lag length tends to adversely affect the size of the ADF test. Conversely, the inclusion of unnecessary (nuisance) parameters when the lag length is set too high will reduce the power of the test.

[24] See also the results in DeJong, Nankervis and Savin (1992).

Box 3.2 Multiple unit root tests.

In Box 2.4 it was stated that if a series must be differenced d times before it becomes stationary, it is said to be integrated of order d, denoted $I(d)$. That is, the series contains d unit roots. Suppose y_t is found to be non-stationary, based on the ADF test using the test procedure outlined in Table 3.2. It has been suggested that rather than assume that the first difference (Δy_t) is stationary, implying that $y_t \sim I(1)$, it is necessary to apply the ADF test to the new variable Δy_t. Failure to reject the null that this new variable is non-stationary would imply that in fact y_t is at least $I(2)$. This procedure of testing from lower to higher orders of integration should continue until the hypothesis of non-stationarity is rejected.

However, Dickey and Pantula (1987) argue that this is an invalid testing procedure, since if $y_t \sim I(2)$, applying the ADF test using (3.5) takes as the alternative hypothesis that y_t is stationary. What needs to be tested first in this instance is whether the variable Δy_t is non-stationary against the alternative that Δy_t is stationary. That is, they suggest that the correct sequential testing procedure is to take the largest number of unit roots likely as the maintained hypothesis (for practical purposes this would usually involve starting with $y_t \sim I(2)$) and then to reduce the order of differencing each time the null hypothesis is rejected until the first time the null is not rejected.

Thus, when $d = 2$ it is necessary to reformulate (3.5) as:

$$\Delta^2 y_t = \psi^* \Delta y_{t-1} + \sum_{i=1}^{p-2} \psi_i \Delta^2 y_{t-i} + \mu + u_t \qquad u_t \sim \text{IID}(0, \sigma^2) \qquad (3.2.1)$$

To test the null hypothesis, we begin by calculating the ADF t-statistic ($\psi^*/\text{SE}(\psi^*)$), which can be compared against the critical values in Table 3.1 (for τ_μ). If $\psi^* = 0$, against the alternative $\psi^* < 0$, is accepted, then Δy_t is non-stationary and y_t contains two unit roots. If the null hypothesis is rejected, then proceed to test the null of one unit root versus the stationary alternative using (3.5).

In practice, it seems intuitive to assume that there would be little difference whichever testing procedure is used, since if $y_t \sim I(2)$, applying the ADF test using (3.5) should see an acceptance of the null 95% of the time (using the 5% critical values from the DF distribution) as long as there is at least one unit root. However, Dickey and Pantula (1987) found that, on the basis of a Monte Carlo study, this was not the case; the ability to reject the null of non-stationarity when there was more than one unit root present (i.e., the series needs $d > 1$ differencing to induce stationarity) decreased when applying an equation such as (3.5) compared with (3.2.2), *but not by very much.* Moreover, the empirical example they considered resulted in a rejection of non-stationarity whichever approach was applied (i.e., testing from lower (higher) to higher (lower) orders of integration), even though the series was judged to be $I(2)$.

Box Table 3.2.1 ADF tests of unit roots: UK money demand data (1963q1–1989q2), seasonally unadjusted.

Variable (and lag length[a])	Test statistic (see Table 3.2 and Box 3.1)					
	τ_τ	$Z(\tau_\tau)$	τ_μ	$Z(\tau_\mu)$	τ	$Z(\tau)$
$\Delta^2 \log$ Real MI	−5.43**	−135.55**	−5.46**	−135.89**	−5.49**	−136.25**
(lag length)	(4)	(4)	(4)	(4)	(4)	(4)
$\Delta^2 \log$ TDE	−5.01**	−126.63**	−5.02**	−126.98**	−5.04**	−127.31**
(lag length)	(11)	(11)	(11)	(11)	(11)	(11)
$\Delta^2 \log P$	−6.58**	−155.54**	−6.61**	−155.81**	−6.65**	−156.04**
(lag length)	(6)	(6)	(6)	(6)	(6)	(6)
$\Delta^2 R$	−5.35**	−105.42**	−5.35**	−105.90**	−5.38**	−106.33**
(lag length)	(11)	(11)	(11)	(11)	(11)	(11)

[a] The lag length was set by AIC + 2 on every occasion (see text for details).
* Rejects the null hypothesis at least at the 10% level.
** Rejects the null hypothesis at least at the 5% level.

Applying (3.2.1), both with and without a constant and/or time trend, to the UK money demand data analysed in Table 3.3, the results shown in Box Table 3.2.1 were obtained.[25] Based on both the ADF and PP results, these suggest that all variables are $I(1)$ and not $I(2)$, since we are able to reject the null of two unit roots when each series is differenced twice.

in that unit root tests must have either high probability of falsely rejecting the null of non-stationarity when the true d.g.p. is a nearly stationary process (poor size properties) or low power against any stationary alternative.[26]

The above problem concerning unit root tests, when there is near equivalence of non-stationary and stationary processes in *finite* samples, is in part due to using critical values based on the DF *asymptotic* distribution. The use of asymptotic critical values based on the strong assumptions of the simple DF model was also seen to be a limitation when considering the distribution of the ADF test statistic. Thus, in Harris (1992b) it was suggested that bootstrap methods may be more applicable when using the ADF test of the unit root. Essentially, this amounts to replicating the underlying d.g.p. of the variable itself by sampling from the residuals of the ADF model and obtaining a sampling distribution (and critical values) for the ADF statistic that is applic-

[25] Note that we started testing with $d = 3$ and the null of non-stationarity was rejected in every case. The results presented therefore refer to the test of $I(2)$ against $I(1)$. We also calculated the ADF τ-statistic since differenced series often have a mean of zero and no deterministic trend.

[26] Put more technically, the unit root test must have power equal to its size against a near-stationary process.

able to the underlying d.g.p. (instead of assuming that the underlying d.g.p. can be approximated asymptotically by equation (3.1)).

More recently though, there have been significant theoretical improvements in devising unit root tests that in principle have good size and power properties. The Ng and Perron (2002) approach to using an information criterion that leads to good size when setting the lag length was discussed earlier. For improvements in power, Elliott, Rothenberg and Stock (1996) have shown that the power of the ADF test can be optimized using a form of de-trending known as generalized least squares (GLS) de-trending (see Box 3.3). Taken together, Ng and Perron (2002) have produced a testing procedure that incorporates both the new information criterion for setting the lag length and GLS de-trending. Applying their approach to the data on UK money demand produces the results presented in Box Table 3.3.1, confirming that each series is $I(1)$.

Another development in unit root-testing that is likely to result in an increasingly powerful test is to use panel unit root procedures (see Chapter 7). This is because the power of the test increases with an increase in the number of panel groups (i.e., cross sections) as compared with the well-known low power of the standard DF and ADF unit root tests against near-unit root alternatives for small samples. Lastly, testing for unit roots is likely to have low power in the presence of asymmetric adjustment; thus asymmetric unit root tests have been developed that take account of this possibility (Enders and Granger, 1998, see Box 3.4).[27]

STRUCTURAL BREAKS AND UNIT ROOT TESTS

Perron (1989) shows that, if a series is stationary around a deterministic time trend that has undergone a permanent shift sometime during the period under consideration, failure to take account of this change in the slope will be mistaken by the usual ADF unit root test as a persistent innovation to a stochastic (non-stationary) trend. That is, a unit root test that does not take account of the break in the series will have (very) low power. There is a similar loss of power if there has been a shift in the intercept (possibly in conjunction with a shift in the slope of the deterministic trend).

If the break(s) in the series are known, then it is relatively simple to adjust the ADF test by including (composite) dummy variables[28] to ensure there are as many deterministic regressors as there are deterministic components in the d.g.p. The relevant critical values for unit root tests involving shifts in the trend

[27] The power of unit root tests is also likely to be lower if the d.g.p. of a series being considered exhibits (G)ARCH effects. This is considered in Chapter 8, where we discuss the results of Seo (1999) in particular.

[28] That is, dummy variables that take on a value of (0, 1) to allow for shifts in the intercept and dummies multiplied by a time trend to take into account any change in the slope of the deterministic trend.

Box 3.3 Dickey–Fuller GLS de-trended test.

Elliott et al. (1996) optimize the power of the ADF unit root test by de-trending. If y_t is the series under investigation, the DF GLS test is based on testing H_0: $\psi^* = 0$ in the regression:

$$\Delta y_t^d = \psi^* y_{t-1}^d + \psi_1^* \Delta y_{t-1}^d + \cdots + \psi_{p-1}^* \Delta y_{t-p+1}^d + u_t \tag{3.3.1}$$

where y_t^d is the de-trended series. De-trending depends on whether a constant or a constant and trend are included in the model. Taking the more general case:

$$y_t^d = y_t - \hat{\beta}_0 - \hat{\beta}_1 t \tag{3.3.2}$$

where $(\hat{\beta}_0, \hat{\beta}_1)$ are obtained by regressing $\bar{y}$ on a constant and time trend (the latter deterministic variable denoted as $\bar{z}$), where:

$$\left.\begin{aligned} \bar{y} &= [y_1, (1 - \bar{\alpha}L)y_2, \ldots, (1 - \bar{\alpha}L)y_T] \\ \bar{z} &= [z_1, (1 - \bar{\alpha}L)z_2, \ldots, (1 - \bar{\alpha}L)z_T] \end{aligned}\right\} \tag{3.3.3}$$

and

$$z_t = (1, t)' \qquad \bar{\alpha} = 1 + \frac{\bar{c}}{T} \tag{3.3.4}$$

where T represents the number of observations for y_t and $\bar{c}$ be fixed at -7 in the model with only a constant (i.e., with drift) and at -13.7 when both a constant and trend term enter the ADF regression.

Elliott et al. (1996) show that de-trending in this way produces a test that has good power properties. Critical values are provided in their paper (see also Maddala and Kim, 1998, p. 114). Box Table 3.3.1 presents the results from using the de-trending procedure and selecting the lag length based on the Ng and Perron (2002) new information criterion (NIC), when applied to UK money demand data. First, the lag lengths set using the NIC are usually lower than those reported in Table 3.3 and Box Table 3.2.1, which used the AIC + 2 method available in *TSP 4.5*. With respect to the variables in levels, the ADF-type test (with GLS de-trending) fails to reject the null of non-stationarity (and therefore confirms the results in Table 3.3). The PP tests provide some evidence that the real money supply and prices are stationary only when a constant enters the regression model. When each series is differenced once, the null of non-stationarity is rejected whichever de-trended test is used, except for inflation (however, there is some suggestion that the regression model for this variable is over-parameterized, which may adversely affect the power of the test). When each variable is differenced twice, only the PP Z-test consistently rejects the null (although the interest rate is clearly stationary), while we were able to reject the null more often using the usual ADF test (cf. Box Table 3.2.1). Thus, over-differencing and de-trending may result in too many AR terms in the test equation, lowering the power of this testing procedure.

Box Table 3.3.1 Tests of unit roots based on de-trending and the Ng–Perron NIC: UK money demand data (1963q1–1989q2), seasonally unadjusted.

Variable	Lag length	$\hat{\psi}^*$	DF GLS	PP $Z(\tau)$	Modified PP $Z(\tau)$
Constant and trend in regression					
log Real M1	6	0.982	−1.24	−10.62	−10.57
log TDE	4	0.893	−2.07	−15.55	−10.81
$\Delta \log P$	1	0.871	−2.25	−10.52	−8.26
R	0	0.944	−1.66	−5.79	−5.55
Δ log Real M1	3	0.707	−2.28	−41.03**	−5.13
Δ log TDE	0	−0.339	−14.44**	−137.90**	−45.57**
$\Delta^2 \log P$	7	0.771	−1.78	−49.14**	−1.12
ΔR	0	0.179	−8.45**	−84.54**	−49.84**
Δ^2 log Real M1	8	0.192	−2.18	−116.27**	−0.39
Δ^2 log TDE	7	0.572	−1.86	−117.46**	0.13
$\Delta^3 \log P$	5	0.831	−1.90	−57.27**	−0.10
$\Delta^2 R$	0	−0.398	−15.35**	−142.55**	−42.93**
Constant only in regression					
log Real M1	6	0.986	−0.83	−10.97*	−10.92*
log TDE	8	1.015	1.58	1.58	1.72
$\Delta \log P$	1	0.872	−2.25	−10.32*	−8.12*
R	0	0.958	−1.49	−4.32	−4.18
Δ log Real M1	3	0.750	−2.11*	−35.84**	−4.54
Δ log TDE	0	−0.336	−14.40**	−137.64**	−45.67**
$\Delta^2 \log P$	7	0.967	−0.45	−15.00**	0.31
ΔR	0	0.175	−8.49**	−84.97	−49.92**
Δ^2 log Real M1	8	0.839	−0.79	−99.79	−0.21
Δ^2 log TDE	8	0.965	−0.33	−94.94**	0.002
$\Delta^3 \log P$	7	0.990	−0.25	−13.01**	0.19
$\Delta^2 R$	0	−0.383	−15.09**	−141.03**	−43.53**

DF GLS refers to the ADF test with GLS de-trending; PP Z is the Phillips–Perron with GLS de-trending; and modified PP Z is the modified PP statistic with de-trending.
Calculated using Gauss code available from Pierre Perron. Note, the econometrics package *Eviews 4.1* has automated the Ng–Perron procedure.
* Rejects the null hypothesis at least at the 5% level.
** Rejects the null hypothesis at least at the 1% level.

In general, though, the Ng–Perron approach confirms that each variable considered here is indeed $I(1)$.

Box 3.4 Asymmetric tests for unit roots.

Enders and Granger (1998) have modified the ADF test to allow the alternative hypothesis of stationarity with asymmetric adjustment. Equation (3.1b) can be generalized for $y_t (= y_t, \ldots, y_T)$ as:

$$\Delta y_t = I_t(\rho_1 - 1)(y_{t-1} - \tau) + (1 - I_t)(\rho_2 - 1)(y_{t-1} - \tau) + u_t \qquad (3.4.1)$$

where I_t is a 0/1 dummy variable that divides the observations on y_t into two subsets:[29]

$$I_t = \begin{cases} 1 & \text{if } \Delta y_{t-1} \geq \tau \\ 0 & \text{if } \Delta y_{t-1} < \tau \end{cases} \qquad (3.4.2)$$

where τ is some threshold value such that estimating equation (3.4.1) maximizes the probability that $\rho_1 \neq \rho_2$ (i.e., there is asymmetric adjustment in the series y_t).[30] To test the unit root hypothesis, the null H_0: $(\rho_1 - 1) = (\rho_2 - 1) = 0$ is examined using an F-test of the joint hypothesis and specially calculated critical values, and if this is rejected it is possible to test whether $\rho_1 = \rho_2$ using a conventional F-statistic. Alternatively, a t-max test (based on the most negative t-value associated with either $(\rho_1 - 1)$ or $(\rho_2 - 1)$) can be used to test for a unit root. Clearly, if the t-value on either $(\rho_1 - 1)$ and/or $(\rho_2 - 1)$ is positive, we would not reject the null and the F-test loses its validity in this situation (as it is a two-sided test).

To find the unknown τ, equation (3.4.1) is estimated (including appropriate lags Δy_{t-i} as additional regressors to ensure u_t is IID) up to T times with values of τ that cover the range of values included in Δy_t; the value of τ that results in an estimated (3.4.1) with the minimum residual sum of squares is chosen as the threshold. Critical values can be calculated by using the above procedures for obtaining the ρ_1, τ (and thus I_t) with typically 10,000 Monte Carlo simulations of a random walk under the null hypothesis.[31]

[29] Note that if we replace Δy_{t-1} in (3.4.2) with y_{t-1}, the model is known as the TAR (threshold autoregressive) model; the version used here is known as the momentum TAR (or MTAR) and is favoured as having more power as a test over the TAR model.

[30] Enders and Granger (1998) actually specified a less general model (allowing for nonzero means in the series):

$$\Delta y_t = I_t(\rho_1 - 1)(y_{t-1} - a_0) + (1 - I_t)(\rho_2 - 1)(y_{t-1} - a_0) + u_t \qquad (3.4.1a)$$

where a_0 is the long-run mean of the series, and:

$$I_t = \begin{cases} 1 & \text{if } \Delta y_{t-1} \geq 0 \\ 0 & \text{if } \Delta y_{t-1} < 0 \end{cases} \qquad (3.4.2b)$$

That is, they specified that the threshold value should be the mean of y_t, while more recently it has been argued that this is suboptimal and instead the threshold τ should be estimated as set out in Box 3.4.

[31] That is, the null is $y_t = y_{t-1} + u_t \qquad u_t \sim \text{IID}(0, 1)$.

Box Table 3.4.1 Tests of unit roots based on asymmetric MTAR: UK money demand data (1963q1–1989q2), seasonally unadjusted.

Variable	Lag length*	τ	$(\rho_1 - 1)$	t-value $(\rho_1 - 1)$	$(\rho_2 - 1)$	t-value $(\rho_2 - 1)$	F-value $(\rho_1 - 1) = (\rho_2 - 1) = 0$
log Real M1	5	0.018	−0.001	−1.65	0.000	1.98	2.56
log TDE	4	0.014	0.001	0.23	0.001	3.75	7.14
$\Delta \log P$	3	−0.003	0.087	2.19	−0.219	−3.72**	7.48
R	0	−0.004	0.010	0.58	−0.038	−1.79	1.76

* Set using the Akaike information criteria (see, for example, Greene, 2000, p. 306).
** Rejects the null at the 1% level (critical value is −3.47 based on our own calculation—see text).

As an example, we have applied the asymmetric test as set out in equations (3.4.1) and (3.4.2) to the UK money demand data used earlier. The AIC was used to set the lag length with the results set out in Box Table 3.4.1. The overall test of the unit root hypothesis is the null H_0: $(\rho_1 - 1) = (\rho_2 - 1) = 0$, using the F-statistic reported, but where either $(\rho_1 - 1)$ and/or $(\rho_2 - 1)$ is positive, the t-max test is preferred. The null of a unit root was not rejected except for the inflation variable.

and/or intercept are found in Perron (1989, 1990). However, it is unlikely that the date of the break will be known a priori, as was assumed by Perron (1989). In such situations it is necessary to test for the possibility of a break using various methods that have been developed in the literature. For example, Perron (1994) considers breaks in the intercept and/or the trend using additive- and innovative outlier (AO/IO) approaches (see below), while Zivot and Andrews (1992) and Banerjee, Lumsdaine and Stock (1992) consider IO models and develop a recursive, rolling or sequential approach. As Perron (1994) pointed out, Zivot-Andrews and Banerjee et al. test the joint hypothesis of a null of a unit root and no break in the series, while his approach is a test of the unit root hypotheses *per se* where the change in slope is allowed under both the null and alternative hypotheses. Thus, we concentrate on the Perron approach here.[32]

One version of the AO model allows for an instantaneous change in the intercept of the deterministic trend of a variable y_t and is referred to as the 'crash model'. That is:

$$y_t = \mu_1 + \beta t + (\mu_2 - \mu_1)DU_t + v_t \tag{3.6}$$

[32] Harris (1995) considered in detail the Banerjee et al. (1992) approach.

where $DU_t = 1$, if $t > T_b$ and 0 otherwise, and T_b $(1 < T_b < T)$ is a single break that occurs at an unknown time. Note that y_t can be any general ARMA process, and under the null it will be assumed that it is non-stationary (i.e., contains a unit root). Another version of the AO model allows both a change in the intercept and the slope of the trend function to take place simultaneously (a sudden change in level followed by a different growth path, such as a productivity slowdown):

$$y_t = \mu_1 + \beta_1 t + (\mu_2 - \mu_1)DU_t + (\beta_2 - \beta_1)DT_t^* + v_t \tag{3.7}$$

where $DT_t^* = t - T_b$, if $t > T_b$ and 0 otherwise.

The IO model is similar, but allows for changes to the trend function to be gradual rather than instantaneous. Thus under the alternative hypothesis that y_t is a stationary variable, the above two AO models would be amended in the IO case such that the terms $[(\mu_2 - \mu_1)DU_t + v_t]$ and $[(\mu_2 - \mu_1)DU_t + (\beta_2 - \beta_1)DT_t^* + v_t]$ in equations (3.6) and (3.7) would be prefixed by the MA polynomial lag operator $B(L) = \theta_0 + \theta_1 L + \theta_2 L^2 + \cdots + \theta_q L^q$. This form of the model therefore permits shifts in the trend function to have a gradual effect on y_t.[33]

Testing whether there has been a structural break in the IO model is more straightforward than for the AO model. For the change in intercept (crash) model, the following regression model is used to test the null that y_t is non-stationary:

$$\Delta y_t = \psi^* y_{t-1} + \sum_{i=1}^{p-1} \psi_i \Delta y_{t-i} + \mu + \beta t + \gamma DU_t + \delta D(T_b)_t + \varepsilon_t$$

$$\varepsilon_t \sim \text{IID}(0, \sigma^2) \tag{3.8}$$

where $D(T_b)_t = 1$, if $t = T_b + 1$ (0 otherwise). For the change in intercept and the slope of the trend (productivity slowdown) model, the following is used:

$$\Delta y_t = \psi^* y_{t-1} + \sum_{i=1}^{p-1} \psi_i \Delta y_{t-i} + \mu + \beta t + \theta DU_t + \gamma DT_t^* + \delta D(T_b)_t + \varepsilon_t$$

$$\varepsilon_t \sim \text{IID}(0, \sigma^2) \tag{3.9}$$

In the case of the AO models, there is a two-step procedure whereby equations (3.6) and/or (3.7) are estimated and the error term $(\hat{v}_t)$ is then used in a second-stage regression:

$$\Delta \hat{v}_t = \psi^* \hat{v}_{t-1} + \sum_{i=1}^{p-1} \psi_i \Delta \hat{v}_{t-i} + \sum_{j=0}^{p-1} d_j D(T_b)_{t-j} + e_t \tag{3.10}$$

The test of the models set out in equations (3.6)–(3.10) of the null that y_t is non-stationary are based on H_0: $\psi^* = 0$ against H_1: $\psi^* < 0$, and the t-statistics for

[33] For more details see Perron (1994).

these tests depend on the break date T_b and the lag length p. To select T_b endogenously, two basic approaches can be used. The first is to select T_b as the value, over all possible break dates, that minimizes the t-statistic for testing $\psi^* = 0$. This test then is most favourable to the alternative hypothesis. An alternative procedure that has become more widely used in the literature on testing for structural breaks is to select T_b as the value, over all possible break dates, that maximizes (or minimizes) the value of the t-statistic for testing $\gamma = 0$ in the regression equations (3.6)–(3.10), noting that γ replaces $(\mu_2 - \mu_1)$ in equation (3.6) and replaces $(\beta_2 - \beta_1)$ in equation (3.7). In the 'crash' model, Perron (1994) chooses T_b so as to minimize the value of the t-statistic for testing $\gamma = 0$ (since he argues we are only interested in sudden crashes); for the 'slowdown' model he chooses T_b so as to maximize the absolute value of the t-statistic (i.e., based on the strongest evidence for a structural change). For the IO model, Harvey, Leybourne and Newbold (2001) have found that a test statistic with more power is achieved by choosing the break date as $T_b + 1$, rather than T_b; we adopt the Harvey et al. (2001) procedure here.[34]

As an example of the approach, the various test statistics that have just been discussed were computed using the money demand data considered earlier. The statistical algorithms for conducting the tests are available as *RATS* programs from Pierre Perron (details are available on this book's website). The choice of lag lengths (p) were based on using the AIC (which is equivalent here to maximizing $\bar{R}^2$ in each regression). Results are reported in Table 3.4, and these show that generally there is little evidence for rejecting the unit root null even after allowing for the possibility of a break in the series. Only the inflation series shows that a break may have affected the power of the ADF test, and by examining the value for γ and the break dates it appears that at least one break occurred in 1973 (see Figure 3.1b), although other breaks in 1966 and 1981 are also apparent, suggesting that testing for more than one structural break may be important for this series. Such tests are being developed in the literature, which should result in additional power for unit root-testing (cf. Clemente, Montanes and Reyes, 1998; Ben-David, Lumsdaine and Papell, 2001).

SEASONAL UNIT ROOTS[35]

Time series data often come in a seasonally *un*adjusted form, and it has been argued that where possible such data are to be preferred to their seasonally adjusted counterparts, since the filters used to adjust for seasonal patterns often distort the underlying properties of the data (see sect. 19.6 in Davidson and MacKinnon, 1993 for some evidence). In particular, there is a tendency for

[34] That is, the RATS programmes available from Pierre Perron for conducting the various IO tests have been amended to choose the break date as $T_b + 1$.

[35] For a thorough treatment of this topic, see Ghysels and Osborn (2001). A more succinct (and general treatment) is presented in Frances and McAleer (1999).

Table 3.4 AO and IO ADF tests of unit roots: UK money demand date (1963q1–1989q2), seasonally unadjusted.

Variable	Model	Break date	Lag length (p)	ψ^*	t_{ψ^*}	γ	t_γ
log Real M1	AO/Crash	1973q4	1	−0.00	−0.03	−0.44	−7.94**
log Real M1	AO/Slowdown	1979q3	1	−0.15	−3.98	−2.06	−22.37**
log Real M1	IO/Crash	1973q2	1	−0.01	−0.56	−0.04	−3.11**
log Real M1	IO/Slowdown	1979q4	1	−0.14	−3.44	0.01	4.17**
log TDE	AO/Crash	1982q2	1	−0.25	−3.81	−0.04	−5.49**
log TDE	AO/Slowdown	1985q1	1	−0.21	−3.57	−0.03	−0.27
log TDE	IO/Crash	1974q1	5	−0.12	−1.97	−0.01	−1.50
log TDE	IO/Slowdown	1972q2	1	−0.23	−3.59	0.00	0.38
$\Delta \log P$	AO/Crash	1981q2	1	−0.38	−4.97**	−0.03	−8.84**
$\Delta \log P$	AO/Slowdown	1973q1	1	−0.60	−7.09**	0.06	11.89**
$\Delta \log P$	IO/Crash	1966q3	1	−0.24	−3.69	0.01	1.51
$\Delta \log P$	IO/Slowdown	1973q2	1	−0.56	−5.97**	−0.01	−3.72**
R	AO/Crash	1985q2	1	−0.15	−2.71	−0.10	−12.33**
R	AO/Slowdown	1977q1	1	−0.14	−3.12	0.22	9.03**
R	IO/Crash	1985q1	1	−0.18	−3.33	−0.02	−2.81**
R	IO/Slowdown	1985q1	1	−0.17	−3.10	0.00	1.65
Δ log Real M1	AO/Crash	1973q3	1	−0.96	−9.71**	−0.04	−3.79**
Δ log Real M1	AO/Slowdown	1972q4	1	−1.02	−10.49**	−0.05	−3.28**
Δ log Real M1	IO/Crash	1973q1	1	−0.98	−9.75**	−0.04	−3.14**
Δ log Real M1	IO/Slowdown	1967q3	1	−0.94	−9.41**	0.00	0.79
Δ log TDE	AO/Crash	1981q3	4	−1.27	−4.34**	0.01	1.21
Δ log TDE	AO/Slowdown	1980q2	4	−1.53	−5.02*	−0.04	−0.87
Δ log TDE	IO/Crash	1973q4	4	−1.59	−5.17**	−0.03	−3.30**
Δ log TDE	IO/Slowdown	1980q3	4	−1.59	−4.69**	0.01	2.03**
$\Delta^2 \log P$	AO/Crash	1975q2	1	−1.51	−17.72**	−0.01	−1.68
$\Delta^2 \log P$	AO/Slowdown	1975q1	1	−1.49	−18.11**	−0.00	−0.49
$\Delta^2 \log P$	IO/Crash	1975q2	1	−1.51	−17.47**	−0.01	−2.74**
$\Delta^2 \log P$	IO/Slowdown	1975q2	1	−1.51	−17.38**	−0.00	−0.44
ΔR	AO/Crash	1980q2	1	−0.85	−8.61**	−0.01	−2.14**
ΔR	AO/Slowdown	1972q3	1	−0.85	−8.69**	0.01	0.70
ΔR	IO/Crash	1977q2	1	−0.89	−8.82**	0.00	0.42
ΔR	IO/Slowdown	1972q1	1	−0.85	−8.45**	0.00	0.39

Critical values are obtained from Perron (1994) for t_{ψ^*} and the Student's t-distribution for t_γ.
* Rejects the null at <10% significance level.
** Rejects the null at <5% significance level.

the OLS estimate of ρ_b in the DF test (3.2) to be biased toward 1 when y_t is a seasonally adjusted series, thus rejecting the null hypothesis of non-stationarity substantially less often than it should according to the critical values in Table 3.1.

Certain variables (e.g., consumption, spending) exhibit strong seasonal patterns that account for a major part of the total variation in the data and that are therefore important when model-building. Figure 3.2 presents the evidence for UK real non-durable consumer expenditure over the period 1971q2 to 1993q1. Panel (a) indicates a large seasonal variation across the year, which explains a considerable amount of the variation in the series, while panels (b) and (c) show that whereas quarter 4 spending (October to December) is always higher than spending in the other quarters, there has been a tendency for the July to September quarter to 'catch up' with quarter 4 from the mid-1980s. Thus, while such patterns may result from stationary seasonal processes, which are conventionally modelled using seasonal dummies that allow some variation, but no persistent change in the seasonal pattern over time, the drifting of the quarters over time may indicate that deterministic seasonal modelling is inadequate. That is, the seasonal processes may be non-stationary if there is a varying and changing seasonal pattern over time. Such processes cannot be captured using deterministic seasonal dummies since the seasonal component drifts substantially over time; instead such a series needs to be seasonal-differenced to achieve stationarity. This is more complicated than considering the possibility of a unit root (non-stationarity) at the zero frequency since there are *four* different unit roots possible in a seasonal process. To see this, consider seasonal-differencing quarterly data using the seasonal difference operator $\Delta_4 y_t = (1 - L^4)y_t = y_t - y_{t-4}$. Note that $(1 - L^4)$ can be factorized as:

$$\begin{aligned}(1 - L^4) &= (1 - L)(1 + L + L^2 + L^3) = (1 - L)(1 + L)(1 + L^2)\\ &= (1 - L)(1 + L)(1 - iL)(1 + iL)\end{aligned} \tag{3.11}$$

with each unit root corresponding to a different cycle in the time domain. The first $(1 - L)$ is the standard unit root considered so far, at the zero frequency. The remaining unit roots are obtained from the MA seasonal filter $S(L) = (1 + L + L^2 + L^3)$, and these correspond to the two-quarter (half-yearly) frequency $(1 + L)$ and a pair of complex conjugate roots at the four-quarter (annual) frequency $(1 \pm iL)$. To simplify the interpretation of the seasonal unit roots, Banerjee et al. (1993, p. 122) show that a simple deterministic process $(1 + L)y_t = 0$ can be rewritten as $y_{t+2} = y_t$ (the process returns to its original value on a cycle with a period of 2), while $(1 - iL)y_t = 0$ can be rewritten as $y_{t+4} = y_t$ (the process returns to its original value on a cycle with a period of 4).

Before considering testing for seasonal unit roots, it is useful to note that Osborn (1990) found only five out of thirty UK macroeconomic series required seasonal-differencing to induce stationarity, implying that seasonal unit roots are not encountered very often and macroeconomic time series can typically be described as $I(1)$ with a deterministic seasonal pattern superimposed (Osborn, 1990, p. 300). However, others have found more evidence in favour of seasonal unit roots (e.g., Franses and Vogelsang, 1998 find that seasonal unit roots were generally present in the real gross domestic product (GDP) series they

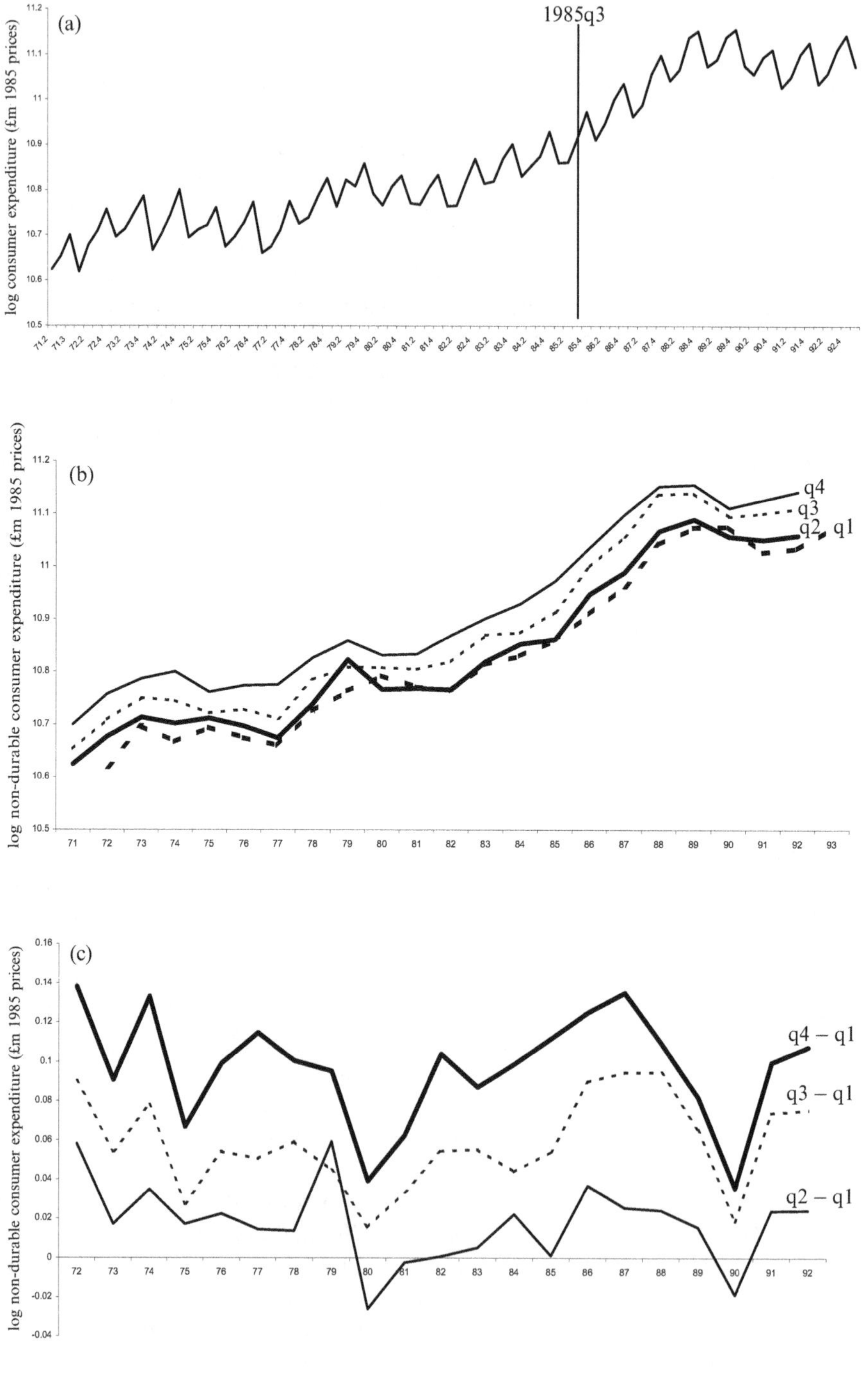

Figure 3.2. Quarterly UK consumer expenditure, seasonally unadjusted, 1971–1993: (a) actual values; (b) four quarters separately; (c) quarters 2–3 minus quarter 1.

considered, even after taking into account the possibility of structural breaks). Second, if all three seasonal unit roots discussed above are actually present, then no two quarters are cointegrated and '... the four quarter series for x go their separate ways in the long run ... the presence of seasonal unit roots begs the question of what sort of economic mechanism would give rise to this failure of cointegration' (Osborn, 1990, p. 300). A third point to note before proceeding concerns the question of whether the usual ADF tests of the null hypothesis of a unit root at the zero frequency are valid, even when other unit roots at other seasonal frequencies are present. Put another way, does the presence of additional roots at other cycles invalidate the non-seasonal unit root test. Ghysels, Lee and Noh (1994) show that the usual ADF test is still valid, as long as a sufficient number of lagged terms are included in the test equation to take account of the seasonal terms in the data. However, they also show (on the basis of Monte Carlo experiments) that the test involves serious size distortions (worse than in the standard ADF case, as discussed earlier).[36]

To incorporate seasonal integration into the definition of integration at the zero frequency (see Box 2.4), it is useful to note as above that seasonal-differencing involves using $(1 - L)$ to difference at the zero frequency d, in order to remove the zero frequency unit roots, and using the seasonal filter $S(L)$ to difference at the seasonal frequency D, in order to remove the seasonal unit roots. Thus, it is said that the stochastic process y_t is integrated of orders d and D (denoted $I(d, D)$) if the series is stationary after first period-differencing d times and seasonal-differencing D times. To test the number of seasonal unit roots in a univariate time series, the common approach is to use the procedure described in Hylleberg, Engle, Granger and Yoo (1990)—HEGY. The following regression is estimated using OLS with tests of the $\pi_i\,(i = 1, \ldots, 4)$ amounting to tests for the various unit roots that may be present in the series:[37]

$$\begin{aligned}\Delta_4 y_t &= \alpha_1 D_{1t} + \alpha_2 D_{2t} + \alpha_3 D_{3t} + \alpha_4 D_{4t} + \pi_1 Z_1 y_{t-1} + \pi_2 Z_2 y_{t-1} + \pi_3 Z_3 y_{t-2} \\ &\quad + \pi_4 Z_3 y_{t-1} + \sum_{i=1}^{p-1} \psi_i \Delta_4 y_{t-i} + \delta t + u_t \qquad u_t \sim \text{IID}(0, \sigma^2) \qquad (3.12)\end{aligned}$$

where D_{qt} is the zero/one dummy corresponding to quarter q and where:

$$\begin{aligned}Z_1 &= (1 + L + L^2 + L^3) \\ Z_2 &= -(1 - L + L^2 - L^3) \\ Z_3 &= -(1 - L^2)\end{aligned}$$

[36] This leads Ghysels et al. (1994) to point out: '... this faces the practical researcher with a difficult choice. Namely, either using unadjusted data resulting in tests with the wrong size, or using adjusted data, with adjustment procedures having adverse effects on power.'

[37] To maximize the power for the non-seasonal unit root, the trend term should be omitted in those cases where its presence is not economically justified (e.g., when variables in rates are being considered such as unemployment rates).

If $\pi_1 = 0$, then the $(1 - L)$ filter is required to remove the unit root at the zero frequency; if $\pi_2 = 0$, then the $(1 + L)$ filter is needed since the series contains a seasonal unit root at the two-quarter (half-yearly) frequency; and when $\pi_3 = \pi_4 = 0$, then the $(1 + L^2)$ filter is needed to remove the seasonal unit roots at the four-quarter (annual) frequency that correspond to $(1 \pm iL)$. Thus, separately testing $\pi_i = 0$, $i = 2, 3, 4$, will determine if there are any seasonal unit roots and at what frequency, while a joint test that $\pi_2 = \pi_3 = \pi_4 = 0$ will test the null that all seasonal roots are present. Lastly, a joint test that all the $\pi_i = 0$, $i = 1, 2, 3, 4$, can be used to test the null that all non-seasonal and seasonal unit roots are present.

Note that the HEGY approach (equation (3.12)), like the standard DF-type approach when only the zero frequency is considered, allows for only one unit root at the zero frequency. That is, we test against a null that at most series is $I(1)$. If y_t is $I(2)$, then (3.12) will not encompass this higher number of unit roots at the zero frequency, and as in the standard DF test it is argued that we need a testing procedure that tests down from the higher to lower orders of integration (cf. Box 3.2 and the Dickey and Pantula, 1987 approach). Franses and Taylor (2000) provide such a testing procedure for determining the order of differencing in seasonal time series processes, while Osborn (1990) provided a HEGY-type test that allows for $y_t \sim I(2)$:

$$\begin{aligned}\Delta_4 \Delta y_t &= \alpha_1 D_{1t} + \alpha_2 D_{2t} + \alpha_3 D_{3t} + \alpha_4 D_{4t} + \pi_1 Z_1 \Delta y_{t-1} + \pi_2 Z_2 \Delta y_{t-1} \\ &\quad + \pi_3 Z_3 \Delta y_{t-2} + \pi_4 Z_3 \Delta y_{t-1} + \sum_{i=1}^{p-1} \psi_i \Delta_4 \Delta y_{t-i} + u_t \qquad u_t \sim \text{IID}(0, \sigma^2)\end{aligned} \tag{3.13}$$

As can be seen, the essential difference between equations (3.12) and (3.13) is that Δy_t rather than y_t enters the test equation, so allowing for more than one unit root at the zero frequency since, if $\pi_i = 0$, then $y_t \sim I(2)$. However, da Silva Lopes (2001) provides an example where starting from the $I(2)$ situation and using either the Osborn (1990) or more general Franses and Taylor (2000) approach leads to a serious loss of power when testing, because over-differencing to encompass the $I(2)$ situation often produces long autoregressions (i.e., nuisance parameters) in the test equation in order to avoid residual autocorrelation problems. The result of this serious power loss is often spurious evidence for (non-seasonal and seasonal) unit roots. Therefore, as a practical (if not strictly theoretically correct) solution da Silva Lopes (2001) suggests starting with the standard Dickey and Pantula (1987) approach (see Box 3.2) that allows $y_t \sim I(2)$, ignoring the possibility of seasonal unit roots to begin with, and, if this is not rejected, then proceeding with the approaches advocated by Osborn and Frances and Taylor. Otherwise, if $y_t \sim I(2)$ is rejected, then da Silva Lopes suggests using the standard HEGY-type test (equation (3.12)) that allows for unit roots at the seasonal and non-seasonal frequencies. He produces some Monte Carlo simulations as evidence that this approach often has higher power as a testing strategy than the more general approaches.

Previous work using UK data has considered whether the consumption function comprises variables with seasonal unit roots (cf. Osborn, Chui, Smith and Birchenall, 1988).[38] The variables considered are real non-durable consumers' expenditure (real C), real personal disposable income (real Y), the inflation rate (π) and end-of-period real liquid assets (real W). These series are plotted in Figure 3.3[39] and exhibit a clear seasonal pattern, especially real consumption (see also Figure 3.2) and real liquid assets. Estimating (3.12) gave the results set out in Table 3.5. Lag lengths were set using the procedures outlined in Ng and Perron (1995) starting from a maximum length of 11. We test both including and excluding the trend term. Based on the results that include a deterministic trend, real consumers' spending appears to have a zero frequency unit root (we cannot reject $\pi_1 = 0$) and a seasonal unit root at the two-quarter frequency (we cannot reject $\pi_2 = 0$), but seasonal unit roots at the four-quarter frequency are absent (since we can reject $\pi_3 = \pi_4 = 0$). The last two columns in Table 3.5 for the first row of results confirm that not all seasonal unit roots are present and that not all unit roots (non-seasonal and seasonal) are present. If the deterministic trend is omitted, then the results for real consumer-spending suggest that there may be seasonal roots at the four-quarter frequency, although the last two columns, which report the joint tests, indicate that not all (seasonal) unit roots are present. Given that a trend term should probably be included to allow for growth, it is likely that the first set of results are more reliable.

The results for real personal disposable income suggest that this variable is $I(1)$ and contains no seasonal unit roots. In contrast, real liquid assets has both seasonal and non-seasonal unit roots, although it is unclear from the results which seasonal roots are present since the individual tests for the two-quarter and four-quarter frequencies do not reject the null, while the overall joint tests suggest that not all (seasonal) roots are present. Finally, inflation (based on the results excluding a deterministic trend) has both a non-seasonal unit root and a root at the half-yearly frequency (the results based on including the trend term allow for the rejection of the zero frequency unit root at the 5% level).

[38] The data is available from the UK Office for National Statistics (ONS) databank and is described in the appendix to the Osborn et al. (1988) paper. Note that total non-durable consumption is used here without excluding any components.

[39] All the variables are converted into natural logarithms. This transformation is standard, and there are important reasons for preferring a model comprising logged variables (Frances and McAleer, 1999, note that exponential growth in levels becomes linear growth, the variance of each series can be stabilized, outliers are less influential and a constant elasticity form of the model is obtained. However, the unit root properties of the data are affected by the log transformation, and we can get different outcomes depending on whether y_t or $\log y_t$ is used. See Frances and McAleer (1998) for more details and a testing procedure.

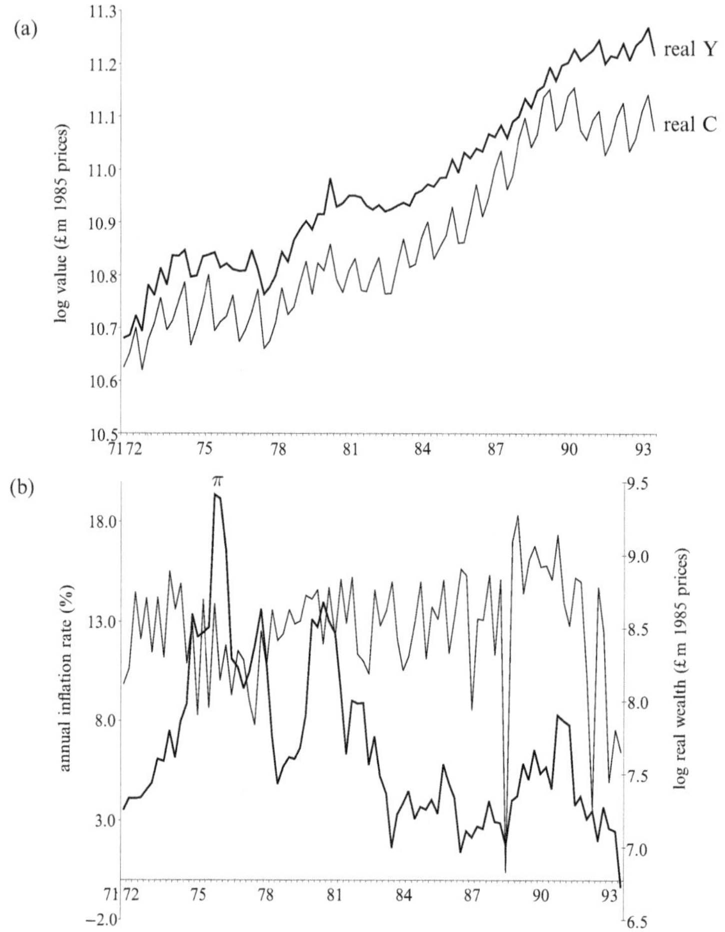

Figure 3.3. Quarterly UK consumption function data, seasonally unadjusted, 1971–1993: (a) log of real income and non-durable consumption; (b) log of real wealth and annual retail inflation rate $[\pi = \log(p_t - p_{t-4})]$.

It is reasonable to conclude that all the variables considered are $I(1, 1)$, except for real personal disposable income which is $I(1, 0)$. As a check, standard ADF tests were undertaken based on (3.5) and (3.3.1 in Box 3.3). These confirm that each series contains a unit root at the zero frequency, providing support for the results obtained using (3.12). Osborn et al. (1988) (using similar unadjusted quarterly data for 1955–1985) report that real W, π and real Y are $I(1, 0)$, while real C was tentatively classified as $I(1, 1)$.

STRUCTURAL BREAKS AND SEASONAL UNIT ROOT TESTS

As in the case with unit root-testing at the zero frequency, if structural breaks are present but are not incorporated into the test regressions, HEGY-type

Table 3.5 Seasonal unit roots tests: UK consumption function data (1971q2–1993q1) based on equation (3.12)).

Variable	Lag length	π_1	π_2	$\pi_3 \cap \pi_4$	$\pi_2 \cap \pi_3 \cap \pi_4$	$\pi_1 \cap \pi_2 \cap \pi_3 \cap \pi_4$
Trend included						
real C	3	−2.93	−2.51	28.48**	41.61*	44.06*
real Y	7	−2.27	−3.64	8.30*	16.78	17.91*
real W	7	−3.00	−2.08	5.08	10.09	17.64*
π	10	−3.49**	−2.10	7.21**	10.92*	12.34*
No trend						
real C	8	−0.11	−1.60	6.28	9.02*	9.01*
real Y	7	0.37	−3.79*	7.46**	15.89*	15.83*
real W	7	−2.75	−2.13	4.82	9.87*	15.69*
π	3	−1.36	−2.51	12.26*	20.19*	20.52*
Trend included						
5% critical value		−3.37	−2.81	6.57	6.03	6.47
1% critical value		−3.97	−3.41	8.86	7.86	8.26
No trend						
5% critical value		−2.81	−2.80	6.62	6.04	5.70
1% critical value		−3.43	−3.40	8.94	7.93	7.42

Note all critical values are taken from Franses and Hobijn (1997)—see Table A.5 in the Statistical Appendix.
* Reject null at 5% significance level, but not 1%.
** Reject null at 1% significance level.

seasonal root tests are biased toward finding too many unit roots (i.e., they suffer from low power). Recent analysis by Smith and Otero (1997), Franses and Vogelsang (1998) and Harvey, Leybourne and Newbold (2002) have extended seasonal unit root-testing to allow for one or more of the seasonal dummy variable coefficients (the D_{qt}) to exhibit structural change (i.e., a shift in the mean).[40] Assuming that there is a single break that occurs at an unknown time T_B (where $1 < T_B < T$), Franses and Vogelsang (1998) assume the following model under the null hypothesis:[41]

$$\Delta_4 y_t = \kappa_1 \Delta_4 DU_{1t} + \kappa_2 \Delta_4 DU_{2t} + \kappa_3 \Delta_4 DU_{3t} + \kappa_4 \Delta_4 DU_{4t} + u_t \qquad u_t \sim \mathrm{IID}(0, \sigma^2) \tag{3.14}$$

[40] Smith and Taylor (2001) have also extended the recursive and rolling regression-based tests for breaks based on Banerjee et al. (1992) to cover seasonal unit roots.
[41] Note that this version of the model under the null hypothesis refers to the AO model, where any shift in the seasonal means is immediate in the effect on y_t. An alternative specification is the IO model, where the right-hand side of equation (3.14) would be enclosed in brackets and prefixed by the MA polynomial lag operator $B(L) = \theta_0 + \theta_1 L + \theta_2 L^2 + \cdots + \theta_q L^q$. This form of the model therefore permits shifts in the seasonal means to have a gradual effect on y_t.

where

$$DU_{qt} = \begin{cases} 1 & (t > T_B) \\ 0 & (t \leq T_B) \end{cases} \qquad q = 1, \ldots, 4$$

The model therefore comprises a non-seasonal and three seasonal unit roots (since $\Delta_4 y_t = (1 - L^4)y_t = y_t - y_{t-4}$ and equation (3.11) shows how this can be factorized into four distinct unit roots), while also allowing for a structural break in each season at time T_B through the DU_{qt} dummies.

In order to test this null hypothesis of an AO break in the seasonal means, Franses and Vogelsang (1998) use a two-step procedure comprising, first, estimation of:

$$\begin{aligned} y_t &= \alpha_1 D_{1t} + \alpha_2 D_{2t} + \alpha_3 D_{3t} + \alpha_4 D_{4t} + \delta_1 DU_{1t} + \delta_2 DU_{2t} + \delta_3 DU_{3t} \\ &\quad + \delta_4 DU_{4t} + e_t \\ &= \sum_{q=1}^{4} \alpha_q D_{qt} + \sum_{q=1}^{4} \delta_q DU_{qt} + e_t \end{aligned} \tag{3.15}$$

and then estimating a HEGY-type equation using the residuals from (3.15):

$$\begin{aligned} \Delta_4 \hat{e}_t &= \pi_1 Z_1 \hat{e}_{t-1} + \pi_2 Z_2 \hat{e}_{t-1} + \pi_3 Z_3 \hat{e}_{t-2} + \pi_4 Z_3 \hat{e}_{t-1} + \sum_{i=1}^{p-1} \psi_i \Delta_4 \hat{e}_{t-i} \\ &\quad + \sum_{q=1}^{4} \theta_q \Delta_4 DU_{q,t} + \sum_{i=1}^{4} \eta_i \Delta_4 DU_{4,t-i} + \varepsilon_t \end{aligned} \tag{3.16}$$

As explained by Franses and Vogelsang (1998), the dummy variables $\Delta_4 DU_{qt}$ and $\Delta_4 DU_{4,t-i}$ are included for essentially technical reasons concerning the limiting distributions in the AO model. The tests of $\pi_1 = 0$ (the unit root at the zero frequency), $\pi_2 = 0$ (a seasonal unit root at the two-quarter (half-yearly) frequency), and $\pi_3 = \pi_4 = 0$ (the seasonal unit roots at the four-quarter (annual) frequency) can be used in the usual way to test the null that non-seasonal and seasonal unit roots are present. The associated test statistics can be denoted t_1 and t_2 for the t-statistics for π_1 and π_2, and F_{34} for the F-test that $\pi_3 = \pi_4 = 0$.

To test the null hypothesis of an IO break in the seasonal means, Frances and Vogelsang (1998) estimate the following:

$$\begin{aligned} \Delta_4 y_t &= \pi_1 Z_1 y_{t-1} + \pi_2 Z_2 y_{t-1} + \pi_3 Z_3 y_{t-2} + \pi_4 Z_3 y_{t-1} + \sum_{i=1}^{p-1} \psi_i \Delta_4 y_{t-i} \\ &\quad + \sum_{q=1}^{4} \theta_q \Delta_4 DU_{qt} + \sum_{q=1}^{4} \mu_q D_{qt} + \sum_{q=1}^{4} \eta_q DU_{qt} + v_t \end{aligned} \tag{3.17}$$

and again the test statistics of interest are denoted t_1 and t_2 for the t-statistics for π_1 and π_2, and F_{34} for the F-test that $\pi_3 = \pi_4 = 0$. The break date T_B is estimated endogenously, and there are essentially two options available: (i) base T_B on the value of t_1, t_2 and F_{34}, which is least favourable to the null that $\pi_1 = 0$, $\pi_2 = 0$ or $\pi_3 = \pi_4 = 0$; or (ii) choose the break date that maximizes the significance of the seasonal mean shift dummy variable coefficients in equations (3.16) or (3.17). The second approach is argued to have the better size and power properties and is denoted:

$$\hat{T}_B = \arg\max F_\delta(T_B) \tag{3.18}$$

Harvey et al. (2002) undertook various Monte Carlo simulations using (3.18) for the AO and IO models and find that, when the IO model is used with quarterly data, equation (3.18) needs to be modified by adding 4 to the right-hand side (i.e., choose the break date four observations later than (3.18) would suggest).

The UK consumption function data discussed in the last section were used to estimate equations (3.11)–(3.13).[42] Lag lengths were set using the procedures outlined in Ng and Perron (1995) starting from a maximum length of 11. We test both including and excluding the trend term. Note that critical values (based on Monte Carlo simulations of the null that $\Delta_4 y_t = \varepsilon_t$, where $\varepsilon_t \sim \text{IID}(0, 1)$) are only available in Harvey et al. (2002) for the model with no trend and the lag length set to zero. Thus, we calculated our own critical values based on 10,000 replications of the null, with $T = 88$ and allowing the lag length to be determined endogenously using the Ng and Perron (1995) approach.[43] The results are reported in Table 3.6. There is clearly some variation with the test outcomes, based on whether the AO or IO model is used, with or without a deterministic trend included. For real consumer-spending, there is evidence of a break around the end of 1985 (see Figure 3.2a), although the results are generally in line with those reported in the last section, when the HEGY model was estimated without allowing for structural change: the variable appears to have a zero frequency unit root (we cannot reject $\pi_1 = 0$) and a seasonal unit root at the two-quarter frequency (we cannot reject $\pi_2 = 0$), but seasonal unit roots at the four-quarter frequency are absent (since we can reject $\pi_3 = \pi_4 = 0$). The results for real personal disposable income confirm that this variable is $I(1)$—although the AO model with trend rejects the null of a unit root at the zero frequency—and the IO model suggests there are no seasonal unit roots at the two-quarter frequency (but there are at the four-quarter frequency, which is in contrast to the results reported in Table 3.5). Broadly, the results for real liquid assets confirm the earlier tests for unit roots without a break, with this variable having both seasonal and non-seasonal unit roots. Lastly, the IO model without a trend confirms that inflation has both a

[42] David Harvey kindly supplied us with his Gauss code in order to estimate the AO and IO models. We have included this on the book's website (along with an amended version that produces new sets of critical values).

[43] Only the critical values obtained with the lag length set by the Ng and Perron approach are reported, although these are not very different when the lag length is set to zero.

Table 3.6 Seasonal unit roots tests with a break in the mean: UK consumption function data (1971q2–1993q1) (based on equations (3.9)–(3.11)).

Variable	Model	Lag length	Break date	t_1	t_2	F_{34}
Real C	AO/T	3	1986q1	−3.45	−2.47	17.33*
Real C	AO/NT	0	1985q3	−0.75	−3.95**	56.47*
Real C	IO/T	3	1985q3	−4.00	−2.61	19.95*
Real C	IO/NT	8	1985q3	−1.38	−1.48	6.42
Real Y	AO/T	6	1987q3	−4.54*	−3.32	9.72
Real Y	AO/NT	2	1985q1	−1.18	−3.43	13.53*
Real Y	IO/T	7	1988q3	−1.98	−3.82**	6.35
Real Y	IO/NT	7	1977q4	0.17	−4.37*	8.08
Real W	AO/T	0	1978q2	−2.28	−3.97**	13.73*
Real W	AO/NT	7	1988q1	−3.25	−1.92	9.12
Real W	IO/T	7	1988q4	−2.85	−1.57	6.04
Real W	IO/NT	7	1988q4	−2.26	−1.56	5.66
π	AO/T	4	1982q1	−3.30	−3.15	7.11
π	AO/NT	4	1982q1	−3.53**	−3.24	7.19
π	IO/T	10	1979q1	−4.83*	−4.60*	12.90**
π	IO/NT	3	1976q3	−1.74	−2.93	29.72*
Critical values						
5%	AO/T			−3.89	−3.53	10.40
1%	AO/T			−4.54	−4.11	13.44
5%	IO/T			−4.08	−3.59	10.28
1%	IO/T			−4.65	−4.22	13.26
5%	AO/NT			−3.46	−3.49	10.17
1%	AO/NT			−4.06	−4.07	13.10
5%	IO/NT			−3.56	−3.59	10.33
1%	IO/NT			−4.18	−4.23	13.56

Note all critical values are based on 10,000 replications with $T = 88$, lag lengths are set by the Ng and Perron (1995) method and $\Delta_4 y_t = \varepsilon_t$, where $\varepsilon_t \sim \text{IID}(0, 1)$.
AO = Additive outlier model; IO = Innovative outlier model; T = Trend included; NT = No trend.
* Reject null at 5% significance level, but not 1%.
** Reject null at 1% significance level.

non-seasonal unit root and a root at the half-yearly frequency, although in general those estimating models that allow for a shift in the seasonal means produce mixed results.

PERIODIC INTEGRATION AND UNIT ROOT-TESTING

The HEGY model for testing (seasonal and non-seasonal) unit roots assumes time-invariant parameters with respect to the seasons covered. If it is assumed that the observations on a variable y_t can be described by a different model for each quarter, the result is a periodic autoregressive model (PAR), comprising an equation for each season:

$$y_t^1 = \mu_t^1 + \phi_1^1 y_{t-1}^1 + \cdots + \phi_p^1 y_{t-p}^1 + \varepsilon_t^1$$
$$y_t^2 = \mu_t^2 + \phi_1^2 y_{t-1}^2 + \cdots + \phi_p^2 y_{t-p}^2 + \varepsilon_t^2$$
$$y_t^3 = \mu_t^3 + \phi_1^3 y_{t-1}^3 + \cdots + \phi_p^3 y_{t-p}^3 + \varepsilon_t^3$$
$$y_t^4 = \mu_t^4 + \phi_1^4 y_{t-1}^4 + \cdots + \phi_p^4 y_{t-p}^4 + \varepsilon_t^4$$

or more concisely as:

$$y_t = \mu_t + \phi_{1,q} y_{t-1} + \cdots + \phi_{p,q} y_{t-p} + \varepsilon_t \tag{3.19}$$

Note that the μ_t comprises the deterministic variables in the model (seasonal dummies and separate seasonal time trends).[44] The PAR(p) model for a quarterly time series has four times the number of autoregressive parameters than are included in a non-periodic AR(p) model, and therefore there is a practical limit when setting the order of p in equation (3.19). Frances and McAleer (1999) point out that PAR(2) or PAR(3) models often suffice where an AR(8) or AR(12) model would be required for the same time series.

To test for a single unit root within a periodic setting, Boswijk and Franses (1996) show that (3.19) can be rewritten as the following regression, whereby the α_q parameters are embedded non-linearly in the model:

$$y_t = \sum_{q=1}^{4} \alpha_q D_{qt} y_{t-1} + \sum_{i=1}^{p-1} \sum_{q=1}^{4} \beta_{iq} D_{qt}(y_{t-1} - \alpha_q y_{t-i-1})$$
$$+ \sum_{q=1}^{4} \mu_q D_{qt} + \sum_{q=1}^{4} \tau_q D_{qt} t \tag{3.20}$$

If $\alpha_1\alpha_2\alpha_3\alpha_4 = 1$ (i.e., $\prod_{q=1}^{4} \alpha_q = 1$), there is a single unit root. The test for this hypothesis is based on a likelihood ratio test $\text{LR} = T\log(\text{RSS}_r/\text{RSS}_u)$, where RSS is the residual sum of squares in the restricted (r) and unrestricted (u) versions of equation (3.20). This test is distributed under the Johansen (1988) distribution,[45] which will be considered in Chapter 5. If this restriction holds (i.e., $\prod_{q=1}^{4} \alpha_q = 1$), then it is possible to test H_0: $\alpha_1 = \alpha_2 = \alpha_3 = 1$, and if this is not rejected, then y_t has a zero frequency unit root. Similarly, if H_0: $\alpha_1 = \alpha_2 = \alpha_3 = -1$ cannot be rejected, y_t has a seasonal unit root -1. Both these tests follow a $\chi^2(3)$ distribution. If both of these null hypotheses are

[44] That is, $\mu_t = \sum_{q=1}^{4} \mu_q D_{qt} + \sum_{q=1}^{4} \tau_q D_{qt} t$.

[45] As will be seen in Chapter 5, the Johansen λ-max test for cointegration is based on testing that the rank of the cointegration space is r versus $r + 1$. In this instance, the test statistic amounts to a test of rank 3 versus rank 4 (appropriate critical values that depend on the deterministic elements included in the model are provided in Tables A10–A12 in the Statistical Appendix at the end of the book).

Table 3.7 Periodic unit roots tests: UK consumption function data (1971q2–1993q1) (based on equation (3.16)).

Variable	LR-statistic	H_0: $\alpha_1 = \alpha_2 = \alpha_3 = 1$	H_0: $\alpha_1 = \alpha_2 = \alpha_3 = -1$
real C	0.07	0.93	381.14[a]
real Y	1.63	2.67	2886.20[a]
real W	6.14	2.88	26.06[a]
π	1.01	0.01	27.07[a]

Note the critical values for the LR test are based on Table A.11 in the Statistical Appendix at the end of the book, while the other tests have a standard $\chi^2(3)$ distribution.
[a] Reject null at 1% significance level.

rejected (i.e., not all the α_q are equal to 1), then y_t is periodically integrated of order 1.[46]

Using UK consumption function data, equation (3.20) was estimated using the non-linear least squares regression algorithm available in *TSP 4.5*; the results are reported in Table 3.7. In all instances, a PAR(3) was used (which on the basis of diagnostic tests seems to be adequate) and the seasonal trends were omitted as they proved insignificant (as well as producing implausible results). The results show that both H_0: $\prod_{q=1}^{4} \alpha_q = 1$ and H_0: $\alpha_1 = \alpha_2 = \alpha_3 = 1$ cannot be rejected, while H_0: $\alpha_1 = \alpha_2 = \alpha_3 = -1$ is clearly rejected, suggesting that each of these variables has only a zero frequency unit root.

CONCLUSION ON UNIT ROOT TESTS

This chapter has shown that, while in principle it is necessary to test for the presence of unit roots in order to avoid the problem of spurious regression, this is by no means a simple exercise. An appropriate testing strategy is based on de-trending the ADF test with the lag structure set by Ng and Perron's (2002) new information criterion. This procedure needs to be amended if there is any evidence of structural breaks in the series under examination, and a testing procedure along the lines outlined in Perron (1994) should then be followed. Similarly, when using seasonally unadjusted data exhibiting strong seasonal patterns that may be changing over time, it is necessary to amend the ADF-type test to allow for possible seasonal unit roots. However, Osborn (1990)

[46] Note that Ghysels, Hall and Lee (1996) develop tests for the hypothesis (that all the α_q are equal to 1) that do not require the restriction $\prod_{q=1}^{4} \alpha_q = 1$. Moreover, Boswijk et al. (1997) allow for more than one unit root and develop a more testing framework that allows for $I(2)$ processes as well as more general testing of non-seasonal and seasonal unit roots. Franses (1994) has developed a multivariate approach (based on the Johansen methodology discussed in Chapter 5) that allows separate tests of hypotheses for zero, seasonal and periodic processes. The latter approach will be considered after the Johansen model has been introduced.

suggested that seasonal unit roots are not encountered very often and macroeconomic times series can typically be described as $I(1)$ with a deterministic seasonal pattern superimposed.

Clearly, the most important problem faced when applying unit root tests is their probable poor size and power properties (i.e., the tendency to over-reject the null when it is true and under-reject the null when it is false, respectively). This problem occurs because of the near equivalence of non-stationary and stationary processes in *finite* samples, which makes it difficult to distinguish between trend-stationary and difference-stationary processes. It is not really possible to make definitive statements like 'real GNP is non-stationary'; rather, unit root tests are more useful for indicating whether the finite sample data used exhibit stationary or non-stationary attributes.[47]

Important Terms and Concepts

DF test	ADF test	Phillips and Perron test
Size and power properties of tests	Structural breaks and unit root tests	Seasonal unit roots
Seasonal-differencing	Multiple unit roots	Asymmetric unit roots

[47] Note also that, if anything, the problems of the size and power of the test are even worse in seasonal unit root models (Ghysels et al., 1994).

4
Cointegration in Single Equations

THE ENGLE–GRANGER (EG) APPROACH

In discussing cointegration in Chapter 2, it was shown that if two time series y_t and x_t are both $I(d)$, then in general any linear combination of the two series will also be $I(d)$; that is, the residuals obtained from regressing y_t on x_t are $I(d)$. If, however, there exists a vector β, such that the disturbance term from the regression ($\varepsilon_t = y_t - \beta x_t$) is of a lower order of integration, $I(d - b)$, where $b > 0$, then Engle and Granger (1987) define y_t and x_t as cointegrated of order (d, b). Thus, if y_t and x_t were both $I(1)$, and $\varepsilon_t \sim I(0)$, the two series would be cointegrated of order $CI(1, 1)$. This implies that if we wish to estimate the long-run relationship between y_t and x_t it is only necessary to estimate the static model:[1]

$$y_t = \beta x_t + \varepsilon_t \tag{4.1}$$

Estimating (4.1) using ordinary least squares (OLS) achieves a consistent[2] estimate of the long-run steady state relationship between the variables in the model and all dynamics and endogeneity issues can be ignored asymptotically. This arises because of what is termed the 'superconsistency' property of the OLS estimator when the series are cointegrated. Before discussing this, recall the following simple dynamic model of short-run adjustment (cf. (2.11)):

$$y_t = \gamma_0 x_t + \gamma_1 x_{t-1} + \alpha y_{t-1} + u_t \tag{4.2}$$

This can be rewritten as:

$$y_t = \beta x_t + \lambda_1 \Delta x_t + \lambda_2 \Delta y_t + v_t \tag{4.3}$$

[1] The issue of whether the model should include an intercept or an intercept and time trend will be discussed in this section when considering the testing strategy for determining whether $\varepsilon_t \sim I(0)$.

[2] That is, as $T \to \infty$, the estimate of β converges to the true β (denoted plim $\hat{\beta} = \beta$). Any bias (and its variance) in finite samples should tend to zero as the sample size T tends to infinity.

where $\beta = (\gamma_0 + \gamma_1/1 - \alpha)$, $\lambda_1 = -(\gamma_1/1 - \alpha)$, $\lambda_2 = -(\alpha/1 - \alpha)$ and $v_t = (u_t/1 - \alpha)$. Thus, estimating the static model (4.1) to obtain an estimate of the long-run parameter β is equivalent to estimating the dynamic model (4.3) without the short-run terms Δx_t, Δy_t. According to the 'superconsistency' property, if y_t and x_t are both non-stationary $I(1)$ variables and $\varepsilon_t \sim I(0)$, then as sample size T gets larger the OLS estimator of β converges to its true value at a much faster rate than the usual OLS estimator with stationary $I(0)$ variables (Stock, 1987). That is, the $I(1)$ variables asymptotically dominate the $I(0)$ variables Δx_t, Δy_t and ε_t. Of course, the omitted dynamic terms (and any bias due to endogeneity) are captured in the residual ε_t, which will consequently be serially correlated.[3] But this is not a problem due to 'superconsistency'.

Nevertheless, in finite samples, it has been shown that bias *is* a problem, and this will be discussed in this section. Moreover, Phillips and Durlauf (1986) have derived the asymptotic distribution of the OLS estimator of β and its associated t-statistic, showing them to be highly complicated and non-normal and thus invalidating standard tests of hypothesis. Thus, so far we have noted that there are problems of finite sample bias and an inability to draw inferences about the significance of the parameters of the static long-run model. A separate issue is whether tests of cointegration based directly on the residuals from (4.1) have good power properties (i.e., they do not under-reject the null when it is false).

To test the null hypothesis that y_t and x_t are not cointegrated amounts, in the Engle–Granger (EG) framework, to directly testing whether $\varepsilon_t \sim I(1)$ against the alternative that $\varepsilon_t \sim I(0)$. There are several tests that can be used, including the Dickey–Fuller (DF) and augmented Dickey–Fuller (ADF) tests discussed at length in the last chapter (comparable Z-tests by Phillips, and Phillips and Perron (PP), are also commonly used, but Monte Carlo work suggests they have poorer size properties and thus they will not be explored here—see Box 3.1). Essentially, Engle and Granger (1987) advocated ADF tests of the following kind:

$$\Delta\hat{\varepsilon}_t = \psi^*\hat{\varepsilon}_{t-1} + \sum_{i=1}^{p-1}\psi_i\Delta\hat{\varepsilon}_{t-i} + \mu + \delta t + \omega_t \qquad \omega_t \sim \text{IID}(0, \sigma^2) \tag{4.4}$$

where the $\hat{\varepsilon}_t$ are obtained from estimating (4.1). The question of the inclusion of trend and/or constant terms in the test regression equation depends on whether a constant or trend term appears in (4.1). That is, deterministic components can be added to *either* (4.1) *or* (4.4), *but not to both*. As with the testing procedure for unit roots generally (cf. Chapter 3), it is important to include a constant if the alternative hypothesis of cointegration allows a non-zero mean for $\hat{\varepsilon}_t(= y_t - \hat{\beta}x_t)$, while in theory a trend should be included if the alternative hypothesis allows a non-zero deterministic trend for $\hat{\varepsilon}_t$. However, Hansen

[3] If there is a simultaneity problem, then $E(x_t, u_t) \neq 0$ is also true.

(1992) has shown on the basis of Monte Carlo experimentation that, irrespective of whether $\hat{\varepsilon}_t$ contains a deterministic trend or not, including a time trend in (4.4) results in a loss of power (i.e., leads to under-rejecting the null of no cointegration when it is false).[4] Since, it is generally unlikely that the $\hat{\varepsilon}_t$ obtained from estimating (4.1) will have a zero mean and given Hansen's results, this form of testing for cointegration should be based on (4.1) and (4.4) with δ set equal to zero.

As with univariate unit root tests, the null hypothesis of a unit root and thus no cointegration (H_0: $\psi^* = 0$) is based on a t-test with a non-normal distribution. However, unless β is already known (and not estimated using (4.1)), it is not possible to use the standard DF tables of critical values. There are two major reasons for this: first, because of the way it is constructed the OLS estimator 'chooses' the residuals in (4.1) to have the smallest sample variance,[5] even if the variables are not cointegrated, making the $\hat{\varepsilon}_t$ appear as stationary as possible. Thus, the standard DF distribution (cf. Table 3.1) would tend to over-reject the null. Second, the distribution of the test statistic under the null is affected by the number of regressors (n) included in (4.1). Thus, different critical values are needed as n changes. Since the critical values also change depending on whether a constant and/or trend are included in (4.4) and with the sample size, there is a large number of permutations, each requiring a different set of critical values with which to test the null hypothesis.

Fortunately, MacKinnon (1991) has linked the critical values for particular tests to a set of parameters of an equation of the response surfaces. That is, with this table of response surfaces (see Table 4.1 for an extract), and the following relation:

$$C(p) = \phi_\infty + \phi_1 T^{-1} + \phi_2 T^2 \tag{4.5}$$

where $C(p)$ is the p per cent critical value, it is possible to obtain the appropriate critical value for any test involving the residuals from an OLS equation where the number of regressors (excluding the constant and trend) lies between $1 \leq n \leq 6$. For instance, the estimated 5% critical value for 105 observations when $n = 3$ in (4.1) and with a constant but no trend included in (4.4) is given by $(-3.7429 - 8.352/105 - 13.41/105^2) \approx -3.82$. Thus, reject the null of no cointegration at the 5% significance level if the t-value associated with ψ^* is more negative than -3.82. Note also that the critical values calculated with $n = 1$ will be the same as those given in Table 3.1 for the univariate DF test.

The residual-based ADF test for cointegration that has just been discussed assumes that the variables in the OLS equation are all $I(1)$, such that the test for cointegration is whether $\varepsilon_t \sim I(1)$ against the alternative that $\varepsilon_t \sim I(0)$. If some of the variables are in fact $I(2)$, then cointegration is still possible if the

[4] Including or excluding the time trend in the model appears to have little effect on the size of the test (i.e., over-rejecting the null when it is true).

[5] The OLS estimator minimizes the (sum of the squared) deviations of the $\hat{\varepsilon}_t$ from the OLS regression line obtained from $y_t = \hat{\beta}x_t$ (i.e., OLS obtains $\hat{\beta}$ that will minimize σ^2).

Table 4.1 Response surfaces for critical values of cointegration tests.

n	Model	% point	ϕ_∞	ϕ_1	ϕ_2
1	No constant, no trend	1	−2.5658	−1.960	−10.04
		5	−1.9393	−0.398	0.0
		10	−1.6156	−0.181	0.0
1	Constant, no trend	1	−3.4336	−5.999	−29.25
		5	−2.8621	−2.738	−8.36
		10	−2.5671	−1.438	−4.48
1	Constant + Trend	1	−3.9638	−8.353	−47.44
		5	−3.4126	−4.039	−17.83
		10	−3.1279	−2.418	−7.58
3	Constant, no trend	1	−4.2981	−13.790	−46.37
		5	−3.7429	−8.352	−13.41
		10	−3.4518	−6.241	−2.79

Source: MacKinnon (1991).

$I(2)$ series cointegrates down to an $I(1)$ variable in order to potentially co-integrate with the other $I(1)$ variables (see Box 2.4). However, Haldrup (1994) shows that the critical values for the ADF test will now depend (particularly in small samples) on the *number* of $I(1)$ and $I(2)$ *regressors* in the equation. Consequently, at the time of testing for cointegration when there is a mix of $I(1)$ and $I(2)$ variables, the critical values provided in Haldrup (1994, table 1) must be used.[6]

A potential problem with using the ADF test can now be considered (although for simplicity of exposition the DF test that involves no lagged values of the dependent variable is presented). Kremers, Ericsson and Dolado (1992) examine the common factor 'problem' of the DF statistic (a problem that applies to any single equation unit root-type cointegration test, such as the Phillips Z-test). Suppose the underlying data-generating process is given by (4.2), with the residuals from (4.1) used to test the null of no cointegration. The DF test comprises:

$$\Delta\hat{\varepsilon}_t = \psi\hat{\varepsilon}_{t-1} + \omega_t \tag{4.6}$$

[6] For instance, he gives the example (which is also used later on—see equation (4.11)) of testing for cointegration in the UK money demand function, where m_t and p_t are potentially $I(2)$. In a test in which homogeneity is not imposed (i.e., m_t and p_t are not combined into $(m_t - p_t)$) so that the OLS regression comprises $m = \beta_0 + \beta_1 p + \beta_2 y - \beta_3 R + \varepsilon$, there is one $I(2)$ regressor and therefore Haldrup's table 1 must be used with $m_1 = 2$ and $m_2 = 1$.

which can be rewritten to obtain the equivalent error correction model (ECM) (evaluated at $\hat{\beta} = \beta$):

$$\left.\begin{aligned} \Delta(y_t - \beta x_t) &= \psi(y_{t-1} - \beta x_{t-1}) + \omega_t \\ \text{or} \qquad \Delta y_t &= \beta \Delta x_t + \psi(y_{t-1} - \beta x_{t-1}) + \omega_t \end{aligned}\right\} \tag{4.7}$$

But this is *not* the unrestricted ECM underlying (4.2); this can be shown to be given by (cf. equation 2.13):

$$\Delta y_t = \gamma_0 \Delta x_t - (1 - \alpha)[y_{t-1} - \beta x_{t-1}] + u_t \tag{4.8}$$

For (4.8) to be the same as (4.7), it is necessary to impose ($\gamma_1 = -\gamma_0 \alpha$), since then (4.2) can be rewritten as:

$$\left.\begin{aligned} (1 - \alpha L)y_t &= (\gamma_0 + \gamma_1 L)x_t + u_t \\ \text{or} \qquad (1 - \alpha L)y_t &= \gamma_0(1 - \alpha L)x_t + u_t \end{aligned}\right\} \tag{4.9}$$

and both sides of this equation contain the common factor $(1 - \alpha L)$. What the DF test imposes through the common factor restriction in (4.9) is that the short-run reaction of y_t to a change in x_t (i.e., γ_0) now becomes the same as the long-run effect (i.e., β) that would occur if the model were in equilibrium.[7] Kremers et al. (1992) point out that if invalid (as is often likely), this restriction imposes a loss of information (and so a loss of power) relative to a test, say, based on the unrestricted ECM.[8]

So why is the EG procedure so popular, given that: (i) this test for cointegration is likely to have lower power against alternative tests; (ii) that its finite sample estimates of long-run relationships are potentially biased; and (iii) inferences cannot be drawn using standard t-statistics about the significance of the parameters of the static long-run model? First, it is of course easy to estimate the static model by OLS and then perform unit root tests on the residuals from this equation. Second, estimating (4.1) is only the first stage of the EG procedure, with stage 2 comprising estimating the short-run ECM itself using the estimates of disequilibrium ($\hat{\varepsilon}_{t-1}$) to obtain information on the speed of adjustment to equilibrium. That is, having obtained ($\hat{\varepsilon}_{t-1} = y_{t-1} - \hat{\beta} x_{t-1}$) from (4.1), it is possible to estimate:

$$\left.\begin{aligned} \Delta y_t &= \gamma_0 \Delta x_t - (1 - \alpha)\hat{\varepsilon}_{t-1} + u_t \\ \text{or} \qquad A(L)\Delta y_t &= B(L)\Delta x_t - (1 - \pi)\hat{\varepsilon}_{t-1} + u \end{aligned}\right\} \tag{4.10}$$

[7] Note that in (4.9) the long-run elasticity between Y and X is $\beta = [\gamma_0(1 - \alpha L)/(1 - \alpha L)] = \gamma_0$, assuming that $\alpha < 1$ (which is necessary for the short-run model to converge to a long-run solution).

[8] They also point out that when using the ADF version of the test, it may be necessary to have a lag length longer than that required in the ECM in order to generate white noise errors, which may lead to poorer size properties (i.e., the likelihood of over-rejecting the null when it is true) for the ADF test than a test (outlined in Box 4.2) based on the unrestricted ECM.

where the second form allows for a general dynamic structure to be determined by the data (see the discussion of (2.14)). Note also that if y_t and x_t are $I(1)$ and cointegration between them exists (thus $\hat{\varepsilon}_t \sim I(0)$), then all the terms in (4.10) are $I(0)$ and statistical inferences using standard t- and F-tests are applicable.

To illustrate the approach, estimating static demand for money equations using seasonally unadjusted data for 1963q1 to 1989q2 produced the following results:[9]

$$m = 0.774p + 1.212y - 3.448R - 2.976 + \varepsilon_1 \qquad R^2 = 0.99, DW = 0.33 \tag{4.11a}$$

$$m - p = 0.769\Delta p + 0.409y - 3.981R + 6.682 + \varepsilon_2 \qquad R^2 = 0.69, DW = 0.24 \tag{4.11b}$$

Using (4.4), with $\mu = \delta = 0$ imposed, the residuals $\hat{\varepsilon}_1$ and $\hat{\varepsilon}_2$ were tested for a unit root under the null hypothesis of no cointegration. The value of p was set by both the Akaike information criterion (AIC) (i.e., equivalent to the maximizing $\bar{R}^2$ approach) and by the formula suggested in Schwert (1989): both produced a similarly long lag length for the ADF test and consequently similar results. The τ-value associated with testing the null hypothesis (that H_0: $\psi^* = 0$ based on the $\hat{\varepsilon}_1$) is -1.56, while the corresponding test statistic for $\hat{\varepsilon}_2$ is -2.62. The critical value for rejecting the null is obtained from Table A.6 and in both instances is -3.09 (at the 10% significance level).[10] These results indicate that there is no long-run stable relationship for money demand. As will be seen, this is in contradiction to some of the results from other tests of cointegration.

TESTING FOR COINTEGRATION WITH A STRUCTURAL BREAK

As with the case of testing for unit roots when there has been a structural break(s), the EG approach will tend to under-reject the null of no cointegration if there is a cointegration relationship that has changed at some (unknown) time during the sample period. That is, a test for cointegration that does not take account of the break in the long-run relationship will have low power.

Gregory and Hansen (1996)—hereafter GH—have extended the EG model to allow for a single break in the cointegration relationship. Rewriting equation

[9] The data are the same as that used previously (e.g., see Figure 3.1) and are based on Hendry and Ericsson (1991). The statistical sources used are discussed by Hendry and Ericsson, although they concentrate on using seasonally adjusted data. The data are reproduced in the Statistical Appendix at the end of the book.

[10] The critical value from Haldrup (1994, table 1), for the case where homogeneity is not imposed (4.11a) and m_t and p_t are both potentially $I(2)$, is -3.93 (at the 10% level).

Box 4.1 Engle–Granger–Yoo 3-step approach.

Engle and Yoo (1991) propose a 'third step' to the standard EG procedure, which seeks to overcome some of the problems inherent in using the static first-step model (4.1) to obtain an estimate of the long-run parameter β. In particular, the latter is generally biased in finite samples and its distribution is generally non-normal, which means that standard t-statistics cannot be used to test hypotheses concerning β. Assuming that there is both a unique conintegration vector *and* weak exogeneity of the right-hand-side variables in the short-run ECM, then the third step provides a correction to the first-stage estimate of β and ensures that it has a normal distribution.

After estimating the static model (cf. (4.1)), a first-stage estimate is obtained of β, which we can label $\hat{\beta}^1$. The residuals from the static model provide estimates of the disequilibrium ($\hat{\varepsilon}_{t-1} = y_{t-1} - \hat{\beta}x_{t-1}$) that then enter the second-stage short-run ECM (cf. (4.10)). The latter itself provides an estimate of the speed-of-adjustment parameter $-(1 - \hat{\alpha})$ and a set of residuals $\hat{u}_t$, which are then used in a third-stage regression:

$$\hat{u}_t = \delta[(1 - \hat{\alpha})x_{t-1}] + v_t \tag{4.1.1}$$

The estimate of $\hat{\delta}$ obtained (together with its standard deviation, which provides the correct standard deviation for $\hat{\beta}^3$ below) is used to correct the first-stage estimates:

$$\hat{\beta}^3 = \hat{\beta}^1 + \hat{\delta} \tag{4.1.2}$$

As an indication of the type of results obtained, the residuals from the first-stage static demand for real money (4.11b) are entered (lagged one period) into a short-run ECM with $\Delta(m - p)_t$ as the dependent variable and an estimate of the speed of adjustment is obtained of -0.05. Thus, each of the (lagged) right-hand-side variables in (4.11b) are multiplied by 0.05 and the new variables form regressors in the third-stage model, with the residuals from the short-run ECM as the dependent variable (cf. (4.1.1)). Using the resultant parameter estimates of $\hat{\delta}$ (and associated standard errors that are used to calculate t-ratios), the corrected long-run relationship come out as:

$$m - p = \underset{(1.90)}{5.082}\Delta p + \underset{(5.28)}{0.813}y - \underset{(3.38)}{5.563}R + \underset{(1.11)}{2.011} + \varepsilon \tag{4.1.3}$$

Comparing these results with (4.16), it can be seen that the EG three-stage approach improves the estimates of y, R and the constant, but the estimate for Δp is still wrongly signed.

(4.1) with the β-vector separated into the intercept and slope parameters (α, β), GH generalize (4.1) to:

$$y_t = \alpha_1 + \alpha_2\varphi_{tk} + \lambda t + \beta_1 x_t + \beta_2 x_t \varphi_{tk} + e_t \tag{4.12}$$

where structural change is included through the dummy variable:

$$\varphi_{tk} = \begin{cases} 0 & \text{if } t \leq k \\ 1 & \text{if } t > k \end{cases} \tag{4.13}$$

where k is the unknown date of the (potential) structural break. Equation (4.12) allows for three alternatives if y_t and x_t cointegrate: (i) a change in the intercept (α) but no change in the slope (β)—thus in equation (4.12) $\lambda = \beta_2 = 0$; (ii) a change in the intercept allowing for a time trend—thus $\beta_2 = 0$ in (4.12); and (iii) a change in the slope vector as well as a change in the intercept—with $\lambda = 0$ in equation (4.12).

Since k is unknown, the ADF test involving $\hat{e}_t$ (the latter obtained from estimating equation (4.12)) is computed for each date within the sample (i.e., $k \in T$), with the largest negative value of the ADF τ-value across all possible break points taken as the relevant statistic for testing the null hypothesis. Critical values are available in table 1 of Gregory and Hansen (1996) and are reproduced in the Statistical Appendix (Table A.7 at the end of the book).[11] Based on estimating the static, real demand-for-money equation using seasonally unadjusted data for 1963q1–1989q2 and allowing the lag length p to be set using the AIC, the results of estimating the GH model are as follows:

$$\begin{aligned} m - p = {} & 1.971\Delta p + 0.831y - 3.343R + 1.823 \\ & - 0.215(1972\text{q}3) + \hat{e} \qquad \text{ADF}(\hat{e}) = -3.41; p = 5 \end{aligned} \tag{4.14a}$$

$$\begin{aligned} m - p = {} & -1.366\Delta p + 1.880y - 2.408R - 0.011t \\ & - 10.003 + 0.164(1983\text{q}3) + \hat{e} \qquad \text{ADF}(\hat{e}) = -4.02; p = 9 \end{aligned} \tag{4.14b}$$

$$\begin{aligned} m - p = {} & -1.242\Delta p + 7.152\Delta p(1973\text{q}3) + 0.174y \\ & + 1.591y(1973\text{q}3) - 1.077R \\ & - 1.295R(1973\text{q}3) + 9.241 \\ & - 18.864(1973\text{q}3) + \hat{e} \qquad \text{ADF}(\hat{e}) = -6.88; p = 1 \end{aligned} \tag{4.14c}$$

Only in the last model, which allows for both a shift in the intercept and slope, is the null of no cointegration rejected at the 5% level of significance; in the other models the null is accepted. The break point in this last model was the third quarter of 1973, and the results suggest that there was a fundamental change in the parameters of the cointegration relationship after this oil price shock.

[11] Note that Gregory and Hansen (1996) also compute critical values for the Phillips Z-test.

ALTERNATIVE APPROACHES

There are a number of alternative tests for cointegration. The simplest is the cointegration regression Durbin–Watson test (CRDW) proposed by Sargan and Bhargava (1983). This is based on the standard Durbin–Watson (DW) statistic obtained from a regression involving (4.1), known to be the uniformly most powerful invariant test[12] of the null hypothesis: that $\hat{\varepsilon}_t$ is a simple non-stationary random walk (i.e., $\hat{\varepsilon}_t = \hat{\varepsilon}_{t-1} + z_t$, where $z_t \sim \text{IN}(0, \sigma^2)$) against the alternative that $\hat{\varepsilon}_t$ is a stationary first-order autoregressive (AR) process (i.e., $\hat{\varepsilon}_t = \rho\hat{\varepsilon}_{t-1} + z_t$, where $|\rho| < 1$ and $z_t \sim \text{IN}(0, \sigma^2)$). In terms of the money demand model, the critical value for rejecting the null of no cointegration is 0.48 (see Sargan and Bhargava, 1983), which is not exceeded in (4.11). However, this critical value is only relevant when $\hat{\varepsilon}_t$ follows a first-order process (i.e., there is no higher-order residual autocorrelation, which is usually present, as in this example). Thus, the CRDW test is generally not a suitable test statistic.[13]

An alternative that has been suggested by Kremers, Ericsson and Dolado (1992) is to directly test the null hypothesis that $\alpha = 1$ in (4.10), which is the error-correction formulation of the model.[14] If this null holds, then there is no cointegration. Under the null hypothesis, such a t-type test has a non-normal distribution, and Kremers et al. (1992) suggest using the MacKinnon critical values associated with the comparable ADF test of the null. Banerjee, Dolado, Galbraith and Hendry (1993), however, show that the distribution of the t-statistic associated with testing $\alpha = 1$ is closer to the normal distribution than it is to the ADF distribution (also, under the alternative hypothesis of cointegration, the t-value is known to be asymptotically normally distributed). However, despite this problem of what set of critical values to use, both Kremers et al. (1992) and Banerjee et al. (1993) show that this approach produces a more powerful test than the ADF test (presumably because no common factor restrictions are imposed). To make the test operational, it is necessary to assume that x_t is weakly exogenous (see p. 94 for a discussion of this property), and an estimate of $\hat{\varepsilon}_{t-1}$ is needed. The latter can either be obtained, for example, from imposing $\beta = 1$ (on theoretical grounds) and thus $\hat{\varepsilon}_{t-1} = y_{t-1} - x_{t-1}$, or an estimate of the long-run relationship must be obtained in advance (i.e., we require an unbiased estimate of β). Another approach equivalent to that suggested by Kremers et al. (1992), is to estimate the unrestricted dynamic model in distributed lag form rather than as an ECM and then

[12] The use of the term 'invariant' means that the test is not affected by a trend entering (4.1).

[13] Note that the CRDW test also suffers from the 'problem' that it imposes a common factor restriction—see the earlier discussion (equations 4.7–4.9) relating to the ADF test on this matter.

[14] In the more general formulation of the ECM, the test amounts to whether the parameter coefficient on the error correction term $\hat{\varepsilon}_{t-1}$ equals zero.

to solve for the long-run model (i.e., to directly estimate equation (4.2) or a more general form and then to solve for equation (4.1)). This procedure is standard in certain econometric packages, in particular *PcGive*, and the output from applying this approach to the money demand model is given in Box 4.2 (see the next section for a discussion of the approach). In line with the results from using the ECM formulation, the test of the null hypothesis of no cointegration is more powerful than using the ADF test. Inder (1993) shows that there are other desirable properties, namely that the unrestricted dynamic model gives '... precise estimates (of long-run parameters) and valid t-statistics, even in the presence of endogenous explanatory variables' (Inder, 1993, p. 68).

Dynamic Models

When the simple dynamic model, as represented by (4.2), is a sufficient representation of the underlying economic relationship, the EG approach of estimating the (static) (4.1) is equivalent to omitting the short-run elements of the dynamic model. As more complicated dynamic models become necessary to capture the relationship between x and y, then estimating the static model to obtain an estimate of the long-run parameter β will push more complicated dynamic terms into the residual ε_t, with the result that the latter can exhibit severe autocorrelation. As has been stated, 'superconsistency' ensures that it is asymptotically valid to omit the stationary $I(0)$ terms in equations like (4.3), but in finite samples the estimates of the long-run relationship will be biased (and, as shown by Phillips, 1986, this is linked to the degree of serial correlation).[15] The Monte Carlo work of Banerjee et al. (1993) and Inder (1993) shows that this bias is often substantial. Thus, it seems reasonable to consider estimating the full model, which includes the dynamics (i.e., (4.2) or its equivalent), since this leads to greater precision in estimating β in finite samples.

One of the results to emerge from the Monte Carlo work is that it is preferable to over-parameterize the dynamic model (i.e., a generous lag length should be chosen) since this reduces any bias when compared with an under-parameterized model, even when the 'true' model involves a simple d.g.p. with few dynamic terms. Thus, the following model should be estimated:

$$A(L)y_t = B(L)x_t + u_t \tag{4.15}$$

where $A(L)$ is the polynomial lag operator $1 - \alpha_1 L - \alpha_2 L^2 - \cdots - \alpha_p L^p$, $B(L)$ is the polynomial lag operator $\gamma_0 + \gamma_1 L + \gamma_2 L^2 + \cdots + \gamma_q L^q$ and $L^r x_t = x_{t-r}$.[16]

[15] Banerjee, Hendry and Smith (1986) show that bias is inversely related to the value R^2 in the static OLS regression model, but they point out that it does not necessarily follow that high values of R^2 imply low biases, since R^2 can always be increased by the addition of more (*ad hoc*) regressors.

[16] For instance, choosing $p = q = 4$ results in the following dynamic model: $y_t = \gamma_0 x_t + \gamma_1 x_{t-1} + \gamma_2 x_{t-2} + \gamma_3 x_{t-3} + \gamma_4 x_{t-4} + \alpha_1 y_{t-1} + \alpha_2 y_{t-2} + \alpha_3 y_{t-3} + \alpha_4 y_{t-4} + u_t$.

Box 4.2 Dynamic analysis and the long-run model: estimates from PcGive.

AR Model estimated:

$$A(L)\,(m-p)_t = B_1(L)y_t + B_2(L)R_2 + B_3(L)\,\Delta p_t + u_t$$

$R^2 = 0.996349$ F(26, 73) = 766:19 [0.0000] $\sigma = 0.0138893$ DW = 2.08
RSS = 0.01408263438 for 27 variables and 100 observations

Information Criteria: SC = -7.62459; HQ = -8.04331; FPE = 0.000244999

Diagnostic tests of the u_t

AR 1- 5 F(5, 68)	=	1.8769	[0.1098]
ARCH 4 F(4, 65)	=	0.67035	[0.6149]
Normality $\chi^2(2)$	=	4.204	[0.1222]
x_i^2 F(49, 23)	=	0.53713	[0.9658]
RESET F(1, 72)	=	0.2299	[0.6331]

Solved Static Long Run equation

	m-p =	-0.3931	+1.052 y	-6.871 R	-7.332 Δp	+0.2379 Seasonal
(SE)		(1.376)	(0.1218)	(0.5737)	(1.693)	(0.1869)

WALD test $\chi^2(4)$ = 155.92 [0.0000] **

Analysis of lag structure

Lag =	0	1	2	3	4	5	Σ
m-p	-1	0.58	0.127	-0.185	0.442	-0.102	-0.138
SE	0	0.123	0.131	0.122	0.123	0.108	0.0311
Constant	-0.0544	0	0	0	0	0	-0.0544
SE	0.185	0	0	0	0	0	0.185
y	-0.00243	0.25	0.0487	-0.385	0.138	0.0969	0.146
SE	0.102	0.112	0.114	0.113	0.119	0.11	0.0281
R	-0.413	-0.355	-0.274	0.0774	0.172	-0.159	-0.952
SE	0.129	0.198	0.2	0.198	0.198	0.147	0.198
Δp	-0.649	0.045	0.103	-0.25	-0.315	0.0502	-1.02
SE	0.24	0.286	0.28	0.276	0.257	0.22	0.241
Seasonal	-0.0119	0.0197	0.0251	0	0	0	0.0329
SE	0.0101	0.0106	0.00916	0	0	0	0.0242

Tests on the significance of each variable

variable	F(num,denom)	Value	Probability	Unit Root t-test
m-p	F(5, 73) =	279.92	[0.0000] **	-4.4577*
Constant	F(1, 73) =	0.086917	[0.7690]	-0.29482
y	F(6, 73) =	7.2548	[0.0000] **	5.1892
R	F(6, 73) =	11.655	[0.0000] **	-4.795
Δp	F(6, 73) =	4.438	[0.0007] **	-4.2184
Seasonal	F(3, 73) =	5.0883	[0.0030] **	1.3642

Tests on the significance of each lag

Lag	F(num,denom)	Value	Probability
1	F(4, 73) =	12.288	[0.0000] **
2	F(4, 73) =	0.84412	[0.5018]
3	F(4, 73) =	3.3472	[0.0143] *
4	F(4, 73) =	5.7811	[0.0004] **
5	F(4, 73) =	0.60177	[0.6626]

COMFAC WALD test statistic table

Order	χ^2df	Value	p-value		Incr. χ^2df	Value	p-value	
5	3	0.55972	[0.9056]		3	0.55972	[0.9056]	
4	6	0.80294	[0.9920]		3	0.24322	[0.9703]	
3	9	2.414	[0.9831]		3	1.6111	[0.6569]	
2	12	13.293	[0.3481]		3	10.879	[0.0124]	*
1	15	34.894	[0.0025]	**	3	21.601	[0.0001]	**

The long-run parameter(s)[17] can be obtained by solving the estimated version of (4.15) for β, which in the simple model (equation (4.2)) amounts to $\beta = (\gamma_0 + \gamma_1/1 - \alpha_1)$.[18] Standard errors of β can be obtained using a (non-linear) algorithm (the procedure used in *PcGive* involves numerical differentiation)), and thus not only are long-run estimates obtained but t-tests concerning the statistical significance of β can also be undertaken. Inder (1993) shows that t-tests of this kind, using critical values from the standard normal distribution, have good size and power properties (even when x_t is endogenous) and therefore valid inferences can be made concerning β.[19]

In addition to providing generally unbiased estimates of the long-run model and valid t-statistics, it is possible to carry out a unit root test of the null hypothesis of no cointegration since the sum of the $\alpha_i\,(i = 1, \ldots, p)$ in (4.15) must be less than one for the dynamic model to converge to a long-run solution. Thus, dividing $(1 - \sum \alpha_i)$ by the sum of their associated standard errors provides a t-type test statistic that can be compared against the critical values given in Banerjee, Dolado and Mestre (1998), in order to test the null hypothesis.[20]

As an example of the approach, recall that when applying unit root tests to the residuals from the static demand-for-money equation, there is no evidence to reject the null hypothesis of no cointegration. Setting $p = q = 5$ and then

[17] If x_t is a single variable, then there is a single long-run parameter β (which may include the long-run estimate of the constant as well as slope—see equation (2.12)—and therefore $\beta = [\beta_0, \beta_1]'$); however, if x_t is a vector of variables, then a vector of long-run parameters is obtained.

[18] In more complicated models, the long-run parameters are the sum of the parameters associated with the variable being considered (i.e., $\sum \gamma_i\,(i = 0, \ldots, q)$ in (4.15)), divided by one minus the sum of the parameters associated with the dependent variable (i.e., $1 - \sum \alpha_i\,(i = 1, \ldots, p)$).

[19] He states that the test statistics based on the simple OLS static model are '... hopelessly unreliable' (p. 67).

[20] Note that dividing the sum of the parameter estimates associated with x (i.e., $\sum \gamma_i$) by the sum of their associated standard errors provides a t-type test of the null hypothesis that there is no significant long-run effect of x on y. This test is *not* equivalent to a test involving the t-values obtained from the solution to the long-run equation, and in small samples it is possible that there will be conflicting outcomes from these alternative approaches.

testing to ensure that this parameterization of (4.15) is general enough to pass various diagnostic tests[21] relating to the properties of the residuals u_t, the following (cf. Box 4.2) long-run relationship is found (with t-values in parentheses):

$$m - p = \underset{(4.33)}{-7.332}\Delta p + \underset{(8.64)}{1.052}y - \underset{(11.98)}{6.871}R - \underset{(0.29)}{0.393} + \underset{(1.27)}{0.238}\text{SEAS} + \varepsilon \qquad (4.16)$$

A Wald test decisively rejects the null that all the long-run coefficients (except the constant term) are zero. The unit root test of the null hypothesis of no cointegration results in a test statistic of −4.46, which rejects the null at the 5% significance level.[22] Thus, this approach suggests that, contrary to the results obtained from the static (4.4), there is a long-run stable relationship for money demand. Furthermore, tests of common factors (COMFAC) in the lag polynomials reject the hypothesis of four common factors, which helps to explain the results from applying the different tests for cointegration. Lastly, it can be seen that the estimates of long-run parameters are also different (cf. equations (4.11b) and (4.16)), with the estimate for Δp wrongly signed and the estimate for real income unexpectedly small in the static model.[23]

Fully Modified Estimators

Using a dynamic modelling procedure results in a more powerful test for cointegration, as well as giving generally unbiased estimates of the long-run relationship and standard t-statistics for conducting statistical hypothesis-testing. In large part the better performance of the dynamic model is the result of not pushing the short-run dynamics into the residual term of the estimated OLS regression. As with the tests for unit roots discussed in the last chapter (Box 3.1), the alternative to modelling the dynamic processes

[21] These diagnostic tests (reported in Box 4.2), and how to interpret them, will be discussed in the section on estimating the short-run model (see p. 96). For now it is sufficient to note that the significance levels for rejecting the null of no serial correlation (AR test, ARCH test, etc.) are given [ ] brackets after each test statistic and are such as to suggest we should have little confidence in rejecting the various null hypotheses.

[22] Note that $(1 - \sum \alpha_i) = -0.138$, with a standard error of 0.0311.

[23] Applying the dynamic modelling approach to the nominal money balances model gives the following lon-run equation:

$$m = \underset{(11.22)}{0.967}p + \underset{(3.82)}{11.153}y - \underset{(7.76)}{6.573}R - \underset{(0.45)}{1.627} + \underset{(1.23)}{0.221}\text{SEAS}$$

while the unit root test for cointegration yields a test statistic of −4.526 (significant at the 5% level). Note that since results discussed in Box 3.2 suggest that m and p are probably $I(2)$, it is assumed that an $I(1)$ cointegration relation between these variables exists that in turn cointegrates with the other $I(1)$ variables in the model (see Box 2.4) to result in an $I(0)$ error term. In (4.16) if $(m - p) \sim I(1)$, as suggested in Box Table 3.2.1, then it is easier to justify the existence of a cointegration relationship for real money demand, given that the other variables are also $I(1)$, including Δp, since $p \sim I(2)$.

is to apply a non-parametric correction to take account of the impact on the residual term of autocorrelation (and possible endogeneity if the right-hand-side variables in the cointegration equation are not weakly exogenous). Such an approach is often termed 'the modified OLS' (see especially Phillips and Hansen, 1990) and amounts to applying adjustments to the OLS estimates of both the long-run parameter(s) β and its associated t-value(s) to take account of any bias, due to autocorrelation and/or endogeneity problems, that shows up in the OLS residuals.[24] Thus, tests involving the modified OLS t-statistics are asymptotically normal.

Inder (1993) found that the modified OLS estimates of the long-run relationship yielded little or no improvement on the precision of the standard OLS estimator. Thus, bias remained a problem in many of his Monte Carlo experiments, leading him to conclude that '... it seems that the semiparametric correction is insufficient to remove the autocorrelation in the error when the data-generating process includes a lagged dependent variable' (p. 61). Furthermore '... Modified OLS gives t-statistics whose sizes are generally no better than the OLS results ... The poor performance of (such) t-statistics suggests that in this case a very large sample is required for the asymptotics to take effect' (p. 66). This is perhaps fortunate since implementation of the Phillips-type non-parametric corrections is somewhat complicated, and Inder's results suggest that there is little to be gained over the static EG approach.

PROBLEMS WITH THE SINGLE EQUATION APPROACH

It was stated in Box 2.4 that if there are $n > 2$ variables in the model, there can be more than one cointegration vector. That is, the variables in a model (e.g., (2.1), which depicts the money demand function) may feature as part of several equilibrium relationships governing the joint evolution of the variables. It is possible for up to $n - 1$ linearly independent cointegration vectors to exist, and only when $n = 2$ is it possible to show that the cointegration vector is unique.

Assuming that there is only one cointegration vector, when in fact there are more, leads to inefficiency in the sense that we can only obtain a linear combination of these vectors when estimating a single equation model. However, the drawbacks of this approach extend beyond its inability to validly estimate the long-run relationships between variables. Even if there is only one cointegration relationship, estimating a single equation is potentially inefficient (i.e., it does not lead to the smallest variance against alternative approaches). As will be seen, information is lost unless each endogenous variable appears on the left-hand side of the estimated equations in the multivariate model, except in

[24] The non-parametric correction for bias due to autocorrelation is akin to the PP correction (Box 3.1); a second correction uses a non-parametric estimate of the long-run covariance between x and y to deal with any endogeneity. It is also possible to correct the unrestricted dynamic model (equation (4.15)) for possible endogeneity using a similar non-parametric correction to that proposed for modified OLS (see Inder, 1993).

the case where all the right-hand-side variables in the cointegration vector are weakly exogenous.

It is useful to extend the single equation ECM to a multivariate framework by defining a vector $\mathbf{z}_t = [y_{1t}, y_{2t}, x_t]'$ and allowing all three variables in $\mathbf{z}_t$ to be potentially endogenous, viz.:

$$\mathbf{z}_t = \mathbf{A}_1\mathbf{z}_{t-1} + \cdots + \mathbf{A}_k\mathbf{z}_{t-k} + \mathbf{u}_t \qquad \mathbf{u}_t \sim \text{IN}(0, \Sigma) \tag{4.17}$$

This is comparable with the single equation dynamic model (4.15) and in a similar way can be reformulated into a *vector* error correction form:

$$\Delta\mathbf{z}_t = \mathbf{\Gamma}_1\Delta\mathbf{z}_{t-1} + \cdots + \mathbf{\Gamma}_{k-1}\Delta\mathbf{z}_{t-k+1} + \mathbf{\Pi}\mathbf{z}_{t-1} + \mathbf{u}_t \tag{4.18}$$

where $\mathbf{\Gamma}_i = -(\mathbf{I} - \mathbf{A}_1 - \cdots - \mathbf{A}_i)$ $(i = 1, \ldots, k-1)$ and $\mathbf{\Pi} = -(\mathbf{I} - \mathbf{A}_1 - \cdots - \mathbf{A}_k)$. The (3×3) $\mathbf{\Pi}$ matrix contains information on long-run relationships; in fact, $\mathbf{\Pi} = \boldsymbol{\alpha}\boldsymbol{\beta}'$, where $\boldsymbol{\alpha}$ represents the speed of adjustment to disequilibrium[25] and $\boldsymbol{\beta}$ is a matrix of long-run coefficients. Thus, the term $\boldsymbol{\beta}'\mathbf{z}_{t-1}$ embedded in (4.18) is equivalent to the error correction term $(y_{t-1} - \beta x_{t-1})$ in (4.8), except that $\boldsymbol{\beta}'\mathbf{z}_{t-1}$ contains up to $(n-1)$ vectors in a multivariate model.[26]

Setting the lag length in (4.18) to $k = 2$ and writing out the model in full gives:

$$\begin{bmatrix} \Delta y_{1t} \\ \Delta y_{2t} \\ \Delta x_t \end{bmatrix} = \Gamma_1 \begin{bmatrix} \Delta y_{1t-1} \\ \Delta y_{2t-1} \\ \Delta x_{t-1} \end{bmatrix} + \begin{bmatrix} \alpha_{11} & \alpha_{12} \\ \alpha_{21} & \alpha_{22} \\ \alpha_{31} & \alpha_{32} \end{bmatrix} \begin{bmatrix} \beta_{11} & \beta_{21} & \beta_{31} \\ \beta_{12} & \beta_{22} & \beta_{32} \end{bmatrix} \begin{bmatrix} y_{1t-1} \\ y_{2t-1} \\ x_{t-1} \end{bmatrix} \tag{4.19}$$

It is now possible to illustrate more fully the problems incurred when estimating only a single equation model. Using (4.19) and writing out just the error correction part of, say, the first equation (i.e., the equation with Δy_{1t} on the left-hand side) gives:[27,28]

[25] See the discussion surrounding $(1 - \alpha_1)$ in (2.13) for an analogous interpretation in the single equation model.

[26] In fact, the matrix $\boldsymbol{\beta}'\mathbf{z}_{t-1}$ contains n column vectors in a multivariate model, but only $(n-1)$ of them can possibly represent long-run relationships and often the number of steady-state vectors is less than $(n-1)$. The whole issue of testing for stationary cointegration vectors in $\boldsymbol{\beta}$ is considered in the next chapter when we test for the reduced rank of $\boldsymbol{\beta}$.

[27] Note that since there are two cointegration relationships, both enter each of the equations in the system. Also, neither of the two equations have been normalized in (4.19), and so all the β_{ij} are included. Normalization, say to obtain a coefficient of 1 on y_{1t-1}, would entail multiplying each long-run relationship by its respective estimate of $1/\beta_{ij}\,(j = 1, 2)$.

[28] Equation (4.20) can also be written as:

$$\alpha_{11}(\beta_{11}y_{1t-1} + \beta_{21}y_{2t-1} + \beta_{31}x_{t-1}) + \alpha_{12}(\beta_{12}y_{1t-1} + \beta_{22}y_{2t-1} + \beta_{32}x_{t-1})$$

which shows clearly the two cointegration vectors with associated speed-of-adjustment terms in the equation for Δy_{1t}.

$$\mathbf{\Pi}_1\mathbf{z}_{t-1} = [(\alpha_{11}\beta_{11} + \alpha_{12}\beta_{12}) \quad (\alpha_{11}\beta_{21} + \alpha_{12}\beta_{22}) \quad (\alpha_{11}\beta_{31} + \alpha_{12}\beta_{32})] \begin{bmatrix} y_{1t-1} \\ y_{2t-1} \\ x_{t-1} \end{bmatrix} \tag{4.20}$$

where $\mathbf{\Pi}_1$ is the first row of $\mathbf{\Pi}$. That is, if only a single equation with Δy_{1t} as the left-hand-side variable is estimated, then it is not possible to obtain an estimate of either of the cointegration vectors since all that can be obtained is an estimate of $\mathbf{\Pi}_1$, which is a linear combination of the two long-run relationships (and this applies equally to the static or dynamic form of the single equation model (cf. equations (4.1) and (4.15)). This result applies whichever element of $\mathbf{z}_t$ is used as the left-hand side in the single equation model, since only estimates of $\mathbf{\Pi}_i$ can be obtained ($i = 1, 2, 3$).

Alternatively, when there is only one cointegration relationship ($\beta_{11}y_{1t-1} + \beta_{21}y_{2t-1} + \beta_{31}x_{t-1}$) rather than two, entering into all three ECMs with differing speeds of adjustment $[a_{11}, \alpha_{21}, \alpha_{31}]'$, then using a single equation approach will obtain an estimate of the cointegration vector, since writing out just the error correction part of, say, the first equation gives:

$$\alpha_{11}(\beta_{11}y_{1t-1} + \beta_{21}y_{2t-1} + \beta_{31}x_{t-1}) \tag{4.21}$$

However, there is information to be gained from estimating the other equations in the system, since α_{21} and α_{31} are not zero. That is, more efficient estimates of $\boldsymbol{\beta}$ can be obtained by using all the information the model has to offer. Indeed, Johansen (1992a) shows that in situations where $\mathbf{z}_t$ is endogenous and there is one cointegration vector, then the variance of the estimator of $\boldsymbol{\beta}_{\text{part}} > \boldsymbol{\beta}_{\text{full}}$, where 'part' refers to a partial estimator (e.g., a single equation OLS estimator) and 'full' refers to a modelling approach that estimates the full system (equation (4.19)).

Only when, say, $\alpha_{21} = \alpha_{31} = 0$ will a single equation estimator of the unique cointegration vector be efficient. Then the cointegration relationship does not enter the other two equations (i.e., Δy_{2t} and Δx_t do not depend on the disequilibrium changes represented by ($\beta_{11}y_{1t-1} + \beta_{21}y_{2t-1} + \beta_{31}x_{t-1}$)). As will be shown in the next chapter, this means that when estimating the parameters of the model (i.e., $\mathbf{\Gamma}_1$, $\mathbf{\Pi}$, $\boldsymbol{\alpha}$, $\boldsymbol{\beta}$) there is no loss of information from *not* modelling the determinants of Δy_{2t} and Δx_t; so, these variables can enter on the right-hand side of a single equation ECM.[29] For now, it is sufficient to state that $\alpha_{21} = \alpha_{31} = 0$ amounts to y_{2t} and x_t being weakly exogenous. When all the right-hand-side variables in a single equation model are weakly exogenous, this approach is sufficient to obtain an efficient estimator of $\boldsymbol{\beta}$ such that (4.15)

[29] More technically, this is referred to as conditioning on these variables.

should provide the same results as a multivariate (or system) estimator (e.g., the Johansen approach, as set out in the next chapter).[30]

As has just been explained, it is only really applicable to use the single equation approach when there is a single unique cointegration vector and when all the right-hand-side variables are weakly exogenous. Inder (1993), on the basis of his Monte Carlo experiments, has suggested that the problem of endogeneity may be relatively unimportant in many situations, but there is still a question as to whether it is possible to perform tests of weak exogeneity in a single equation framework. Urbain (1992) suggests that the usual approach based on a Wu–Hausman-type orthogonality test is unlikely to provide clear results. This approach amounts to regressing the right-hand-side variable of interest (e.g., Δy_{2t}) on all the lagged first-differenced variables in the model (e.g., $\sum_i^{k-1} \Delta \mathbf{z}_{t-i}$)[31] and then testing whether the residuals from this equation are significant in the short-run ECM (cf. equation (4.10)). That is, if Δy_{2t} is weakly exogenous, then the residuals from the equation determining it will be orthogonal to (i.e., non-correlated with) the short-run ECM determining Δy_{1t}. However, Urbain (1992) points out that orthogonality will be present anyway (on the basis of the multivariate normal distribution) and suggests that it would be more appropriate to test whether the error correction term embedded in the short-run ECM (i.e., $\hat{\boldsymbol{\varepsilon}}_{t-1} = \hat{\boldsymbol{\beta}}_1' \mathbf{z}_{t-1}$) is significant in the equation determining Δy_{2t}. As mentioned previously, if Δy_{2t} is weakly exogenous, then it does not depend on the disequilibrium changes represented by the $\boldsymbol{\varepsilon}_{t-1}$. However, even though it is possible in principle to test for weak exogeneity, there is still the more important issue of how many possible $(n-1)$ cointegration relations exist in a model that includes n variables. Since this must be established, it is better to undertake testing for weak exogeneity as part of a multivariate procedure. As will be seen, this can be done easily using the Johansen approach.

As an example of the single equation approach when there is more than one cointegration relationship, consider the UK purchasing power parity (PPP) and uncovered interest rate parity (UIP) model estimated by Johansen and Juselius (1992). This model is examined in detail in the next chapter, where multivariate testing suggests that there are at least two cointegration relationships between the five variables p_1 (the UK wholesale price index), p_2 (trade-weighted foreign wholesale price index), e (UK effective exchange rate), i_1 (3-month UK treasury bill rate) and i_2 (3-month Eurodollar interest rate). Theory suggests that if PPP holds in the goods market (i.e., internationally produced goods are perfect substitutes for domestic goods), we should expect

[30] Note that estimating the long-run relationship using a static model (equation (4.1)) will not produce the same result because of small sample bias (i.e., both (4.15) and (4.18) incorporate short-run adjustments). In fact, with weak exogeneity assumed, (4.15) and (4.18) are equivalent.

[31] Other variables known to determine Δy_{2t}, but not already included in the model since they are assumed exogenous to it, may also enter.

to find *in the long run* that price differentials between two countries are equal to differences in the nominal exchange rate ($p_1 - p_2 = e$), while UIP in the capital market relates the interest rates of the two countries to expected changes in exchange rates ($i_1 - i_2 = e^e - e$). If markets are efficient, expected changes in exchange rates will be increasingly influenced by deviations from long-run PPP (especially as the forecast horizon grows—see Juselius, 1995) and thus $e^e = (p_1 - p_2)$, providing a link between the capital and the goods market. If parity holds in the long run we should expect $(i_1 - i_2) = (p_1 - p_2 - e)$ and estimated parameter values of $(\pm)1$ for all the variables in the model.

Estimating the static model using seasonally unadjusted data for 1972q1 to 1987q2 produced the following result:

$$p_1 = 1.442p_2 + 0.468e - 0.937i_1 + 1.114i_2 + \varepsilon \qquad R^2 = 0.99,\ \text{DW} = 0.19 \tag{4.22}$$

and using (4.4), with $\delta = 0$ imposed, the residuals $\hat{\varepsilon}$ were tested for a unit root under the null hypothesis of no cointegration. The τ-value associated with testing the null hypothesis (that H_0: $\psi^* = 0$ based on the $\hat{\varepsilon}$) was -2.40, while the critical value for rejecting the null is -4.64 (at the 5% significance level obtained from Table A.6 with $n = 5$ and $T = 62$). Thus, these results indicate that there is no long-run stable relationship.[32]

Setting $p = q = 5$ and then testing to ensure that this parameterization of (4.15) is general enough to pass various diagnostic tests relating to the properties of the residuals $\hat{u}_t$, the following long-run relationship is found using the dynamic modelling approach (with t-values in parentheses):

$$p_1 = \underset{(29.92)}{1.331}p_2 + \underset{(8.51)}{0.402}e + \underset{(3.48)}{3.765}i_1 - \underset{(0.88)}{0.606}i_2 + \varepsilon \tag{4.23}$$

A Wald test decisively rejects the null that all of the long-run coefficients are zero. However, the unit root test of the null hypothesis of no cointegration results in a test statistic of -2.97, which does reject the null at the 10% significance level (based on a critical value of -3.65 obtained from table 2 in Banerjee, Lumsdaine and Stock, 1998). Thus, using the single equation approach, cointegration is not established and the estimates of long-run parameters seem remote from their expected values.

ESTIMATING THE SHORT-RUN DYNAMIC MODEL

Having obtained an estimate of the long-run relationship, the second stage of the EG procedure comprises estimating the short-run ECM itself (e.g., equation (4.10)) using the estimates of disequilibrium ($\hat{\varepsilon}_{t-1}$) to obtain information on the speed of adjustment to equilibrium. The $\hat{\varepsilon}_{t-1}$ associated with the cointegration relations obtained from the static and dynamic models (equa-

[32] Note that the CRDW test also fails to reject the null.

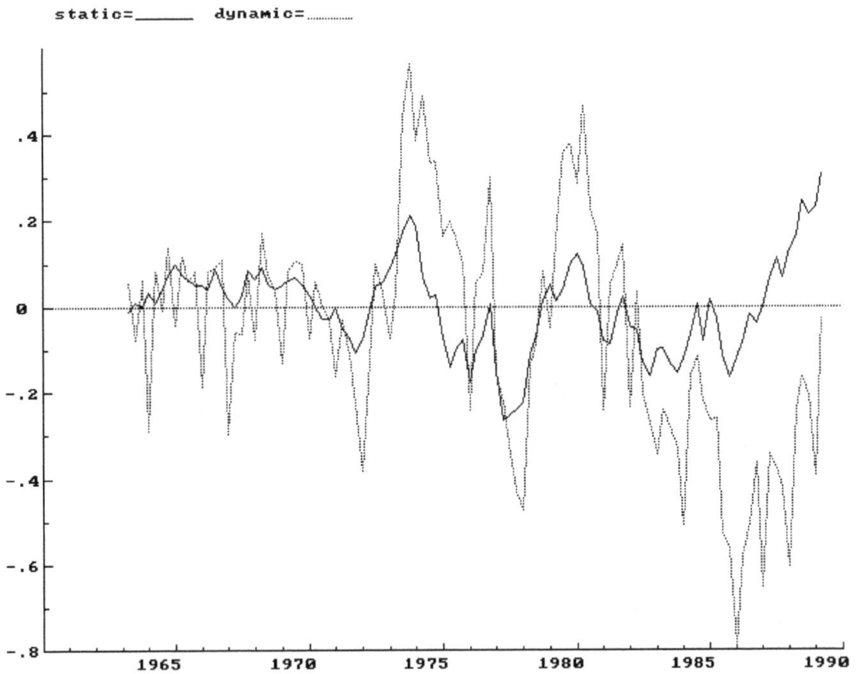

Figure 4.1. Cointegration relations for UK money supply based on equations (4.11b) and (4.16).

tions (4.11b) and (4.16)) are plotted in Figure 4.1. These show that real M1 was considerably off its equilibrium value (which occurs when $\hat{\varepsilon}_{t-1} = 0$), especially (according to the dynamic approach) after 1982. Thus, it will be interesting to see whether the money supply adjusts quickly or slowly to such disequilibrium.

The initial model (denoted Model 1) is the AR distributed lag model with $p = q = 5$ used to obtain $\hat{\varepsilon}_{t-1} = (m - p)_{t-1} + 7.332\Delta p_{t-1} - 1.052y_{t-1} + 6.871R_{t-1} + 0.393 - 0.238\text{SEAS}$ (see Box 4.2). Model 2 is the equivalent short-run ECM obtained by setting $p = q = 4$ in (4.10). Next the Hendry-type 'general-to-specific' procedure is used to reduce this short-run ECM to its parsimonious form (see Ericsson, Hendry and Tran, 1992 for full details relating to this data set). This resulted in Models 3–6 and involved dropping insignificant variables and reparameterizing the estimated equation as follows:

- Model 3: since $\Delta R_{t-1} = \Delta R_{t-2} = \Delta R_{t-3} = \Delta R_{t-4} = 0$, these variables are dropped.
- Model 4: since $\Delta p_t = -\Delta p_{t-1}$, these variables are dropped and $\Delta^2 p_t$ is introduced instead; since $\Delta p_{t-2} = \Delta p_{t-3} = \Delta p_{t-4} = 0$ these variables are also dropped.

Table 4.2 F-statistics for the sequential reduction from the fifth-order AR model in Box 4.2.

Model reduction	Degrees of freedom	Test statistic [significance level]
Model 1 → 2:	$F(3, 73)$	0.01906 [0.9964]
Model 1 → 3:	$F(7, 73)$	0.46212 [0.8587]
Model 2 → 3:	$F(4, 76)$	0.82641 [0.5124]
Model 1 → 4:	$F(11, 73)$	0.64029 [0.7885]
Model 2 → 4:	$F(8, 76)$	0.90842 [0.5142]
Model 3 → 4:	$F(4, 80)$	0.99911 [0.4131]
Model 1 → 5:	$F(15, 73)$	0.72135 [0.7553]
Model 2 → 5:	$F(12, 76)$	0.93305 [0.5192]
Model 3 → 5:	$F(8, 80)$	0.99501 [0.4465]
Model 4 → 5:	$F(4, 84)$	0.99096 [0.4171]
Model 1 → 6:	$F(17, 73)$	0.75495 [0.7364]
Model 2 → 6:	$F(14, 76)$	0.94940 [0.5118]
Model 3 → 6:	$F(10, 80)$	1.00730 [0.4447]
Model 4 → 6:	$F(6, 84)$	1.01290 [0.4226]
Model 5 → 6:	$F(2, 88)$	1.05720 [0.3518]

- Model 5: since $\Delta y_{t-2} = -\Delta y_{t-3}$, these variables are dropped and $\Delta^2 y_{t-2}$ is introduced instead; also as $\Delta y_t = \Delta y_{t-1} = \Delta y_{t-4} = 0$ these variables are dropped.
- Model 6: since $\Delta(m-p)_{t-1} = \Delta(m-p)_{t-2} = \Delta(m-p)_{t-3}$, these variables are replaced by $[(m-p)_t - (m-p)_{t-3}]/3$ instead.

The F-statistics (and associated probabilities of rejecting the null in square brackets) for testing each model in the sequential reduction process are given in Table 4.2. The complete reduction from Model 1 to Model 6 is not rejected with $F_{17,73} = 0.75$ [0.74] and none of the reductions between model pairs reject at the 5% significance level. The final model obtained was:

$$\begin{aligned}\Delta(m-p)_t = {} & \underset{(1.360)}{0.005} - \underset{(4.717)}{0.880}\Delta^2 p_t + \underset{(3.203)}{0.149}\Delta^2 y_{t-2} - \underset{(5.025)}{0.646}\Delta_3(m-p)_t/3 \\ & + \underset{(3.395)}{0.188}\Delta(m-p)_{t-4} - \underset{(3.517)}{0.387}\Delta R_t - \underset{(10.802)}{0.116}\varepsilon_{t-1} - \underset{(2.312)}{0.012}\text{SEAS}_{1t} \\ & - \underset{(4.476)}{0.022}\text{SEAS}_{2t} + \underset{(1.710)}{0.012}\text{SEAS}_{3t}\end{aligned} \tag{4.24}$$

Diagnostics

$R^2 = 0.833$; $F(9, 90) = 50.044$ [0.0000]; $\sigma = 0.0135641$; DW $= 2.15$; AR 1–5 $F(5, 85) = 1.0355$ [0.4021]; ARCH 4 $F(4, 82) = 0.70884$ [0.5882]; X_i^2 $F(15, 74) = 0.786\,57$ [0.6881]; $X_i * X_j$ $F(48, 41) = 0.702\,69$ [0.8804]; RESET $F(1, 89) = 0.260\,72$ [0.6109]; normality $\chi^2(2) = 3.4735$ [0.1761].

None of the diagnostic tests reported are significant at the 95% critical value (except the F-test in which all the slope coefficients are zero), and therefore there is nothing to suggest that the model is mis-specified. These tests cover, respectively, the goodness of fit of the model (i.e., what percentage of the total variation in the dependent variable is explained by the independent variables); an F-test in which all the right-hand-side explanatory variables except the constant have zero parameter coefficients; the standard deviation of the regression; the DW test for first-order autocorrelation (which is strictly not valid in a model with lagged dependent variables); a Breusch–Godfrey Lagrange multiplier (LM) test for serial autocorrelation up to the fifth lag, obtained by regressing the residuals from the original model on all the regressors of that model and the lagged residuals; an autoregressive conditional heteroscedastic (ARCH) test, obtained by regressing the squared residuals from the model on their lags (here up to the fourth lag) and a constant; White's test for heteroscedasticity, involving the auxiliary regression of the squared residuals on the original regressors and all their squares; White's heteroscedasticity/functional for the mis-specification test, based on the auxiliary regression of the squared residuals on all squares and cross products of the original regressors; Ramsey's RESET general test of mis-specification, obtained by adding powers of the fitted values from the model (e.g., $\hat{y}_t^2$, $\hat{y}_t^3$, etc.) to the original regression equation; and the Jarque–Bera test for normality. Significance levels for rejecting the null hypothesis are given in [ ] brackets. Full references for each test are available in most standard econometric texts, such as Johnston and Dinardo (1997). Econometric software packages, which usually contain similar batteries of tests, also provide good references and explanations.

Another important aspect of diagnostic checking is testing for structural breaks in the model, which would be evidence that the parameter estimates are non-constant. Sequential 1-step-ahead Chow tests[33] and 1-step-ahead residuals ($u_t = y_t - \mathbf{x}_t'\hat{\boldsymbol{\beta}}_t$) can be obtained from applying recursive least squares to the model over successive time periods by increasing the sample period by one additional observation for each estimation. Plots of these Chow tests and residuals are given in Figure 4.2 for the estimated short-run ECM. The graph of 1-step-ahead residuals are shown bordered by two standard deviations from the mean of zero (i.e., $0 \pm 2\sigma_t$), and points outside this region are either outliers or are associated with coefficient changes. There is some evidence to suggest that there is a problem around the 1983q3 observation. The Chow tests also suggest that parameter instability is evident around the 1973q2 and 1983q3 time periods.

Returning to (4.24), the speed-of-adjustment coefficient indicates that the UK money supply adjusted relatively slowly to changes to the underlying equilibrium relationship since the parameter estimate on $\hat{\varepsilon}_{t-1}$ shows that

[33] These are calculated as the *change* in the sum of the squared residuals ($\sum u_t^2$) from the model as it is estimated over successive time periods (adjusted for degrees of freedom) and an F-test that β changes is obtained.

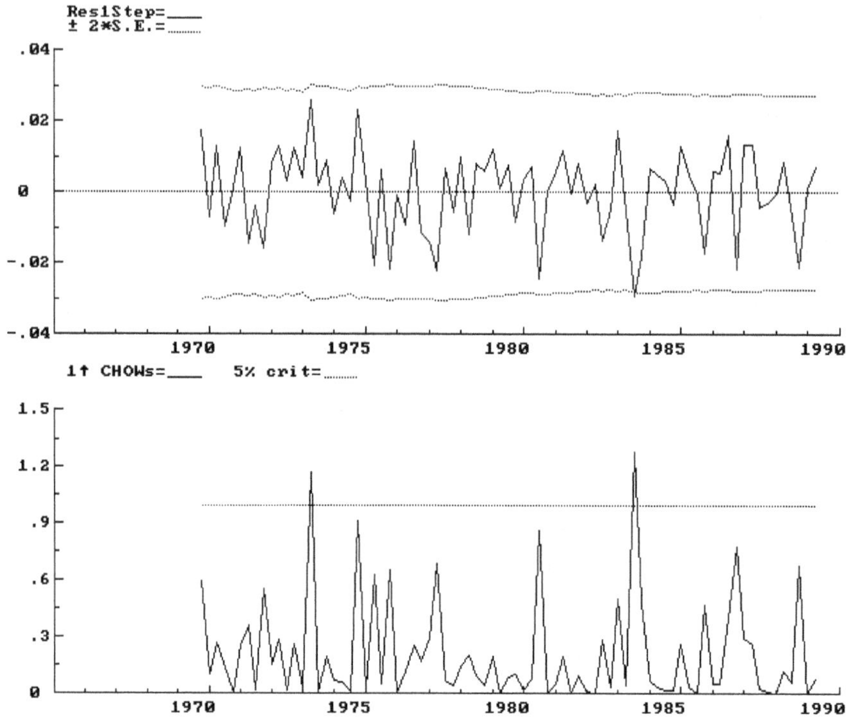

Figure 4.2. Diagnostic testing of the short-run ECM: 1-step-ahead residuals and chow tests.

economic agents removed only 11.6% of the resulting disequilibrium each period. This helps to explain the considerable deviations from equilibrium depicted in Figure 4.1.

SEASONAL COINTEGRATION[34]

If series exhibit strong seasonal patterns they may contain seasonal unit roots; consequently, any potential cointegration may occur at seasonal cycles as well as (or instead of) at the zero frequency domain. In cases where there are seasonal unit roots in the series and the cointegration relation is thought to be a long-run (zero frequency) relation between the series, the cointegration regression of, say, c_t on y_t using (4.1) gives inconsistent estimates. Thus, in such a situation it is necessary to test for the long-run relationship using data that has been adjusted using the seasonal filter $S(L) = (1 + L + L^2 + L^3)$ in order to remove the seasonal unit roots and leave the zero frequency unit root corresponding to $(1 - L)$. That is, when series have unit roots at both the zero and

[34] The reader is advised to review the discussion of seasonal unit roots in Chapter 3 (p. 63) before tackling this section.

seasonal frequencies (i.e., are all $I(1, 1)$), the static model test for cointegration between, for example, c_t and y_t becomes:

$$(Z_1c_t) = \beta_1(Z_1y_t) + \varepsilon_t \tag{4.25}$$

where $Z_1 = (1 + L + L^2 + L^3)$, β_1 is the long-run relationship at the zero frequency and the standard test of the null hypothesis of no cointegration is to directly test whether $\varepsilon_t \sim I(1)$ against the alternative that $\varepsilon_t \sim I(0)$. Thus, the equivalent of (4.4) can be estimated using the $\hat{\varepsilon}_t$ obtained from estimating (4.25):

$$\Delta\hat{\varepsilon}_t = \pi_1\hat{\varepsilon}_{t-1}\sum_{i=1}^{p-1}\psi_i\Delta\hat{\varepsilon}_{t-i} + \mu + \delta t + \omega_t \qquad \omega_t \sim \text{IID}(0, \sigma^2) \tag{4.26}$$

with the issue of whether to include a trend and/or constant terms in the test regression remaining the same. The test statistic is a t-type test of H_0: $\pi_1 = 0$ against H_1: $\pi_1 < 0$, with critical values given by MacKinnon (cf. Table 4.1).

To test for seasonal cointegration at the two-quarter (half-yearly) frequency $(1 + L)$, requires leaving in the seasonal root at this cycle using Z_2 and estimating:

$$(Z_2c_t) = \beta_2(Z_2y_t) + v_t \tag{4.27}$$

where $Z_2 = -(1 - L + L^2 - L^3)$ and β_2 is the long-run relationship at the two-quarter frequency. Testing the null hypothesis of no cointegration uses the residuals $\hat{v}_t$ from (4.27) and the following version of the ADF test:

$$(\hat{v}_t + \hat{v}_{t-1}) = \pi_2(-\hat{v}_{t-1}) + \sum_{i=1}^{p-1}\psi_i(\hat{v}_{t-i} + \hat{v}_{t-i-1})$$
$$+ \mu + \sum_{i=1}^{3}\delta_i D_{it} + \omega_t \qquad \omega_t \sim \text{IID}(0, \sigma^2) \tag{4.28}$$

where D_{qt} is the zero/one dummy corresponding to quarter q. The test statistic is a t-type test of H_0: $\pi_2 = 0$ against H_1: $\pi_2 < 0$, with critical values given by MacKinnon (cf. Table A.6).

Finally, testing for seasonal cointegration at the four-quarter (annual) frequency $(1 \pm iL)$ requires leaving in the seasonal roots at this cycle using Z_3 and estimating:

$$(Z_3c_t) = \beta_3(Z_3y_t) + \beta_4(Z_3y_{t-1}) + \zeta_t \tag{4.29}$$

where $Z_3 = -(1 - L^2)$ and β_3 and β_4 are the long-run relationships at the four-quarter frequency. Testing the null hypothesis of no cointegration uses the residuals $\hat{\zeta}_t$ from (4.29) and the following version of the ADF test:

$$(\hat{\zeta}_t + \hat{\zeta}_{t-2}) = \pi_3(-\hat{\zeta}_{t-2}) + \pi_4(-\hat{\zeta}_{t-1}) + \sum_{i=1}^{p-1}\psi_i(\hat{\zeta}_{t-i} + \hat{\zeta}_{t-i-1})$$
$$+ \mu + \sum_{i=1}^{3}\delta_i D_{it} + \omega_t \qquad \omega_t \sim \text{IID}(0, \sigma^2) \tag{4.30}$$

Table 4.3 Test for cointegration at frequencies 0, $\frac{1}{2}$, $\frac{1}{4}$, $\frac{3}{4}$: UK consumption function data (1971q2–1993q1) (based on equations (4.26), (4.28) and (4.30)).

Variables	Deterministic components included[a]	t_{π_1}	t_{π_2}	t_{π_3}	t_{π_4}	$F_{\pi_3 \cap \pi_4}$
c_t, y_t	I+TR/SD	−2.36	−2.43	−3.46	−2.48[b]	10.24[b]
c_t, y_t	I	−2.33	−1.63	−1.91	−1.37	2.86
c_t, w_t	I+TR/SD	−1.20	−3.50	−3.58	−3.12[d]	13.16[c]
c_t, w_t	I	1.69	−2.76	−1.58	−0.91	1.70
$c_t, y_t, w_t, \pi_t,$	I+TR/SD	−2.01	−3.12	−3.58	−2.20	9.79
$c_t, y_t, w_t, \pi_t,$	I	−1.95	−2.77	−2.56	−1.06	3.93

[a] TR = trend, I = intercept, SD = seasonal dummies.
[b] Rejects null at 5% significance level.
[c] Rejects null at 2.5% significance level.
[d] Rejects null at 1% significance level.

where the test of the null hypothesis requires a joint F-test H_0: $\pi_3 = \pi_4 = 0$. Critical values for this test and individual t-tests of H_0: π_3, H_0: $\pi_4 = 0$, when there are two variables in the cointegration equation, are given in Engle, Granger, Hylleberg and Lee (1993, table A.1).

Assuming that cointegration occurs at all frequencies (i.e., $[\hat{\varepsilon}_t, \hat{v}_t, \hat{\zeta}_t] \sim I(0)$) in (4.25), (4.27) and (4.29), the following short-run ECM for c_t and y_t (see Engle et al., 1993) can be estimated:

$$(1 - L^4)c_t = \Delta_4 c_t = \sum_{j=0}^{q} a_j \Delta_4 y_{t-j} + \sum_{i=1}^{p} b_i \Delta_4 c_{t-i} + \gamma_1 \hat{\varepsilon}_{t-1} + \gamma_2 \hat{v}_{t-1}$$
$$+ (\gamma_3 + \gamma_4 L)\hat{\zeta}_{t-1} + u_t \tag{4.31}$$

where the γ_i are speed-of-adjustment parameters and it is assumed that y_t is weakly exogenous.[35]

In the last chapter, tests for seasonal integration using UK data suggested that both real consumer-spending, real liquid assets and inflation are $I(1, 1)$. The results for real personal disposable income suggest that it does not have any seasonal unit roots (i.e., it is $I(1, 0)$). Tests for seasonal cointegration are reported in Table 4.3; these suggest that cointegration between c_t, y_t, w_t, and π_t (and subgroups) can be rejected at the zero (or long-run) frequency and at the two-quarter frequency.[36] However, there is evidence to suggest that variables are cointegrated at the four-quarter (or annual) frequency, given the values of

[35] Otherwise, the term $\Delta_4 y_t$ on the right-hand side of the ECM would not be allowed and we could write a second ECM with $\Delta_4 y_t$ as the dependent variable. The latter would have the same cointegration relations, but the speed-of-adjustment parameters γ_i would potentially be of a different magnitude.
[36] Note lag lengths set to maximize R^2, and in accordance with the arguments in Schwert (1989), are used. Results reported in Table 4.3 are based on max-$\bar{R}^2$.

the F-statistics obtained.[37] Similar results were obtained using Japanese data for c_t and y_t by Engle et al. (1993), and they argued: '... if a slightly impatient borrowing-constrained consumer has the habit of using his bonus payments to replace worn out clothes, furniture, etc., when the payment occurs, one may expect cointegration at the annual frequency' (p. 292). Given that such bonus payments are not typical in the British labour market, some other (although similar) rationale has to be sought. Lastly, these results confirm those in Hylleberg, Engle, Granger and Yoo (1990), who also found some evidence of seasonal cointegration between c_t and y_t at the half-yearly frequency using UK data.

PERIODIC COINTEGRATION

If the individual time series display periodic integration (e.g., the observations on a variable y_t can be described by a different model for each quarter—see Chapter 3), then there may exist stationary relationships between the variables at different frequencies that require the estimation of a periodic cointegration model. A single equation approach has been developed by Boswijk and Franses (1995), viz:

$$\Delta_4 y_t = \sum_{q=1}^{4} \alpha_q D_{qt}(y_{t-4} - \boldsymbol{\beta}_q \mathbf{x}_{t-4}) + \sum_{q=1}^{4} \mu_q D_{qt} + \sum_{q=1}^{4} \tau_q D_{qt} t \tag{4.32}$$

where $\mathbf{x}_t$ is a vector of explanatory variables and D_{qt} is the zero/one dummy corresponding to quarter q. The last two terms in (4.32) comprise the deterministic part of the model (seasonal intercepts and seasonal time trends), which may be omitted. Equation (4.32) is also typically augmented with lagged values of $\Delta_4 y_t$ and current and lagged values of $\Delta_4 \mathbf{x}_t$, to capture the dynamics of the model. The α_q and $\boldsymbol{\beta}_q$ parameters determine the speed of adjustment and long-run relationship between y_t and $\mathbf{x}_t$ as in the usual ECM (although here there are four different models, one for each season, and $\boldsymbol{\beta}_q \neq 1$ will result in periodic cointegration).

Equation (4.32) can be estimated using non-linear least squares and full or partial periodic cointegration can be tested using Wald-type tests. The test for partial periodic cointegration for quarter q involves the null H_{0q}: $(\alpha_q, \beta_q) = 0$ against the alternative H_{1q}: $(\alpha_q, \beta_q) \neq 0$, while the full test comprises H_0: $\Sigma\alpha_q = \Sigma\beta_q = 0$, against the alternative H_1: $(\Sigma\alpha_q, \Sigma\beta_q) \neq 0$. The test statistics are:

$$\left.\begin{aligned} \text{Wald}_q &= (T - k)(\text{RSS}_{0q} - \text{RSS}_1)/\text{RSS}_1 \\ \text{and} \quad \text{Wald} &= (T - k)(\text{RSS}_0 - \text{RSS}_1)/\text{RSS}_1 \end{aligned}\right\} \tag{4.33}$$

[37] Note that because critical values for cointegration equations involving more than two variables are not available at the four-quarter frequency, it is not possible to draw any definite conclusions surrounding the tests of the full consumption function model.

Table 4.4 Wald tests for periodic cointegration: UK consumption function data (1971q2–1993q1) (based on equation (4.32)).

Variables	Wald_1	Wald_2	Wald_3	Wald_4	Wald_5
c_t, w_t	8.53	8.92	4.34	2.83	22.50
y_t, w_t	3.21	12.89*	3.76	10.80	28.13

* Rejects null at 10% significant level. Critical values at the 10% level for Wald_q and Wald are 12.38 and 38.97, respectively (Boswijk and Franses, 1995, tables A1 and A2).

where T is the sample size, k the number of estimated parameters in (4.32) and where RSS_{0q}, RSS_0 and RSS_1 denote the residual sum of squares under H_{0q}, H_0 and H_1, respectively. Critical values are provided in Boswijk and Franses (1995, tables A1 and A2).

Using the UK consumption function data for 1971q2 to 1993q1, equation (4.32) was estimated with y_t equal to the log of real consumer-spending (excluding non-durables) and $\mathbf{x}_t$ comprising the log of real income, real wealth and annual retail inflation. We were not able to reject the null of no periodic cointegration for any quarter (or the full model comprising all quarters), whether the deterministic components in (4.32) were included or excluded. The most significant results obtained from pairing variables are reported in Table 4.4, with models including seasonal intercepts and time trends. Only with real income as the dependent variable and real wealth as its determinant is there any evidence of periodic cointegration in quarter 2 (although rejection is only at the 10 per cent significance level). Perhaps these results are not surprising, given that in Table 3.7 there was no evidence of periodic integration.

ASYMMETRIC TESTS FOR COINTEGRATION

To recap the standard EG approach to testing for cointegration, it is assumed that there is at most a single long-run relationship between y and x; that is:

$$y_t = \beta_0 + \beta_1 x_t + \varepsilon_t \tag{4.34}$$

Assuming y_t and x_t are both $I(1)$, then Engle and Granger (1987) show that cointegration exists if $\varepsilon_t \sim I(0)$. The long-run model in equation (4.34) is associated with a short-run ECM based on symmetric adjustment, with the second-step EG test for cointegration based on the OLS estimate of ρ in equation (4.35):[38]

$$\Delta\hat{\varepsilon}_t = \rho\hat{\varepsilon}_{t-1} + v_t \qquad v_t \sim \text{IID}(0, \sigma^2) \tag{4.35}$$

[38] Note that for simplicity here we have adopted the DF version of the test, rather than the ADF (see equation (4.4)). Lagged values of $\Delta\hat{\varepsilon}_{t-i}$ would need to enter the right-hand side of (4.35) to ensure that v_t has the desired properties stated in the equation.

If the null hypothesis of no cointegration H_0: $\rho = 0$ can be rejected in favour of H_1: $\rho < 0$, then equations (4.34) and (4.35) jointly imply the following ECMs:

$$A(L)\Delta y_t = B(L)\Delta x_{t-1} - (1-\alpha_1)ec_{t-1} + \omega_t \qquad \omega_t \sim \text{IID}(0, \sigma^2) \tag{4.36a}$$

$$A(L)\Delta xt = B(L)\Delta y_{t-1} - (1-\alpha_2)ec_{t-1} + \omega_t^* \qquad \omega_t^* \sim \text{IID}(0, \sigma^2) \tag{4.36b}$$

where

$$ec_{t-1} = \hat{\varepsilon}_{t-1} = y_{t-1} - \hat{\beta}_0 - \hat{\beta}_1 x_{t-1}$$

and $A(L)$ and $B(L)$ are polynomial lag operators.

Equation (4.36) implies that any short-run changes in y_t and x_t due to disequilibrium $(1-\alpha_i)$ are strictly proportional to the absolute value of the error correction term. If, however, adjustment to disequilibrium is asymmetric, then Enders and Granger (1998) and Enders and Siklos (2001) show that an alternative specification for equation (4.35) (called the momentum threshold autoregressive model) can be written as:

$$\Delta\hat{\varepsilon}_t = I_t\rho_1\hat{\varepsilon}_{t-1} + (1-I_t)\rho_2\hat{\varepsilon}_{t-1} + v_t^* \qquad v_t^* \sim \text{IID}(0, \sigma^2) \tag{4.37}$$

where I_t is the Heaviside indicator function based on threshold value τ:[39]

$$I_t = \begin{cases} 1 & \text{if } \Delta\hat{\varepsilon}_{t-1} \geq \tau \\ 0 & \text{if } \Delta\hat{\varepsilon}_{t-1} < \tau \end{cases} \tag{4.38}$$

The asymmetric version of the ECM, then, replaces the single error correction term in equation (4.36) (ec_{t-1}) with two error correction terms multiplied by I_t and $(1-I_t)$, respectively.

To test the null hypothesis of no cointegration against the alternative of cointegration with asymmetry, the null H_0: $(\rho_1 - 1) = (\rho_2 - 1) = 0$ is examined using an F-test of the joint hypothesis and specially calculated critical values, and if this is rejected it is possible to test whether $\rho_1 = \rho_2$ using a conventional F-statistic. Alternatively, a t-max test (based on the most negative t-value associated with either $(\rho_1 - 1)$ or $(\rho_2 - 1)$) can be used to test for a unit root. Clearly, if the t-value on either $(\rho_1 - 1)$ and/or $(\rho_2 - 1)$ is positive, we would not reject the null and the F-test loses its validity in this situation (as it is a two-sided test).

To find the unknown τ, equation (4.37) is estimated (including appropriate lags $\Delta\hat{\varepsilon}_{t-i}$ as additional regressors to ensure v_t^* is IID) up to T times with values of τ that cover the range of values included in $\Delta\hat{\varepsilon}_t$; the value of τ that results in

[39] Enders and Siklos (2001) also specified the TAR model, whereby the Heaviside indicator function becomes:

$$I_t = \begin{cases} 1 & \text{if } \hat{\varepsilon}_{t-1} \geq 0 \\ 0 & \text{if } \hat{\varepsilon}_{t-1} < 0 \end{cases} \tag{4.38a}$$

See also Box 3.4.

Table 4.5 Tests of cointegration[a] based on asymmetric MTAR: US interest rate data (1960q1–1999q3).

Variable	Lag length	τ	$(\rho_1 - 1)$	t-value $(\rho_1 - 1)$	$(\rho_2 - 1)$	t-value $(\rho_2 - 1)$	F-value $(\rho_1 - 1) = (\rho_2 - 1) = 0$
$\hat{\varepsilon}_t$	1	−0.330	−0.102	−2.45	−0.359	−4.11	11.07
$\hat{\varepsilon}_t$	2	−0.330	−0.083	−1.93	−0.340	−3.87	8.86
$\hat{\varepsilon}_t$	6[b]	−0.330	−0.136	−2.88	−0.405	−4.21	10.67

[a] t-max 5% critical value is −3.42; F-test 5% critical value is 6.40 based on own calculation (see text).
[b] Set using the AIC (see, for example Greene, 2000, p. 306). Other lag lengths included for compatibility with Enders and Siklos (2001).

an estimated (4.37) with the minimum residual sum of squares is chosen as the threshold.[40]

As an example, we have applied the asymmetrical test as set out in equations (4.37) and (4.38) to the data set used by Enders and Siklos (2001) to test for asymmetric adjustment in the US term structure of interest rates (i.e., y_t comprises the 3-month US Treasury bill rate and x_t comprises the yield on 10-year Government bonds, from 1960q1 to 1999q3). The AIC was used to set the lag length at the time of estimating equation (4.37) when lagged values of the dependent variable are allowed to enter as additional regressors. The results are set out in Table 4.5. The overall test of the unit root hypothesis is the null H_0: $(\rho_1 - 1) = (\rho_2 - 1) = 0$ using the F-statistic reported, but where either $(\rho_1 - 1)$ and/or $(\rho_2 - 1)$ is positive, the t-max test is preferred. The null of no cointegration was rejected at each lag length selected, using both the t-max and F-test, and thus a standard F-test that H_0: $\rho_1 = \rho_2$ was conducted. Given the parameter estimates obtained for $(\rho_1 - 1)$ and $(\rho_2 - 1)$, not surprisingly the F-statistic exceeds the 1% critical value in every instance, indicating that the term structure of interest rates adjusts asymmetrically to disequilibrium depending on whether the long-run relationship is above or below the threshold in any given time period. Figure 4.3 plots the cointegration residuals (i.e., $\hat{\varepsilon}_t$) and τ, and this shows different patterns for the disequilibrium term above and below the threshold.

Finally, we estimated the ECM (equation (4.36)), with $\hat{\varepsilon}_{t-1}$ obtained from estimating equation (4.34)[41] and I_t set using equation (4.38) with $\tau = -0.33$,

[40] Critical values can be obtained by using the above procedures for obtaining the ρ_1, τ (and thus I_t) with typically 10,000 Monte Carlo simulations of a random walk under the null hypothesis (i.e., $y_t = y_{t-1} + u_t$ where $u_t \sim \text{IID}(0, 1)$).
[41] Note that the estimated equation was $y_t = -0.816 + 0.928x_t$, where y_t is the US short-run interest rate and x_t is the long-run interest rate.

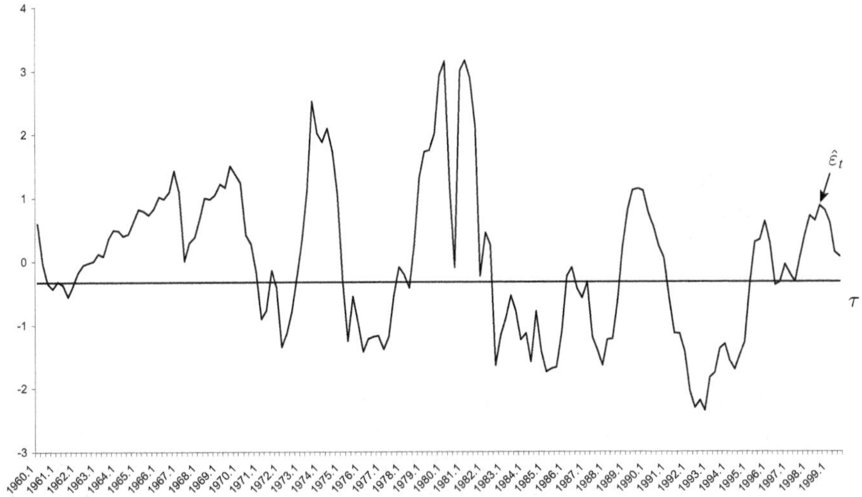

Figure 4.3. Cointegration residuals from MTAR model.

obtaining the following results:

$$\Delta y_t = \underset{(0.007)}{0.004} + \underset{(4.64)}{0.387}\Delta y_{t-1} - \underset{(-3.89)}{0.302}\Delta y_{t-2} + \underset{(4.37)}{0.368}\Delta y_{t-3}$$

$$+ \underset{(4.55)}{0.471}\Delta y_{t-5} - \underset{(-3.05)}{0.470}\Delta x_{t-5} - \underset{(-1.85)}{0.124}I_t\hat{\varepsilon}_{t-1} - \underset{(-2.67)}{0.124}(1 - I_t)\hat{\varepsilon}_{t-1} \quad (4.39a)$$

Diagnostics

$\bar{R}^2 = 0.252$; DW $= 1.84$; AR 1–5 LM $= 6.53$ [0.258]; ARCH $= 0.069$ [0.794]; Chow test $= 1.163$ [0.326]; RESET2 $= 3.554$ [0.061]; Jarque–Bera test $=$ 195.269 [0.000].

$$\Delta x_t = \underset{(0.369)}{0.014} + \underset{(2.61)}{0.184}\Delta y_{t-5} - \underset{(-4.08)}{0.440}\Delta x_{t-5} + \underset{(2.58)}{0.100}I_t\hat{\varepsilon}_{t-1} + \underset{(1.15)}{0.092}(1 - I_t)\hat{\varepsilon}_{t-1} \quad (4.39b)$$

Diagnostics

$\bar{R}^2 = 0.121$; DW $= 1.68$; AR 1–5 LM $= 7.91$ [0.161]; ARCH $= 3.886$ [0.049]; Chow test $= 1.090$ [0.369]; RESET2 $= 1.105$ [0.295]; Jarque–Bera test $=$ 36.031 [0.000].

Concentrating on the speed-of-adjustment coefficients (allowing for asymmetric adjustment) for the short-term interest rate equation (4.39a), when disequilibrium is above the threshold (i.e., $\hat{\varepsilon}_{t-1} = y_{t-1} + 0.816 - 0.928x_{t-1} > -0.33$ and short-term rates are too high with regard to the long run), adjustment in short-term interest rates to restore the long-run equilibrium is relatively slow (economic agents removed only 12.4% of the disequilibrium each period); when disequilibrium is below the threshold then adjustment is faster (with over 32% catch-up each period). The results for the long-term interest rate suggest that adjustment is significantly different from zero only when disequilibrium is above the threshold. In this instance the short-run increase in long-term rates is such that some 10% catch-up is achieved each period to eradicate the long-run imbalance between short- and long-term interest rates.

CONCLUSIONS

Testing for cointegration using a single equation is problematic. If there are $n > 2$ variables in the model and if $n - 1$ of them are not weakly exogenous, the single equation approach can be misleading, particularly if there is more than one cointegration relationship present. If single equation methods are to be used, it would seem that the unrestricted dynamic modelling approach is most likely to produce unbiased estimates of the long-run relationship, with appropriate t- and F-statistics. The test of cointegration associated with this approach is also more powerful against alternatives, such as the usual EG static model. However, given that the number of cointegration vectors is unknown and given the need to allow all variables to be potentially endogenous (and then testing for exogeneity), there seems little advantage to *starting* from the single equation model. Rather, the multivariate vector autoregression (VAR) approach developed by Johansen (1988) is the more obvious place to begin testing for cointegration.

Important Terms and Concepts

EG approach	Superconsistency	Finite sample bias
Residual-based ADF test for cointegration	Common factors	Fully modified estimators
Dynamic single equation models	Cointegration vector	Seasonal cointegration
Speed-of-adjustment to equilibrium	Diagnostic checking	Periodic cointegration
Asymmetric threshold cointegration		

5
Cointegration in Multivariate Systems

The Johansen technique is an essential tool for applied economists who wish to estimate time series models. The implication that non-stationary variables can lead to spurious regressions unless at least one cointegration vector is present means that some form of testing for cointegration is almost mandatory. Earlier use of the Engle–Granger (EG) procedure (Chapter 4) has generally given way to the determination of cointegration rank, given the consequences for the EG approach if more than one cointegration relationship exists. In this chapter we implement Johansen's (1988, 1995a) technique using *PcGive 10.1*.[1]

The problems facing the user who wishes to implement the technique include, *inter alia*:

- testing the order of integration of each variable that enters the multivariate model;
- setting the appropriate lag length of the vector autoregression (VAR) model (in order to ensure Gaussian error terms in the vector error correction model—VECM) and determining whether the system should be conditioned on any predetermined $I(0)$ variables (including dummies to take account of possible policy interventions);
- testing for reduced rank, including the issue of testing whether the system should be treated as an $I(2)$ rather than an $I(1)$ system;
- identifying whether there are trends in the data and therefore whether deterministic variables (a constant and trend) should enter the cointegration space or not;
- testing for weak exogeneity (which leads to the modelling of a partial system with exogenous $I(1)$ variables);
- testing for unique cointegration vectors and joint tests involving restrictions on $\boldsymbol{\alpha}$ and $\boldsymbol{\beta}$.

[1] *PcGive 10.1, Modelling Dynamic Systems Using PcGive*, developed by Jurgen A. Doornik and David F. Hendry, distributed as part of *Oxmetrics* by Timberlake Consultants Ltd (info@timberlake.co.uk).

Each of these will be considered in turn and examples provided (in particular based on the purchasing power parity—PPP—and uncovered interest rate parity—UIP—model estimated by Johansen and Juselius (1992) as discussed in the last chapter, and the UK money demand model). However, it is necessary first to briefly outline the Johansen model and the method of reduced rank regression used to estimate it.

THE JOHANSEN APPROACH

The multivariate autoregressive (AR) model was discussed briefly in the last chapter when considering the deficiencies of the single equation cointegration approach. Defining a vector $\mathbf{z}_t$ of n potentially endogenous variables, it is possible to specify the following data-generating process (d.g.p.) and model $\mathbf{z}_t$ as an unrestricted vector autoregression (VAR) involving up to k lags of $\mathbf{z}_t$:

$$\mathbf{z}_t = \mathbf{A}_1\mathbf{z}_{t-1} + \cdots + \mathbf{A}_k\mathbf{z}_{t-k} + \mathbf{u}_t \qquad \mathbf{u}_t \sim \text{IN}(0, \Sigma) \tag{5.1}$$

where $\mathbf{z}_t$ is $(n \times 1)$ and each of the $\mathbf{A}_i$ is an $(n \times n)$ matrix of parameters. This type of VAR model has been advocated most notably by Sims (1980) as a way to estimate dynamic relationships among jointly endogenous variables without imposing strong a priori restrictions (such as particular structural relationships and/or the exogeneity of some of the variables). The system is in a reduced form with each variable in $\mathbf{z}_t$ regressed on only lagged values of both itself and all the other variables in the system. Thus, ordinary least-squares (OLS) is an efficient way to estimate each equation comprising (5.1) since the right-hand side of each equation in the system comprises a common set of (lagged and thus predetermined) regressors.

Equation (5.1) can be reformulated into a VECM form:

$$\Delta\mathbf{z}_t = \Gamma_1\Delta\mathbf{z}_{t-1} + \cdots + \Gamma_{k-1}\Delta\mathbf{z}_{t-k+1} + \Pi\mathbf{z}_{t-k} + \mathbf{u}_t \tag{5.2}$$

where $\Gamma_i = -(\mathbf{I} - \mathbf{A}_1 - \cdots - \mathbf{A}_i)$ $(i = 1, \ldots, k-1)$ and $\Pi = -(\mathbf{I} - \mathbf{A}_1 - \cdots - \mathbf{A}_k)$. This way of specifying the system contains information on both the short- and long-run adjustment to changes in $\mathbf{z}_t$, via the estimates of $\hat{\mathbf{\Gamma}}_i$ and $\hat{\mathbf{\Pi}}$, respectively. As will be seen, $\Pi = \boldsymbol{\alpha}\boldsymbol{\beta}'$, where $\boldsymbol{\alpha}$ represents the speed of adjustment to disequilibrium and $\boldsymbol{\beta}$ is a matrix of long-run coefficients such that the term $\boldsymbol{\beta}'\mathbf{z}_{t-k}$ embedded in (5.2) represents up to $(n-1)$ cointegration relationships in the multivariate model, which ensures that the $\mathbf{z}_t$ converge with their long-run steady state solutions. Assuming $\mathbf{z}_t$ is a vector of non-stationary $I(1)$ variables, then all the terms in (5.2) that involve $\Delta\mathbf{z}_{t-i}$ are $I(0)$ while $\Pi\mathbf{z}_{t-k}$ must also be stationary for $\mathbf{u}_t \sim I(0)$ to be 'white noise'. There are three instances when the requirement that $\Pi\mathbf{z}_{t-k} \sim I(0)$ is met; first, when all the variables in $\mathbf{z}_t$ are in fact stationary, which is an uninteresting case in the present context since it implies that there is no problem of spurious regression and the appropriate modelling strategy is to estimate the standard Sims-type VAR in levels (i.e., equation (5.1)). The second instance is when there is no cointegration at all, implying that there are no linear combinations of the $\mathbf{z}_t$ that are $I(0)$, and consequently Π is an $(n \times n)$ matrix of zeros. In this case, the appropriate model is a VAR in first-differences involving no long-run elements. The third way for $\Pi \mathbf{z}_{t-k}$ to be $I(0)$ is when there exists up to $(n-1)$ cointegration relationships: $\boldsymbol{\beta}' \mathbf{z}_{t-k} \sim I(0)$. In this instance $r \leq (n-1)$ cointegration vectors exist in $\boldsymbol{\beta}$ (i.e., r columns of $\boldsymbol{\beta}$ form r linearly independent combinations of the variables in $\mathbf{z}_t$, each of which is stationary), together with $(n-r)$ non-stationary vectors (i.e., $n-r$ columns of $\boldsymbol{\beta}$ form $I(1)$ common trends). Only the cointegration vectors in $\boldsymbol{\beta}$ enter (5.2), otherwise $\Pi \mathbf{z}_{t-k}$ would not be $I(0)$, which implies that the last $(n-r)$ columns of $\boldsymbol{\alpha}$ are insignificantly small (i.e., effectively zero).[2] Thus the typical problem faced (determining how many $r \leq (n-1)$ cointegration vectors exist in $\boldsymbol{\beta}$) amounts to equivalently testing which columns of $\boldsymbol{\alpha}$ are zero. Consequently, testing for cointegration amounts to a consideration of the rank of Π (i.e., finding the number of r linearly independent columns in Π).

To recap, if Π has full rank (i.e., there are $r = n$ linearly independent columns), then the variables in $\mathbf{z}_t$ are $I(0)$, while if the rank of Π is zero, then there are no cointegration relationships. Neither of these two cases is particularly interesting. More usually, Π has reduced rank (i.e. there are $r \leq (n-1)$ cointegration vectors present). On p. 122 we shall consider actual tests for the (reduced) rank of Π, which, as noted earlier, are equivalent to testing which columns of $\boldsymbol{\alpha}$ are zero. However, this presupposes that it is possible to factorize Π into $\Pi = \boldsymbol{\alpha}\boldsymbol{\beta}'$, where $\boldsymbol{\alpha}$ and $\boldsymbol{\beta}$ can both be reduced in dimension to $(n \times r)$.[3] It is generally not possible to apply ordinary regression techniques to the individual equations comprising the system in (5.2), since what is obtained is an $(n \times n)$ estimate of Π.[4,5] Rather, Johansen (1988)

[2] Each of the r cointegration vectors in $\boldsymbol{\beta}$ is associated with a particular column in $\boldsymbol{\alpha}$ that must contain at least one non-zero element. See (4.19) for a simple example.

[3] Note that once we know how many r linearly independent columns there are in Π (i.e., once we know its rank), we then know that the last $(n-r)$ columns of $\boldsymbol{\alpha}$ are (effectively) zero and thus that the last $(n-r)$ columns of $\boldsymbol{\beta}$ are non-stationary and do not enter (5.2). Thus, it is in this sense that we can then reduce the dimensions of $\boldsymbol{\alpha}$ and $\boldsymbol{\beta}$ to $(n \times r)$.

[4] That is, even if say the last $(n-r)$ columns of $\boldsymbol{\alpha}$ are insignificantly small, such that there are only r columns in $\boldsymbol{\alpha}$ that are *significantly* different from zero, estimates of $\Pi (= \boldsymbol{\alpha}\boldsymbol{\beta}')$ obtained using standard regression techniques are likely to be of full rank $(n \times n)$ in any practical situation (given that the last $(n-r)$ columns in $\boldsymbol{\beta}$ representing the common trends will be non-zero and these will combine with the last $(n-r)$ columns of $\boldsymbol{\alpha}$, which are insignificantly small, but nevertheless likely to be non-zero). Thus, an inability to factorize Π would mean that we could not carry out tests of the rank of Π based on testing directly the number of non-zero columns in $\boldsymbol{\alpha}$. Factorization is achieved by a procedure based on reduced rank regression involving canonical correlations (see Box 5.1).

[5] Kleibergen and van Dijk (1994) have developed an approach based on directly estimating Π using OLS and then decomposing it. However, it is unclear whether this approach has any particular advantages over Johansen's, given that the procedure is not straightforward.

obtains estimates of $\boldsymbol{\alpha}$ and $\boldsymbol{\beta}$ using the procedure known as reduced rank regression. Since this is quite complicated, the details are confined to Box 5.1.

TESTING THE ORDER OF INTEGRATION OF THE VARIABLES

When using times series data, it is often assumed that the data are non-stationary and thus that a stationary cointegration relationship(s) needs to be found in order to avoid the problem of spurious regression. However, it is clear from the discussion in Chapter 3 that unit root tests often suffer from poor size and power properties (i.e., the tendency to over-reject the null hypothesis of non-stationarity when it is true and under-reject the null when it is false, respectively). This has meant that in practical applications, it is quite common for there to be tests for cointegration even when the preceding unit root analysis suggests that the properties of the variables in the equation(s) are unbalanced (i.e., they cannot cointegrate down to a common lower order of integration—see Box 2.4).[6] This might be justified on the grounds that the unit root tests are not reliable, and consequently the variables may indeed all be, say, $I(1)$. However, it is not necessary for all the variables in the model to have the same order of integration (unless $n = 2$), but it is important to understand and take account of the implications when all the variables are not $I(1)$.

Indeed, it is possible that cointegration is present when there is a mix of $I(0)$, $I(1)$ and $I(2)$ variables in the model. Stationary $I(0)$ variables might play a key role in establishing a sensible long-run relationship between non-stationary variables, especially if theory a priori suggests that such variables should be included.[7] However, in the multivariate model, for every stationary variable included, the number of cointegration equations will increase correspondingly. To see this, recall from the above discussion of the Johansen procedure that testing for cointegration amounts to a consideration of the rank of Π (i.e., finding the number of r linearly independent columns in Π). Since each $I(0)$ variable is stationary by itself, it forms a 'cointegration relation' by itself and consequently forms a linearly independent column in Π. To take the argument one step further, suppose we have two $I(0)$ variables in the model such that we

[6] In Box 2.4 it was stated that, for cointegration to exist, a subset of the higher order series must cointegrate to the order of the lower order series. So, if $y_t \sim I(1)$, $x_t \sim I(2)$ and $z_t \sim I(2)$, then as long as we can find a cointegration relationship between x_t and z_t such that $v_t(= x_t - \lambda z_t) \sim I(1)$, then v_t can potentially cointegrate with y_t to obtain $w_t(= y_t - \xi v_t) \sim I(0)$. Note that this presupposes that there are in fact two cointegration relationships suggesting that unbalanced equations should always be estimated in a multivariate framework.

[7] For example, if wages and labour market variables are $I(1)$, it might be necessary to include the relationship between wage inflation and the unemployment rate—the Phillips Curve—to obtain cointegration relations.

Box 5.1 The Johansen method of reduced rank regression.

Rewriting (5.2) as:

$$\Delta\mathbf{z}_t + \boldsymbol{\alpha\beta}'\mathbf{z}_{t-k} = \Gamma_1\Delta\mathbf{z}_{t-1} + \cdots + \Gamma_{k-1}\Delta\mathbf{z}_{t-k+1} + \mathbf{u}_t \qquad (5.1.1)$$

it is possible to correct for short-run dynamics (i.e., take out their effect) by regressing $\Delta\mathbf{z}_t$ and $\mathbf{z}_{t-k}$ separately on the right-hand side of (5.1.1). That is, the vectors $\mathbf{R}_{0t}$ and $\mathbf{R}_{kt}$ are obtained from:

$$\Delta\mathbf{z}_t = P_1\Delta\mathbf{z}_{t-1} + \cdots + P_{k-1}\Delta\mathbf{z}_{t-k+1} + \mathbf{R}_{0t} \qquad (5.1.2)$$

$$\mathbf{z}_{t-k} = T_1\Delta\mathbf{z}_{t-1} + \cdots + T_{k-1}\Delta\mathbf{z}_{t-k+1} + \mathbf{R}_{kt} \qquad (5.1.3)$$

which can then be used to form residual (product moment) matrices:

$$\mathbf{S}_{ij} = T^{-1}\sum_{i=1}^{T}\mathbf{R}_{it}\mathbf{R}'_{jt} \qquad i, j = 0, k \qquad (5.1.4)$$

The maximum likelihood estimate of β is obtained as the eigenvectors corresponding to the r largest eigenvalues from solving the equation:

$$|\lambda\mathbf{S}_{kk} - \mathbf{S}_{k0}\mathbf{S}_{00}^{-1}\mathbf{S}_{0k}| = 0 \qquad (5.1.5)$$

which gives the n eigenvalues $\hat{\lambda}_1 > \hat{\lambda}_2 > \cdots > \hat{\lambda}_n$ and the corresponding eigenvectors $\hat{\mathbf{V}} = (\hat{\mathbf{v}}_1, \ldots, \hat{\mathbf{v}}_n)$.[8] Those r elements in $\hat{\mathbf{V}}$ that determine the linear combinations of stationary relationships can be denoted $\hat{\boldsymbol{\beta}} = (\hat{\mathbf{v}}_1, \ldots, \hat{\mathbf{v}}_r)$ (i.e., these are the cointegration vectors). This is because the eigenvalues are the *largest* squared canonical correlations between the 'levels' residuals $\mathbf{R}_{kt}$ and the 'difference' residuals $\mathbf{R}_{0t}$; that is, we obtain estimates of all the distinct $\hat{\mathbf{v}}_i'\mathbf{z}_t (i = 1, \ldots, r)$ combinations of the $I(1)$ levels of $\mathbf{z}_t$ that produce high correlations with the stationary $\Delta\mathbf{z}_t \sim I(0)$ elements in (5.2), such combinations being the cointegration vectors by virtue of the fact that they must themselves be $I(0)$ to achieve a high correlation. Thus the magnitude of $\hat{\lambda}_i$ is a measure of how strongly the cointegration relations $\hat{\mathbf{v}}_i'\mathbf{z}_t$ (which we can now denote as $\hat{\boldsymbol{\beta}}_i'\mathbf{z}_t$) are correlated with the stationary part of the model. The last $(n - r)$ combinations obtained from solving (5.1.5) (i.e., $\hat{\mathbf{v}}_i'\mathbf{z}_t$ $(i = r + 1, \ldots, n)$, indicate the non-stationary combinations, and theoretically these are uncorrelated with the stationary elements in (5.2). Consequently, for the eigenvectors corresponding to the non-stationary part of the model, $\hat{\lambda}_i = 0$ for $i = r + 1, \ldots, n$. So, for example, Johansen (1992b) points out that the test that $r = 1$ is really a test that $\hat{\lambda}_2 = \hat{\lambda}_3 = \cdots = \hat{\lambda}_n = 0$, whereas $\hat{\lambda}_1 > 0$. Since he also shows that $\hat{\lambda}_i = \hat{\boldsymbol{\alpha}}_i'\mathbf{S}_{00}^{-1}\hat{\boldsymbol{\alpha}}_i$, a test involving these eigenvalues (which we shall see is the standard way to test for cointegration) is equivalent to testing that the $\boldsymbol{\alpha}_i$ are insignificantly small for $i = r + 1, \ldots, n$. Finally, note that estimates of $\hat{\boldsymbol{\alpha}} = \mathbf{S}_{0k}\hat{\boldsymbol{\beta}}$.

[8] Note that $\mathbf{V}$ is normalized such that $\mathbf{V}'\mathbf{S}_{kk}\mathbf{V} = \mathbf{I}$.

can find a linear combination (i.e., a single $\boldsymbol{\beta}_i$) that cointegrates. This does not imply that these two $I(0)$ variables form only one cointegration relationship, since we could linearly combine the two columns of $\boldsymbol{\beta}$, each containing just the one $I(0)$ variable, to obtain the cointegration relationship being sought.[9] Thus the practical implication of including $I(0)$ variables is that cointegration rank will increase and a number of the cointegration vectors in $\boldsymbol{\beta}$ should contain only one variable. Knowledge of this (or at least the expectation) may help in interpreting the initial (unrestricted) results obtained from using the Johansen approach.

If the model contains $I(2)$ variables, the situation becomes far more complicated. Some (or all) of the $I(2)$ variables may cointegrate down to $I(1)$ space and then further cointegrate with other $I(1)$ variables to obtain a cointegration vector(s). Thus, the presence of variables that require to be differenced *twice* to induce stationarity does not preclude the possibility of stationary relationships in the model.[10] However, applying the standard Johansen approach, which is designed to handle $I(1)$ and $I(0)$ variables, will not provide the necessary stationary vectors. When there are $I(2)$ variables in the model, we must either replace them with an $I(1)$ alternative through some form of differencing (e.g., if money supply and prices are $I(2)$, we could reformulate the model to consider real money $m_t - p_t$), or it will be necessary to use the approach developed by Johansen (1995b) for $I(2)$ models. Again, knowing that there are $I(2)$ variables in the model can help in formulating the right approach to estimating cointegration relationships in such situations.

FORMULATION OF THE DYNAMIC MODEL

So far, the VECM to be estimated (equation (5.2)) contains no deterministic components (such as an intercept and trend, or seasonal dummies). There is

[9] Recall that in the extreme if Π has full rank (i.e., there are $r = n$ linearly independent columns), then all the variables in $\mathbf{z}_t$ are $I(0)$. Note that this points to a problem regarding what is meant by cointegration between $I(0)$ variables, since there are potentially an infinite number of ways we can combine these variables, and each time (by definition) the relationship formed is $I(0)$. This is not a problem when the variables are $I(1)$, since Engle and Granger (1987) have shown that linear combinations of non-stationary variables are in general also non-stationary unless we can find some $\boldsymbol{\beta}_i$ that results in a cointegration relationship.

[10] Johansen (1995b) shows that if the number of cointegration relations exceeds the number of $I(2)$ common trends in $\boldsymbol{\beta}$, then combinations of the variables in $\mathbf{z}_t$ can be stationary by themselves. If this condition is not met, then it should still be possible to combine some of the $I(1)$ vectors in $\boldsymbol{\beta}$ with suitable combinations of the $I(2)$ variables to form stationary vectors. This is the situation known as polynomial cointegration—or multicointegration—and we discuss this briefly in Box 5.3. Even if such combinations exist, there will of course still remain $I(1)$ and/or $I(2)$ vectors that are non-stationary 'common trends'.

also the issue of setting the appropriate lag length of the $\Delta \mathbf{z}_{t-k+1}$ to ensure that the residuals are Gaussian (i.e., they do not suffer from autocorrelation, non-normality, etc.). Setting the value of k is also bound up with the issue of whether there are variables that only affect the short-run behaviour of the model and that, if they are omitted, will become part of the error term $\mathbf{u}_t$. Residual mis-specification can arise as a consequence of omitting these important conditioning variables, and increasing the lag length k is often not the solution (as it usually is when, for example, autocorrelation is present).[11,12] The question of whether there are trends in the data and therefore whether deterministic variables (a constant and trend) should enter the cointegration space or not will be taken up after considering how to test for the number of cointegration vectors in the model, since testing for the inclusion of these deterministic components is undertaken *jointly* with testing for cointegration rank. In this section, we consider the other issues surrounding the appropriate value for k.

For notational simplicity, assume that $k = 2$ and that there exist other variables that are both weakly exogenous and insignificant in the long-run cointegration space such that we can condition on the set of such $I(0)$ variables $\mathbf{D}_t$. The latter will only affect the short-run model, and it is possible to rewrite (5.2) as:

$$\Delta \mathbf{z}_t = \Gamma_1 \Delta \mathbf{z}_{t-1} + \Pi \mathbf{z}_{t-2} + \Psi \mathbf{D}_t + \mathbf{u}_t \tag{5.3}$$

The variables in $\mathbf{D}_t$ are often included to take account of short-run 'shocks' to the system, such as policy interventions and the impact of the two oil price shocks in the 1970s that had an important effect on macroeconomic conditions. Such variables often enter as dummy variables, including seasonal dummies when the data are observed more frequently than annually.[13] Seasonal

[11] Indeed, if residual autocorrelation is due to omitted conditioning variables increasing the value of k results in potentially harmful over-parameterization which affects the estimates of cointegration rank (including the $\boldsymbol{\beta}$), making it difficult to interpret economically the cointegration relations present, as well as significantly reducing the power of the test (if the lag length is too large, then too few cointegration relations are found).

[12] Note, however, that in the general case of setting the value of k, Monte Carlo evidence suggests that tests of cointegration rank (see p. 122) are relatively robust to over-parameterization, while setting too small a value of k severely distorts the size of the tests (Cheung and Lai, 1993). More recent Monte Carlo evidence is presented in Lutkepohl and Saikkonen (1999), confirming that there are often severe size distortions when k is too small and power losses if k is too large. Their recommendation was to choose the lag length using information criteria selection procedures (e.g., the AIC) '... which tend to find a balance between a good approximation of the DGP and an efficient use of the sample information' (Lutkepohl and Saikkonen, 1999, p. 184).

[13] Since seasonal adjustment methods have an effect on the trend behaviour of individual series, it is argued that *un*adjusted data are preferable. For example, Lee and Siklos (1997) show that seasonal adjustment can lead to less cointegration, while Ermini and Chang (1996) show that seasonal adjustment can induce spurious cointegration.

dummies are centred to ensure that they sum to zero over time,[14] and thus they do not affect the underlying asymptotic distributions upon which tests (including tests for cointegration rank) depend. However, it is worth noting at the outset that including any other dummy or dummy-type variable *will* affect the underlying distribution of test statistics, such that the critical values for these tests are different depending on the number of dummies included. This will mean that the published critical values provided by Johansen and others (e.g., Osterwald-Lenum, 1992; Pesaran, Shin and Smith, 2000) are only indicative in such situations.[15]

As an example, consider the PPP and UIP model estimated using UK data by Johansen and Juselius (1992). This was set out briefly in the last chapter and comprises the five variables p_1 (the UK wholesale price index), p_2 (trade-weighted foreign wholesale price index), e (UK effective exchange rate), i_1 (3-month UK Treasury bill rate) and i_2 (3-month Eurodollar interest rate). Using OLS to estimate the system denoted by (5.3) and restricting $\mathbf{D}_t$ to include only seasonal dummies and an intercept produces the output in Table 5.1 (*PcGive 10.1* was used,[16] leaving the cointegration rank unrestricted as $r = n$). The diagnostic tests[17] involve F-tests for the hypotheses: that the i-period lag ($F_{k=i}$) is zero; that there is no serial correlation (F_{ar}, against fourth-order autoregression); that there is no autoregressive conditional heteroscedasticity (ARCH) (FARCH, against fourth order); that there is no heteroscedasticity (F_{het}); and lastly a χ^2-test for normality (χ^2_{nd}: see Doornik and Hansen, 1993). Analogous system (vector) tests are also reported (see the *PcGive* manual), with the last test F_{ur} representing the test against the significance of the regressors in $\mathbf{D}_t$.

The results based on $k = 2$ indicate that the second period lag is significant in at least one of the equations in the model (and cointegration analysis requires the model to have a common lag length). Non-normal residuals are a problem in the equations determining p_2 and i_2. The impact of the outlier observations is seen more clearly in Figure 5.1. Increasing the lag length to $k = 3$ (or higher) has little impact and the additional lags are generally not significant (although the choice of k based on the Akaike information criterion

[14] For example, the usual quarterly (0, 1) dummies for each period (S_{1t}, S_{2t}, S_{3t} and S_{4t}) are entered as $(S_{it} - S_{1t})$, $i = 1, \ldots, 4$.

[15] Johansen and Nielsen (1993) derive the asymptotic distributions for some models with dummy variables that can be simulated via a program called *DisCo* (written in Pascal).

[16] Note that *PcGive* actually estimates the VAR model in levels (see equation (5.1)) rather than the equivalent VECM in first differences with the lagged $\mathbf{z}_{t-k}$ (see equation (5.2)). This needs to be borne in mind when conducting any hypothesis tests with respect to the regressors in the model, since the usual t- and F-tests are not normally distributed in a system containing non-stationary I(I) variables in levels (see Chapter 2).

[17] Most of these were considered in the last chapter. Note that hypothesis tests with respect to the residuals of the model are valid, since these are stationary $I(0)$ on the presumption that there are cointegration relationships in the data set. The F-tests (that the i-period lag ($F_{k=i}$) is zero) are only indicative (see the previous footnote).

Table 5.1 Model evaluation diagnostics: PPP and UIP model using UK data (only an intercept and seasonal dummies in $\mathbf{D}_t$).

Statistic	p_1	p_2	e	i_1	i_2
Lag length = 2					
$F_{k=1}(5, 42)$	20.49**	11.91**	14.11**	20.94**	6.51**
$F_{k=2}(5, 42)$	2.03	1.59	1.04	3.89**	0.88
σ	0.85%	1.23%	3.32%	1.23%	1.45%
$F_{\text{ar}}(4, 42)$	1.10	0.34	1.76	0.85	2.36
$F_{\text{arch}}(4, 38)$	2.53	0.03	0.59	0.41	1.59
$F_{\text{het}}(20, 25)$	1.09	2.07*	0.33	0.92	1.57
$\chi^2_{\text{nd}}(2)$	7.71*	68.87**	1.63	2.59	23.56**
Multivariate tests: $F_{\text{ar}}(100, 111) = 1.28$; $F_{\text{het}}(300, 176) = 0.86$; $\chi^2_{\text{nd}}(10) = 97.68$**; $F_{\text{ur}}(50, 194) = 120.12$**; AIC = −42.2045; HQ = −41.2487					
Lag length = 3					
$F_{k=1}(5, 36)$	22.47**	12.11**	12.59**	13.98**	6.72**
$F_{k=2}(5, 36)$	3.23*	0.70	1.75	2.99*	3.15*
$F_{k=3}(5, 36)$	1.37	1.86	1.64	2.09	3.42*
σ	0.78%	1.20%	3.35%	1.23%	1.30%
$F_{\text{ar}}(4, 36)$	1.52	1.56	1.50	0.99	1.18
$F_{\text{arch}}(4, 32)$	1.90	0.02	0.31	1.51	2.07
$F_{\text{het}}(30, 9)$	0.41	0.78	0.24	0.53	0.92
$\chi^2_{\text{nd}}(2)$	4.15	72.30**	8.32*	2.58	19.43**
Multivariate tests: $F_{\text{ar}}(100, 82) = 1.02$; $\chi^2_{\text{het}}(450) = 494.53$; $\chi^2_{\text{nd}}(10) = 96.44$**; $F_{\text{ur}}(75, 176) = 74.38$**; AIC = −42.4480; HQ = −41.1422					

* Rejects null hypothesis at 5% significance level.
** Rejects null hypothesis at 1% significance level.

(AIC) would in fact result in $k = 4$, whereas in contrast the Hannan–Quinn (HQ) criterion suggests that $k = 1$ is to be preferred).[18]

Johansen and Juselius (1992) argued that by looking at residual plots the above problems of excess kurtosis were found to coincide with significant changes in the oil price, and thus they conditioned their model on Δpo_t and Δpo_{t-1}, where po measures the world price of crude oil. These $I(0)$ variables were presumed to be exogenous and to have only a short-run effect, and thus they are presumed to enter $\mathbf{D}_t$ only. The residual diagnostics that now result are

[18] When information criteria suggest different values of k, Johansen et al. (2000) note that it is common practice to prefer the HQ criterion. However, like others, we have set $k = 2$ in our subsequent analysis mainly because setting k at different values results in implausible estimates of the cointegration vectors. Clearly, this present example of cointegration analysis lacks sufficient observations with too many variables to estimate and is a prime candidate for conditioning on exogenous variables—something we discuss on pp. 135ff.

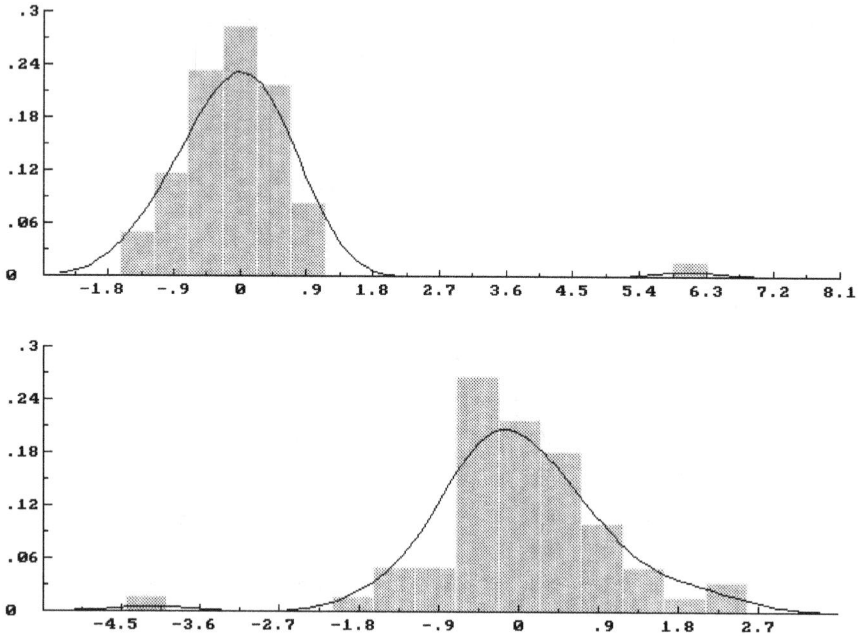

Figure 5.1. Residual densities for p_2 and i_2: excluding Δpo_t, Δpo_{t-1} and D_{usa} in the model.

shown in the top half of Table 5.2, and Figure 5.2. There is a significant reduction in the kurtosis associated with the foreign wholesale price index,[19] but little change in the residuals of the Eurodollar interest rate equation. Johansen and Juselius (1992) stopped at this point in terms of the specification of $\mathbf{D}_t$, arguing that if these two variables prove to be weakly exogenous (as was the case for p_2), then non-normality is less of a problem since we can condition on the weakly exogenous variables (although they remain in the long-run model) and therefore improve the stochastic properties of the model. In practice, as will be seen on pp. 135ff when we consider testing for weak exogeneity, this means that the exogenous variables only enter the right-hand side of (5.2) and do not therefore have to be modelled themselves, which is an advantage especially '... if there have been many interventions during the period and the weakly exogenous variable exhibits all the "problematic" data features' (Hansen and Juselius, 1994).

The residual plot for i_2 indicates that the outlier problem is associated with the first quarter of 1979 and especially the second quarter of 1980. Thus, a second dummy was included taking on the value of 1 for both these periods and labelled D_{usa} (since it coincided in the later period with depository institutions deregulation and the Monetary Control Act in the USA, which had a

[19] The variable Δpo_t is highly significant in the equation determining p_2.

Table 5.2 Model evaluation diagnostics: PPP and UIP model using UK data (1972q1–1987q2) (lag length $k = 2$).

Statistic	p_1	p_2	e	i_1	i_2
Intercept, seasonal dummies and Δpo_t, Δpo_{t-1} in $\mathbf{D}_t$					
$F_{k=1}(5, 40)$	16.65**	13.07**	11.95**	19.53**	6.15**
$F_{k=2}(5, 40)$	1.42	1.14	0.72	3.59**	0.68
$\hat{\sigma}$	0.80%	0.83%	3.35%	1.24%	1.47%
$F_{ar}(4, 40)$	1.16	1.59	1.53	0.56	2.94
$F_{arch}(4, 36)$	1.48	0.49	0.46	0.37	1.70
$F_{het}(20, 23)$	0.60	1.34	0.30	0.79	1.34
$\chi^2_{nd}(2)$	5.75	12.19**	1.17	3.74	23.29**
Multivariate tests: $F_{ar}(100, 102) = 1.13$; $F_{het}(300, 152) = 0.64$; $\chi^2_{nd}(10) = 46.23$**; $F_{ur}(50, 185) = 130.90$**; AIC $= -42.2045$; HQ $= -41.7876$					
Intercept, seasonal dummies, Δpo_t, Δpo_{t-1} and D_{usa} in $\mathbf{D}_t$					
$F_{k=1}(5, 39)$	16.62**	12.77**	11.32**	17.88**	9.35**
$F_{k=2}(5, 39)$	1.48	1.21	0.74	2.96*	0.83
σ	0.81%	0.83%	3.34%	1.25%	1.33%
$F_{ar}(4, 39)$	1.16	1.54	1.94	0.51	2.03
$F_{arch}(4, 35)$	1.39	0.47	0.22	0.32	0.82
$F_{het}(20, 22)$	0.59	1.27	0.28	0.68	0.68
$\chi^2_{nd}(2)$	5.30	12.31**	2.03	4.37	4.24
Multivariate tests: $F_{ar}(100, 97) = 1.24$; $F_{het}(300, 140) = 0.54$; $\chi^2_{nd}(10) = 26.24$**; $F_{ur}(50, 181) = 132.74$**; AIC $= -43.0151$; HQ $= -41.8550$					

* Rejects null hypothesis at 5% significance level.
** Rejects null hypothesis at 1% significance level.

strong impact on interest rate determination outside the USA). The new set of residual diagnostics are reported in the lower half of Table 5.2 and Figure 5.3, showing yet a further improvement in the stochastic properties of the model.

A different example of the problems associated with specifying the value of k and the elements in $\mathbf{D}_t$ involves OLS estimation of the demand-for-money model. Setting $k = 2$ and restricting $\mathbf{D}_t$ to include only seasonal dummies and an intercept, the results as set out in Table 5.3 are obtained. The null hypothesis of no serial correlation is rejected in the univariate case for the real money supply and real output (cf. the F_{ar} statistics against fifth-order autoregression) and for the system as a whole. There is also some evidence that the residuals from the real output and inflation equations are non-normally distributed. Increasing the lag length to $k = 4$ produces the results in the second half of Table 5.3 (as well as minimizing the AIC); the extra lags on $(m - p)_t$ and y_t are significant[20] and serial correlation is no longer a problem, although the test for

[20] Note again the comments in previous footnotes about hypothesis-testing with respect to non-stationary variables.

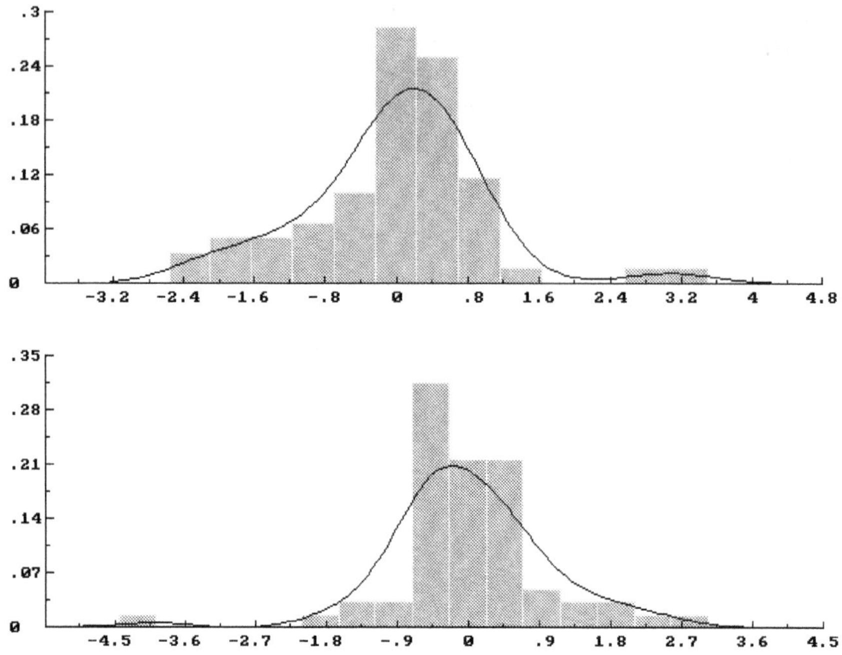

Figure 5.2. Residual densities for p_2 and i_2: including Δpo_t, Δpo_{t-1}, but excluding D_{usa} in the model.

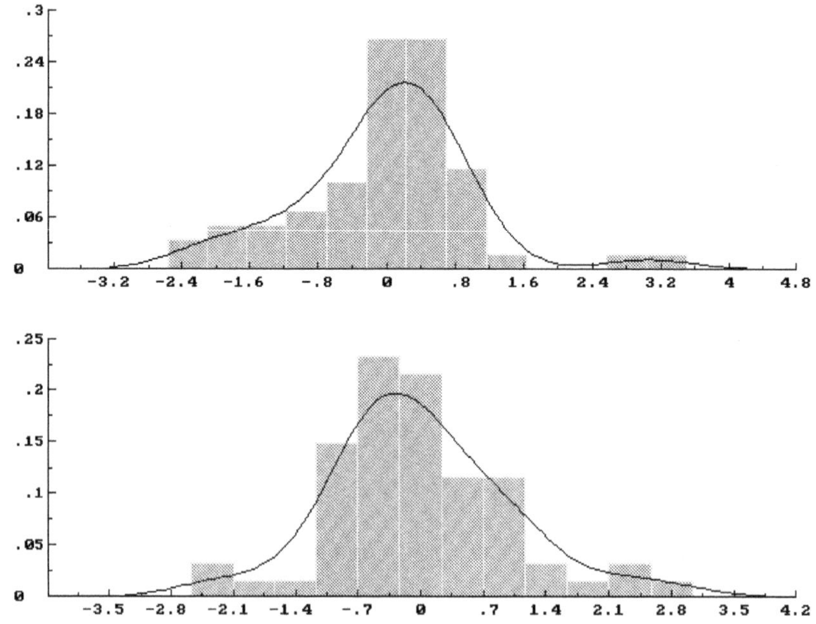

Figure 5.3. Residual densities for p_2 and i_2: including Δpo_t, Δpo_{t-1} and D_{usa} in the model.

Table 5.3 Model evaluation diagnostics: UK demand for money (1963q1–1989q2) (only an intercept and seasonal dummies in $\mathbf{D}_t$).

Statistic	$m-p$	y	Δp	R
Lag length = 2				
$F_{k=1}(4, 88)$	12.22**	10.36**	5.80**	12.22**
$F_{k=2}(4, 88)$	5.10**	6.00**	5.33**	5.10**
σ	2.00%	1.71%	0.77%	1.31%
$F_{ar}(5, 86)$	4.19**	2.77*	0.51	0.34
$F_{arch}(4, 83)$	0.78	0.87	1.14	2.42
$F_{het}(16, 74)$	0.94	1.00	0.78	1.79*
$\chi^2_{nd}(2)$	3.39	7.88*	6.26*	3.04
Multivariate tests: $F_{ar}(80, 270) = 2.02$**; $F_{het}(160, 574) = 1.09$; $\chi^2_{nd}(8) = 19.54$*; $F_{ur}(32, 326) = 248.47$**; AIC $= -34.5196$				
Lag length = 4				
$F_{k=1}(4, 78)$	9.25**	9.79**	5.95**	23.60**
$F_{k=2}(4, 78)$	2.56*	1.41	3.33*	1.39
$F_{k=3}(4, 78)$	1.59	4.52**	0.37	0.18
$F_{k=4}(4, 78)$	4.79**	5.18**	1.71	0.72
σ	1.62%	1.58%	0.73%	1.36%
$F_{ar}(5, 76)$	1.92	1.66	0.93	1.04
$F_{arch}(4, 73)$	1.02	1.09	0.64	3.31*
$F_{het}(32, 48)$	0.52	0.73	0.76	0.89
$\chi^2_{nd}(2)$	2.50	5.28	5.44	2.82
Multivariate tests: $F_{ar}(80, 231) = 0.96$; $F_{het}(320, 400) = 0.59$; $\chi^2_{nd}(8) = 18.76$*; $F_{ur}(64, 307) = 124.42$**; AIC $= -34.8381$				

* Rejects null hypothesis at 5% significance level.
** Rejects null hypothesis at 1% significance level.

ARCH is significant for the interest rate equation. Checking the plot of the residuals for the latter indicates outliers associated with the first two quarters of 1977, and adding a dummy to cover this period removes the ARCH process.[21] Alternatively, on the assumption that the interest rate is weakly exogenous, it may be appropriate to condition on R instead of adding the extra dummy variable, especially if no economic rationale is available to justify its inclusion.[22]

[21] It is fairly common for conditional heteroscedasticity to lead to heavy tailed distributions.

[22] Hendry and Doornik (1994) estimated a similar model to the present one, using seasonally adjusted data, and introduced two extra dummies into $\mathbf{D}_t$, one to account for the two oil price shocks in the 1970s and the other to account for the Barber boom in 1973 and the tight monetary policy introduced in 1979 (see Hendry and Doornik, 1994, fn. 1). These dummies are significant in the model estimated here, but their inclusion has little impact on the short-run model other than to introduce mild autocorrelation into the real output equation. This points to a potential trade-off that often occurs in terms of setting the value of k and introducing $I(0)$ variables into $\mathbf{D}_t$.

TESTING FOR REDUCED RANK

It was stated earlier that if a model contains $\mathbf{z}_t$, a vector of non-stationary $I(1)$ variables, then $\Pi\mathbf{z}_{t-k}$ in (5.2) contains the stationary long-run error correction relations and must be stationary for $\mathbf{u}_t \sim I(0)$ to be 'white noise'. The occurs when $\Pi(=\boldsymbol{\alpha\beta}')$ has reduced rank; that is, there are $r \leq (n-1)$ cointegration vectors present in $\boldsymbol{\beta}$ so that testing for cointegration amounts to finding the number of r linearly independent columns in Π, which is equivalent to testing that the last $(n-r)$ columns of $\boldsymbol{\alpha}$ are insignificantly small (i.e., effectively zero). In Box 5.1, it is shown that Johansen's maximum likelihood approach to solving this problem amounts to a reduced rank regression, which provides n eigenvalues $\hat{\lambda}_1 > \hat{\lambda}_2 > \cdots > \hat{\lambda}_n$ and *their corresponding* eigenvectors $\hat{\mathbf{V}} = (\hat{\mathbf{v}}_1, \cdots, \hat{\mathbf{v}}_n)$. Those r elements in $\hat{\mathbf{V}}$ that determine the linear combinations of stationary relationships can be denoted $\hat{\boldsymbol{\beta}} = (\hat{\mathbf{v}}_1, \ldots, \hat{\mathbf{v}}_r)$; that is, the distinct $\hat{\mathbf{v}}_i'\mathbf{z}_t$ $(i = 1, \ldots, r)$ combinations of the $I(1)$ levels of $\mathbf{z}_t$ that produce high correlations with the stationary $\Delta\mathbf{z}_t \sim I(0)$ elements in (5.2) are the cointegration vectors by virtue of the fact that they must themselves be $I(0)$ to achieve a high correlation. Since each eigenvector $\hat{\mathbf{v}}_i$ has a corresponding eigenvalue, then the magnitude of $\hat{\lambda}_i$ is a measure of how strongly the cointegration relations $\hat{\mathbf{v}}_i'\mathbf{z}_t$ (which we can now denote as $\hat{\boldsymbol{\beta}}_i'\mathbf{z}_t$) are correlated with the stationary part of the model. The last $(n-r)$ combinations obtained from the Johansen approach (i.e., $\hat{\mathbf{v}}_i'\mathbf{z}_t$ $(i = r+1, \ldots, n)$), indicate the non-stationary combinations and theoretically are uncorrelated with the stationary elements in (5.2). Consequently, for the eigenvectors corresponding to the non-stationary part of the model, $\lambda_i = 0$ for $i = r+1, \ldots, n$.

Thus to test the null hypothesis that there are at most r cointegration vectors (and thus $(n-r)$ unit roots) amounts to:

$$H_0\colon \lambda_i = 0 \qquad i = r+1, \ldots, n$$

where only the first r eigenvalues are non-zero. This restriction can be imposed for different values of r, and then the log of the maximized likelihood function for the restricted model is compared with the log of the maximized likelihood function of the unrestricted model and a standard likelihood ratio test computed (although with a non-standard distribution). That is, it is possible to test the null hypothesis using what has become known as the *trace* statistic:

$$\lambda_{\text{trace}} = -2\log(Q) = -T\sum_{i=r+1}^{n}\log(1-\hat{\lambda}_i) \qquad r = 0, 1, 2, \ldots, n-2, n-1 \tag{5.4}$$

where Q = (Restricted maximized likelihood ÷ Unrestricted maximized likelihood). Asymptotic critical values are provided in Osterwald-Lenum (1992), Pesaran et al. (2000) and Doornik (1999) although if dummy variables enter the deterministic part of the multivariate model (i.e., $\mathbf{D}_t$ above), then these critical values are only indicative. Similarly, if the practitioner only has a small sample

Table 5.4 Tests of the cointegration rank for the PPP and UIP model using UK data (1972q1–1987q2).[a]

H_0: r	$n-r$	$\hat{\lambda}_i$	λ_{max} test	λ_{max} (0.95)	Trace test	λ_{trace} (0.95)
0	5	0.407	31.37	33.6	83.26*	70.5
1	4	0.307	22.02	27.4	51.89*	48.9
2	3	0.249	17.20	21.1	29.87	31.5
3	2	0.122	7.82	14.9	12.68	17.9
4	1	0.078	4.85	8.1	4.85	8.1

[a] See Johansen and Juselius (1992, table 2).
* Denotes rejection at the 5% significance level (based on critical values in Pesaran et al. 2000, table 6c—see also the Statistical Appendix at the end of this book).

of observations on $\mathbf{z}_t$, then there are likely to be problems with the power and size properties of the above test when using asymptotic critical values. The implications of this, and other similar problems with the trace statistic, are considered on p. 124 and in footnote 23.

Another test of the significance of the largest λ_r is the so-called maximal eigenvalue or λ-max statistic:

$$\lambda_{max} = -T\log(1-\hat{\lambda}_{r+1}) \qquad r = 0, 1, 2, \ldots, n-2, n-1 \tag{5.5}$$

This tests that there are r cointegration vectors against the alternative that $r+1$ exist. Since the sequence of trace tests $(\lambda_0, \lambda_1, \ldots, \lambda_{n-1})$ leads to a consistent test procedure and consistency is not available for the λ-max test, it is usually current practice to only use the trace statistic when testing for cointegration rank (although initially we present both tests for completeness).[23] An example of testing for the reduced rank of Π is now presented to make clear the use of the tests outlined above.

The results obtained from applying the Johansen reduced rank regression approach (see Box 5.1) to the PPP and UIP model discussed above (with intercept, seasonal dummies and Δpo_t, Δpo_{t-1}, D_{usa} in $\mathbf{D}_t$ and $k=2$) are given in Table 5.4. The various hypotheses to be tested, from no cointegration (i.e., $r=0$ or alternatively $n-r=5$) to increasing numbers of cointegration vectors are presented in columns 1 and 2. The eigenvalues associated with the combinations of the $I(1)$ levels of $\mathbf{z}_t$ are in column 3, ordered from highest to lowest. Next come the λ_{max} statistics that test whether $r=0$ against $r=1$ or $r=1$ against $r=2$, etc. That is, a test of the significance of the largest λ_r is

[23] Note that Lutkepohl et al. (2001) have looked at the small-sample properties of the trace and λ-max tests, concluding that the former sometimes has poorer size properties while the λ-max test often suffers from loss of power. In general, they conclude: '... our overall recommendation is to use the trace tests if one wants to apply just one test version. Of course there is nothing wrong with the common practice of using both versions simultaneously' (p. 304).

performed, and the present results suggest that the hypothesis of no cointegration ($r = 0$) cannot be rejected at the 5% level (with the 5% critical values given in column 5). The λ_{trace} statistics test the null that $r = q$ ($q = 0, 1, 2, \ldots, n-1$) against the unrestricted alternative that $r = n$. On the basis of this test it is possible to accept that there are two cointegration vectors, since the trace statistic associated with the null hypothesis that $r = 1$ is rejected, but the null hypothesis that $r = 2$ is not rejected. This apparent contradiction in the tests for cointegration rank is not uncommon. As has already been stated, the inclusion of dummy or dummy-type variables in $\mathbf{D}_t$ affects the underlying distribution of the test statistics, such that the critical values for these tests are different depending on the number of dummies included. The problem of small samples has also been mentioned, and Reimers (1992) suggests that in such a situation the Johansen procedure over-rejects when the null is true. Thus he suggests taking account of the number of parameters to be estimated in the model and making an adjustment for degrees of freedom by replacing T in (5.4) and (5.5) by $T - nk$, where T is the sample size, n is the number of variables in the model and k is the lag length set when estimating (5.2).[24] Using both Reimers adjusted trace and λ_{max} statistics, we could not reject the null of no cointegration given that we would now be using a value of $T - nk = 50$ rather than $T = 60$ in calculating the test statistics. However, as pointed out by Doornik and Hendry (1994), it is unclear whether this is the preferred correction, although Cheung and Lai (1993) report that their results '... support that the finite-sample bias of Johansen's tests is a positive function of $T/(T - nk)$ ... furthermore, the finite-sample bias toward over-rejection of the no cointegration hypothesis magnifies with increasing values of n and k.' More recently, Johansen (2002a, 2002b) has considered the issue of correcting the rank test statistics in small samples, finding that a Bartlett-type correction that depends on the parameters of the VECM ($\boldsymbol{\Gamma}$, $\boldsymbol{\alpha}$, $\boldsymbol{\beta}$, $\boldsymbol{\Sigma}$—see equation 5.2), as well as the degrees of freedom, is a theoretical improvement for calculating appropriate critical values. However, simulations (based on Monte Carlo experiments) provided some mixed results. An alternative to using such a correction factor would be to simulate the exact distribution based on the d.g.p. underlying the model being considered, using bootstrap methods, but again this is not without problems (see Harris and Judge, 1998, for a discussion).[25]

The Monte Carlo experiments reported in Cheung and Lai (1993) also

[24] Cheung and Lai (1993) note that '... an equivalent way to make finite-sample corrections is to adjust the critical values and not the test statistics.' The scaling factor used to adjust the critical values is $T/(T - nk)$.

[25] The bootstrap approach in effect amounts to undertaking the same type of Monte Carlo work that generated the tables of critical values for the trace (and λ-max) test, but for the purposes of calculating critical values relevant to a particular data set (based on unknown d.g.p.s). However, the results in Harris and Judge (1998) suggest that the bootstrap test statistic has poor size properties.

suggest that '... between Johansen's two LR [likelihood ratio] tests for cointegration, the trace test shows more robustness to both skewness and excess kurtosis in (the residuals) than the maximal eigenvalue (λ_{max}) test.'[26] Since the PPP and UIP model suffers from excess kurtosis, it may be preferable to place greater weight on the trace test. However, it is also important to use any additional information that can support the choice of r. Juselius (1995) suggests looking at the dynamics of the VAR model (equation (5.1)) and in particular whether it converges in the long run. Thus the eigenvalues (i.e., roots) of what is termed the companion matrix (**A**) are considered since these provide additional confirmation of how many $(n - r)$ roots are on the unit circle and thus the number of r cointegration relations. The matrix **A** is defined by:

$$\mathbf{A} = \begin{bmatrix} \mathbf{A}_1 & \mathbf{A}_2 & \cdots & \mathbf{A}_{k-1} & \mathbf{A}_k \\ \mathbf{I}_n & 0 & \cdots & 0 & 0 \\ 0 & \mathbf{I}_n & \cdots & 0 & 0 \\ 0 & 0 & \cdots & \mathbf{I}_n & 0 \end{bmatrix}$$

where $\mathbf{A}_i$ is defined by (5.1) and $\mathbf{I}_n$ is the n-dimensional identity matrix. There are 10 roots of the companion matrix in the present example, since $n \times k = 10$. The moduli[27] of the three largest roots are 0.979, 0.918 and 0.918, respectively, indicating that all roots are inside the unit circle with the three largest close to unity. This suggests that $(n - r) = 3$ and thus there are two cointegration relations. The fact that all roots are inside the unit circle is consistent with $\mathbf{z}_t$ comprising $I(1)$ processes, although it is certainly possible that the largest root is not significantly different from 1. If any of the roots are on or outside the unit circle, this would tend to indicate an $I(2)$ model, requiring second-order differencing to achieve stationarity.[28]

The estimates of $\hat{\boldsymbol{\alpha}}$ and $\hat{\boldsymbol{\beta}}$ obtained from applying the Johansen technique (using the *PcGive 10.1* program) are presented in Box 5.2.[29] Note that the $\hat{\boldsymbol{\beta}}$-matrix is presented in normalized form, with the latter having one element of each row of $\boldsymbol{\beta}'$ set equal to -1 (along the diagonal in this instance). This is

[26] 'Fat tails' due to generalized ARCH (GARCH) processes are also likely to affect the small-sample properties of the trace and maximal eigenvalue tests. This is discussed in Chapter 8, when we look at modelling financial models using cointegration techniques.
[27] Recall that the roots of the characteristic equation used to solve for the eigenvalues (or characteristic roots) can be complex (i.e., contain a real and imaginary part $h \pm vi$, where h and v are two real numbers and i is an imaginary number) and the modulus is the absolute value of the complex root and is calculated as $\sqrt{(h^2 + v^2)}$.
[28] Formal testing of the $I(2)$ model is considered in Box 5.3.
[29] Note, for simplicity and in line with common practice, that the full rank (5×5) matrices are labelled $\hat{\alpha}$ and $\hat{\beta}$ in Box 5.2, although it might be more appropriate to label them as $\mathbf{V} = (v_1, \ldots, v_n)$ and $\mathbf{W} = (w_1, \ldots, w_n)$, where the v_i are the eigenvectors obtained from with Johansen procedure with associated weights w_i. Only the first r elements in **W** and **V** that are associated with stationary relationships should be labelled $\hat{\alpha}$ and $\hat{\beta}$, with the latter having reduced rank.

Box 5.2 Output from* PcGive 10.1 *for PPP and UIP models.

Normalised

β'

p_1	p_2	e	i_1	i_2
-1.000	0.774	0.781	2.861	1.749
0.079	-1.000	-0.332	1.601	-1.982
-1.075	1.639	-1.000	-0.078	-0.766
-2.236	0.410	4.588	-1.000	-1.872
4.009	3.079	1.442	0.786	-1.000

α

0.076	0.009	0.011	0.003	0.003
0.024	-0.022	-0.020	-0.006	-0.005
-0.147	-0.070	0.135	0.011	-0.006
-0.060	-0.099	-0.009	0.004	-0.013
-0.041	0.096	-0.027	0.000	0.007

T-VALUES FOR α

3.622	0.308	0.538	0.972	0.808
1.097	-0.699	-0.982	-1.709	-1.160
-1.697	-0.552	1.655	0.825	-0.371
-1.856	-2.071	-0.308	0.683	-1.994
-1.204	1.898	-0.823	-0.065	1.009

achieved by simply dividing each row by the chosen element. Normalizing the $\hat{\boldsymbol{\beta}}$-matrix leads to a normalized $\hat{\boldsymbol{\alpha}}$-matrix, and different normalizations applied to $\hat{\boldsymbol{\beta}}$ lead to different values in the $\hat{\boldsymbol{\alpha}}$ matrix. Figure 5.4 plots the first four relations associated with the first four rows in $\hat{\boldsymbol{\beta}}'$ to see if any of the $\hat{\boldsymbol{\beta}}_i'\mathbf{z}_t$ are stationary. The first two vectors correspond to the most stationary relations in the model, but there is some evidence that both relationships are upward trending. The other two vectors are clearly non-stationary. The plots in Figure 5.5 present a different version of the same relations as in Figure 5.4 since, instead of multiplying the $\hat{\boldsymbol{\beta}}_i'$ by $\mathbf{z}_t$, where $\mathbf{z}_t$ captures all the short-run dynamics (including seasonals) in the model, the $\hat{\boldsymbol{\beta}}_i$ are multiplied by a vector $\mathbf{R}_{kt}$ that is equivalent to $\mathbf{z}_t$, but with all the short-run dynamic effects removed (i.e., $\mathbf{R}_{kt} = \mathbf{z}_{t-k} - (\hat{\boldsymbol{\Gamma}}_1\Delta\mathbf{z}_{t-1} + \cdots + \hat{\boldsymbol{\Gamma}}_{k-1}\Delta\mathbf{z}_{t-k+1})$—see equations (5.2) and (5.1.3)). The first two graphs in Figure 5.5 now suggest that the first two vectors are stationary, confirming that $r = 2$. Note, however, the advice given by Hansen and Juselius (1994) that when '... $\boldsymbol{\beta}'\mathbf{z}_t$ and $\boldsymbol{\beta}'\mathbf{R}_{kt}$ look widely different, in particular if the former looks **I**(1) whereas the latter looks stationary, it is a good idea to check whether your data vector $\mathbf{z}_t$ is second order instead of first order nonstationary.'

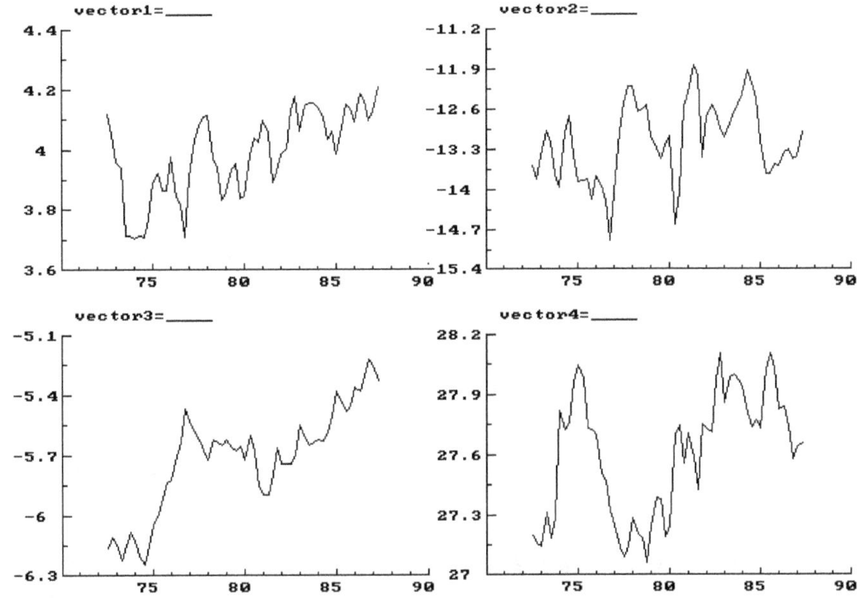

Figure 5.4. Plots of the relations $\hat{\mathbf{v}}_i'\mathbf{z}_t$ (those that cointegrate can be denoted as $\hat{\boldsymbol{\beta}}_i'\mathbf{z}_t$).

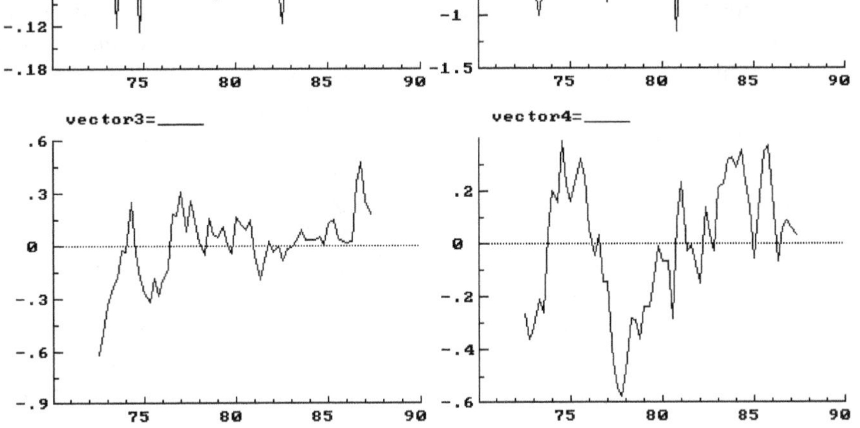

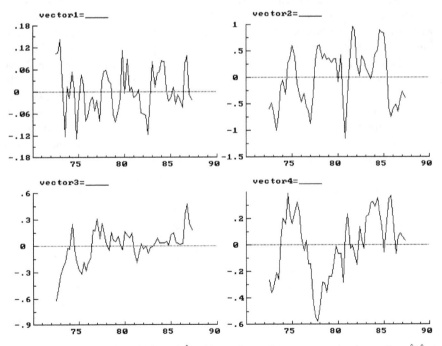

Figure 5.5. Plots of the relations $\hat{\mathbf{v}}_i\hat{\mathbf{R}}_{kt}$ (those that cointegrate can be denoted as $\hat{\boldsymbol{\beta}}_i'\hat{\mathbf{R}}_{kt}$).

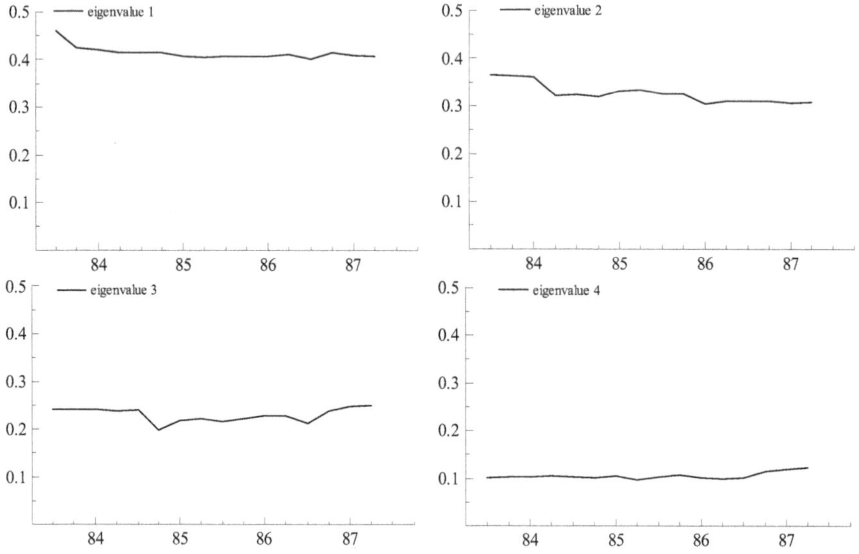

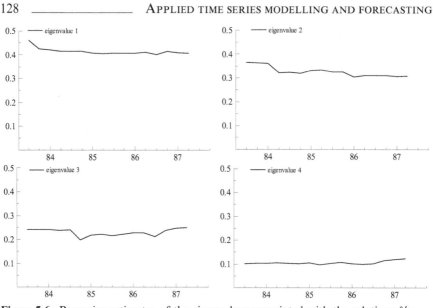

Figure 5.6. Recursive estimates of the eigenvalues associated with the relations $\hat{\mathbf{v}}_i'\mathbf{z}_t$.

As another check of the adequacy of the model, Figure 5.6 plots recursive estimates of the first four non-zero eigenvalues. This type of graph corresponds to a standard plot of parameter estimates in the usual regression model since non-constancy of $\hat{\boldsymbol{\alpha}}$ or $\hat{\boldsymbol{\beta}}$ should be reflected in non-constancy of the $\hat{\lambda}_i$. If there were breaks in the cointegration vectors, then generally this would result in too low a rank order being established for $\hat{\boldsymbol{\Pi}}$, as the break would likely be 'mistaken' for non-stationarity. Generally, for the PPP and UIP model there is no evidence of parameter instability due to, for example, the failure to account for structural breaks. More formal tests for structural breaks are being developed—for example, Inoue (1999) allows for a break in the deterministic components in the VECM (see equation (5.6) and the next section), but not in $\hat{\boldsymbol{\alpha}}$ or $\hat{\boldsymbol{\beta}}$. Johansen, Mosconi and Nielson (2000) discuss the implication of such deterministic breaks on the test statistics for cointegration rank. In contrast, Quintos (1997) tests whether there has been a change in the rank of $\hat{\boldsymbol{\Pi}}$ over the sample period (i.e., the number of cointegration vectors changes over time). Lutkepohl, Saikkonen and Trenkler (2001) compare two types of tests for the cointegration rank of a VAR process with a deterministic shift in the level at some known point in time. Lastly, Gabriel, Psaradakis and Sola (2002) advocate the use of Markov switching techniques that allow multiple regime shifts as a way for testing for (multiple) breaks in $\hat{\boldsymbol{\alpha}}$ and/or $\hat{\boldsymbol{\beta}}$.

As an example of a likely $I(2)$ system, consider the UK demand-for-money model again, but in terms of nominal money balances. Applying the Johansen approach to seasonally *un*adjusted data for the 1963q1 to 1989q2[30] period

[30] Including centred seasonal dummies and a constant in $\mathbf{D}_t$.

results in one cointegration vector being accepted after testing for reduced rank, with the largest eigenvalue of the companion matrix having a modulus of 1.007. Estimating the real money demand model with the potentially $I(2)$ variables m_t and p_t replaced by $(m-p)_t$ also produces support for a single cointegration relationship, but this time with the largest eigenvalue of the companion matrix having a modulus of 0.991. Johansen (1995b) has developed a more exact test for whether the model contains any $I(2)$ variables (see Box 5.3), but the procedure is not yet fully available in *PcGive 10.1* (Box 5.3 indicates what currently can be modelled in terms of an $I(2)$ system). If there are $I(2)$ variables and the rank test procedure outlined above for the $I(1)$ model indicates that there are cointegration relationships, then they are valid, but not necessarily stationary, which has implications for the next stage of econometric modelling (e.g., estimating dynamic error correction models that include these cointegration relationships). In such a situation, as noted above, it is necessary to replace the $I(2)$ variables with $I(1)$ alternatives through some form of differencing or to use the approach for $I(2)$ variables developed by, for example, Johansen (1995a, chap. 9) and Paruolo (1996).

Lastly, having determined how many cointegration vectors there are, it is now necessary to consider whether they are unique and consequently whether they tell us anything about the structural economic relationships underlying the long-run model. The PPP and UIP model (see Box 5.2) appears to have two cointegration vectors (i.e., the first two rows of $\boldsymbol{\beta}'$, since these correspond to the largest eigenvalues and thus have the highest correlation with the stationary part of the model). As Johansen and Juselius (1992) point out, the first vector seems to contain the assumed PPP relation in the first three variables and the second to contain the interest rate differential in the last two variables. However, when interpreting the cointegration vectors obtained from the Johansen approach it needs to be stressed that what the reduced rank regression procedure provides is information on how many unique cointegration vectors *span* the cointegration space, while any linear combination of the stationary vectors is itself a stationary vector and thus the estimates produced for any particular column in $\boldsymbol{\beta}$ are not necessarily unique. This can easily be seen by noting that $\boldsymbol{\alpha\beta}' = \boldsymbol{\alpha\xi}^1\boldsymbol{\xi\beta}' = \boldsymbol{\alpha}^*\boldsymbol{\beta}'^*$, where $\boldsymbol{\xi}$ is any $r \times r$ non-singular matrix. Thus, if we can find a ξ-matrix that transforms $\boldsymbol{\beta}$ into $\boldsymbol{\beta}^*$, we still have the same unique number of cointegration vectors, but the vectors themselves are not unique. This is very important, and it would be a major limitation if we could not determine unique structural relationships for each cointegration vector (assuming such uniqueness exists). Fortunately, it is possible to test for unique vectors (see p. 152) as well as to test more generally to see if particular relationships span the cointegration space (e.g., does the $(1, -1, -1, *, *)'$ vector exist anywhere within the space spanned by the two vectors comprising the PPP model).[31]

[31] Note that * denotes an unrestricted value.

Box 5.3 Formal testing of the I(2) model using Johansen's two-step approach.

There is an additional condition (associated with *just* the non-stationary $(n-r)$ part of the model) that (5.2) must satisfy for the model to contain only $I(1)$ variables; that is:

$$\text{rank}(\boldsymbol{\alpha}'_{\perp}\boldsymbol{\Gamma}\boldsymbol{\beta}_{\perp}) = n - r \qquad \text{when } \boldsymbol{\Gamma} = \mathbf{I}_n - \sum_{j=1}^{k} \boldsymbol{\Gamma}_i \tag{5.3.1}$$

where $\boldsymbol{\Gamma}$ is the mean lag matrix of (5.2) and $\boldsymbol{\alpha}_{\perp}$ and $\boldsymbol{\beta}_{\perp}$ are $n \times (n-r)$ orthogonal matrices to $\boldsymbol{\alpha}$ and $\boldsymbol{\beta}$ such that $\boldsymbol{\alpha}'_{\perp}\boldsymbol{\alpha} = 0$ and $\boldsymbol{\beta}'_{\perp}\boldsymbol{\beta} = 0$. If this condition is met, then the non-stationary part of the model comprises $(n-r)$ linearly independent $I(1)$ relations, which can be added to the r linearity independent stationary relations contained in the reduced rank matrix $\boldsymbol{\Pi}(=\boldsymbol{\alpha}\boldsymbol{\beta}')$. If the condition is not met, then $(\boldsymbol{\alpha}'_{\perp}\boldsymbol{\Gamma}\boldsymbol{\beta}_{\perp})$ has a reduced rank of $s_1 < (n-r)$ and the overall model will contain r cointegration relations, s_1 common $I(1)$ trends and $s_2 = (n - r - s_1)$ common $I(2)$ trends. The problem now becomes one of separating out the three dimensions of the model.

First, note that when there are $I(2)$ trends present, the appropriate VECM model is the second-differenced version akin to (5.2), viz.:

$$\Delta^2 \mathbf{z}_t = \boldsymbol{\Gamma}\Delta\mathbf{z}_{t-1} + \boldsymbol{\Gamma}_1^*\Delta^2\mathbf{z}_{t-1} + \cdots + \boldsymbol{\Gamma}_{k-2}^*\Delta^2\mathbf{z}_{t-k+2} + \boldsymbol{\Pi}\mathbf{z}_{t-k} + \mathbf{u}_t \tag{5.3.2}$$

Johansen (1995b) proposes a two-step procedure to determine the dimensions of r, s_1 and s_2. The first step is to proceed as in the case of the standard $I(1)$ model and obtain estimates of $\hat{r}$, $\hat{\boldsymbol{\alpha}}$ and $\hat{\boldsymbol{\beta}}$ (i.e., in terms of testing for cointegration rank, this step uses a reduced rank regression procedure based on (5.2) in order to determine the number of cointegration relations in the model). The second step amounts to determining the rank of $(\boldsymbol{\alpha}'_{\perp}\boldsymbol{\Gamma}\boldsymbol{\beta}_{\perp})$, which is conditional on having estimates of $\hat{\boldsymbol{\alpha}}$ and $\hat{\boldsymbol{\beta}}$, and uses a reduced rank regression procedure based on (5.3.2) after it has been multiplied through by $\boldsymbol{\alpha}'_{\perp}$:

$$\boldsymbol{\alpha}'_{\perp}\Delta^2\mathbf{z}_t = \boldsymbol{\alpha}'_{\perp}\boldsymbol{\Gamma}\Delta\mathbf{z}_{t-1} + \boldsymbol{\alpha}'_{\perp}\boldsymbol{\Gamma}_1^*\Delta^2\mathbf{z}_{t-1} + \cdots + \boldsymbol{\alpha}'_{\perp}\boldsymbol{\Gamma}_{k-2}^*\Delta^2\mathbf{z}_{t-k+2} + \boldsymbol{\alpha}'_{\perp}\mathbf{u}_t \tag{5.3.3}$$

Note that the term involving the stationary long-run relations $\boldsymbol{\Pi}\mathbf{z}_{t-k}$ has dropped out since $\alpha'_{\perp}\Pi = (\alpha'_{\perp}\alpha)\beta' = 0$ and that (5.3.3) comprises a $(n-r) \times (n-r)$-dimensional system of equations in only first- and second-order differences. That is, the second step only operates on the non-stationary part of the model, and from it we can determine s_1, the rank of $(\boldsymbol{\alpha}'_{\perp}\boldsymbol{\Gamma}\boldsymbol{\beta}_{\perp})$. In fact, the reduced rank analysis of (5.3.3) provides $(n-r)$ eigenvalues $\mu_1 > \mu_2 > \cdots > \mu_{n-r}$ that can be used to test the null hypothesis that there are at most s_1 common $I(1)$ trends (and thus

$s_2 = (n - r - s_1)$ common $I(2)$ trends) using a likelihood ratio test statistic equivalent to the trace statistic in the standard $I(1)$ approach:

$$Q_{r,s_1} = -T \sum_{i=s+1}^{n-r} \log(1 - \hat{\lambda}_i) \qquad s = 0, 1, 2, \ldots, n - r - 1 \tag{5.3.4}$$

Note that this tests for the rank s_1 conditional on the value of r, and thus tests are carried out after having determined the number of cointegration vectors in the model. The critical values are the same as those given in Osterwald-Lenum (1992), since Johansen has shown that Q_{r,s_1} and λ_{trace} have the same asymptotic distributions. However, the above test is conditional on r being known, but since this is not known in practice Paruolo (1996) has developed a joint test of s_1 and r. That is, it is more relevant to test H_{r,s_1} against H_r using the joint test statistic:

$$S_{r,s_1} = -2\log Q(H_{r,s_1}|H_r) = Q_{r,s_1} + Q_r \tag{5.3.5}$$

The critical values for this test are available (depending on the deterministic components in the model) in Paruolo (1996) and Johansen (1995b), while Doornik (1999) provides approximations for use in *PcGive 10.1*.

As an example of the $I(2)$ approach, we use step 1 of Johansen's two-step reduced rank regression procedure available in *PcGive 10.1* and seasonally unadjusted UK money demand data to obtain the results presented in Box Table 5.3.1 (note we substitute m_t and p_t for $(m - p)_t$ in this model and omit Δp_t, since it is likely that $m_t, p_t \sim I(2)$ while $(m - p)_t \sim I(1)$). Each row of test statistics involving Q_{r,s_1} has been obtained after setting r (i.e., the rank of Π). Thus, for $r = 0$, the options available for testing in the non-stationary part of the model are from zero to three common $I(1)$ trends (or, reading along the last row of the table, from four to zero common $I(2)$ trends). Thus, we start in the top left-hand corner of Box Table 5.3.1, and under $r = 0$ we start by testing the null that $s_1 = 0$, which with a test statistic of 242.23 rejects the null at better than the 1% significance level. Next (under $r = 0$) we test $s_1 = 1$, and so on, each time rejecting the null. Moving to the row where $r = 1$ is the maintained hypothesis, we again

Box Table 5.3.1 The results of the $I(2)$ analysis of UK money demand data.

r	Q_{r,s_1}				$Q_r = \lambda_{\text{trace}}$	λ_{trace} (0.95)	$n = r$
0	242.23** $s_1=0$	176.90** $s_1=1$	135.85** $s_1=2$	120.54** $s_1=3$	114.38**	48.88	4
1		105.80** $s_1=0$	41.32 $s_1=1$	33.44 $s_1=2$	27.14	31.51	3
2			35.74 $s_1=0$	19.12 $s_1=1$	11.36	17.86	2
3				13.06 $s_1=0$	0.08	8.07	1
$s_2 = n - r - s_1$	4	3	2	1	0		

** Rejects at the 1% significance level.

test first $s_1 = 0$, then $s_1 = 1$ and so on. The first time the null cannot be rejected provides our joint result on $Q_{r,s_1} + Q_r$. In the present situation, when $r = 1$,[32] allowing for at most three non-stationary columns in $\boldsymbol{\beta}$, we test for the rank of the non-stationary part of the model and find that, when testing the null that $s_1 = 1$, we cannot reject at the 5% significance level. This suggests that the model comprises a single comon $I(1)$ trend and $s_2(= n - r - s_1 = 2)$ common $I(1)$ trends. Since we have an $I(2)$ system (i.e., $\text{rank}(\boldsymbol{\alpha}'_{\perp}\boldsymbol{\Gamma}\boldsymbol{\beta}_{\perp}) < n - r$) and defining $z_t = [x_{1t}, x_{2t}]$ where $x_{1t} \sim I(1)$ and $x_{2t} \sim I(2)$, Banerjee, Cockerill and Russell (2001) point out that r cointegrating relationships are further decomposable into r_0 directly co-integrating relationships, where the levels of the $I(2)$ variables cointegrate directly with an $I(0)$ variable, and r_1 polynomial cointegrating relationships, where the levels of x_{2t} cointegrate with the differences of the levels and (possibly) with the levels of the $x_{1t} \sim I(1)$ to give an $I(0)$ variable:

$$\boldsymbol{\beta}'_0 x_{2t} \sim I(0) \qquad \text{where } \boldsymbol{\beta}_0 \text{ is } n \times r_0 \text{ with rank } r_0 \tag{5.3.6}$$

$$\boldsymbol{\beta}'_1 x_{2t} + \boldsymbol{\beta}'_2 \Delta x_{2t} + \boldsymbol{\beta}'_3 x_{1t} \sim I(0) \qquad \text{where } \boldsymbol{\beta}_i \ (i = 1, \ldots, 3) \text{ are } n \times r_1 \tag{5.3.7}$$

$$r_0 + r_1 = r \tag{5.3.8}$$

In equation (5.3.7), $\boldsymbol{\beta}'_1 x_{2t}$ is integrated of order 1 (implying $x_{2t} \sim CI(2, 1)$), which cointegrates with either the $I(1)$ variables in the model (x_{1t}) and/or the differenced $I(2)$ variables (with $\Delta x_{2t} \sim I(1)$). Generally, the number of polynomial cointegrating relationships equals the number of $I(2)$ common trends in the system (implying that since $r = r_0 + r_1$, then $r_1 \equiv s_2(= n - r - s_1)$), which in the present situation with $s_2 = 2$ is not feasible (given that we have found that $r = 1$). Thus, the results are somewhat ambiguous, and economic reasoning would suggest a plausible outcome is at most one common $I(2)$ trend in the model forming a relationship as depicted by (5.3.7).[33]

DETERMINISTIC COMPONENTS IN THE MULTIVARIATE MODEL

In discussing the formulation of the dynamic model, the question of whether an intercept and trend should enter the short- and/or long-run model was raised.

[32] Note that the standard trace test of the $I(1)$ model confirms that $r = 1$, since the test statistic of $27.14 < 31.54$ (the critical value obtained from Pesaran et al. (2000, table 6c)).

[33] Note that *PcGive 10.1* only is currently programmed to undertake testing for the $I(2)$ system; it does not undertake step 2 of Johansen's procedure and allow testing of the eigenvectors (however, this procedure is available as an additional download to the *Cats in Rats* econometric program, distributed by Estima—see the Appendix at the end of the book).

For notational simplicity assuming that $k = 2$ and omitting the other deterministic variables in $\mathbf{D}_t$, we can expand the VECM (equation (5.2)) to include the various options that need to be considered:

$$\Delta\mathbf{z}_t = \Gamma_1 \Delta\mathbf{z}_{t-1} + \boldsymbol{\alpha} \begin{bmatrix} \boldsymbol{\beta} \\ \mu_1 \\ \delta_1 \end{bmatrix} \tilde{\mathbf{z}}_{t-k} + \boldsymbol{\alpha}_\perp \mu_2 + \boldsymbol{\alpha}_\perp \delta_2 t + \mathbf{u}_t \tag{5.6}$$

where $\tilde{\mathbf{z}}'_{t-k} = (\mathbf{z}'_{t-k}, 1, t)$. Although it is possible to specify a model (denoted here as Model 1) where $\delta_1 = \delta_2 = \mu_1 = \mu_2 = 0$ (i.e., there are no deterministic components in the data or in the cointegration relations), this is unlikely to occur in practice, especially as the intercept is generally needed to account for the units of measurement of the variables in $\mathbf{z}_t$.[34] There are three models that can realistically be considered:

- If there are no linear trends in the levels of the data, such that the first-differenced series have a zero mean, then $\delta_1 = \delta_2 = \mu_2 = 0$. Thus, the intercept is restricted to the long-run model (i.e., the cointegration space) to account for the units of measurement of the variables in $\mathbf{z}_t$. The critical values for this model are available in Osterwald-Lenum (1992), although Pesaran et al. (2000, table 6b[35]) have extended these to allow for (weakly) exogenous $I(1)$ variables to enter the model such that the endogenous model set out in equation (5.6) is a special case where the number of exogenous variables (k) equals 0. Doornik (1999) has also produced critical values using the Gamma distribution, and these are the default option in the econometrics package *PcGive 10.1*. For consistency, we shall label this Model 2.[36]
- If there are linear trends in the levels of the data, then we specify a model that allows the non-stationary relationships in the model to drift, so $\delta_1 = \delta_2 = 0$. However, it is assumed that the intercept in the cointegration vectors is cancelled by the intercept in the short-run model, leaving only an intercept in the short-run model (i.e., in estimating (5.6), μ_1 combines with μ_2 to provide an overall intercept contained in the short-run model). The critical values for this Model 3 are in Table 6c in Pesaran et al. (2000).
- If there are no quadratic trends in the levels of the data, then there will be no time trend in the short-run model, but if there is some long-run linear growth that the model cannot account for, given the chosen data set, then we allow for a linear trend in the cointegration vectors. Thus, the only restriction imposed is $\delta_2 = 0$ and the cointegration space includes time as a

[34] Note that critical values for this Model 1 are available in Pesaran et al. (2000, table 6(a)). For the model specified here with no exogenous $I(1)$ variables—see next section—the appropriate values are those when $k = 0$.

[35] Reproduced in the Statistic Appendix at the end of this book as Table A.10.

[36] As stated in the text, Model 1 coincides with $\delta_1 = \delta_2 = \mu_1 = \mu_2 = 0$.

trend-stationary variable, to take account of unknown exogenous growth (e.g., technical progress).[37,38] For Model 4, the critical values are available in table 6d in Pesaran et al. (2000).

Another model (Model 5) that could be considered is to extend Model 4 to allow for linear trends in the short-run model, determining $\Delta \mathbf{z}_t$ and thus quadratic trends in $\mathbf{z}_t$. Thus δ_2 is also unrestricted, although this is economically hard to justify (especially since if the variables are entered in logs, this would imply an implausible ever-increasing or decreasing rate of change).

The question of which model (2–4) should be used is not easily answered a priori;[39] the vector $\mathbf{z}_t$ could be plotted in levels (and first differences) and examined for trends so that variables like interest rates, which show no indication to drift upward or downward over time, might require the intercept to be restricted to lie in the cointegration space. However, plots of the data would provide little information on whether Model 4 should be used, since this choice arises when the available data cannot account for other unmeasured factors that induce autonomous growth in (some or all of the variables) in $\mathbf{z}_t$. Thus, Johansen (1992b) suggests the need to test the joint hypothesis of both the rank order and the deterministic components, based on the so-called Pantula principle. That is, all three models are estimated and the results are presented from the most restrictive alternative (i.e., $r = 0$ and Model 2) through to the least restrictive alternative (i.e., $r = n - 1$ and Model 4). The test procedure is then to move through from the least restrictive model and at each stage to compare the trace test statistic to its critical value and only stop the first time the null hypothesis is not rejected.[40]

As an example, consider the UK real money demand model, with seasonally unadjusted data ($k = 4$ and seasonal dummies are included in $\mathbf{D}_t$). The results from estimating Models 2–4 and then applying the Pantula principle are given in Table 5.5. Starting with the most restrictive model, the rank test

[37] Note that one of the other variables in $\mathbf{z}_t$ may also be trend-stationary and form a cointegration relationship with time, so adding the trend to the cointegration space is necessary.

[38] Note, in this form of the deterministic model, that the constant in the cointegration space again cancels out with the intercept in the short-run model.

[39] The question of which model to use when testing for the rank of Π is important in practice. Gonzalo and Lee (1998) show that when variables are trending (but this is not taken into account in the deterministic component of the model), this will often lead to spurious rejection of no cointegration (or low cointegration rank) using the Johansen procedure. Similarly, variables that are $I(0)$, but are wrongly included as $I(1)$, can also lead to poor size of the trace test. Thus, the authors advocate using the EG single equation test as a check, since it does not seem to suffer from poor size in such instances.

[40] An alternative approach (used commonly) is to estimate Model 4 and then test down to see if the null hypothesis (that the trend should be excluded) is valid. It is not clear which approach is to be preferred, although the Pantula Principle is a joint test of deterministic components and the rank order.

Table 5.5 Determining cointegration rank and the model for the deterministic components using the trace test: UK real demand-for-money data (1963q1–1989q2).

H_0:	r	$n-r$	Model 2		Model 3		Model 4
	0	4	123.77	→	90.99		111.31
	1	3	48.77		16.26*		35.83
	2	2	10.77		6.34		13.27
	3	1	3.49		0.42	→	3.36

statistic of 123.77 exceeds its 95% critical value of 53.48. Then proceed to the next most restrictive model (keeping to the same value of r), as shown by the arrow in the table, which again exceeds its critical value in Pesaran et al (2000, table 6c). Moving through the table row by row from left to right, the first time the null is not rejected is indicated by the *. Thus, we would accept that there is one cointegration vector and there are deterministic trends in the levels of the data (Model 3). Looking at Figure 3.1, this choice of Model 3 may not be obvious, given that real money supply, real total domestic expenditure and the inflation and interest rates are not strongly trending for most of the period covered.

Having now considered the full set of $I(0)$ variables to enter $\mathbf{D}_t$ (i.e., dummies as well as constant and trend components), we can proceed to testing restrictions on the $\boldsymbol{\alpha}$ and $\boldsymbol{\beta}$. First, we test for weak exogeneity and then for linear hypotheses on the cointegration relations. This leads to tests for unique cointegration vectors and finally joint tests involving restrictions on $\boldsymbol{\alpha}$ and $\boldsymbol{\beta}$.

TESTING FOR WEAK EXOGENEITY AND VECM WITH EXOGENOUS $I(1)$ VARIABLES

In the VECM (5.2), it has been shown that the Π matrix contains information on long-run relationships, where $\Pi = \boldsymbol{\alpha\beta}'$, $\boldsymbol{\alpha}$ represents the speed of adjustment to disequilibrium and $\boldsymbol{\beta}$ is a matrix of long-run coefficients. Furthermore, it was explained that if there are $r \leq (n-1)$ cointegration vectors in $\boldsymbol{\beta}$, then this implies that the last $(n-r)$ columns of $\boldsymbol{\alpha}$ are zero.[41] Thus the typical problem faced, of determining how many $r \leq (n-1)$ cointegration vectors exist in $\boldsymbol{\beta}$, amounts to equivalently testing which columns of $\boldsymbol{\alpha}$ are zero.

Turning to the role of the non-zero columns of $\boldsymbol{\alpha}$, suppose that $r = 1$ and $\mathbf{z}_t = [y_{1t}, y_{2t}, x_t]'$: then $\boldsymbol{\alpha} = [\alpha_{11}, \alpha_{21}, \alpha_{31}]'$.[42] The first term in $\boldsymbol{\alpha}$ represents the

[41] Recall that each of the r cointegration vectors in $\boldsymbol{\beta}$ is associated with a particular column in $\boldsymbol{\alpha}$ that must contain at least one non-zero element. See (4.19) for a simple example.

[42] As shown in the last chapter, when discussing the problems of using a single equation approach to cointegration.

speed at which Δy_{1t}, the dependent variable in the first equation of the VECM, adjusts toward the single long-run cointegration relationship $(\beta_{11}y_{1t-1} + \beta_{21}y_{2t-1} + \beta_{31}x_{t-1})$, α_{21} represents the speed at which Δy_{2t} adjusts and α_{31} shows how fast Δx_t responds to the disequilibrium changes represented by the cointegration vector.[43] More generally, each of the r non-zero columns of $\boldsymbol{\alpha}$ contains information on which cointegration vector enters which short-run equation and on the speed of the short-run response to disequilibrium.

Taking things a step further, the presence of *all* zeros in row i of α_{ij}, $j = 1, \ldots, r$, indicates that the cointegration vectors in $\boldsymbol{\beta}$ do not enter the equation determining Δz_{it}. As is shown in Box 5.4, this means that when estimating the parameters of the model (i.e., the Γ_i, Π, $\boldsymbol{\alpha}$, $\boldsymbol{\beta}$) there is no loss of information from *not* modelling the determinants of Δz_{it}; thus, this variable is weakly exogenous *to the system* and can enter on the right-hand side of the VECM. For example, suppose $\mathbf{z}_t = [y_{1t}, y_{2t}, x_t]'$ and $r = 2$ (and for ease of exposition let $k = 2$); then repeating (4.19) by writing out the VECM in full gives:

$$\begin{bmatrix} \Delta y_{1t} \\ \Delta y_{2t} \\ \Delta x_t \end{bmatrix} = \Gamma_1 \begin{bmatrix} \Delta y_{1t-1} \\ \Delta y_{2t-1} \\ \Delta x_{t-1} \end{bmatrix} + \begin{bmatrix} \alpha_{11} & \alpha_{12} \\ \alpha_{21} & \alpha_{22} \\ \alpha_{31} & \alpha_{32} \end{bmatrix} \begin{bmatrix} \beta_{11} & \beta_{21} & \beta_{31} \\ \beta_{12} & \beta_{22} & \beta_{32} \end{bmatrix} \begin{bmatrix} y_{1t-1} \\ y_{2t-1} \\ x_{t-1} \end{bmatrix} \tag{5.7}$$

If $\alpha_{3j} = 0$, $j = 1, 2$, then the equation for Δx_t contains no information about the long-run $\boldsymbol{\beta}$, since the cointegration relationships do not enter into this equation. It is therefore valid to condition on the weakly exogenous variable x_t and proceed with the following partial (conditional model) version of the VECM:

$$\Delta \mathbf{y}_t = \Gamma_0 \Delta x_t + \tilde{\boldsymbol{\Gamma}}_1 \Delta \mathbf{z}_{t-1} + \boldsymbol{\alpha}_1 \boldsymbol{\beta}' \mathbf{z}_{t-2} + \hat{\mathbf{u}}_t \tag{5.8}$$

where $\mathbf{y}_t = [y_{1t}, y_{2t}]'$ and $\boldsymbol{\alpha}_1$ is equal to $\boldsymbol{\alpha}$ with $\alpha_{31} = \alpha_{32} = 0$. Note that the weakly exogenous variable x_t remains in the long-run model (i.e., the cointegration vectors), although its short-run behaviour is not modelled because of its exclusion from the vector on the left-hand side of the equation.[44]

[43] See the discussion in Chapter 2 on short-run models for more information on the role of the speed-of-adjustment parameter.

[44] Note that if x_t is both weakly exogenous and insignificant in the long-run cointegration space (the latter can be tested when imposing restrictions on the $\boldsymbol{\beta}$), then we can condition on x_t by confining it to lie within the short-run model. Then (5.8) can be reformulated as:

$$\Delta \mathbf{y}_t = \Gamma_0 \Delta x_t + \Gamma_1 \Delta \mathbf{z}_{t-1} + \boldsymbol{\alpha\beta}' \mathbf{y}_{t-2} + \mathbf{u}_t$$

where x_{t-2} has been removed from the vector determining the long-run relations.

Box 5.4 Conditional and marginal models.

If the vector $\mathbf{z}_t = [y_{1t}, y_{2t}, x_t]'$ is decomposed into $\mathbf{y}_t = [y_{1t}, y_{2t}]'$ and x_t, Johansen (1992d) shows that (5.3), ignoring $\mathbf{D}_t$, can be decomposed into the conditional model for $\mathbf{y}_t$ given x_t:

$$\Delta\mathbf{y}_t = \boldsymbol{\omega}\Delta x_t + (\boldsymbol{\Gamma}_{y1} - \boldsymbol{\omega}\boldsymbol{\Gamma}_{x1})\Delta\mathbf{z}_{t-1} + (\boldsymbol{\alpha}_y - \boldsymbol{\omega}\boldsymbol{\alpha}_x)\boldsymbol{\beta}'\mathbf{z}_{t-2} + \mathbf{u}_{yt} - \boldsymbol{\omega}\mathbf{u}_{xt} \quad (5.4.1)$$

and the marginal model for x_t:

$$\Delta x_t = \boldsymbol{\Gamma}_{x1}\Delta\mathbf{z}_{t-1} + \boldsymbol{\alpha}_x\boldsymbol{\beta}'\mathbf{z}_{t-2} + \mathbf{u}_{xt} \quad (5.4.2)$$

where $\boldsymbol{\omega} = \Omega_{yx}\Omega_{yx}^{-1}$. Note that estimating this model *as a system* is equivalent to estimating the full model, as can be seen by simply substituting (5.4.2) into (5.4.1). Also, all the cointegration relations $\boldsymbol{\beta}'\mathbf{z}_t$ enter into the marginal as well as conditional models.

If $\alpha_x = 0$ (i.e., the rows of $\boldsymbol{\alpha}$ corresponding to x_t are zero: $\alpha_{3j} = 0$ for $j = 1, 2$), then (5.4.1) and (5.4.2) reduce to:

$$\Delta\mathbf{y}_t = \boldsymbol{\omega}\Delta x_t + (\boldsymbol{\Gamma}_{y1} - \boldsymbol{\omega}\boldsymbol{\Gamma}_{x1})\Delta\mathbf{z}_{t-1} + \boldsymbol{\alpha}_y\boldsymbol{\beta}'\mathbf{z}_{t-2} + \mathbf{u}_{yt} - \boldsymbol{\omega}\mathbf{u}_{xt} \quad (5.4.3)$$

and

$$\Delta x_t = \boldsymbol{\Gamma}_{x1}\Delta\mathbf{z}_{t-1} + \mathbf{u}_{xt} \quad (5.4.4)$$

When this holds, x_t is said to be weakly exogenous with respect to $\boldsymbol{\beta}$, since by the definition of weak exogeneity due to Engle, Hendry and Richard (1983), two necessary conditions are fulfilled. First, the parameters of interest (here $\boldsymbol{\beta}$) are functions only of the parameters in the conditional model, because $\boldsymbol{\beta}$ now only enters (5.4.3). Second, the parameters in the conditional and marginal models must be variation-free in that they do not have joint restrictions, and this is guaranteed by the properties of the Gaussian distribution.

Lastly, note that (5.4.4) shows that both Δy_{t-1} and Δx_{t-1} determine Δx_t, since $\Delta\mathbf{z}_{t-1}$ features on the right-hand side of the equation. Thus, x_t is only weakly exogenous with respect to $\boldsymbol{\beta}$. However, if x_t is not Granger-caused by $\mathbf{y}_t$, then x_t is strongly exogenous with respect to $\boldsymbol{\beta}$. This is true if the coefficients of $\Delta\mathbf{y}_{t-1}$ are zero such that we can replace $\Delta\mathbf{z}_{t-1}$ with Δx_{t-1} in (5.4.4).

There are at least two potential advantages from estimating the multivariate model having conditioned on the weakly exogenous variables. In particular, if the weakly exogenous variables exhibit all the 'problematic' data features (see the earlier section on determining the elements in $\mathbf{D}_t$), then conditioning on these variables will usually ensure that the rest of the system determining $\Delta \mathbf{y}_t$ has better stochastic properties (in terms of the residuals of the short-run equations being free of problems). This is linked to the second advantage, which becomes apparent when the short-run model is also of interest, since the number of short-run variables in the VECM will be reduced. However, it is not usually prudent to start with the modelling of a conditional system unless weak exogeneity is assured (e.g., by economic theory), although when estimating even small econometric models the number of variables involved (and the typical short time series available) may mean that estimating the conditional model is a more viable option (cf. Greenslade, Hall and Henry, 2002; Pesaran et al., 2000). The estimates of $\boldsymbol{\alpha}$ and $\boldsymbol{\beta}$ are the same as when estimating the full model with weak exogeneity restrictions on $\boldsymbol{\alpha}$, but the asymptotic distributions of the rank test statistics are different; thus Pesaran et al. (2000) have computed appropriate rank test statistics allowing for exogenous $I(1)$ regressors in the long-run model. More importantly, though, we will usually want to test for weak exogeneity in the full model rather than to assume it. Thus, conditional models are usually estimated after determining the restrictions to be placed on $\boldsymbol{\alpha}$ (and $\boldsymbol{\beta}$), and then the appropriate critical values for testing for cointegration are those available in Pesaran et al. (2000, table 6), reproduced as Tables A.10–A.12 in the Statistical Appendix at the end of this book.

So far, weak exogeneity has been discussed in terms of $\mathbf{x}_t$ being weakly exogenous in every cointegration vector. This is the usual way in which exogeneity and endogeneity are established, with variables classified on the basis of their role in all the equations in the system. However, it is possible to consider whether $\mathbf{x}_t$ is weakly exogenous with respect to the parameters of a particular cointegration vector. Thus, for instance, there may be two cointegration vectors and tests for weak exogeneity may involve hypotheses that some vector $\mathbf{x}_{1t}$ is weakly exogenous with respect to the parameters of the first cointegration vector, while a second vector $\mathbf{x}_{2t}$ (which may or may not be the same as $\mathbf{x}_{1t}$) is weakly exogenous with respect to the parameters of the second cointegration vector. Indeed, it is possible to test each $\alpha_{ij}\,(i = 1, \ldots, n;$ $j = 1, \ldots, r)$ separately and to talk about the corresponding variable x_{it} being weakly exogenous with respect to cointegration vector j. This is valid, as long as weak exogeneity is clearly defined with respect to a single cointegration vector (and not to the full model, which may comprise more than one long-run relationship among the variables in the model), since accepting the hypothesis that some $\alpha_{ij} = 0$ really amounts to finding that the particular cointegration vector j does not enter into the short-run equation determining the associated variable Δx_{it}.[45]

It is also important to stress that testing for weak exogeneity in a particular cointegration vector presumes that this vector represents a structural long-run

[45] The next chapter will illustrate the role of testing individual α_{ij} and show up the potential confusion that arises from labelling these as tests of 'weak exogeneity'.

relationship between the variables in the model and not a linear combination,[46] in which case $\boldsymbol{\alpha}$ will also be a linear combination of the speed-of-adjustment coefficients, and testing for weak exogeneity in this context is not particularly meaningful. This suggests that in practice testing for restrictions involving $\boldsymbol{\alpha}$ should almost always be done alongside testing for restrictions that identify $\boldsymbol{\beta}$. We shall return to this on p. 155.

It is usually not valid to condition the VECM on x_{it} unless this variable is weakly exogenous in the full system, although there are exceptions to this rule. For instance, suppose $n = 4$ and that one of the cointegration vectors, say the first one, has associated with it the following: $\boldsymbol{\alpha}_1' = [*, 0, 0, 0]$, where the * denotes an unrestricted parameter. Then all the variables in the cointegration vector (except the first, y_{1t}) are weakly exogenous with respect to $\boldsymbol{\beta}_1$, and if we are only interested in this first cointegration relationship, then it is valid to abandon the multivariate model and move to a single equation approach and condition on the weakly exogenous variables (i.e., they move to the right-hand side of the equation and are contemporaneous with the dependent variable).[47] If the other cointegration vectors do not enter the short-run model determining Δy_{1t} (which will be true when $\alpha_{i,j}' = [0, *, *, *]$ for $j \neq 1$), then y_{1t} can be said to be weakly exogenous in these other cointegration vectors, and it is appropriate to concentrate on the first vector of interest only. However, if other cointegration vectors *do* enter the model determining Δy_{1t}, we might not want to move to the single equation approach if modelling the system might be appropriate (see the discussion of structural VAR-modelling in the next chapter).

To test for weak exogeneity in the system as a whole requires a test of the hypothesis that H: $\alpha_{ij} = 0$ for $j = 1, \ldots, r$ (i.e., row i contains zeros). This test is conducted in *PcGive 10.1* by placing row restrictions on $\boldsymbol{\alpha}$ to give a new restricted model and then using a likelihood ratio test involving the restricted and unrestricted models to ascertain whether the restrictions are valid (see the discussion on p. 122 of testing for reduced rank for details). The form of the restrictions is straightforward using the 'general restrictors' editor[48] that allows the relevant rows of $\boldsymbol{\alpha}$ to be set to zero (see the Appendix to the book for details on how this is done in *PcGive 10.1*). Imposing row restrictions results in $(n - 1)$

[46] Recall that the reduced rank regression procedure provides information on how many unique cointegration vectors *span* the cointegration space, while any linear combination of the stationary vectors is itself a stationary vector and thus the estimates produced for any particular column in $\boldsymbol{\beta}$ are not necessarily unique.

[47] See the discussion in the last chapter about the appropriateness of the single equation model.

[48] This imposition of 'general restrictions' requires the use of a testing procedure such as H: $\{\boldsymbol{\alpha} = f(\boldsymbol{\alpha}^u)\}$ where $\boldsymbol{\alpha}$ is expressed as a function of the unrestricted elements in $\boldsymbol{\alpha}$. This function may even be non-linear. The software package *PcGive 10.1* makes use of a switching algorithm that can solve this kind of problem using a numerical optimization procedure (see Doornik and Hendry, 2001, for further details).

new eigenvalues λ_i^* for the restricted model, which are used in the LR test statistic comprising:[49]

$$-2\log(Q) = T\sum_{i=1}^{r}\log\left\{\frac{(1-\hat{\lambda}_i^*)}{(1-\hat{\lambda}_i)}\right\} \tag{5.9}$$

This test statistic is compared with the χ^2 distribution with $(r \times (n-m))$ degrees of freedom[50] in order to obtain the significance level for rejecting the null hypothesis. As with the testing procedure for reduced rank, it has been suggested that the above LR statistic should be corrected for degrees of freedom, which involves replacing T, the sample size, by $T - (l/n)$, where l is the number of parameters estimated in the reduced rank regression model.[51] Psaradakis (1994) found, on the basis of Monte Carlo testing, that such a modification improved the small-sample behaviour of LR statistics.

The first example of testing for weak exogeneity to be considered is the UK money demand model, with seasonally unadjusted data ($k = 4$ and seasonal dummies are included in $\mathbf{D}_t$). It has already been established (Table 5.5) that it is possible to accept that there is one cointegration vector (and deterministic trends in the levels of the data). The estimates of $\boldsymbol{\alpha}$ and $\boldsymbol{\beta}$ obtained from applying the Johansen technique are presented in Box 5.5; note that only the normalized $\boldsymbol{\beta}$ (and consequently $\boldsymbol{\alpha}$) corresponding to $r = 1$ is presented.[52] We test the null hypothesis that y_t, Δp_t and R_t are weakly exogenous, and thus there are three row restrictions imposed on $\boldsymbol{\alpha}$:[53]

$$\boldsymbol{\alpha}' = [* \quad 0 \quad 0 \quad 0] \tag{5.10}$$

[49] An alternative approach is to set the restrictions by specifying an $(n \times m)$ matrix $\mathbf{A}$ of linear restrictions, where $(n - m)$ equals the number of row restrictions imposed on $\boldsymbol{\alpha}$, such that the null hypothesis amounts to testing whether $\boldsymbol{\alpha} = \mathbf{A}\alpha_0$. Inposing the restrictions reduces $\boldsymbol{\alpha}$ to an $(m \times n)$ matrix $\boldsymbol{\alpha}_0$. It is also useful to note that these same restrictions in $\mathbf{A}$ could be imposed by specifying an $(n \times (n-m))$ matrix $\mathbf{B}$ such that $\mathbf{B}'\boldsymbol{\alpha} = 0$. Clearly, $\mathbf{B}$ must be orthogonal to $\mathbf{A}$ (i.e., $\mathbf{B}'\mathbf{A} = \mathbf{A}'_{\perp}\mathbf{A} = 0$). Both the matrices $\mathbf{A}$ and $\mathbf{B}$ are used in the mechanics of restricting the Johansen reduced rank regression model, thereby obtaining $(n - 1)$ new eigenvalues λ_i^* for the restricted model, which are used in the LR test statistic comprising equation (5.9) below. Although both are used to solve the reduced rank regression, the user will only have to specify either $\mathbf{A}$ or $\mathbf{B}$ (e.g., *PcGive 10.1* has an option to use $\mathbf{A}$, while other programmes use $\mathbf{B}$). As already stated, in *PcGive* it is much easier to impose restrictions on the $\boldsymbol{\alpha}$ directly using the 'general restrictors' editor, rather than specifying $\mathbf{A}$ (although the latter is still available as an option).

[50] Note that $(n - m)$ equals the number of row restrictions imposed on $\boldsymbol{\alpha}$.

[51] That is, $l = ((k \times n) + \text{Number of deterministic components}) \times n$.

[52] Since $r = 1$ and normalizing on the variable $m - p$, standard errors (and hence t-statistics) are available for $\boldsymbol{\beta}'$.

[53] For readers wishing to specify the alternative procedure involving the setting of the matrices $\mathbf{A}$ and $\mathbf{B}$, see Harris (1995, eqn (5.10)).

Box 5.5 *Output from* PcGive 10.1 *for the UK money demand model.*

```
Eigenv.   Trace     H0: r=   vn-r=
0.5228    90.99**      0       4
0.0936    16.26        1       3
0.0569     6.34        2       2
0.0041     0.42        3       1
** rejects at <1% significance level (critical values from Doornik,
1999))

Normalised (Based on 1 cointegration vector; t-values in parenthesis)

    β'
    m - p       y         Δp         R
   -1.000     1.073     -7.325     -6.808
             (14.98)    (-6.57)   (-16.72)

    α'
    0.167     0.007     -0.016     -0.007
   (8.53)    (0.36)    (-1.74)    (-0.43)

Testing Restrictions on α

The LR test, χ²(3) = 3.76, p-value = 0.29

    β'
    m - p       y         Δp         R
   -1.000     1.097     -7.780     -6.835
             (14.61)    (-6.65)   (-16.01)

    α'
    0.148     0.000      0.000      0.000
   (9.42)    (0.00)     (0.00)     (0.00)
```

The largest new eigenvalue $\hat{\lambda}_1^*$ for the restricted model along with $\hat{\lambda}_1$ from the unrestricted model are used to compute:

$$-2\log(Q) = 101\log\left\{\frac{(1-0.5047)}{(1-0.5228)}\right\} = 3.76 \tag{5.11}$$

which does not exceed $\chi^2(3) = 7.81$. If the LR statistic is corrected for degrees of freedom, which involves replacing T by $T - (l/n)$ in (5.9), then LR = 3.02, which again does not reject the null.

Separate tests on each of the adjustment parameters could also be conducted; for instance, testing H: $\boldsymbol{\alpha}_{41} = 0$ requires:

$$\boldsymbol{\alpha}' = [0 \quad * \quad * \quad *] \tag{5.12}$$

since there is only one restriction imposed on $\boldsymbol{\alpha}$. However, it is not necessary to conduct these individual tests, which are distributed under the χ^2 distribution with 1 degree of freedom, since t-values associated with each $\boldsymbol{\alpha}_{ij}$ are automatically reported (see Box 5.5). Initially, before testing any restrictions on $\boldsymbol{\alpha}$, the t-values would have suggested that weak exogeneity for y, Δp and R was likely to hold. Since it does, this confirms that it is valid to condition on these variables and use a single equation estimator of the cointegration vector. Comparison of the Johansen multivariate estimator of $\boldsymbol{\beta}'_{\text{full}} = [-1.0, 1.073, -7.325, -6.808]$ with the estimate in (4.16) of $\boldsymbol{\beta}'_{\text{part}} = [-1.0, 1.052, -7.332, -6.871]$ shows that the two approaches are equivalent.

As a second example of testing for weak exogeneity, consider the PPP and UIP model of Johansen and Juselius (1992), where $n = 5$ and $r = 2$. Looking at the results in Box 5.2, the t-values on the α_{ij} when $r = 2$ (i.e., the first two columns of $\boldsymbol{\alpha}$) suggest that either or both of the following hypotheses might be valid: H: α_{2j} for $j = 1, 2$ and H: $\alpha_{3j} = 0$ for $j = 1, 2$. The first test involves:

$$\boldsymbol{\alpha}' = \begin{bmatrix} * & 0 & * & * & * \\ * & 0 & * & * & * \end{bmatrix} \tag{5.13}$$

The largest new eigenvalues for the restricted model along with $\hat{\lambda}_i$ from the unrestricted model are used to compute the LR test, which equals 1.336, which does not exceed $\chi^2(2)$.[54] If the LR statistic is corrected for degrees of freedom, which involves replacing T by $T - (l/n)$, then LR $= 1.305$, which again does not reject the null. The second test is very similar and simply requires swapping around columns 2 and 3 in (5.13). The joint test that H: $\alpha_{2j} = \alpha_{3j} = 0$ for $j = 1$, 2 imposes two row restrictions on $\boldsymbol{\alpha}$:

$$\boldsymbol{\alpha}' = \begin{bmatrix} * & 0 & 0 & * & * \\ * & 0 & 0 & * & * \end{bmatrix} \tag{5.14}$$

and results in the two new eigenvalues for this version of the restricted model along with $\hat{\lambda}_i$ from the unrestricted model giving a value for the LR statistic of 4.683, which does not exceed $\chi^2(4)$. Thus, on the basis of these tests, both p_2 (trade-weighted foreign wholesale price index) and e (the UK effective exchange rate) are weakly exogenous.

Finally, if we wish to test restrictions on each α_{ij} ($i = 1, \ldots, n; j = 1, \ldots, r$) separately, when $r > 1$ or when only a subset of $\boldsymbol{\alpha}$ do not involve the restriction that row i contains all zeros, then the 'general restrictions' approach in *PcGive* is very flexible and simple to implement.

TESTING FOR LINEAR HYPOTHESES ON COINTEGRATION RELATIONS

Earlier it was stated that having determined how many cointegration vectors there are, it is necessary to consider whether they are unique and consequently whether they tell us anything about the structural economic relationships

[54] Note that the degrees of freedom were calculated using $(r \times (n - m)) = 2$.

underlying the long-run model. Since the Johansen reduced rank regression procedure only determines how many unique cointegration vectors *span* the cointegration space and since any linear combination of the stationary vectors is also a stationary vector, the estimates produced for any particular column in $\boldsymbol{\beta}$ are not necessarily unique. Therefore, it will be necessary to impose restrictions motivated by economic arguments (e.g., that some of the β_{ij} are zero or that homogeneity restrictions are needed such as $\beta_{1j} = -\beta_{2j}$) and then test whether the columns of $\boldsymbol{\beta}$ are identified. Testing for identification will be followed up in the next section.

Hypotheses about $\boldsymbol{\beta}$ can be formulated directly in *PcGive 10.1* using the 'general restrictions' editor. An example from Johansen and Juselius (1994) associated with the following version of $\boldsymbol{\beta}$, of dimension (6×3), involves various homogeneity and zero restrictions:

$$\boldsymbol{\beta} = \begin{bmatrix} a & 0 & 0 \\ * & * & * \\ -a & * & * \\ 1 & 1 & 0 \\ 0 & -1 & 1 \\ * & * & * \end{bmatrix} \tag{5.15}$$

The restrictions placed on the vectors in the first example are as follows: the two restrictions on $\boldsymbol{\beta}_1$ comprise a homogeneity constraint $(\beta_{11} = -\beta_{31})$ and constrain $\beta_{51} = 0$. The cointegration vector is normalized by setting $\beta_{41} = 1$, which is a restriction, but not a constraint. There are also two constraints each placed on $\boldsymbol{\beta}_2$ and $\boldsymbol{\beta}_3$ (plus one normalization), and since all three cointegration vectors have exactly two constraints plus one normalization (thus three restrictions) this results in a just-identified model, as explained in Box 5.6. The major consequence of this is that since there is no change in the log-likelihood function of a just-identified system, no LR test of the restrictions is possible.

All the restrictions on $\boldsymbol{\beta}$ will be tested jointly[55] (i.e., all the restricted cointegration vectors are estimated together comprising one joint test of their validity). The outcome, assuming identification, will be unique cointegration vectors. However, testing joint restrictions involving all of the separate $\boldsymbol{\beta}_i$ spanning the entire cointegration space is sometimes not the best way to start when testing restrictions, unless economic theory is particularly informative on the hypotheses that should be tested. Instead, Johansen and Juselius (1992) suggested more general tests of hypotheses:

1 The same restrictions are placed on all the cointegration vectors spanning $\boldsymbol{\beta}$. Thus, this general hypothesis can be used to test whether a particular structure holds in all the cointegration relations.

[55] Except, as just stated, in the just-identified model.

Box 5.6 Testing for identification of cointegration vectors.

Hypotheses about $\boldsymbol{\beta}$ can be formulated as follows:

$$H_\beta: \boldsymbol{\beta} = (\mathbf{H}_1\boldsymbol{\varphi}_1, \mathbf{H}_2\boldsymbol{\varphi}_2, \ldots, \mathbf{H}_r\boldsymbol{\varphi}_r) \tag{5.6.1}$$

where the matrices $\mathbf{H}_1, \ldots, \mathbf{H}_r$, expressing the linear economic hypotheses to be tested on each of the r cointegration relations, are $(n \times s_i)$ matrices and each $\boldsymbol{\varphi}_i$ is an $(s_i \times 1)$ vector of parameters to be estimated in the ith cointegration relations. Since there are s_i unrestricted parameters in $\boldsymbol{\beta}_i$, then $\mathbf{H}_i$ imposes k_i restrictions such that $(k_i + s_i = n)$. Note that it is possible to impose the same restrictions in $\mathbf{H}_i$ by specifying an $(n \times k_i)$ matrix $\mathbf{R}_i$ such that $\mathbf{R}_i'\boldsymbol{\beta}_i = 0$. Since this is equivalent to $\boldsymbol{\beta}_i = \mathbf{H}_i\varphi_i$, this implies that $\mathbf{R}_i$ is orthogonal to $\mathbf{H}_i$ and consequently $\mathbf{R}_i'\mathbf{H}_i = \mathbf{R}_i'\mathbf{R}_{i\perp} = 0$. In practice both will be needed when testing uniqueness since identification depends upon finding the rank of $(\mathbf{R}_i'\mathbf{H}_j)$ for $i \neq j$.

Identification here is defined in Johansen (1992c) and Johansen and Juselius (1994) with respect to the linear restrictions specified in $\mathbf{R}_i$ and $\mathbf{H}_i$ (see equation (5.6.1)). The first vector in the cointegration space is identified if:

$$\text{rank}(\mathbf{R}_1'\boldsymbol{\beta}_1, \mathbf{R}_1'\boldsymbol{\beta}_2, \ldots, \mathbf{R}_1'\boldsymbol{\beta}_r) = \text{rank}(\mathbf{R}_1'\mathbf{H}_1\boldsymbol{\varphi}_1, \mathbf{R}_1'\mathbf{H}_2\boldsymbol{\varphi}_2, \ldots, \mathbf{R}_1'\mathbf{H}_r\boldsymbol{\varphi}_r) = r - 1 \tag{5.6.2}$$

Johansen (1992c) generalizes (5.6.2) to provide a definition for a set of restrictions that identify the unique vectors. Specifically, his theorem 3 states that the restrictions $\mathbf{R}_1, \ldots, \mathbf{R}_r$ are identifying if (and only if), for $k = 1, \ldots, r - 1$ and for any set of indices $1 \leq i_1 < \cdots < i_k \leq r$ not containing i, it holds that

$$\text{rank}(\mathbf{R}_i'\mathbf{H}_{i_1}, \ldots, \mathbf{R}_i'\mathbf{H}_{i_k}) \geq k \tag{5.6.3}$$

If (5.6.3) is satisfied for a particular value of i, then the restrictions $\mathbf{R}_i$ identify vector i.

Two Cointegration Vectors

Where $r = 2$, so that hypotheses about $\boldsymbol{\beta}$ can be formulated as H_β: $\boldsymbol{\beta} = (\mathbf{H}_1\boldsymbol{\varphi}_1, \mathbf{H}_2\boldsymbol{\varphi}_2)$, then (5.6.3) is satisfied and $\mathbf{R}_1$ and $\mathbf{R}_2$ identify the vectors in $\boldsymbol{\beta}$ if:

$$\text{rank}(\mathbf{R}_1'\mathbf{H}_2) \geq 1 \quad \text{and} \quad \text{rank}(\mathbf{R}_2'\mathbf{H}_1) \geq 1 \tag{5.6.4}$$

As an illustration, we shall consider restrictions on the PPP and UIP models (results using *PcGive 10.1* are reported in the main text, and here we shall formally show how to test for identification). Box Table 5.6.1 provides various restricted forms for $\boldsymbol{\beta}$ that were set out in the main text (and originally suggested by Johansen and Juselius, 1992).

Box Table 5.6.1 Specifying restrictions on $\boldsymbol{\beta}$ (when $r = 2$).

$\boldsymbol{\beta}^1 = (\mathbf{H}_1\boldsymbol{\varphi}_1, \mathbf{H}_2\boldsymbol{\varphi}_2)$

$$\boldsymbol{\beta}^1 = \begin{bmatrix} 1 & 0 \\ -1 & 0 \\ -1 & 0 \\ * & 1 \\ * & -1 \end{bmatrix} \quad \mathbf{R}_1 = \begin{bmatrix} 1 & 1 \\ 1 & 0 \\ 0 & 1 \\ 0 & 0 \\ 0 & 0 \end{bmatrix} \quad \mathbf{H}_1 = \begin{bmatrix} 1 & 0 & 0 \\ -1 & 0 & 0 \\ -1 & 0 & 0 \\ 0 & 1 & 0 \\ 0 & 0 & 1 \end{bmatrix} \quad \mathbf{R}_2 = \begin{bmatrix} 1 & 0 & 0 & 0 \\ 0 & 1 & 0 & 0 \\ 0 & 0 & 1 & 0 \\ 0 & 0 & 0 & 1 \\ 0 & 0 & 0 & 1 \end{bmatrix} \quad \mathbf{H}_2 = \begin{bmatrix} 0 \\ 0 \\ 0 \\ 1 \\ -1 \end{bmatrix}$$

$\boldsymbol{\beta}^2 = (\mathbf{H}_1\boldsymbol{\varphi}_1, \mathbf{H}_2\boldsymbol{\varphi}_2)$

$$\boldsymbol{\beta}^2 = \begin{bmatrix} 1 & 0 \\ -1 & 0 \\ -1 & 0 \\ 0 & 1 \\ 0 & -1 \end{bmatrix} \quad \mathbf{R}_1 = \begin{bmatrix} 1 & 1 & 0 & 0 \\ 1 & 0 & 0 & 0 \\ 0 & 1 & 0 & 0 \\ 0 & 0 & 1 & 0 \\ 0 & 0 & 0 & 1 \end{bmatrix} \quad \mathbf{H}_1 = \begin{bmatrix} 1 \\ -1 \\ -1 \\ 0 \\ 0 \end{bmatrix} \quad \mathbf{R}_2 = \begin{bmatrix} 1 & 0 & 0 & 0 \\ 0 & 1 & 0 & 0 \\ 0 & 0 & 1 & 0 \\ 0 & 0 & 0 & 1 \\ 0 & 0 & 0 & 1 \end{bmatrix} \quad \mathbf{H}_2 = \begin{bmatrix} 0 \\ 0 \\ 0 \\ 1 \\ -1 \end{bmatrix}$$

$\boldsymbol{\beta}^3 = (\mathbf{H}_1\boldsymbol{\varphi}_1, \mathbf{H}_2\boldsymbol{\varphi}_2)$

$$\boldsymbol{\beta}^3 = \begin{bmatrix} 1 & 0 \\ -1 & 0 \\ -1 & 0 \\ * & 1 \\ 0 & -1 \end{bmatrix} \quad \mathbf{R}_1 = \begin{bmatrix} 1 & 1 & 0 \\ 1 & 0 & 0 \\ 0 & 1 & 0 \\ 0 & 0 & 0 \\ 0 & 0 & 1 \end{bmatrix} \quad \mathbf{H}_1 = \begin{bmatrix} 1 & 0 \\ -1 & 0 \\ -1 & 0 \\ 0 & 1 \\ 0 & 0 \end{bmatrix} \quad \mathbf{R}_2 = \begin{bmatrix} 1 & 0 & 0 & 0 \\ 0 & 1 & 0 & 0 \\ 0 & 0 & 1 & 0 \\ 0 & 0 & 0 & 1 \\ 0 & 0 & 0 & 1 \end{bmatrix} \quad \mathbf{H}_2 = \begin{bmatrix} 0 \\ 0 \\ 0 \\ 1 \\ -1 \end{bmatrix}$$

The restrictions placed on the vectors in the first example (relating to $\boldsymbol{\beta}^1$) are as follows: the two restrictions on the first column vector comprise homogeneity constraints ($\beta_{11} = -\beta_{21}$ and $\beta_{11} = -\beta_{31}$). The cointegration vector is normalized by setting $\beta_{11} = 1$, which is a restriction, but not a constraint. Since ($k_i + s_i = 2 = 3 = 5$), this results in the following dimensions: $\mathbf{R}_1(5 \times 2)$ and $\mathbf{H}_1(5 \times 3)$.[56] $\mathbf{H}_1$ expresses the linear economic hypothesis to be tested on the first column vector in $\boldsymbol{\beta}^1$; its first column imposing the homogeneity constraints, while columns 2 to 3 in turn locate the unrestricted elements of the cointegration vector (i.e., β_{41} and β_{51}). In contrast, each column of $\mathbf{R}_1$ imposes a homogeneity constraint. Determining the elements of $\mathbf{R}_2$ and its counterpart $\mathbf{H}_2$ proceeds in a similar fashion. Since ($k_i + s_i = 4 + 1 = 5$), this results in the following dimensions: $\mathbf{R}_2(5 \times 4)$ and $\mathbf{H}_2(5 \times 1)$. $\mathbf{H}_2$ imposes the homogeneity constraint ($\beta_{42} = -\beta_{52}$), and since there are no other columns other parameters are set to zero; the first three columns of $\mathbf{R}_2$ impose the constraint that the elements picked out are zero, while the last column imposes a homogeneity constraint. Formulating the restricions on the vectors in $\boldsymbol{\beta}^2$ and $\boldsymbol{\beta}^3$ is equally straightforward: in practice, it is useful to start by writing out the restricted $\boldsymbol{\beta}$ as in Box Table 5.6.1 and then determine the dimensions of k_i and s_i.

[56] Recall that $\mathbf{R}_i(n \times k_i)$ and $\mathbf{H}_i(n \times s_i)$, where k_i represents the number of restricted parameters and s_i the number of unrestricted parameters, such that $(k_i + s_i = n)$.

Box Table 5.6.2 Rank conditions (Equation (5.6.3)) for identifying cointegration vectors (when $r = 2$).

Vector	$\text{rank}(\mathbf{R}_1'\mathbf{H}_2)$	$\text{rank}(\mathbf{R}_2'\mathbf{H}_1)$
$\boldsymbol{\beta}^1$	0	2
$\boldsymbol{\beta}^2$	1	1
$\boldsymbol{\beta}^3$	1	2

Applying (5.6.4) to the restrictions as set out in Box Table 5.6.1, we obtain the rank of the various matrices as set out in Box Table 5.6.2. All the cointegration vectors are identified except the first vector in $\boldsymbol{\beta}^1$, where $\text{rank}(\mathbf{R}_1'\mathbf{H}_2) < 1$. This occurs because it is possible to take a linear combination of $\mathbf{H}_1$ and $\mathbf{H}_2$ that would remove either β_{41} or β_{51} from $\boldsymbol{\beta}^1$ and yet *jointly* the restricted vectors are a valid representation of the two cointegration vectors in $\boldsymbol{\beta}^1$. In effect, as Johansen and Juselius (1994) point out: "... the space spanned by $\mathbf{H}_2$ is contained in the space spanned by $\mathbf{H}_1$ ... and within this set-up we can only estimate uniquely the impact of a linear combination of (β_{41} or β_{51}) in the first relation." An example of how this might happen in practice is given in the main text.

Three Cointegration Vectors

When $r = 3$, things are more complicated because there are more linear combinations of the $\mathbf{R}_i'\mathbf{H}_i$ to be considered. Hypotheses about $\boldsymbol{\beta}$ can be formulated as H_β: $\boldsymbol{\beta} = (\mathbf{H}_1\boldsymbol{\varphi}_1, \mathbf{H}_2\boldsymbol{\varphi}_2, \mathbf{H}_3\boldsymbol{\varphi}_3)$, and $\mathbf{R}_1$, $\mathbf{H}_2$ and $\mathbf{H}_3$ identify the *first* vector in $\boldsymbol{\beta}$ if:

$$\text{rank}(\mathbf{R}_1'\mathbf{H}_2) \geq 1 \quad \text{and} \quad \text{rank}(\mathbf{R}_1'\mathbf{H}_3) \geq 1 \quad \text{and} \quad \text{rank}(\mathbf{R}_1'(\mathbf{H}_2 : \mathbf{H}_3)) \geq 2 \tag{5.6.5}$$

where $\mathbf{H}_2 : \mathbf{H}_3$ denotes the concatenation of these two matrices. For ease of computation, the problem is reformulated in terms of equivalent symmetric matrices and defined thus:

$$\mathbf{M}_{i.j.m} = \mathbf{H}_j'\mathbf{H}_m - \mathbf{H}_j'\mathbf{H}_i(\mathbf{H}_i'\mathbf{H}_i)^{-1}\mathbf{H}_i'\mathbf{H}_m \qquad \text{for } i, j, m = 1, 2, 3$$

and in terms of (5.6.5) we now have:

$$\text{rank}(\mathbf{M}_{1.22}) \geq 1 \qquad \text{rank}(\mathbf{M}_{1.33}) \geq 1 \qquad \text{rank}\begin{bmatrix} M_{1.22} & M_{1.23} \\ M_{1.32} & M_{1.33} \end{bmatrix} \geq 2 \tag{5.6.6}$$

Similar expressions can be used to check if $\mathbf{R}_1$, $\mathbf{R}_2$ and $\mathbf{R}_3$ identify the other vectors $i = 2$, 3 in $\boldsymbol{\beta}$.[57] To illustrate the way in which $\mathbf{R}_i$ and $\mathbf{H}_i$ are for-

[57] Most statistical software programs can handle these types of calculations with ease. An example using SHAZAM, based on the second example in Box Table 5.6.3, can be found in the appendix to this chapter.

mulated and identification proceeds when $r = 3$, Box Table 5.6.3 presents examples from Johansen and Juselins (1994) associated with the following four versions of $\boldsymbol{\beta}$ of dimension (6×3), involving the following, various homogeneity and zero restrictions:

$$\boldsymbol{\beta}^1 = \begin{bmatrix} a & 0 & 0 \\ * & * & * \\ -a & * & * \\ 1 & 1 & 0 \\ 0 & -1 & 1 \\ * & * & * \end{bmatrix} \quad \boldsymbol{\beta}^2 = \begin{bmatrix} a & 0 & 0 \\ 1 & 0 & 0 \\ -a & 0 & * \\ 0 & 1 & 0 \\ 0 & 1 & 1 \\ * & 0 & * \end{bmatrix}$$

$$\boldsymbol{\beta}^3 = \begin{bmatrix} 1 & 0 & 0 \\ -1 & 0 & 0 \\ -1 & 0 & * \\ * & 1 & 0 \\ * & -1 & 1 \\ * & 0 & * \end{bmatrix} \quad \boldsymbol{\beta}^4 = \begin{bmatrix} 1 & 0 & 0 \\ -1 & 0 & 0 \\ -1 & 0 & * \\ * & 1 & 0 \\ 0 & 1 & 1 \\ * & 0 & * \end{bmatrix} \tag{5.6.7}$$

The restrictions placed on the vectors in the first example are as follows: the two restrictions on the first column vector in $\boldsymbol{\beta}^1$ comprise a homogeneity constraint ($\beta_{11} = -\beta_{31}$) and $\beta_{51} = 0$. The cointegration vector is normalized by setting $\beta_{41} = 1$, which is not a constraint. Since ($k_i + s_i = 2 + 4 = 6$), this results in the following dimensions $\mathbf{R}_1(6 \times 2)$ and $\mathbf{H}_1(6 \times 4)$. $\mathbf{H}_1$ expresses the linear economic hypothesis to be tested on the first column vector in $\boldsymbol{\beta}^1$, its first column imposing the homogeneity constraint, while columns 2 to 4 in turn locate the unrestricted elements of the cointegration vector (i.e., β_{21}, β_{41} and β_{61}). In contrast, the first column of $\mathbf{R}_1$ imposes the homogeneity constraint while the second column imposes the zero restriction. Determining the elements of $\mathbf{R}_2$ and $\mathbf{R}_3$ and their counterparts $\mathbf{H}_2$ and $\mathbf{H}_3$ proceeds in a similar fashion. Formulating the restrictions on the vectors in $\boldsymbol{\beta}^i$ ($i = 2, \ldots, 4$) proceeds in a similar fashion.

The results from applying the test of identification in (5.6.6) for each vector are reported in Box Table 5.6.4. The cointegration space represented by $\boldsymbol{\beta}^1$ is identified since the necessary conditions are satisfied. However, this is a special case in that $r - 1 = 2$ restrictions have been imposed through $\mathbf{H}_1$, $\mathbf{H}_2$ and $\mathbf{H}_3$, on each cointegration vector. Thus, given that these restrictions are identifying, it can be said that the model is just-identified. Since the

Box Table 5.6.3 Specifying restrictions on β (when $r = 3$).

$\boldsymbol{\beta}^1 = (\mathbf{H}_1\boldsymbol{\varphi}_1, \mathbf{H}_2\boldsymbol{\varphi}_2, \mathbf{H}_3\boldsymbol{\varphi}_3)$

$$\mathbf{H}_1 = \begin{bmatrix} 1 & 0 & 0 & 0 \\ 0 & 1 & 0 & 0 \\ -1 & 0 & 0 & 0 \\ 0 & 0 & 1 & 0 \\ 0 & 0 & 0 & 0 \\ 0 & 0 & 0 & 1 \end{bmatrix} \quad \mathbf{H}_2 = \begin{bmatrix} 0 & 0 & 0 & 0 \\ 1 & 0 & 0 & 0 \\ 0 & 1 & 0 & 0 \\ 0 & 0 & 1 & 0 \\ 0 & 0 & -1 & 0 \\ 0 & 0 & 0 & 1 \end{bmatrix} \quad \mathbf{H}_3 = \begin{bmatrix} 0 & 0 & 0 & 0 \\ 1 & 0 & 0 & 0 \\ 0 & 1 & 0 & 0 \\ 0 & 0 & 0 & 0 \\ 0 & 0 & 1 & 0 \\ 0 & 0 & 0 & 1 \end{bmatrix}$$

$$\mathbf{R}_1 = \begin{bmatrix} 1 & 0 \\ 0 & 0 \\ 1 & 0 \\ 0 & 0 \\ 0 & 1 \\ 0 & 0 \end{bmatrix} \quad \mathbf{R}_2 = \begin{bmatrix} 0 & 1 \\ 0 & 0 \\ 0 & 0 \\ 1 & 0 \\ 1 & 0 \\ 0 & 0 \end{bmatrix} \quad \mathbf{R}_3 = \begin{bmatrix} 1 & 0 \\ 0 & 0 \\ 0 & 0 \\ 0 & 1 \\ 0 & 0 \\ 0 & 0 \end{bmatrix}$$

$\boldsymbol{\beta}^2 = (\mathbf{H}_1\boldsymbol{\varphi}_1, \mathbf{H}_2\boldsymbol{\varphi}_2, \mathbf{H}_3\boldsymbol{\varphi}_3)$

$$\mathbf{H}_1 = \begin{bmatrix} 1 & 0 & 0 \\ 0 & 1 & 0 \\ -1 & 0 & 0 \\ 0 & 0 & 0 \\ 0 & 0 & 0 \\ 0 & 0 & 1 \end{bmatrix} \quad \mathbf{H}_2 = \begin{bmatrix} 0 \\ 0 \\ 0 \\ 1 \\ -1 \\ 0 \end{bmatrix} \quad \mathbf{H}_3 = \begin{bmatrix} 0 & 0 & 0 \\ 0 & 0 & 0 \\ 1 & 0 & 0 \\ 0 & 0 & 0 \\ 0 & 1 & 0 \\ 0 & 0 & 1 \end{bmatrix}$$

$$\mathbf{R}_1 = \begin{bmatrix} 1 & 0 & 0 \\ 0 & 0 & 0 \\ 1 & 0 & 0 \\ 0 & 1 & 0 \\ 0 & 0 & 1 \\ 0 & 0 & 0 \end{bmatrix} \quad \mathbf{R}_2 = \begin{bmatrix} 0 & 1 & 0 & 0 & 0 \\ 0 & 0 & 1 & 0 & 0 \\ 0 & 0 & 0 & 1 & 0 \\ 1 & 0 & 0 & 0 & 0 \\ 1 & 0 & 0 & 0 & 0 \\ 0 & 0 & 0 & 0 & 1 \end{bmatrix} \quad \mathbf{R}_3 = \begin{bmatrix} 1 & 0 & 0 \\ 0 & 1 & 0 \\ 0 & 0 & 0 \\ 0 & 0 & 1 \\ 0 & 0 & 0 \\ 0 & 0 & 0 \end{bmatrix}$$

$\boldsymbol{\beta}^3 = (\mathbf{H}_1\boldsymbol{\varphi}_1, \mathbf{H}_2\boldsymbol{\varphi}_2, \mathbf{H}_3\boldsymbol{\varphi}_3)$

$$\mathbf{H}_1 = \begin{bmatrix} 1 & 0 & 0 & 0 \\ -1 & 0 & 0 & 0 \\ -1 & 0 & 0 & 0 \\ 0 & 1 & 0 & 0 \\ 0 & 0 & 1 & 0 \\ 0 & 0 & 0 & 1 \end{bmatrix} \quad \mathbf{H}_2 = \begin{bmatrix} 0 \\ 0 \\ 0 \\ 1 \\ -1 \\ 0 \end{bmatrix} \quad \mathbf{H}_3 = \begin{bmatrix} 0 & 0 & 0 \\ 0 & 0 & 0 \\ 1 & 0 & 0 \\ 0 & 0 & 0 \\ 0 & 1 & 0 \\ 0 & 0 & 1 \end{bmatrix}$$

$$\mathbf{R}_1 = \begin{bmatrix} 1 & 1 \\ 1 & 0 \\ 0 & 1 \\ 0 & 0 \\ 0 & 0 \\ 0 & 0 \end{bmatrix} \quad \mathbf{R}_2 = \begin{bmatrix} 1 & 0 & 0 & 0 & 0 \\ 0 & 1 & 0 & 0 & 0 \\ 0 & 0 & 1 & 0 & 0 \\ 0 & 0 & 0 & 1 & 0 \\ 0 & 0 & 0 & 1 & 0 \\ 0 & 0 & 0 & 0 & 1 \end{bmatrix} \quad \mathbf{R}_3 = \begin{bmatrix} 1 & 0 & 0 \\ 0 & 1 & 0 \\ 0 & 0 & 0 \\ 0 & 0 & 1 \\ 0 & 0 & 0 \\ 0 & 0 & 0 \end{bmatrix}$$

$\boldsymbol{\beta}^4 = (\mathbf{H}_1\boldsymbol{\varphi}_1, \mathbf{H}_2\boldsymbol{\varphi}_2, \mathbf{H}_3\boldsymbol{\varphi}_3)$

$$\mathbf{H}_1 = \begin{bmatrix} 1 & 0 & 0 \\ -1 & 0 & 0 \\ -1 & 0 & 0 \\ 0 & 1 & 0 \\ 0 & 0 & 0 \\ 0 & 0 & 1 \end{bmatrix} \quad \mathbf{H}_2 = \begin{bmatrix} 0 \\ 0 \\ 0 \\ 1 \\ -1 \\ 0 \end{bmatrix} \quad \mathbf{H}_3 = \begin{bmatrix} 0 & 0 & 0 \\ 0 & 0 & 0 \\ 1 & 0 & 0 \\ 0 & 0 & 0 \\ 0 & 1 & 0 \\ 0 & 0 & 1 \end{bmatrix}$$

$$\mathbf{R}_1 = \begin{bmatrix} 1 & 1 & 0 \\ 1 & 0 & 0 \\ 0 & 1 & 0 \\ 0 & 0 & 0 \\ 0 & 0 & 1 \\ 0 & 0 & 0 \end{bmatrix} \quad \mathbf{R}_2 = \begin{bmatrix} 1 & 0 & 0 & 0 & 0 \\ 0 & 1 & 0 & 0 & 0 \\ 0 & 0 & 1 & 0 & 0 \\ 0 & 0 & 0 & 1 & 0 \\ 0 & 0 & 0 & 1 & 0 \\ 0 & 0 & 0 & 0 & 1 \end{bmatrix} \quad \mathbf{R}_3 = \begin{bmatrix} 1 & 0 & 0 \\ 0 & 1 & 0 \\ 0 & 0 & 0 \\ 0 & 0 & 1 \\ 0 & 0 & 0 \\ 0 & 0 & 0 \end{bmatrix}$$

Box Table 5.6.4 Bank conditions (equation (5.6.3)) for identifying cointegration vectors (when $r = 3$).

Rank $\mathbf{M}_{i,j,m}$	$\boldsymbol{\beta}^1$	$\boldsymbol{\beta}^2$	$\boldsymbol{\beta}^3$	$\boldsymbol{\beta}^4$
Hypothesis $\boldsymbol{\beta}_1 = \mathbf{H}_1\boldsymbol{\varphi}_1$				
1.22	2	1	0	1
1.33	2	2	1	2
1.23	2	3	2	2
Hypothesis $\boldsymbol{\beta}_2 = \mathbf{H}_2\boldsymbol{\varphi}_2$				
2.11	2	3	3	3
2.33	1	3	3	3
2.13	2	5	4	4
Hypothesis $\boldsymbol{\beta}_3 = \mathbf{H}_3\boldsymbol{\varphi}_3$				
3.11	2	2	2	2
3.22	1	2	1	1
3.12	2	3	2	2

likelihood function for the exactly identified model is not changed, no testing of the hypotheses is involved. The second example involves over-identification, since the number of restrictions $k_i > r - 1$. Again the cointegration space represented by $\boldsymbol{\beta}^2$ is identified since the necessary conditions are satisfied (cf. Box Table 5.6.4). The test of whether restrictions are valid is based on an LR test[58] involving $v = \Sigma_i(n - r + 1 - s_i)$ degrees of freedom. In this case, where $(n - r + 1) = 4$, then $v = (4 - 3) + (4 - 1) + (4 - 3) = 5$, and thus the test statistic is distributed as $\chi^2(5)$.

[58] This test is not computed in the same way as the more general tests, since the solution of the reduced rank regression now involves numerical optimization based on a switching algorithm that concentrates the likelihood function on $\boldsymbol{\alpha}$ and $\boldsymbol{\beta}$, respectively.

In the next example concerning $\boldsymbol{\beta}^3$, the rank condition involving $\mathbf{H}_1$ is not satisfied since the rank of $\mathbf{M}_{1.22} = 0$. This occurs because it is possible to take a linear combination of $\mathbf{H}_1$ and $\mathbf{H}_2$ that would remove either β_{41} or β_{51} from $\boldsymbol{\beta}_1^3$, and yet *jointly* the restricted $\boldsymbol{\beta}_1^3$ and $\boldsymbol{\beta}_2^3$ are a valid representation of the first two cointegration vectors in $\boldsymbol{\beta}^3$. Although $\boldsymbol{\beta}^3 = (\mathbf{H}_1\boldsymbol{\varphi}_1, \mathbf{H}_2\boldsymbol{\varphi}_2, \mathbf{H}_3\boldsymbol{\varphi}_3)$ is not identified, the restrictions on the cointegration space are valid and can be tested using an LR test. Note, however, that in this instance $v = (4-3) + (4-1) + (4-3) = 5$ rather than $v = (4-4) + (4-1) + (4-3) = 4$ (i.e., $s_i = 3$ in $\mathbf{H}_1$, since there are three and not two restrictions imposed because of the lack of identification).

The last example, concern $\boldsymbol{\beta}^4$, is the same as the previous example except that the additional restriction (that $\beta_{51} = 0$) is imposed to achieve an identified model. Thus, when the system is not identified, the rank condition tests often provide information to suggest what needs to be done to identify the model.

2 If r_1 cointegration vectors are assumed to be known, the remaining r_2 vectors can be left unrestricted. If there is more than one 'known' cointegration vector (so that $r_1 > 1$ in the first group), then the test can be expanded to cover each 'known' vector plus the remaining 'unknown' vectors. In the limit, when all cointegration vectors are 'known' this test would be equivalent to the hypotheses tested using, for example, equation (5.15).

These general tests of hypotheses are now illustrated using the PPP and UIP model estimated by Johansen and Juselius (1992). The results already presented in Table 5.4 indicate that it is plausible to set $r = 2$, with the first cointegration vector seeming to contain the PPP relation among the first three variables and the second to contain the interest rate differential among the last two variables. So, the first general hypothesis is that the PPP relationship $[a_{1j}, -a_{2j}, -a_{3j}, *, *]$, for $j = 1, \ldots, r$, holds in both vectors. This requires testing:[59]

$$\boldsymbol{\beta}' = \begin{bmatrix} 1 & -1 & -1 & * & * \\ 1 & -1 & -1 & * & * \end{bmatrix} \tag{5.16}$$

A second test is for only the UIP relationship $[*, *, *, a_{4j}, -a_{5j}]$ to enter all cointegration vectors, thus imposing one restriction (i.e., $a_{4j} = -a_{5j}$) on each cointegration vector; that is:

$$\boldsymbol{\beta}' = \begin{bmatrix} * & * & * & 1 & -1 \\ * & * & * & 1 & -1 \end{bmatrix} \tag{5.17}$$

The results for the above two hypotheses, together with the restricted $\boldsymbol{\beta}$, are

[59] Note that normalizing each vector such that the first element equals 1 is not a constraint.

Table 5.6 Testing some general restrictions on cointegration vectors in the PPP and UIP model.[a]

Test		Restricted $\boldsymbol{\beta}$					LR statistic	Probability of accepting null
		p_1	p_2	e	i_1	i_2		
$\mathbf{H}_1$	$\boldsymbol{\beta}_1$	1.000	−1.000	−1.000	−3.604	−1.359	$\chi^2(4) = 3.92$	0.42
	$\boldsymbol{\beta}_2$	1.000	−1.000	−1.000	1.000	−4.594		
$\mathbf{H}_2$	$\boldsymbol{\beta}_1$	1.000	−1.422	0.966	1.000	−1.000	$\chi^2(2) = 13.77$	0.00
	$\boldsymbol{\beta}_2$	0.666	−0.951	0.514	1.000	−1.000		
$\mathbf{H}_3$	$\boldsymbol{\beta}_1$	1.000	−1.000	−1.000	0.000	0.000	$\chi^2(3) = 17.11$	0.00
	$\boldsymbol{\beta}_2$	−0.307	0.287	0.275	1.000	0.613		
$\mathbf{H}_4$	$\boldsymbol{\beta}_1$	1.000	−0.934	−0.896	−5.596	0.559	$\chi^2(3) = 4.32$	0.23
	$\boldsymbol{\beta}_2$	0.000	0.000	0.000	1.000	−1.000		

[a] The first vector is always normalized on p_1 and the other vector is normalized on i_1.

given in Table 5.6. The PPP relationship appears to hold in both cointegration relationships, but the hypothesis that only the interest rate differential enters both vectors is strongly rejected.

On the basis of these results, Johansen and Juselius (1992) went on to test if the PPP and UIP relationships were stationary by themselves (i.e., whether one cointegration vector can be specified as $\mathbf{H}_3 = [1, -1, -1, 0, 0]'$ and the other as $\mathbf{H}_4 = [0, 0, 0, 1, -1]'$).[60] Testing for a 'known' cointegration vector, with the other vector unrestricted, involves:

$$\boldsymbol{\beta}' = \begin{bmatrix} 1 & -1 & -1 & 0 & 0 \\ * & * & * & * & * \end{bmatrix} \qquad \boldsymbol{\beta}' = \begin{bmatrix} 0 & 0 & 0 & 1 & -1 \\ * & * & * & * & * \end{bmatrix} \tag{5.18}$$

The resulting test is based on the χ^2 distribution with $(r_1 \times (n - r))$ degrees of freedom. The results for the tests are also given in Table 5.6, and the hypothesis that one of the cointegration vectors represents only the PPP relationship is rejected, while there is support for the idea that one of the vectors contains a stationary relationship between just the interest rate variables.

The results obtained so far suggest that the PPP relationship exists in both cointegration, vectors, but not on its own, while the opposite is true for the UIP relationship. This might at first seem contradictory, since hypothesis $\mathbf{H}_4$ would suggest that the PPP relationship does not exist in the cointegration vector containing the UIP relationship, and yet $\mathbf{H}_1$ was not rejected. A reconciliation of the apparent contradiction requires the PPP relationship to be insignificant in the UIP cointegration relationship, and this seems to be supported by the estimate of $\boldsymbol{\beta}_2$ in $\mathbf{H}_1$. These results are informative from the point

[60] It would obviously be feasible (even desirable) to test for these jointly by specifying restrictions on both cointegration vectors (see equation 5.20).

of view of formulating hypotheses about whether there are unique vectors in the cointegration space, and we take this up again in the next two sections.

TESTING FOR UNIQUE COINTEGRATION VECTORS

It has already been pointed out that since the Johansen approach as outlined comprises estimating a reduced-form unrestricted VECM, it only provides information on the uniqueness of the cointegration *space*. Thus it is necessary to impose restrictions motivated by economic arguments to obtain unique *vectors* lying within that space, and then test whether the columns of $\boldsymbol{\beta}$ are identified in terms of the long-run *structural* relations between the economic variables in the model.[61] Identification is formally defined and discussed in Box 5.6. Here we illustrate testing for unique cointegration vectors and report the outcome of whether identification is achieved.

Before doing so, it is important to note that there are different strategies that can be used to achieve uniqueness/identification, involving a balance between the (strict) imposition of known economic relationships and an *ad hoc* testing strategy that involves, for example, dropping elements of $\boldsymbol{\beta}$, testing to insure that such restrictions are accepted using LR tests and proceeding until uniqueness happens to be achieved. For example, Garratt, Lee, Pesaran and Shin (1999) argue that developing the structural long-run relationships between the variables in the model needs to be based *ex ante* on economic theory, before estimation takes place, rather than '... the more usual approach where the starting point is an unrestricted VAR model, with some vague priors about the nature of the long-run relations' (p. 15). They give an example of deriving testable hypotheses from developing such a model from theory (see also Garratt, Lee, Pesaran and Shin, 2001) and then testing to ensure the structure is accepted using the type of tests considered later on.

However, in certain circumstances, there may be insufficient theory on which to proceed or the *ex ante* relationships suggested by theory are rejected. Or, alternatively, one or more elements of a cointegration vector may be statistically insignificant (and therefore can be potentially removed), since to leave the insignificant variable in the relation (assuming that the theory from which it is derived is correct) will lead to under-identification.[62] Thus, it is important to note that it is not strictly necessary to always derive the structural relations (i.e., the unique cointegration vectors) beforehand, as Davidson (1998) shows.

[61] Of course, when $r = 1$, then the space is uniquely defined by a single vector. Note also that it may not be possible to identify unique vectors, and this does not invalidate the long-run stationary relationships between the variables in the cointegration space.

[62] As Davidson (1998) points out, if theory is incorrect (or at least uninformative), a cointegration vector containing an insignificant variable(s) '... can be of no interest to us', based on his Theorem 3.

He introduces the concept of an irreducibly cointegrated (IC) relationship comprising a set of $I(1)$ variables that are cointegrated; but, dropping any of the variables leaves a set that is not cointegrated. He shows that if a structural cointegrating relation is identified (by the rank condition—see Box 5.6), then it must also be irreducible, indicating that at least some IC vectors are structural. Not all IC relations are structural, but those that are not are called 'solved relations' and involve linear combinations of structural vectors. In certain circumstances IC relations will always be structural (e.g., if an IC relation contains a variable that appears in no other IC relation, or if an IC relation contains strictly fewer variables than all those others having variables in common with it); thus '... it is possible ... to discover structural economic relationships directly from data analysis, without the use of any theory' (Davidson, 1998, pp. 93–94). Thus, the concept of IC relationships suggests that a strategy for identification could involve dropping (one by one) the variables from reduced form (i.e., unrestricted) cointegration vectors to obtain the sets of relationships that are IC and then testing to see which of these is identified. In most situations, combining as much prior economic theory as possible with a testing strategy that seeks to ensure that relationships are unique should suffice. Finally, it is worth noting that, as a general rule, if restrictions are imposed that involve each cointegration vector having at least one variable unique to it, then the relationships will always be identified. Thus, to just-identify the model, there must be r^2 restrictions imposed comprising $r^2 - r$ constraints on parameters in the model plus a further r normalizations that are not constraints. For example, when $r = 3$, each cointegration vector must include two constraints—typically placed to ensure that each vector has at least one variable unique to it—plus a further normalization of one of the variables in the vector. When the model is just-identified, each vector has the same number of restrictions and there is no overall additional constraint on the log-likelihood function for the new model, thus a test of the restrictions is not possible. Often further restrictions are imposed on the cointegration vectors to obtain an over-identified model that does constrain the log-likelihood function and thus leads to an LR test of the overall constraints imposed.

Following Johansen (1992c) and Johansen and Juselius (1994), identification is achieved if when applying the restrictions of the first cointegration vector to the other $r - 1$ vectors the result is a matrix of rank $r - 1$ (i.e., a matrix with $r - 1$ independent columns). Put another way, '... it is not possible by taking linear combinations of for instance $\boldsymbol{\beta}_2, \ldots, \boldsymbol{\beta}_r$ to construct a vector and hence an equation which is restricted in the same way as $\boldsymbol{\beta}_1$ and in this sense could be confused with the equation defined by $\boldsymbol{\beta}_1$. Hence, $\boldsymbol{\beta}_1$ can be (uniquely) recognised among all linear combinations of $\boldsymbol{\beta}_1$' (Johansen, 1992c).

As an example, consider the PPP and UIP model and the tests of restrictions undertaken in the last section. The general hypotheses tested suggest that the PPP relationship is significant in one vector while the UIP relationship exists on its own in the other vector. Thus, it would appear valid to specify the following:

$$\boldsymbol{\beta}' = \begin{bmatrix} 1 & -1 & -1 & * & * \\ 0 & 0 & 0 & 1 & -1 \end{bmatrix} \tag{5.19}$$

Using the 'general restrictions' editor in *PcGive 10.1* gives an LR test statistic of 6.45, which is not very significant under the $\chi^2(5)$.[63] However, identification is not achieved—and this relates to the fact that the first vector is not identified (Box 5.6 provides the outcome from formally testing for identification). This occurs because it is possible to take a linear combination of the two cointegration vectors in $\boldsymbol{\beta}$, which would remove either β_{41} or β_{51}, and yet *jointly* the restricted vectors are a valid representation of the two cointegration vectors in $\boldsymbol{\beta}$. In effect, the space spanned by the second vector is contained in the space spanned by the first such that we can only estimate uniquely the impact of a linear combination of β_{41} or β_{51} in the first relation. To see this clearly, consider the following linear combination of the first two vectors:

$$\begin{bmatrix} 1.000 \\ -1.000 \\ -1.000 \\ 1.893 \\ 1.893 \end{bmatrix} + 1.893 \times \begin{bmatrix} 0.000 \\ 0.000 \\ 0.000 \\ 1.000 \\ -1.000 \end{bmatrix} = \begin{bmatrix} 1.000 \\ -1.000 \\ -1.000 \\ 3.786 \\ 0.000 \end{bmatrix}$$

To overcome under-identification, we can reformulate the problem as:

$$\boldsymbol{\beta}' = \begin{bmatrix} 1 & -1 & -1 & 0 & 0 \\ 0 & 0 & 0 & 1 & -1 \end{bmatrix} \tag{5.20}$$

where because each vector has at least one variable unique to it means that the model is clearly identified, but the test of these restrictions results in an LR test statistic of 26.99, which is highly significant under the $\chi^2(6)$ distribution. The compromise position is to specify:

$$\boldsymbol{\beta}' = \begin{bmatrix} 1 & -1 & -1 & * & 0 \\ 0 & 0 & 0 & 1 & -1 \end{bmatrix} \tag{5.21}$$

which is identified with an LR test statistic of 6.45, which is not very significant under the $\chi^2(5)$ distribution, lending support to the general hypotheses. Thus, imposing a structure on the PPP and UIP model suggests that the PPP relationship exists in one vector along with the UK interest rate (but not as covered interest parity), while the UIP relationship uniquely forms the second cointegration vector.

When the cointegration space is uniquely identified, *PcGive 10.1* will calculate the 'standard errors' associated with each freely estimated β_{ij}. In the last

[63] Note that the degrees of freedom are, as in Box 5.6, calculated as $v = (5 - 2 + 1 - 2) + (5 - 2 + 1 - 1) = 5$, since $s_1 = 2$ and not 3.

model estimated there is only one such parameter and it has a coefficient value of −4.646 and standard error of 0.556. The standard errors can be used to calculate Wald (or t) tests of hypotheses about the β_{ij} that are asymptotically distributed as $\chi^2(1)$. Thus, if it was meaningful to test that the interest rate variable in the PPP cointegration vector is −5, then we can use the following Wald test:

$$\left(\frac{-4.646 - (-5)}{0.556}\right)^2 = 0.40$$

which does not reject this hypothesis since $\chi^2_{0.95}(1) = 3.84$.

JOINT TESTS OF RESTRICTIONS ON $\boldsymbol{\alpha}$ AND $\boldsymbol{\beta}$

It is now possible to jointly test restrictions on both the cointegration vectors and the speed-of-adjustment parameters. However, care is needed when doing this, since some forms of constraint on $\boldsymbol{\alpha}$ can induce a failure of identification of $\boldsymbol{\beta}$, and vice versa.[64] Having obtained results in the PPP and UIP model that accept the various hypotheses that H_0: $\alpha_{2j} = \alpha_{3j} = 0$ for $j = 1, 2$ and that the two vectors in $\boldsymbol{\beta}$ comprise [1, −1, −1, *, 0] and [0, 0, 0, 1, −1], these various restrictions can be pooled. It is also possible (but not reported here) to add one further restriction, that the 3-month Treasury bill rate (i_1) is weakly exogenous, and in total accept the joint null hypothesis: H_0: $\alpha_{2j} = \alpha_{3j} = \alpha_{4j} = 0$ for $j = 1, 2$.[65]

Pooling the various restrictions gives the results reported in the first part of Box 5.7. The overall LR test does not significantly reject the null and therefore these joint restrictions are satisfied.[66] On the basis of these results, the last step is to condition on the weakly exogenous variables and then check that imposing the various restrictions has not altered the model's underlying properties. The conditional estimates, when p_2, e and i_1 are weakly exogenous, are also reported in Box 5.7 and indicate that there is significant overall change in the model after applying the conditioning, with substantial improvement in the (not reported) diagnostic tests of the residuals (primarily because we can now validly condition on the non-normal foreign wholesale price index and exchange rate, p_2 and e).[67] Plots of the restricted cointegration relations and

[64] Restrictions on $\boldsymbol{\alpha}$ can also have implications for the dynamic stability of the short-run model, as Fischer (1993) shows.

[65] This additional constraint would not have been obvious from the results in Box 5.2.

[66] Note that deriving the degrees of freedom in this test is not straightforward, although in this instance adding together the degrees of freedom from the separate tests provides the appropriate value. When the model is not identified, then v is only approximate.

[67] Note also that we can only reject the null of $r = 1$ at the 10% significance level using the appropriate critical values in Pesaran et al. (2000) when there are exogenous $I(1)$ regressors in the model, although the 5% critical value is 16.90 (and we get a test statistic of 16.03).

Box 5.7 *Testing joint restrictions on α and β:* PcGive 10.1 output for the PPP and UIP models.

Testing Restrictions on α and β

The LR test, $\chi^2(11) = 13.81$, p-value = 0.24

Normalised (Based on 2 cointegration vectors; t-values in parenthesis for unrestricted variables)

β′

p_1	p_2	e	i_1	i_2
1.000	-1.000	-1.000	-4.250	0.000
			(-7.66)	
0.000	0.000	0.000	1.000	-1.000

α′

-0.072	0.000	0.000	0.000	0.074
(-4.39)				(2.85)
-0.074	0.000	0.000	0.000	0.415
(-1.21)				(4.26)

Conditional Model : p_2, e and i_1 weekly exogenous

Eigenv.	Trace	H_0: r=	n-r=
0.3846	45.16**	0	2
0.2344	16.03*	1	1

**/* rejects at 5%/10% significance level (critical values from Pesaran et. al. (2000, Table 6c)

(i) 3-month UK Treasury bill rate enters PPP vector

The LR test, χ^2 (5) = 8.65 , p-value = 0.12

Normalised (Based on 2 cointegration vectors; t-values in parenthesis for unrestricted variables)

β′

p_1	i_2	p_2	e	i_1
1.000	0.000	-1.000	-1.000	-1.049
				(-1.28)
0.000	-1.000	0.000	0.000	1.000

α′

-0.071	0.086
(-3.94)	(2.94)
-0.026	-0.303
(-0.41)	(-3.02)

(ii) 3-month UK Treasury bill rate excluded from PPP vector

The LR test, χ^2 (6) = 9.36 , p-value = 0.15

Normalised (Based on 2 cointegration vectors; t-values in parenthesis for unrestricted variables)

β′

p_1	i_2	p_2	e	i_1
1.000	0.000	-1.000	-1.000	0.000
0.000	-1.000	0.000	0.000	1.000

α′

-0.070	0.096
(-3.62)	(3.21)
0.021	-0.373
(0.31)	(-3.69)

recursive eigenvalues (again not shown) suggest that the model performs much better than in its unrestricted form, and indeed the first cointegration vector (and recursive eigenvalues associated with this vector) now looks more stationary.

However, the conditional model suggests that the Treasury bill rate is now redundant in the PPP vector (with a t-statistic of -1.28). Thus, excluding this variable from the first vector in $\boldsymbol{\beta}$ produces the last set of results in Box 5.7. The test of restrictions is accepted and the end result is one PPP relationship in the first cointegration vector and the UIP relationship only in the second vector (recall in the unrestricted model—equation (5.20)—this was rejected).

SEASONAL UNIT ROOTS

Franses (1994) developed a multivariate approach to testing for seasonal unit roots in a univariate series. Since this involves an adaptation of the Johansen approach it can now be considered. The approach amounts to taking a single times series x_t and rewriting it as s annual series each based on a separate season s. When dealing with quarterly data, we obtain the vector $\mathbf{X}_T = [X_{1T}, X_{2T}, X_{3T}, X_{4T}]'$, where X_{iT} contains all the observations from quarter i for $t = 1, \ldots, T$. Writing this as a VECM (cf. (5.2)) gives:

$$\Delta \mathbf{X}_T = \Gamma_1 \Delta \mathbf{X}_{T-1} + \cdots + \Gamma_{k-1} \Delta \mathbf{X}_{T-k+1} + \Pi \mathbf{X}_{T-k} + \Psi \mathbf{D}_t + \mathbf{u}_t \tag{5.22}$$

where $\mathbf{D}_t$ contains an intercept for each short-run equation and in practice it is likely that $k = 1$. This model can be estimated in the usual way, based on the Johansen reduced rank regression approach, and reduced rank tests (equations (5.4) and (5.5)) applied to determine the number of cointegration vectors contained in the model. If $r = 4$, then Π has full rank and there are no units roots (seasonal or otherwise) in x_t and hence the series (being stationary) does not require any differencing. If $r = 0$, then all the unit roots $(1, -1, -i, -i)$ are contained in x_t (see the discussion of equation (3.11)), and this series needs to be differenced by $(1 - L^4)$. If $0 < r < 4$, then roots at different frequencies are present and various tests of hypotheses can be conducted involving the cointegration vectors, which will determine the type of unit roots present. These are summarized in Table 5.7 (table 1 in Franses, 1994). Note that if the various tests of the rank of Π are accepted, but the hypotheses concerning the form of the restrictions on the cointegration vectors in Table 5.7 are rejected, then this is evidence of the periodically integrated model with time-varying seasonal parameters. Franses (1994) provides the critical values of the tests for reduced rank when the sample is $T = 25$, 50 and the constant term is restricted or unrestricted to lie in the cointegration space, since these are not the same as in the standard Johansen approach.[68] He also applies his approach to the

[68] These are reproduced as Tables A.13 to A.16 in the Statistical Appendix at the end of the book.

Table 5.7 Testing for (non) seasonal unit roots using the Johansen approach (source: Franses, 1994).

Rank of Π	Restricted $\boldsymbol{\beta}'$ matrix	Cointegration vectors	Differencing filter	(Non) seasonal unit roots
3	$\boldsymbol{\beta}_1' = \begin{bmatrix} -1 & 0 & 0 \\ 1 & -1 & 0 \\ 0 & 1 & -1 \\ 0 & 0 & 1 \end{bmatrix}$	$X_{2T} - X_{1T}$ $X_{3T} - X_{2T}$ $X_{4T} - X_{3T}$	$(1 - L)$	1
3	$\boldsymbol{\beta}_2' = \begin{bmatrix} 1 & 0 & 0 \\ 1 & 1 & 0 \\ 0 & 1 & 1 \\ 0 & 0 & 1 \end{bmatrix}$	$X_{2T} + X_{1T}$ $X_{3T} + X_{2T}$ $X_{4T} + X_{3T}$	$(1 + L)$	-1
2	$\boldsymbol{\beta}_1' = \begin{bmatrix} -1 & 0 \\ 0 & -1 \\ 1 & 0 \\ 0 & 1 \end{bmatrix}$	$X_{3T} - X_{1T}$ $X_{4T} - X_{2T}$	$(1 - L^2)$	$1, -1$
2	$\boldsymbol{\beta}_2' = \begin{bmatrix} 1 & 0 \\ 0 & 1 \\ 1 & 0 \\ 0 & 1 \end{bmatrix}$	$X_{3T} + X_{1T}$ $X_{4T} + X_{2T}$	$(1 + L^2)$	$1, -i$
1	$\boldsymbol{\beta}_1' = \begin{bmatrix} -1 \\ 1 \\ -1 \\ 1 \end{bmatrix}$	$X_{4T} - X_{3T} + X_{2T} - X_{1T}$	$(1 - L)(1 + L^2)$	$1, i, -i$
1	$\boldsymbol{\beta}_2' = \begin{bmatrix} 1 \\ 1 \\ 1 \\ 1 \end{bmatrix}$	$X_{4T} + X_{3T} + X_{2T} + X_{1T}$	$(1 + L)(1 + L^2)$	$-1, i, -i$
0			$(1 - L^4)$	$1, -1, i, -i$

Table 5.8 Multivariate tests for (non-) seasonal unit roots using UK consumption function data (1971q2–1993q1).

Variable	Rank of Π^a	LR test of restrictions on $\boldsymbol{\beta}_1'$	LR test of restrictions on $\boldsymbol{\beta}_2'$
log real C	2	$\chi^2(4) = 10.15$*	$\chi^2(4) = 28.12$**
log real Y	2	$\chi^2(4) = 21.47$**	$\chi^2(4) = 39.50$**
log real W	3	$\chi^2(3) = 3.28$	$\chi^2(3) = 9.95$*
π	3	$\chi^2(3) = 17.69$**	$\chi^2(3) = 25.76$**

[a] Based on trace test and critical values given in Table A.13 in the Statistical Appendix at the end of this book.
* Denotes rejection at the 5% significance level.
** Denotes rejection at the 10% significance level.

Japanese consumption function data used in Engle, Granger, Hylleberg and Lee (1993), finding no evidence of seasonal unit roots in the data.

Table 5.8 presents the result when this approach is applied to the consumption function data analysed in Chapter 3. With respect to consumer-spending and real output, there are two unit roots, but, since the restrictions on the elements of $\boldsymbol{\beta}$ are rejected, this would imply periodic integration. The wealth variable would appear to have one unit root at the zero frequency, while retail price inflation also has one unit root, although this would seem to involve periodic integration. The results obtained based on a single equation test of periodic integration (Table 3.7) found that each of these variables has only a zero frequency unit root; this is clearly at odds (except for real wealth) with the multivariate results presented here.

SEASONAL COINTEGRATION

Engle et al.'s (1993) single equation approach to modelling seasonal cointegration was covered in the last chapter. Using the Johansen multivariate approach, it is possible to test for a long-run relationship between the variables in a model at the zero, two-quarter (bi-annual) frequency and four-quarter (annual) frequencies, since Lee (1992) and Lee and Siklos (1995) extended the basic VECM form to a multivariate form of the Hylleberg, Engle, Granger and Yoo approach:

$$\begin{aligned}\Delta_4 \mathbf{z}_t = {} & \Gamma_1 \Delta_4 \mathbf{z}_{t-1} + \cdots + \Gamma_{k-4} \Delta_4 \mathbf{z}_{t-k+4} + \Pi_1 \mathbf{z}_{1,t-1} + \Pi_2 \mathbf{z}_{2,t-1} + \Pi_3 \mathbf{z}_{3,t-2} \\ & + \Pi_4 \mathbf{z}_{3,t-1} + \Upsilon_1 \mathbf{D}_{1t} + \Upsilon_2 \mathbf{D}_{2t} + \Upsilon_3 \mathbf{D}_{3t} + \Upsilon_4 \mathbf{D}_{4t} + \mathbf{u}_t \end{aligned} \tag{5.23}$$

where $\mathbf{D}_{qt}$ is the zero/one vector of dummies corresponding to quarter q and where:

$$\begin{aligned} \mathbf{z}_{1t} &= (1 + L + L^2 + L^3)\mathbf{z}_t && \text{(zero frequency)} \\ \mathbf{z}_{2t} &= (1 - L + L^2 - L^3)\mathbf{z}_t && \text{(bi-annual frequency, } \pi/2) \\ \mathbf{z}_{3t} &= (1 - L^2)\mathbf{z}_t && \text{(annual frequency, } \pi) \end{aligned}$$

Table 5.9 Seasonal cointegration tests for four-dimensional UK consumption function data (1971q2–1993q1): trace test statistics. Critical values were taken from Franses and Kunst (1999, table 3), where the sources are discussed.

	No dummies[a]			Unrestricted dummies[a]			Restricted dummies[b]		
H_0:	0	π	$\pi/2$	0	π	$\pi/2$	0	π	$\pi/2$
$r = 0$	45.57*	42.14	55.17	42.99	52.60	95.31	42.99	51.79*	93.17*
5%	47.2	NA	NA	47.2	NA	NA	50.2	54.4	64.9
10%	43.8	NA	NA	43.8	NA	NA	46.5	51.0	61.0
$r = 1$	24.10	20.48	23.97*	24.95	32.07*	60.82**	24.95	31.25	60.00**
5%	29.4	26.2	24.0	29.4	34.4	40.6	30.4	34.9	43.2
10%	26.7	23.4	21.2	26.7	31.3	37.1	27.7	32.0	40.2
$r = 2$	10.48	4.49	3.52	10.33	16.88	29.23**	10.33	16.48	28.88**
5%	15.3	13.0	12.3	15.3	19.3	24.3	15.5	20.1	26.4
10%	13.3	11.1	10.3	13.3	17.0	21.6	13.6	17.8	23.9
$r = 3$	1.20	0.06	1.00	1.21	3.89	4.46	1.21	3.91	4.73
5%	3.8	4.3	4.4	3.8	8.6	11.9	3.8	8.8	12.6
10%	2.7	3.1	3.1	2.7	6.9	9.9	2.8	7.3	10.8

Note 0, π and $\pi/2$ refer to the zero, annual and bi-annual frequencies, respectively.
* Rejects null at 10% level.
** Rejects null at 5% level.
[a] Refers to the model by Lee (1992) and extended by Lee and Siklos (1995).
[b] Refers to the model by Franses and Kunst (1999).

and the ranks of the $n \times n$ matrices $\mathbf{\Pi}_i = \boldsymbol{\alpha}_i \boldsymbol{\beta}_i'$ determine how many cointegration relations there are and at which frequency. Note that equation (5.23) allows either for no deterministic seasonal dummies to enter the model ($\Upsilon_i = 0$) or there are no restrictions on these dummies. Franses and Kunst (1998) impose specific restrictions on the seasonal dummies and force them to enter the cointegration space (see their equation (3)), arguing that this is a more theoretically justifiable way to deal with seasonal intercepts.

Estimating equation (5.23) with different treatments of the seasonal dummy intercepts and using the UK consumption function data discussed in Chapter 3, we obtain the trace statistics reported in Table 5.9.[69] In all three forms of the model, there is no (or only weak) evidence of cointegration at the zero frequency. In the model with seasonal dummies, there is evidence that there are possibly one (the restricted model) or two (unrestricted model) co-integration vectors at the annual frequency, although the results are not statistically strong. For all models there is evidence that we can reject the null that there are at most 1 or 2 cointegration vectors at the bi-annual

[69] Robert Kunst was kind enough to provide the Gauss code in order to undertake these estimations.

Table 5.10 Cointegration vectors for UK consumption function data (1971q2–1993q1).

				Seasonal dummies	
log real C	log real Y	log real W	π	cost(πt)	cos($\pi(t-1)/2$)
Zero frequency					
−1.00	−1.04	1.02	−1.56		
Annual frequency					
−1.00	0.37	−1.00	0.40	−0.75	
Bi-annual frequency					
−1.00	−0.32	−1.11	−0.96	−0.11	−0.11
0.60	−1.00	−0.43	−0.64	−1.03	−1.03
0.14	0.23	−1.00	−0.82	−0.03	0.60

frequency (the results are particularly strong when seasonal dummies enter the model in either a restricted or unrestricted form, since we find $r = 3$). These results are different from those we obtained when using the single equation EG-type approach; the latter could find no evidence to suggest the variables cointegrate at the two-quarter (bi-annual) frequency, although we now find strong evidence for this using the multivariate approach.

Finally, Table 5.10 reports the most stationary cointegration vectors obtained from estimating the restricted dummies version of the model. As is usual in these cases, it is difficult to interpret these relationships: which is one of the major criticisms of the multivariate seasonal cointegration approach.

CONCLUSIONS

The Johansen approach to testing for cointegration is widely accessible to applied economists. However, in undertaking this type of analysis it is important to spend some time in formulating the dynamic model in terms of which deterministic components (intercept, trend and dummy variables) should enter, setting the correct lag length of the VAR and using all the information available when testing for the reduced rank and thus the number of cointegration vectors in the system. There is also the issue of modelling the $I(2)$ system, when there are $I(2)$ variables in the model.

Testing for weak exogeneity is now fairly standard, and the more general tests of linear hypotheses on cointegration vectors are also relatively straightforward. The most important issue is the ability to formulate unique cointegration vectors, which involves testing for identification. This is crucial, since the unrestricted estimates of $\boldsymbol{\beta}$ are often hard to interpret in terms of their economic information. In fact, what is increasingly obvious is the need to ensure that prior information motivated by economic arguments forms the basis for imposing restrictions, and not the other way around. To give just a single example of this, Clements and Mizon (1991) estimated a model of the UK labour market involving real average earnings per person-hour (w), the inflation rate (Δp), productivity (y), average hours (a) and the unemployment rate (u). The unrestricted model that they obtained from the Johansen approach was:

$$\boldsymbol{\beta} = \begin{array}{c} \begin{array}{ccccc} w & \Delta p & y & a & u \end{array} \\ \begin{bmatrix} 1 & -0.740 & -0.643 & 6.017 & -9.822 \\ 8.801 & 1 & -0.495 & -7.289 & 14.553 \\ -2.031 & 1.298 & 1 & -5.897 & 7.828 \\ 0.756 & 2.128 & -0.383 & 1 & 12.837 \\ 0.344 & -0.093 & -0.101 & 0.259 & 1 \end{bmatrix} \end{array}$$

On the basis of testing for reduced rank, they found that there were probably three stationary relationships in the model. In terms of their unrestricted results, it is difficult to make immediate sense of all but perhaps the first vector, which seems to be a fairly standard wage equation. Although they do not test for unique cointegration vectors or formally test for identification, they do (on the basis of prior economic information) transform the unrestricted space into the following:

$$\boldsymbol{\beta}' = \begin{array}{c} \begin{array}{ccccc} w & \Delta p & y & a & u \end{array} \\ \begin{bmatrix} 1 & 0.000 & -1.000 & 5.983 & 0.112 \\ 0.037 & 0.000 & 0.037 & 1 & 0.001 \\ 0.100 & -1 & -0.100 & -0.050 & -0.009 \end{bmatrix} \end{array}$$

These restrictions[70] define a system quite different from the original, with the average hours and inflation vectors essentially containing nothing but these variables, while the wage equation remains (minus the inflation variable). This seems more reasonable than the unrestricted estimates and probably would not have been apparent from a more general *ad hoc* approach to imposing restrictions on $\boldsymbol{\beta}$.

But this is a difficult area since the practitioner justifiably wants to limit the number of variables that can enter the model in order to simplify the cointegration relationships, but economic theory may suggest a plethora of relevant variables. Economic models are also subject to debate and part of the role of applied work is to test competing hypotheses. These problems are not new, but

[70] It is hard to be conclusive, because of a lack of information on the restrictions actually imposed (they were arrived at by choosing ξ such that $\boldsymbol{\alpha\beta}' = \boldsymbol{\alpha}\xi^{-1}\xi\boldsymbol{\beta}' = \boldsymbol{\alpha}^*\boldsymbol{\beta}'^*$, where ξ is any $r \times r$ non-singular matrix). However, it appears from applying the test given in (5.6.3) that the third vector is not identified due to the fact that the space spanned by the second vector is contained in the space spanned by this third vector.

the relative newness and difficulty of implementing the Johansen approach gives them a renewed emphasis.

Important Terms and Concepts

Johansen technique	Reduced rank regression	Cointegration relationship
VAR model	VECM model	Testing for cointegration rank
Conditioning on weakly exogenous variables	$I(2)$ models	Pantula principle
Testing for weak exogeneity	Cointegration space	Unique cointegration vectors
Identification of the long-run model		

APPENDIX 1 PROGRAMMING IN SHAZAM: TESTING IDENTIFICATION RESTRICTIONS IN β

```
* See Table 6, Johansen and Juselius (1994)
read h1 / rows=6 cols=3 list
 1 0 0
 0 1 0
-1 0 0
 0 0 0
 0 0 0
 0 0 1
read h2 / rows=6 cols=1 list
 0
 0
 0
 1
-1
 0
read h3 / rows=6 cols=3 list
0 0 0
0 0 0
1 0 0
0 0 0
0 1 0
0 0 1

*****************
* First equation *
*****************
*defining equation 14 in Johansen 1992
matrix m1_22=(h2'h2)-(h2'h1*inv(h1'h1)*h1'h2)
matrix m1_33=(h3'h3)-(h3'h1*inv(h1'h1)*h1'h3)
matrix m1_23=(h2'h3)-(h2'h1*inv(h1'h1)*h1'h3)
matrix m1_32=(h3'h2)-(h3'h1*inv(h1'h1)*h1'h2)
matrix s1=m1_22|m1_23
matrix s2=1_m32|m1_33
matrix m1=(s1'|s2')'

matrix rm1_22=rank(m1_22)'
matrix rm1_33=rank(m1_33)'
matrix rm1_23=rank(m1)'
print rm1_22 rm1_33 rm1_23

******************
* Second equation *
******************
matrix m2_11=(h1'h1)-(h1'h2*inv(h2'h2)*h2'h1)
matrix m2_33=(h3'h3)-(h3'h2*inv(h2'h2)*h2'h3)
matrix m2_13=(h1'h3)-(h1'h2*inv(h2'h2)*h1'h3)
matrix m2_31=(h3'h1)-(h3'h2*inv(h2'h2)*h2'h1)
matrix s1=m2_11|m2_13
matrix s2=m2_31|m2_33
matrix m1=(s1'|s2')'
matrix rm2_11=rank(m2_11)'
matrix rm2_33=rank(m2_33)'
matrix rm2_13=rank(m1)'
print rm2_11 rm2_33 rm2_13

*****************
* Third equation *
*****************
matrix m3_11=(h1'h1)-(h1'h3*inv(h3'h3)*h3'h1)
matrix m3_22=(h2'h2)-(h2'h3*inv(h3'h3)*h3'h2)
matrix m3_12=(h1'h2)-(h1'h3*inv(h3'h3)*h3'h2)
matrix m3_21=(h2'h1)-(h2'h3*inv(h3'h3)*h3'h1)
matrix s1=m3_11|m3_12
matrix s2=m3_21|m23_2
matrix m1=(s1'|s2')'
matrix rm3_11=rank(m3_11)'
matrix rm3_22=rank(m3_22)'
matrix rm3_12=rank(m1)'
print rm3_11 rm3_22 rm3_12
stop
```

6
Modelling the Short-run Multivariate System

INTRODUCTION

Obtaining long-run estimates of the cointegration relationships is only a first step to estimating the complete model. The short-run structure of the model is also important in terms of the information it conveys on the short-run adjustment behaviour of economic variables, and this is likely to be at least as interesting from a policy viewpoint as estimates of the long run. Another important aspect of modelling both the short- and long-run structures of the system is that we can attempt to model the contemporaneous interactions between variables (i.e., we can estimate a simultaneous system), and this then provides an additional layer of valuable information (see Hendry and Doornik, 1994, for a full discussion of this and related issues). The approach adopted here amounts to the following steps and is greatly influenced by the Hendry approach of general-to-specific modelling:

- use the Johansen approach to obtain the long-run cointegration relationships between the variables in the system;
- estimate the short-run vector autoregression (VAR) in error correction form (hence vector error correction model—VECM) with the cointegration relationships explicitly included and obtain a parsimonious representation of the system. This is by custom denoted the parsimonious VAR (PVAR), but seems more aptly designated a parsimonious VECM (PVECM);
- condition on any (weakly) exogenous variables thus obtaining a conditional PVECM model; and
- model any simultaneous effects between the variables in the (conditional) model and test to ensure that the resulting restricted model parsimoniously encompasses the PVECM.

To illustrate these steps the small, UK monetary model presented in Hendry and Doornik (1994) is used (with seasonally *un*adjusted data). Although the final version estimated is different the purpose here is to illustrate the methodology involved, rather than to argue with their model of the money demand function.[1] It will also become apparent that no attempt is made to discuss in depth the full implications and procedures of dynamic modelling. That is beyond the scope of this book, so what follows is in the way of an introduction to (and illustration of) the topic.

Finally, we conclude the chapter with some general comments on structural VAR-modelling, particularly as it relates to the estimation of macroeconomic models.

ESTIMATING THE LONG-RUN COINTEGRATION RELATIONSHIPS

The Johansen approach for obtaining estimates of the long-run relationships between the variables ($\mathbf{z}_t$) in the multivariate model was discussed extensively in the last chapter. Here we present a slightly different version of the UK money demand model that was used to illustrate the approach, as a first step toward estimating the short-run dynamic model.

In the last chapter, it was possible to identify a single cointegration vector describing the stationary relationship between the following $I(1)$ variables: $m - p, y, \Delta p$ and R. Hendry and Mizon (1993) allow for a time trend in the cointegration vectors to take account of long-run exogenous growth not already included in the model.[2] Taking a similar approach with the seasonally unadjusted data set produced the results in Table 6.1 (*PcGive 10.1* was used and all the test statistics reported were defined in the last chapter—thus, for brevity, explanations are not repeated here); both the trace and $\lambda_{\max}$ tests for reduced rank indicate that it is possible to reject the null hypothesis that $r = 1$ at only the 10% level of significance (although both test statistics only just fall short of the 5% critical values). As before the lag length for the VAR is set at $k = 4$, and it was found necessary to condition on a set of $I(0)$ variables $\mathbf{D}_t$,

[1] Of course, economic justification of the final model is usually necessary, but less attention is paid to this aspect of modelling in the example to be presented.

[2] Recall that, on the basis of applying the Pantula principle to testing which version of the deterministic component should be used, it was possible to accept that there is only one cointegration vector and there are deterministic trends in the levels of the data (denoted Model 3). A test for exclusion of the trend term results (using *Microfit 4.0*) in an LR test statistic of 19.35, which is highly significant; in *PcGive 10.1* a model reduction test produces $F(4, 74) = 5.59$, which is again able to reject the exclusion of the trend at better than the 5% significance level. Thus the trend is certainly accepted by the model. Finally, note that the Hendry and Mizon model includes *two* cointegration vectors and a linear trend in the cointegration space.

Table 6.1 Tests of the cointegration rank[a] for the UK money demand data (1963q1–1989q2).

$H_0: r$	$n-r$	λ_i	λ_{max}test	$\lambda_{max}(0.95)$	Trace test	$\lambda_{trace}(0.95)$
0	4	0.586	89.01**	31.8	130.80**	63.0
1	3	0.221	25.24*	25.4	41.76*	42.3
2	2	0.105	11.20	19.2	16.52	25.8
3	1	0.051	5.32	12.4	5.32	12.4

[a] See the discussion of Table 5.4
* Denotes rejection at the 10% significance level.
** Denotes rejection at the 5% significance level.

which included centred seasonal dummy variables and three (impulse) dummies that take account of outliers in the data. Hendry and Mizon include dummies labelled DOIL and DOUT to account for the 'Barber Boom' and the two oil price shocks in the 1970s. Here it was found necessary to include three separate dummies that took on a value of one in 1973q3, 1974q2 and 1977q1. The first two (denoted D_1 and D_2) were necessary to 'induce' normal residuals in the equation determining Δp, while the third dummy (denoted D_3) was sufficient to account for an outlier in the interest rate equation.[3] The model evaluation diagnostic tests are provided in Table 6.2 and show that, generally, the residuals can be considered Gaussian (the only remaining system problem is the rejection of normality at the 5% level). Actual and fitted values for each equation are given in Figure 6.1, while Figures 6.2 and 6.3 present various plots associated with diagnostic testing of the residuals, confirming that, generally, the performance of the VECM is satisfactory.

The two normalized cointegration vectors obtained were $\boldsymbol{\beta}_1' = [1, 0.029, 4.440, 8.063, -0.007]$ and $\boldsymbol{\beta}_2' = [-0.113, 1, -2.893, 0.208, -0.006]$, where the ordering of the elements is $m-p$, y, Δp, R and a time trend. Clearly, the inclusion of the time trend has an adverse (multicollinear) effect on the estimate for y in the money demand function (cf. $\boldsymbol{\beta}_1$). Plots of the cointegration vectors (including actual and fitted values) and recursive estimates of the eigenvalues are presented in Figures 6.4 and 6.5. These indicate that the first two vectors look stationary (although the money demand vector is less so), while the common trends vectors are non-stationary. Estimates of these vectors are relatively stable over time (as shown by the recursively

[3] Note that there is little effect here from ignoring these outliers, but at other times 'factoring out' outliers can be important in terms of the estimates of the cointegration relations. When this occurs, and assuming that there is little prior knowledge available to justify the dummy variables, it becomes a moot point whether conditioning in this fashion is valid. If there are genuine outliers, then it would seem justifiable to 'drop' such observations in terms of their influence on the model. The alternative would be to include other variables that can explain the outliers.

Table 6.2 Model evaluation diagnostics:[a] the UK money demand data (1963q1–1989q2) (an intercept, seasonal dummies and three impulse dummies in $\mathbf{D}_t$; a time trend in the cointegration space).

Statistic	$m-p$	y	Δp	R
Lag length = 4				
$F_{k=1}(4,74)$	8.74**	8.99**	2.12	27.09**
$F_{k=2}(4,74)$	2.02	1.00	2.82*	2.10
$F_{k=3}(4,74)$	1.56	2.87*	0.54	0.05
$F_{k=4}(4,74)$	6.21**	3.28*	0.89	0.66
σ	1.54%	1.61%	0.61%	1.26%
$F_{\text{ar}}(5,72)$	1.29	1.97	1.05	0.98
$F_{\text{arch}}(4,69)$	0.76	1.12	0.73	1.68
$F_{\text{het}}(34,42)$	0.35	0.65	0.88	0.94
$\chi^2_{\text{nd}}(2)$	3.52	5.02	4.62	1.10

Multivariate tests: $F_{\text{ar}}(80,215)=0.93$; $F_{\text{het}}(340,345)=0.53$; $\chi^2_{\text{nd}}(8)=16.42$*; $F_{\text{ur}}(68,292)=127.58$**; AIC $=-35.2067$.

[a] See the discussion of Tables 5.1 and 5.3 on p. 116.
* Denotes rejection at the 5% significance level.
** Denotes rejection at the 1% significance level.

obtained eigenvalues, which were generally constant). Thus, the following tests of hypotheses were conducted with respected to $\boldsymbol{\beta}$:

$$\boldsymbol{\beta}' = \begin{bmatrix} -1 & 1 & * & * & 0 \\ 0 & -1 & * & * & * \end{bmatrix}$$

These satisfy the conditions for identification,[4] as can be determined from the fact that each vector has at least one variable unique to it. The tests of the restrictions on the cointegration vectors were conducted jointly with a test of the hypothesis that y and R are weakly exogenous (i.e., $H: \alpha_{2j} = \alpha_{4j} = 0$ for $j = 1, 2$). The results, obtained using *PcGive 10.1*, are given in Box 6.1, indicating that the restrictions are acceptable. It is also possible to test whether Δp is 'weakly exogenous' in the money demand equation (i.e., $H: \alpha_{31} = 0$) and separately whether $m-p$ is 'weakly exogenous' in the other equation (i.e., $H: \alpha_{12} = 0$). The overall likelihood ratio (LR) test statistic obtained when these additional restrictions are imposed is a test statistic of 6.82, which is not very significant under the $\chi^2(7)$ distribution.[5] This indicates that only the money demand long-run relationship enters the short-run error correction

[4] In terms of Box 5.6, $\text{rank}(\mathbf{R}_1'\mathbf{H}_2) = 2$ and $\text{rank}(\mathbf{R}_2'\mathbf{H}_1) = 1$ (i.e., both have a rank at least equal to 1).

[5] This use of the term 'weakly exogeneous' when testing the significance of a single element in $\boldsymbol{\alpha}$ will be clarified when estimating the structural short-run model below, where we find evidence to suggest that in a system of simultaneous equations there is support for the notion that changes in prices 'cause' changes in the money supply.

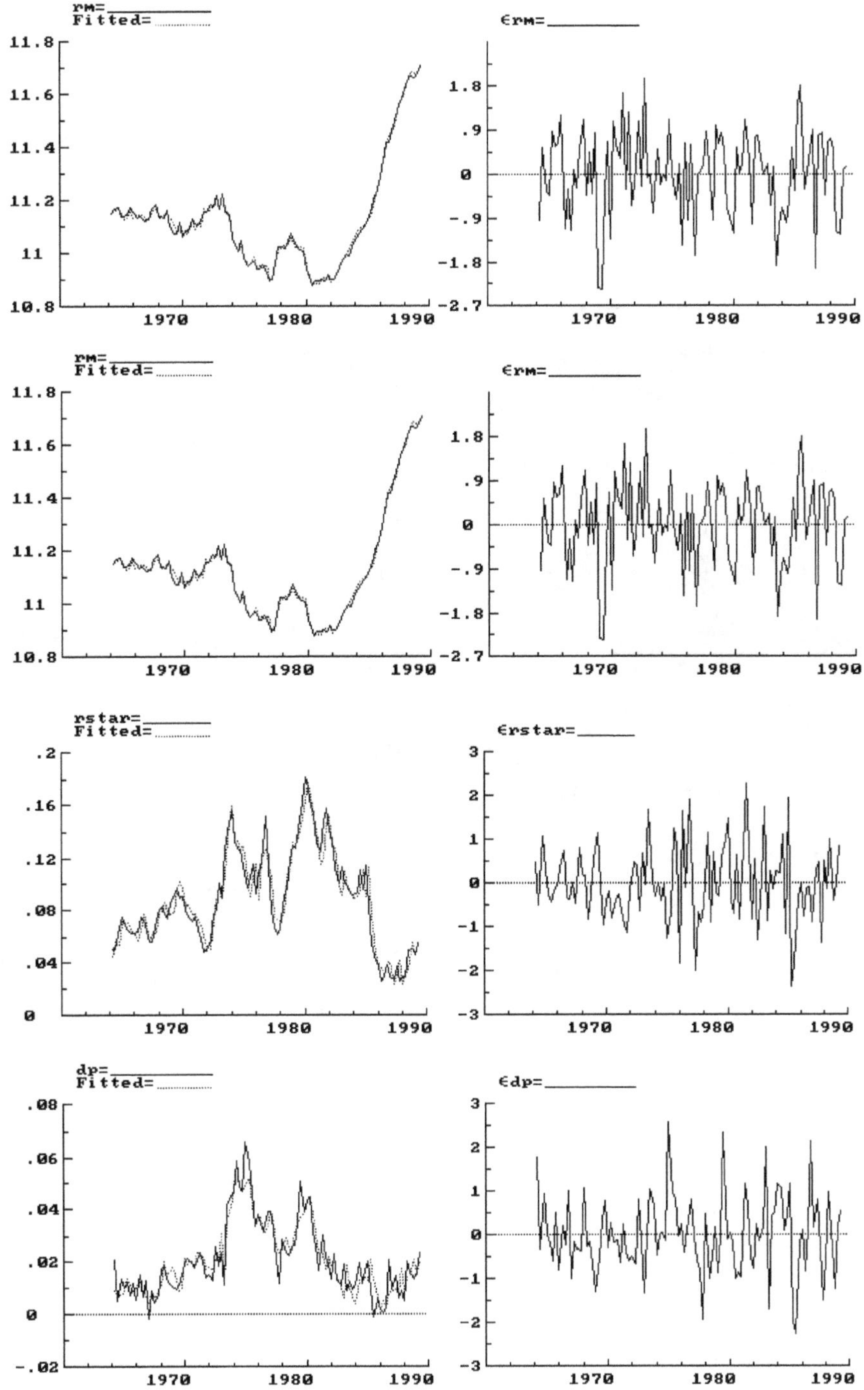

Figure 6.1. Actual and fitted values and scaled residuals.

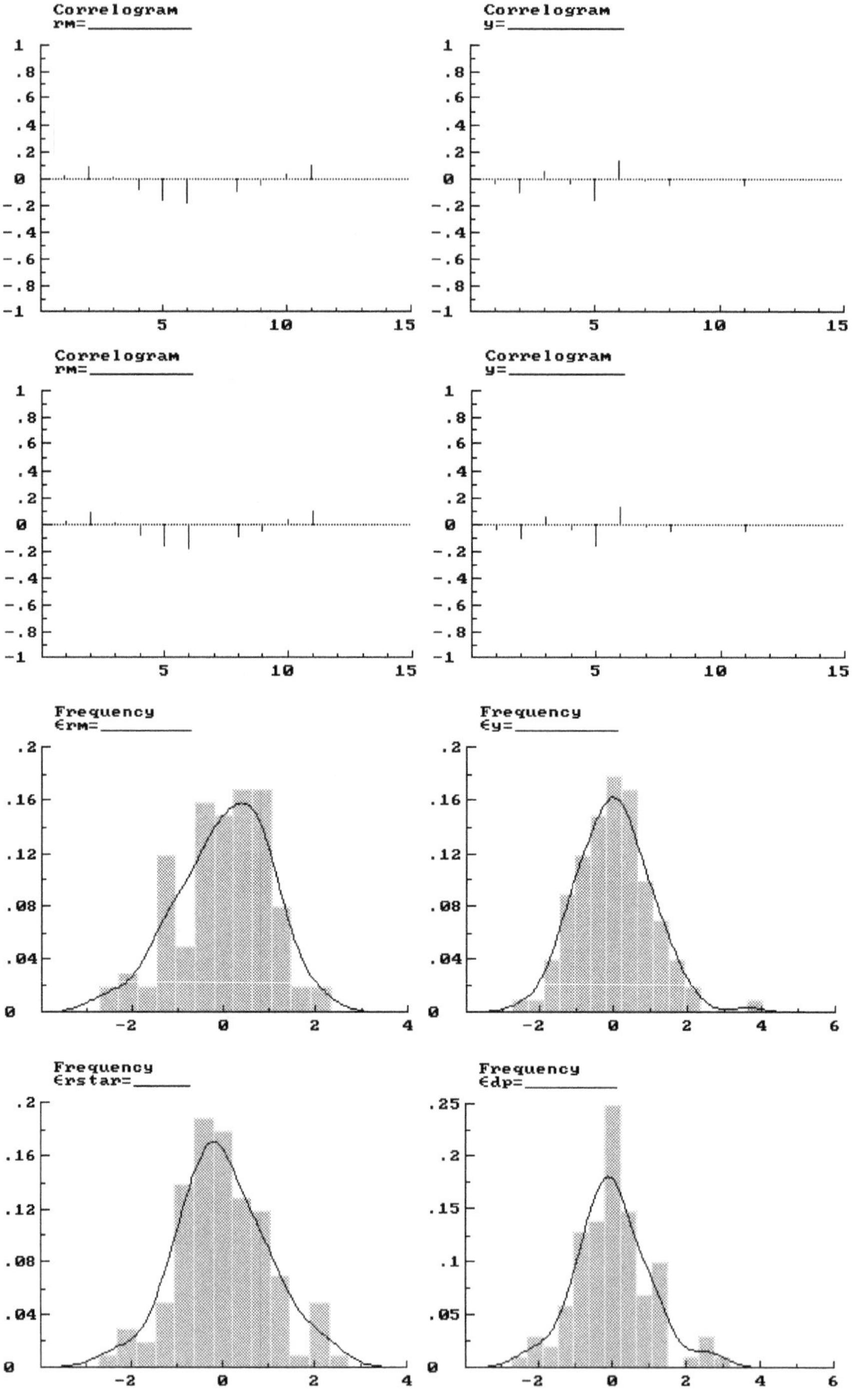

Figure 6.2. Diagnostic graphs of the residuals: correlogram and distribution.

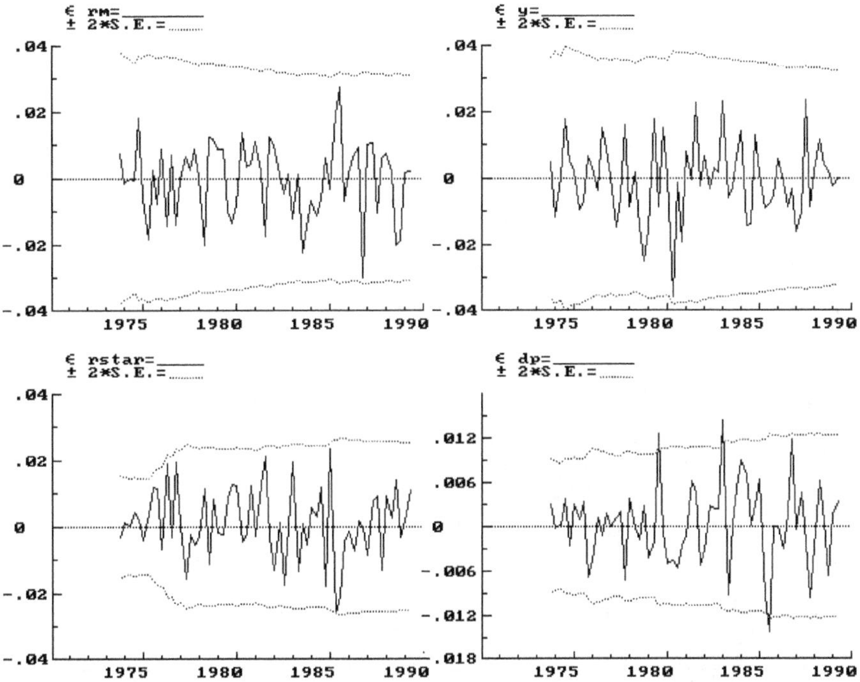

Figure 6.3. Diagnostic graphs of the residuals: one-step residuals.

model (ECM) determining $\Delta(m-p)$, while only the second cointegration relationship enters a short-run ECM determining $\Delta^2 p$.

Thus, the outcome of the cointegration analysis is the following two long-run relationships:

$$\left.\begin{aligned} \hat{\boldsymbol{\beta}}_1'\tilde{\mathbf{z}} &= m - p - y + 6.14\Delta p + 6.71R \\ \hat{\boldsymbol{\beta}}_2'\tilde{\mathbf{z}} &= y - 0.007t - 2.54\Delta p + 1.22R \end{aligned}\right\} \quad (6.1)$$

which define the error correction terms to be included when estimating the VECM. Note that $\tilde{\mathbf{z}}_t = [(m-p)_t, y_t, \Delta p_t, R_t, t]'$, while $\mathbf{z}_t$ has no time trend in the vector.

To reiterate, the first relationship is the standard money demand relationship, while the second vector is deemed to represent 'excess demand' with the deviation of output from trend having a significant positive relationship to inflation and a negative one to the interest rate. Note that Figure 6.4 shows that disequilibrium is large in the money demand equation (as can be seen by comparing the actual and fitted values), but less so in the 'excess demand' relation, although since all the speed-of-adjustment parameters are small in value (cf. the estimates of $\boldsymbol{\alpha}$ in Box 6.1), both the money supply and

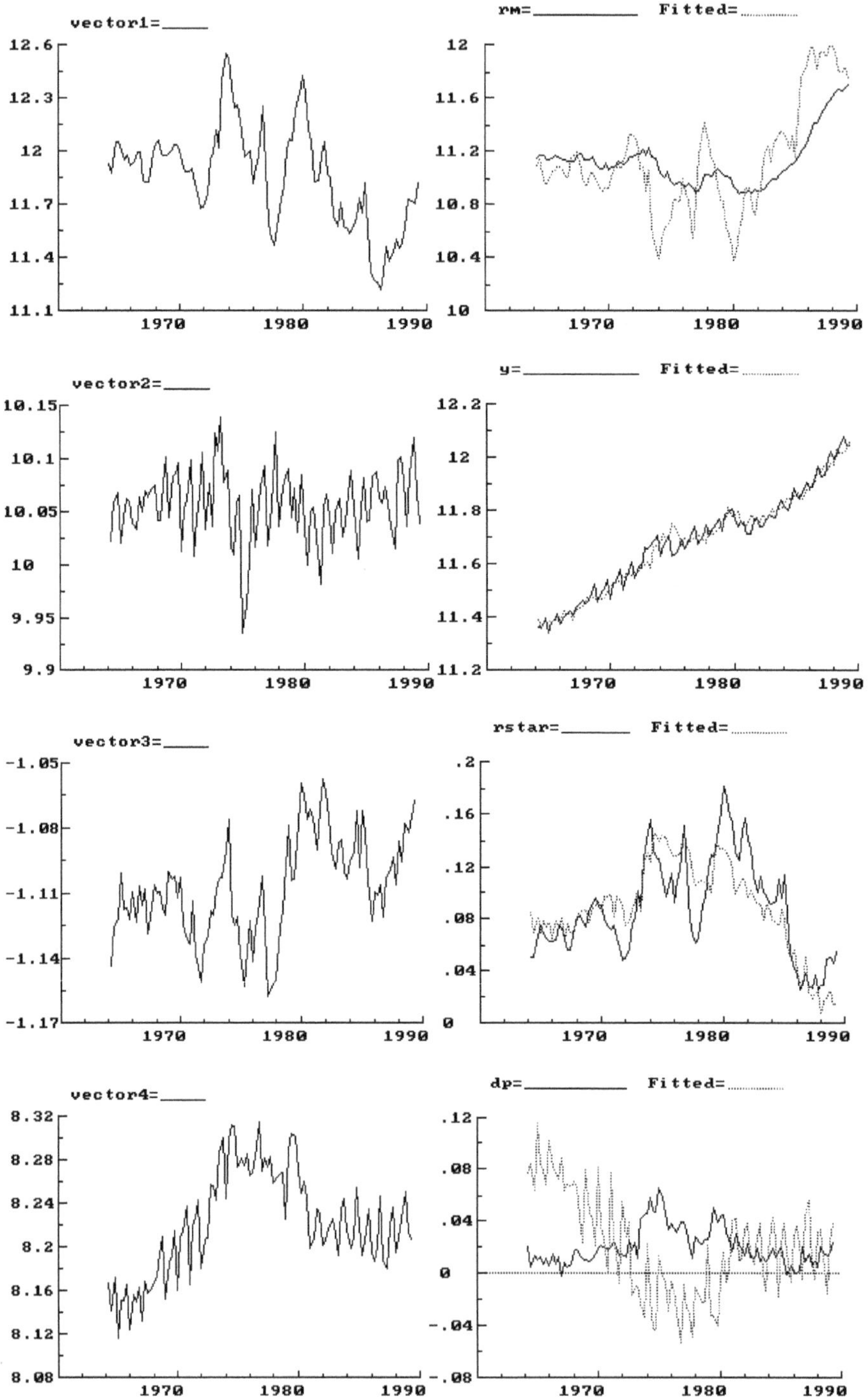

Figure 6.4. Plots of the relations $\mathbf{v}_i'\mathbf{Z}_t$ (those that cointegrate can be denoted as $\hat{\boldsymbol{\beta}}_i'\mathbf{z}_t$).

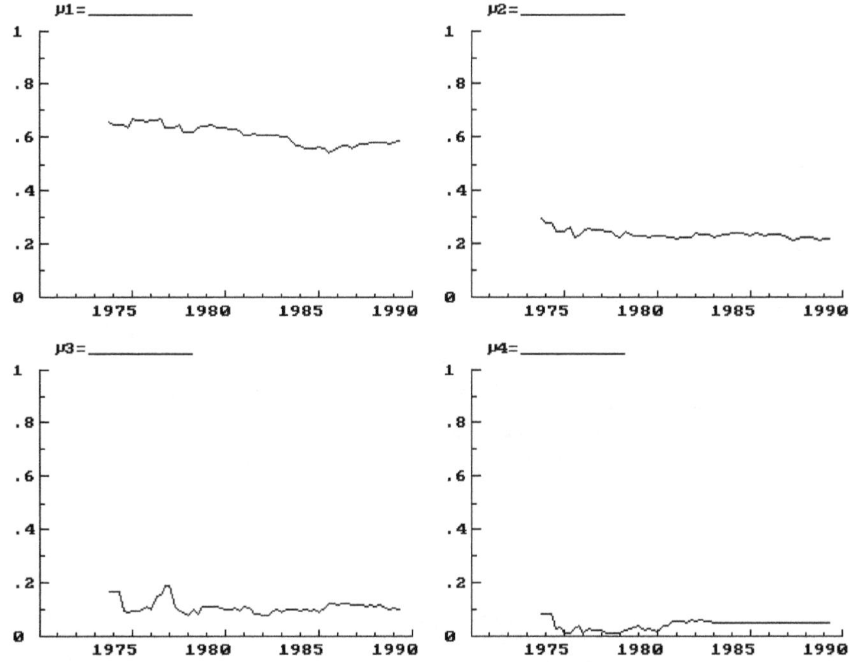

Figure 6.5. Recursive estimates of the eigenvalues associated with the relations $\mathbf{v}_i'\mathbf{z}_t$.

inflation adjust relatively slowly to changes to the underlying equilibrium relationship.

PARSIMONIOUS VECM

Having obtained the long-run cointegration relations using the Johansen approach, it is now possible to reformulate the above model and estimate the VECM with the error correction terms explicitly included:

$$\Delta \mathbf{z}_t = \Gamma_1 \Delta \mathbf{z}_{t-1} + \Gamma_2 \Delta \mathbf{z}_{t-2} + \Gamma_3 \Delta \mathbf{z}_{t-3} + \boldsymbol{\alpha}(\hat{\boldsymbol{\beta}}_1' \tilde{\mathbf{z}}_{t-1} + \hat{\boldsymbol{\beta}}_2' \tilde{\mathbf{z}}_{t-1}) + \Psi \mathbf{D}_t + \mathbf{u}_t \quad (6.2)$$

It makes no difference whether $\tilde{\mathbf{z}}_t$ enters the error correction term with a lag of $t-1$ or $t-k$, since these two forms of (6.2) can be shown to be equivalent. At this stage no separate restrictions are placed on each α_{ij} (even though the above testing of weak exogeneity in the long-run model indicates that only one cointegration relationship is present in each equation and therefore that it is appropriate to place restrictions on $\boldsymbol{\alpha}$). Thus ordinary least squares (OLS) is still an efficient way to estimate each equation comprising (6.2),

Box 6.1 Testing joint restrictions on α and β: PcGive 10.1 output for the UK money demand model.

Testing Restrictions on α and β

The LR test, $\chi^2(5) = 3.60$, p-value = 0.61

Normalised (Based on 2 cointegration vector; t-values in parenthesis)

β'

m - p	y	Δp	R	time
-1.000	1.000	-6.541	-6.657	0.000
		(-7.37)	(-19.64)	
0.000	-1.000	2.809	-1.136	0.007
		(6.02)	(-5.87)	(32.46)

α'

0.179	0.000	-0.012	0.000
(9.63)		(-1.49)	
0.083	0.000	-0.152	0.000
(1.12)		(-4.91)	

Testing Restrictions on α and β

The LR test, $\chi^2(7) = 6.82$, p-value = 0.45

Normalised (Based on 2 cointegration vector; t-values in parenthesis)

β'

m - p	y	Δp	R	time
-1.000	1.000	-6.142	-6.713	0.000
		(-7.21)	(-20.63)	
0.000	-1.000	2.539	-1.225	0.007
		(5.84)	(-6.80)	(35.59)

α'

0.179	0.000	0.000	0.000
(10.32)			
0.000	0.000	-0.152	0.000
		(-5.52)	

given that each has a common set of (lagged) regressors. Since all the variables in the model are now $I(0)$, statistical inference using standard t- and F-tests is valid.

Estimating the multivariate system denoted by (6.2) confirms the above

Table 6.3 Certain model evaluation diagnostics relating to equation (6.2) (an intercept, seasonal dummies and three impulse dummies in $\mathbf{D}_t$).

Statistic	$\Delta(m-p)$	Δy	$\Delta^2 p$	ΔR
Lag length = 3				
$F_{i=1}(4, 77)$	4.64**	1.98	5.24**	3.17*
$F_{i=2}(4, 77)$	7.61**	0.71	2.02	0.30
$F_{i=3}(4, 77)$	6.34**	3.22*	0.98	0.59
t-tests of significance				
$\boldsymbol{\beta}_1'\mathbf{z}_{t-1}$	−7.63**	−0.35	0.70	−0.35
$\boldsymbol{\beta}_2'\mathbf{z}_{t-1}$	−1.62	−0.13	4.99**	1.42

* Denotes rejection at the 5% significance level.
** Denotes rejection at the 1% significance level.

tests of weak exogeneity[6] and tests whether all the (common) lagged $\Delta\mathbf{z}_{t-i}$ are significant in every equation (see Table 6.3). Thus, parsimony can be achieved by removing the insignificant regressors and testing whether this reduction in the model is supported by an F-test.[7] In fact dropping all non-significant lagged terms in Table 6.3 gave a test statistic of $F(24, 269) = 1.21$, which results in an acceptance of the null hypothesis that the omitted regressors have zero coefficients. Finally, the resultant model was checked in terms of diagnostic tests on the residuals (cf. Table 6.2)[8] together with checks that parameter constancy holds (involving graphs of the recursive properties of the model, such as one-step residuals and Chow F-tests for break points in the individual equations and in the system as a whole). Although these tests are not reported here, the parsimonious reduced-form system is (generally) congruent as defined by the Hendry general-to-specific approach to modelling.

[6] By considering the statistical significance of the $\Delta\mathbf{z}_{t-i}$ in each equation, it is also possible to test whether each variable in the model Granger-causes any other variable. Lagged values of ΔR are not significant in the equation determining Δy (hence interest rates do not Granger-cause output), while output does not Granger-cause inflation. Lastly, lagged values of $\Delta(m-p)$, Δy and $\Delta^2 p$ are not significant in the equation determining ΔR. Thus, since y and R are weakly exogenous in the system, we can surmise that interest rates are strongly exogenous with respect to output and output is strongly exogenous with respect to inflation.

[7] Note that we retain a common set of (lagged) regressors—deletions are with respect to all equations, thus OLS is still applicable.

[8] These were 'acceptable', except that the test for autoregressive conditional heteroseedasticity (ARCH) in the interest rate equation rejects the null at less than the 1% significance level, while there are some problems of non-normal residuals in the output equation. Thus, a model conditioning on these variables would be useful.

CONDITIONAL PVECM

From tests involving the long-run model as well as tests of the significance of the error correction terms in the PVECM, it is possible to accept that y and R are weakly exogenous in the system under investigation. Therefore, we can condition on these two variables, assuming that we are more concerned with modelling money demand and inflation. Hendry and Doornik (1994) retain the full system and thus continue to model the weakly exogenous variables.[9] Thus, our system is now defined as (see also equation (5.8)):

$$\begin{aligned}\Delta\mathbf{y}_t &= \Gamma_0\Delta\mathbf{x}_t + \Gamma_1\Delta\mathbf{z}_{t-1} + \Gamma_2\Delta\mathbf{z}_{t-2} + \Gamma_3\Delta\mathbf{z}_{t-3} \\ &\quad + \boldsymbol{\alpha}_1(\hat{\boldsymbol{\beta}}_1'\tilde{\mathbf{z}}_{t-1} + \hat{\boldsymbol{\beta}}_2'\tilde{\mathbf{z}}_{t-1}) + \Psi\mathbf{D}_t + \mathbf{u}_t \end{aligned} \tag{6.3}$$

where $\mathbf{y}_t = [(m-p)_t, \Delta p_t]'$ and $\mathbf{x}_t = [Y_t, R_t]'$ and $\boldsymbol{\alpha}_1$ is equal to $\boldsymbol{\alpha}$ with $\alpha_{2j} = \alpha_{4j} = 0$ for $j = 1, 2$. It is possible to test for a parsimonious version of (6.3), where non-significant (common) lagged $\Delta\mathbf{z}_{t-i}$ are removed and the resulting reduction in the model is supported by an F-test.

The results from estimating the parsimonious version of the conditional model are given in Table 6.4. The various diagnostic tests of the residuals indicate that the model has the desired properties for OLS estimation, other than an indication that the rate of inflation equation has non-normal errors. However, multivariate tests are satisfactory.[10] The correlation of actual and fitted values is 0.90 and 0.81, respectively, for the $\Delta(m-p)_t$ and $\Delta^2 p_t$ equations. Earlier tests indicated that the money demand error correction term (cointegration relationship) is only significant in the first equation, while the 'excess demand' ECM is only significant in the second equation; however, both long-run cointegration relations appear to be significant in the money demand equation in Table 6.4. The coefficients attached to these terms (i.e., the speed of adjustment to disequilibrium) are not dissimilar to those obtained using the Johansen approach (see Box 6.1), except for the second relation in the model for the real money demand.

STRUCTURAL MODELLING

A major feature of the last model is the rather large correlation of −0.21 between the residuals of the two equations. This suggests that the money demand and rate of inflation equations are not independent of each other, but rather that there are simultaneous effects between $\Delta(m-p)_t$ and $\Delta^2 p_t$ that could be modelled by imposing some structure on the conditional PVECM.[11] That is, it might seem reasonable to presume that $\Delta(m-p)_t$ con-

[9] In fact, their estimated equations for Δy_t and ΔR_t amount to marginal equations where each dependent variable is regressed on lags of itself, the DOIL dummy and the 'excess demand' cointegration vector.

[10] Plots and graphs including recursive statistics are also satisfactory, although not shown here.

[11] Alternatively, as Doornik and Hendry (2001) state, the observed correlation between the residuals may result from other influences, such as cross-correlated random shocks or common omitted variables.

Table 6.4 OLS estimates of the conditional model.

Variable	$\Delta(m-p)_t$		$\Delta^2 p_t$	
	Coefficient	t-values	Coefficient	t-values
ΔR_t	−0.537	−4.56	0.152	3.43
ΔR_{t-1}	0.521	3.26	−0.151	−2.53
$\Delta^2 p_{t-1}$	0.604	2.86	−0.355	−4.49
$\Delta(m-p)_{t-1}$	−0.370	−4.27	0.074	2.27
$\Delta(m-p)_{t-2}$	−0.420	−4.72	0.143	4.28
$\Delta(m-p)_{t-3}$	−0.374	−5.20	0.051	1.91
$\hat{\boldsymbol{\beta}}'_1\tilde{\mathbf{z}}_{t-1}$	−0.174	−10.40	0.006	0.95
$\hat{\boldsymbol{\beta}}'_2\tilde{\mathbf{z}}_{t-1}$	−0.133	−2.25	0.154	6.94
D_1	−0.010	−0.62	0.015	2.54
D_2	0.059	3.64	−0.025	−4.09
Constant	1.549	2.31	−1.751	−6.96
SEAS[a]	−0.021	−4.05	−0.004	−2.03
SEAS_{t-1}	−0.009	−1.64	0.007	3.40
SEAS_{t-2}	−0.008	−1.39	0.003	1.54
Diagnostics				
$\hat{\sigma}$	1.46%		0.55%	
$F_{\text{ar}}(5.82)$[b]	1.17		1.19	
$F_{\text{arch}}(4, 79)$	0.48		0.76	
$F_{\text{het}}(16, 70)$	0.80		0.84	
$\chi^2_{\text{nd}}(2)$	1.34		6.83*	

Multivariate tests: $F_{\text{ar}}(20, 152) = 1.29$; $F_{\text{het}}(48, 203) = 0.76$; $\chi^2_{\text{nd}}(4) = 6.97$; $F_{\text{ur}}(16, 172) = 24.01$**

[a] SEAS = Seasonal dummies.
[b] See the discussion of Tables 5.1 and 5.3.
* Denotes rejection at the 5% significance level.
** Denotes rejection at the 1% significance level.

temporaneously depends on $\Delta^2 p_t$. To ignore this information, if it is correct, means that OLS estimation of the PVECM will be inconsistent.

Estimation of a structural model requires the inclusion of those endogenous variables that determine other endogenous variables, as additional right-hand-side regressors in the relevant equation (see Box 6.2 for a discussion of structural models and their identification). The model also requires to be identified, which among other requirements means that no more than $\ell = (n \times (k-1)) + r$ regressors can enter any equation and no more than $n \times \ell$ unknowns can enter the model (excluding intercepts and other deterministic components in $\mathbf{D}_t$).[12] Identification also requires that no equation can be

[12] Recall that n is the number of variables in $\mathbf{z}_t$, k is the lag length of the VAR and r is the number of cointegration relationships that enter the short-run ECM.

Box 6.2 Structural models and identification.

The structural VECM counterpart of the example used here requires the reduced form (6.2) to be reformulated as:

$$\begin{aligned}\mathbf{A}_0\Delta\mathbf{z}_t &= \mathbf{A}_1\Delta\mathbf{z}_{t-1} + \mathbf{A}_2\Delta\mathbf{z}_{t-2} + \mathbf{A}_3\Delta\mathbf{z}_{t-3} + \mathbf{a}(\hat{\boldsymbol{\beta}}_1'\tilde{\mathbf{z}}_{t-1} + \hat{\boldsymbol{\beta}}_2'\tilde{\mathbf{z}}_{t-1}) \\ &\quad + \tilde{\boldsymbol{\Psi}}\mathbf{D}_t + \varepsilon_t \qquad (6.2.1) \\ \varepsilon_t &\sim \text{IN}(0, \Omega)\end{aligned}$$

where $\mathbf{A}_i = \mathbf{A}_0\Gamma_i$ for $i = 1, 2$ and 3, $\mathbf{a} = \mathbf{A}_0\boldsymbol{\alpha}$; $\boldsymbol{\Psi} = \mathbf{A}_0\boldsymbol{\Psi}$; $\Omega = \mathbf{A}_0\Sigma\mathbf{A}_0'$; and $\varepsilon_t = \mathbf{A}_0\mathbf{u}_t$. That is, (6.2.1) is obtained by pre-multiplying the reduced form through by the $(n \times n)$ matrix $\mathbf{A}_0$, where the latter specifies the structure that links the endogenous variables in the model. To see this, assume for the moment that $k = 2$ (this will simplify notation by removing the terms involving $\mathbf{A}_2\Delta\mathbf{z}_{t-2}$ and $\mathbf{A}_3\Delta\mathbf{z}_{t-3}$), ignore the term $\tilde{\boldsymbol{\Psi}}\mathbf{D}_t$ and write out the left-hand side of the structural VECM given in (6.2.1):

$$\begin{bmatrix} 1 & A_{12} & A_{13} & A_{14} \\ A_{21} & 1 & A_{23} & A_{24} \\ A_{31} & A_{32} & 1 & A_{34} \\ A_{41} & A_{42} & A_{43} & 1 \end{bmatrix} \begin{bmatrix} \Delta(m-p)_t \\ \Delta y_t \\ \Delta^2 p_t \\ \Delta R_t \end{bmatrix} = \mathbf{A}_1\Delta\mathbf{z}_{t-1} + \mathbf{a}(\hat{\boldsymbol{\beta}}_1'\tilde{\mathbf{z}}_{t-1} + \hat{\boldsymbol{\beta}}_2'\tilde{\mathbf{z}}_{t-1}) + \varepsilon_t \qquad (6.2.2)$$

As can be seen, the parameters A_{ij} contemporaneously link all the endogenous variables in $\mathbf{z}_t$. To proceed to the identification of the short-run dynamic model, (6.2.1) can be rewritten in compact notation as:

$$\mathbf{A}'\mathbf{X}_t = \tilde{\boldsymbol{\Psi}}\mathbf{D}_t + \varepsilon_t \qquad (6.2.3)$$

where $\mathbf{A}' = [\mathbf{A}_0, \mathbf{A}_1, \mathbf{A}_2, \mathbf{A}_3, \mathbf{a}]$ is a $((n + l) \times n)$ matrix, with $l = (n \times (k-1)) + r$, and where $\mathbf{X}_t' = [\Delta\mathbf{z}_t', \Delta\mathbf{z}_{t-1}', \Delta\mathbf{z}_{t-2}', \Delta\mathbf{z}_{t-3}', \tilde{\mathbf{z}}_{t-1}'\hat{\boldsymbol{\beta}}]$. Identification in the short-run model requires restrictions on the structural equations and, in particular, restrictions on $\mathbf{A}$. These restrictions are typically determined by economic theory, and as Johnston (1984, p. 453, his italics) explains '... the most common restrictions are *exclusion* restrictions, which specify that certain variables do *not* appear in certain equations.' However, homogeneity restrictions are also fairly common, and in general Johansen and Juselius (1994) show that identifying restrictions on the columns of $\mathbf{A}$, denoted as $(\mathbf{A}_1, \ldots, \mathbf{A}_{n+l})$, take the form:

$$A = (\mathbf{H}_1\boldsymbol{\varphi}_1, \mathbf{H}_2\boldsymbol{\varphi}_2, \ldots, \mathbf{H}_{n+l}\boldsymbol{\varphi}_{n+l}) \qquad (6.2.4)$$

which can be checked by the rank order condition as set out in (5.6.3), with $k = n - 1$, together with the computational procedure they suggest for obtaining the rank orders (see the discussion in the last chapter surrounding equation 5.6.3).

a linear combination of other equations, and thus the actual location of the restrictions placed on an unrestricted structural VECM (which has $n \times (n + l)$ potential regressors) is an important element in identifying unique short-run equations. As a very general guide, each equation in the model requires at least one unique predetermined variable (entering with a non-zero coefficient) to identify it, and in the example used here we know from earlier testing that the money demand error correction term enters only the equation determining $\Delta(m-p)_t$, while the 'excess demand' term only enters the $\Delta^2 p_t$ equation.[13]

Estimating the structural model and then dropping insignificant regressors gave the estimates reported in Table 6.5. The χ^2 test of the null hypothesis that these regressors are zero resulted in a test statistic of 4.54 (with 2 degrees of freedom), and the null is consequently accepted. More importantly, since the structural model has 25 parameters against 28 in the conditional PVECM (Table 6.4) the LR test of over-identifying restrictions is given by $\chi^2(3) = 5.57$, which does not reject. So the structural model can be said to parsimoniously encompass the conditional PVECM. Other tests of whether the model is congruent with the data evidence are provided in Table 6.5 and in Figures 6.6–6.9. The model has generally constant coefficients (Figure 6.7 shows one-step residuals and Figure 6.8 shows Chow tests for breaks in the series) and approximately 'white noise', normally distributed errors (cf. the test statistics in Table 6.5). The model appears to 'fit' the data quite well (Figure 6.6), and the parameter estimates are generally sensible (and not very different to those in Hendry and Doornik, 1994). In economic terms the model supports the contention that causality is from output, interest rates and prices to money.[14,15] Moreover, the correlation between the structural residuals

[13] Given the results of the parsimonious conditional model, the 'excess demand' term is a candidate for inclusion in the equation determining $\Delta(m-p)_t$, although when we allow for its inclusion it is once again insignificant. Note that we could achieve identification by omitting other variables that proved insignificant in the parsimonious model.

[14] Note that this highlights the care that needs to be taken when speaking of weak exogeneity with respect to variables in a single equation. Earlier tests involving the long-run model found that y and R are weakly exogenous to the system, Δp is weakly exogenous in the money demand equation and $m - p$ is weakly exogenous in the price equation. However, what the latter tests actually established was that the money demand cointegration relationship does not enter the short-run model determining Δp and the 'excess demand' long-run relationship does not enter the short-run equation determining $m - p$. Clearly, the FIML results suggest that changes in prices cause changes in the money supply.

[15] Changing the simultaneous model around so that $\Delta(m-p)_t$ enters as a regressor in the equation determining $\Delta^2 p_t$ is unsuccessful. First, the test of over-identifying restrictions is $\chi^2(6) = 14.67$, which rejects at the 5% level. Thus, this form of the structural model can*not* be said to parsimoniously encompass the conditional PVECM. Moreover, the coefficient on $\Delta(m-p)_t$ is not significantly different from zero in the $\Delta^2 p_t$ equation, and the correlation between the structural residuals obtained from the FIML model is now -0.29, indicating a failure to model the structure underlying the data evidence that is available.

Table 6.5 Full information maximum likelihood (FIML) estimates of the conditional model.

Variable	$\Delta(m-p)_t$		$\Delta^2 p_t$	
	Coefficient	t-values	Coefficient	t-values
$\Delta^2 p_t$	−1.152	−4.09	—	—
ΔR_t	−0.331	−2.65	0.160	3.60
ΔR_{t-1}	0.400	2.65	−0.102	
$\Delta^2 p_{t-1}$	—		−0.347	−4.61
$\Delta(m-p)_{t-1}$	−0.298	−3.23	0.065	2.52
$\Delta(m-p)_{t-2}$	−0.249	−3.17	0.127	4.73
$\Delta(m-p)_{t-3}$	−0.333	−4.82	—	—
$\hat{\boldsymbol{\beta}}_1'\tilde{\mathbf{z}}_{t-1}$	−0.164	−10.80	—	—
$\hat{\boldsymbol{\beta}}_2'\tilde{\mathbf{z}}_{t-1}$	—	—	0.151	7.22
D_1	0.007	0.41	0.013	2.24
D_2	0.036	2.16	−0.026	−4.25
Constant	0.037	10.30	−1.720	−7.23
SEAS[a]	−0.023	−4.76	−0.002	−1.30
SEAS_{t-1}	−0.001	−0.20	0.009	4.93
SEAS_{t-2}	−0.003	−0.56	0.005	2.80
Diagnostics				
$\hat{\sigma}$	1.45%		0.55%	

Multivariate tests:[b] $F_{\text{ar}}(20, 156) = 1.22$; $F_{\text{het}}(48, 208) = 0.79$; $\chi^2_{\text{nd}}(4) = 7.44$.

[a] SEAS = Seasonal.
[b] See the discussion of Tables 5.1 and 5.3.

obtained from the FIML model is 0.01, indicating some success in modelling the structure underlying the data evidence that is available. Figure 6.9 shows dynamic (ex-post) forecasts for the last two years of the data (together with a small sample of the pre-forecast data); none of the forecasts lie outside their individual confidence bars, and therefore constancy of the model is readily accepted. The root mean square error (and mean absolute error) values (see Chapter 8 for a discussion of forecast evaluation tests) for $\Delta(r-m)_t$ and $\Delta^2 p_t$ are 0.018 (0.147) and 0.005 (0.072), respectively. When sets of variables are cointegrated, their out-of-sample forecasts are tied together as well, and thus forecasts tend to be better than when no cointegration restrictions are imposed (Lin and Tsay, 1996). However, Hendry and Clements (2002) point out that if the cointegration vectors are unstable (non-constant over time), then mean shifts can have a particularly detrimental effect on forecasting. There is little evidence (cf. Figure 6.5) of any instability in the long-run part of the model considered here.

While the forecasts produced in Figure 6.9 are included more as a diagnostic tool for the adequacy of the model, out-of-sample forecasts require that

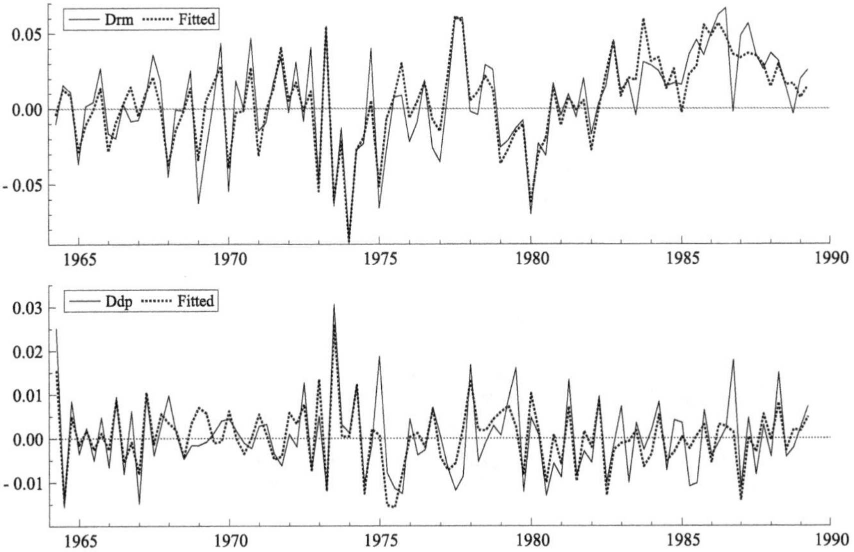

Figure 6.6. Actual and fitted values: short-run model.

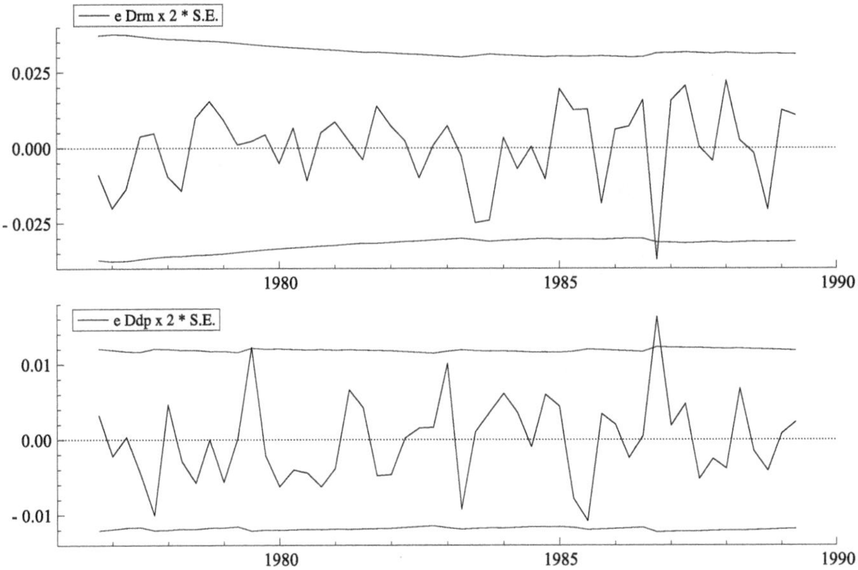

Figure 6.7. Diagnostic one-step residuals: short-run model.

the cointegration vectors are stable and that the variables 'driving' the model are not only weakly exogenous but also strongly exogenous, otherwise the forecasts are not meaningful. That is, past values of the endogenous variables in the model should not determine the interest rate (ΔR_t) in the structural model estimated in Table 6.5. To check for strong exogeneity, we test whether lagged values of $\Delta^2 p_{t-i}$, and $\Delta(m-p)_{t-i}$, are significant in a model

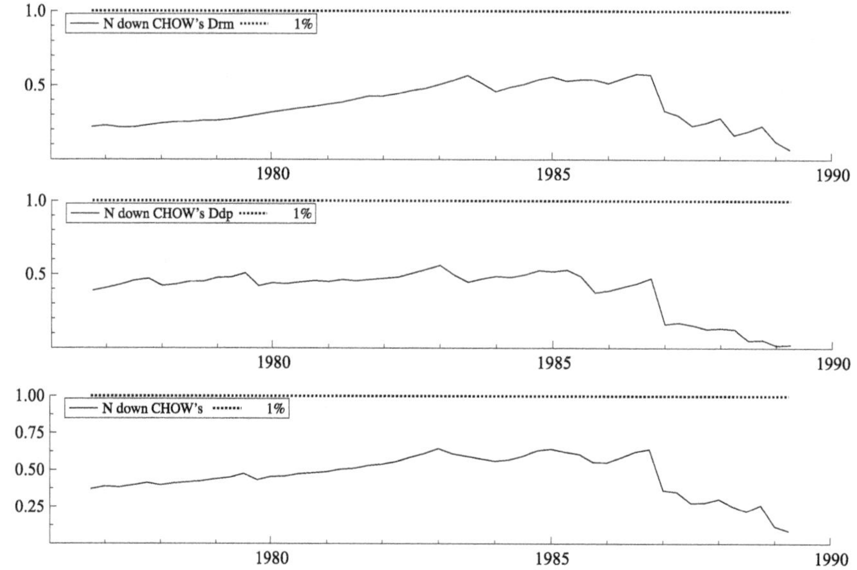

Figure 6.8. Diagnostic Chow tests of parameter stability: short-run model.

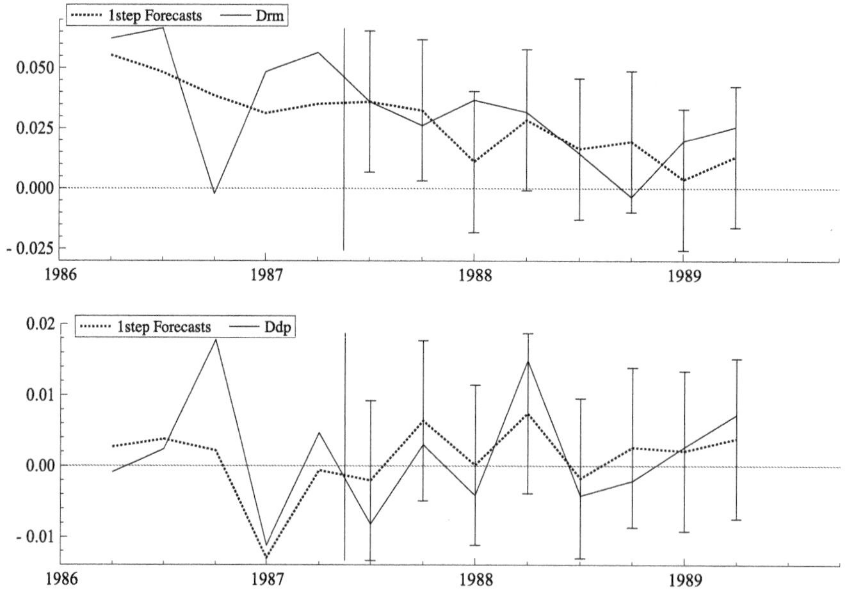

Figure 6.9. One-step model-based forecasts: short-run model.

determining ΔR_t (when the lags ΔR_{t-i} are also included as determinants). If we can accept $H_0 : \Delta(m-p)_{t-i} = 0$, then the money supply is said not to Granger-cause interest rates and R_t is strongly exogenous with respect to $(m-p)_t$ (given that it has already been established that interest rates are weakly exogenous—

see Chapter 1 for a discussion of exogeneity). Undertaking such a test (with i set equal to 3) produced an $F(8, 84)$ statistic of 1.67, which is not significant at the 10% level. Similarly, the test statistic for whether inflation Granger-causes interest rates was $F(4, 84) = 1.11$. Therefore we can conclude that interest rates are strongly exogenous in this model.

One further test of exogeneity is whether interest rates are super-exogenous, as this is important for policy purposes in order to avoid the Lucas Critique (see Chapter 1). Hendry (1995, p. 536) constructed a policy dummy (Pol_t) to take account of regime shifts in interest rates (taking on a value of unity in 1973q3, 1976q4 and 1985q1; -1 in 1977q1 and 1985q2; and 0.5 in 1979q3 and 1979q4), and when we use this to estimate the marginal model ΔR_t we obtain the following outcome (which is almost identical to Hendry's results):

$$\Delta R_t = \underset{(-0.59)}{-0.001} + \underset{(3.55)}{0.291}\Delta R_{t-1} + \underset{(7.28)}{0.035}Pol_t \tag{6.4}$$

Diagnostics

$R^2 = 0.371$; $F(2, 98) = 28.84$ [0.000]; $\sigma = 0.011$; DW $= 2.16$; AR 1–5 $F(5, 93) = 1.93$ [0.097]; ARCH 4 $F(4, 90) = 2.025$ [0.097]; X_i^2 $F(4, 93) = 0.338$ [0.851]; RESET $F(1, 97) = 0.760$ [0.386]; normality $\chi^2(2) = 0.222$ [0.895]; instability tests 0.431 (variance), 0.760 (joint).

The variable Pol_t and the residuals from equation (6.4) were then added to the structural model determining $\Delta^2 p_t$, and $\Delta(m - p)_t$; we find that Pol_t is significant in the equation determining $\Delta^2 p_t$ and the residuals from the interest rate equation are significant in both structural equations. Thus ΔR_t is not strongly exogenous in this model, in contrast to the findings presented in Hendry (1995).

Finally, estimates of the coefficients attached to error correction terms again confirm that the speed of adjustment to long-run changes in the variables is slow but significant. As to short-run adjustments to shocks (i.e., a standard error increase in the structural residuals of the equations determining $\Delta(m - p)_t$ and $\Delta^2 p_t$ in Table 6.5), Figure 6.10 plots the impulse responses of the model with the top half of the diagram showing the impact of a shock in the money supply and the lower half a shock in inflation. Changes in the money supply take longer to work through the system than do changes in inflation, whichever equation is shocked. It clearly takes up to 3 years to return the system to short-run equilibrium. Figure 6.11 produces the impact of the shocks as accumulated responses (rather than period-by-period responses), showing that in all situations the positive shocks persist in terms of increasing the money supply and inflation in the long run, but that the long-run properties of the model (encapsulated in the cointegration vectors) act immediately to bring the model back near to its pre-shock position. If we were to use an

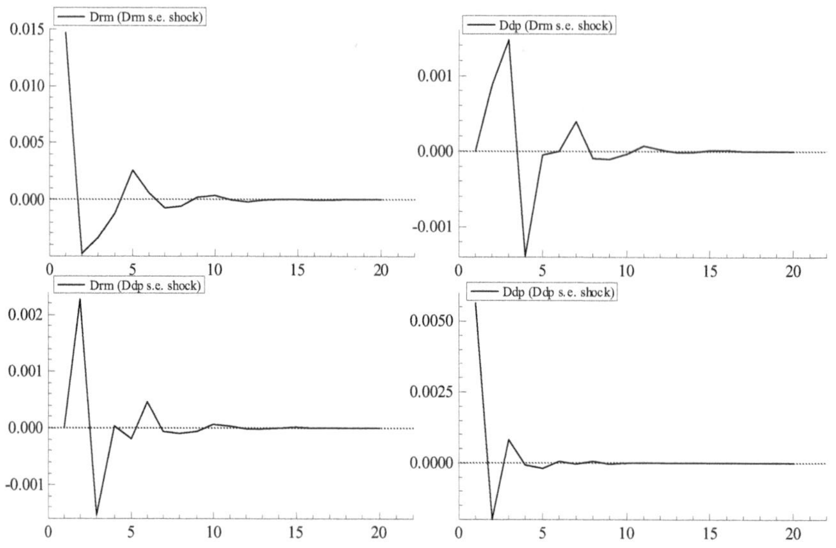

Figure 6.10. Impulse response shocks.

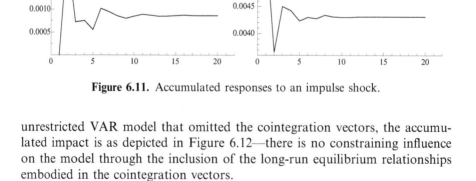

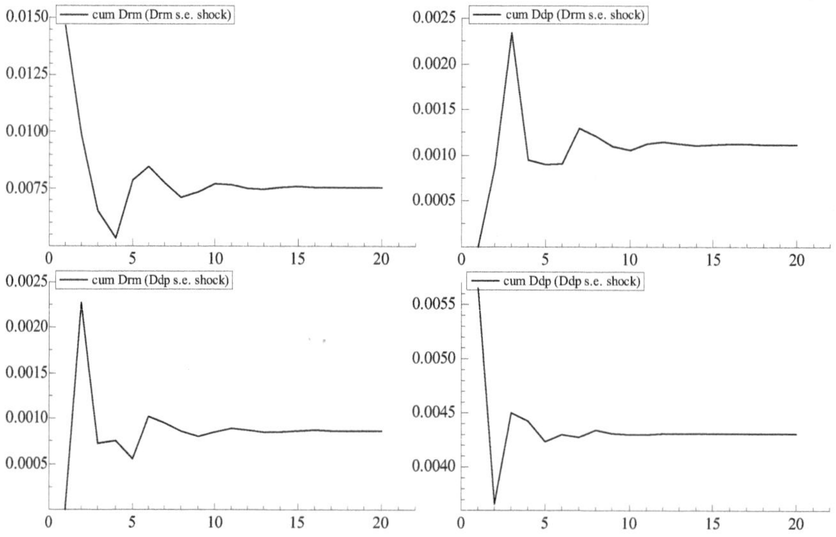

Figure 6.11. Accumulated responses to an impulse shock.

unrestricted VAR model that omitted the cointegration vectors, the accumulated impact is as depicted in Figure 6.12—there is no constraining influence on the model through the inclusion of the long-run equilibrium relationships embodied in the cointegration vectors.

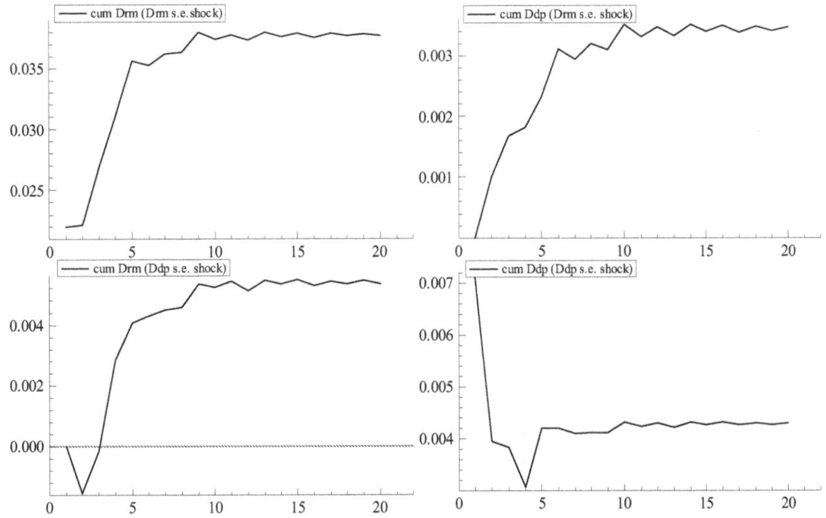

Figure 6.12. Accumulated responses to an impulse shock (unrestricted VAR model).

STRUCTURAL MACROECONOMIC MODELLING

The applied researcher typically wants to model the economic relationships between variables in order to (i) test economic theories (i.e., understand the nature of these relationships) and (ii) to predict what would happen to the model in the event of a change in (one or more of) its variables. The latter might be induced by structural shocks that are fully exogenous to the system (such as an 'output shock' due to oil price rises) or changes in variables may be due to government policy. With respect to policy impacts, the model needs to be robust to the Lucas Critique (see Chapter 1), and it has been argued that this can only be achieved when policy effects are unanticipated (i.e., exogenous), much in the same way as structural shocks are orthogonal to the model.

In order to proceed with structural macroeconomic modelling, it is important to note that while in principle there exists a set of structural relationships describing the model (equation (6.5)), typically we do not have enough information on these 'deep parameters' (i.e., the structural parameters), but rather the modeller has to start from a reduced-form model. Consider the following structural macroeconomic model:[16]

$$\mathbf{A}\mathbf{z}_t = \mathbf{C}(L)\mathbf{z}_{t-1} + \mathbf{B}\boldsymbol{\varepsilon}_t \tag{6.5}$$

where $\mathbf{z}$ is a vector of macroeconomic variables, some of which are endogenous (such as output, prices and (un)employment), with the remainder comprising (policy) variables controlled by government (such as the money supply and interest rates) or determined outside the system (e.g., world demand and

[16] This example is based on Favero (2001, chap. 6).

inflation). The matrices of parameters comprise: $\mathbf{A}$ (the contemporaneous relations among the variables in the model), the lag polynomial $\mathbf{C}(L)$ that allows dynamic adjustment and $\mathbf{B}$ (the contemporaneous relationships among the structural disturbances $\boldsymbol{\varepsilon}_t$ such that when $\mathbf{B} = \mathbf{I}_n$, the identity matrix, then shocks to one variable do not directly impact on other variables in the model).

Since the structural model is not directly observable, a reduced form of the underlying structural model can be estimated instead:

$$\mathbf{z}_t = \mathbf{A}^{-1}\mathbf{C}(L)\mathbf{z}_{t-1} + \mathbf{u}_t \tag{6.6}$$

where

$$\mathbf{A}\mathbf{u}_t = \mathbf{B}\boldsymbol{\varepsilon}_t \tag{6.7}$$

Equation (6.7) shows that the disturbances in the reduced-form model $\mathbf{u}_t$ are a complicated mixture of the underlying structural shocks and are not easy to interpret unless a direct link can be made to the structural shocks (in the same way, the rest of the reduced-form parameters in the model are also difficult to relate to a specific economic structure).

There are different solutions to the problem of relating (6.6) back to (6.5). The VAR-modelling approach of Sims (1980) was intended primarily to analyse the impact of (structural) shocks in the model, so he suggested the following approach to just-identifying the model:

$$A = \begin{bmatrix} 1 & 0 & 0 & 0 \\ a_{21} & 1 & 0 & 0 \\ \vdots & \vdots & 1 & \vdots \\ a_{n1} & \cdots & a_{nn-1} & 1 \end{bmatrix} \qquad B = \begin{bmatrix} b_{11} & 0 & 0 & 0 \\ 0 & b_{22} & 0 & 0 \\ \vdots & \vdots & b_{ii} & \vdots \\ 0 & 0 & 0 & b_{nn} \end{bmatrix} \tag{6.8}$$

The restriction on $\mathbf{A}$ is called the Choleski factorization and ensures that there is a strict causal ordering in the contemporaneous relationships between the endogenous variables, with the most endogenous variable (i.e., the one affected most by the others) ordered last in the model. The formulation of $\mathbf{B}$ ensures that the shocks are independent of each other. Of course, there may be little or no justification for these imposed restrictions in economic terms, and indeed the only way to know if they are justified is by recourse to economic theory. Different orderings of the variables in $\mathbf{z}_t$ will produce different orthogonalized impulse responses. Thus, it is difficult to interpret these responses in economic terms.

Another problem with the Sims' approach is that it often ignores the long-run structural relationships in the model by not converting the VAR to a VECM. If $I(1)$ variables are cointegrated, then omitting such information leads to a mis-specified model and in any case limits our ability to say very much about economic theories (i.e., understand the nature of the equilibrium relationships between the variables in the model).

The structural VAR approach extends the Sims' approach in that it attempts to use economic theory to identify the restrictions needed in $\mathbf{A}$

and **B**. However, Levtchenkova, Pagan and Robertson (1999) argue that '... although the interpretation offered in support of restrictions ... ostensibly arises from some prior economic theory, in practice most ... come from past empirical work or introspection.' Moreover, such restrictions do not help in identifying the long-run relationships among the n variables in the model, and in anything other than a small macroeconomic model the number of restrictions needed is large $[n(n-1)/2]$, and it is unlikely that enough information would be available for identification based on theory.

An alternative approach to this problem of identification in macroeconomic models is to use a structural cointegrating VAR approach, whereby the first step is to identify the cointegration vectors spanning the long run. As discussed in the last chapter, Garratt, Lee, Pesaran and Shin (1999, 2001) argue that developing the structural long-run relationships between the variables in the model needs to be based *ex ante* on economic theory, before estimation takes place, rather than '... the more usual approach where the starting point is an unrestricted VAR model, with some vague priors about the nature of the long-run relations' (p. 15). They give an example of deriving testable hypotheses from developing such a model from theory and then testing to ensure the structure is accepted using the type of tests considered in Chapter 5. These structural cointegrating relationships are then embedded in the unrestricted VAR of the macroeconomic model. While, in principle, the short-run restrictions (in **A** and **B**) can be imposed (thus obtaining a short-run structural model), the problem still remains of what information is available on which to base such restrictions. Thus Garratt et al. (1999) attempt to get around the problem by suggesting the use of a more general method of analysing impulse responses that does not rely on the use of identifying restrictions (and that is not dependent on the ordering of the variables in the model). Thus, they favour the use of the generalized impulse response analysis (Pesaran and Shin, 1998). As long as there is a *constant* mapping between $\boldsymbol{\varepsilon}_t$ in equation (6.7) and $\mathbf{u}_t$, then '... the analysis of the shocks to the estimated equations provides insights into the response of the macroeconomic model to the underlying structural shocks, taking into account the contemporaneous effects that such shocks might have on the different variables in the model. While this analysis cannot provide an understanding of the response of the Macroeconomy to specified structural shocks ... it does provide a meaningful characterisation of the dynamic responses of the macroeconomy to "realistic" shocks' (Garratt et al., 1999, p. 13). For a discussion of the relationship and differences between orthogonalized and generalized impulse responses, see Pesaran and Shin (1998).

Important Terms and Concepts

Short-run VAR	Dynamic modelling	PVAR (or PVECM)
Conditional VAR-modelling	Structural VAR-modelling	Simultaneous effects
FIML	Non-linear constraints	Identification of the short-run structural model

7
Panel Data Models and Cointegration

INTRODUCTION

Until now, our concern has been with time series data and the use of appropriate procedures to estimate models using such data, especially when the data may be non-stationary (i.e., contain a unit root(s)). However, panel data (i.e., cross-sectional time series data with $i = 1, \ldots, N$ 'individuals' in each time period and with $t = 1, \ldots, T$ observations for each individual over time) are increasingly being used in both macro- as well as the more traditional micro-level studies of economic problems. At the macro-level there is increasing use of cross-country data to study such topics as purchasing power parity (cf. Pedroni, 2001) and growth convergence (cf. McCoskey, 2002), as well as familiar issues such as whether real gross domestic product data contain unit roots (cf. Rapach, 2002). Micro-based panel data (such as those generated by national household surveys or surveys of firms) are also widely used where typically the data comprise large N and small T.

Baltagi (2001) considers some of the major advantages (as well as limitations) of using panel data, such as how they allow for heterogeneity in individuals, firms, regions and countries, which is absent when using aggregated time series data. They also give more variability, which often leads to less collinearity among variables, while cross sections of time series provide more degrees of freedom and more efficiency (more reliable parameter results) when estimating models. The dynamics of adjustment are better handled using panels especially in micro-based studies involving individuals, and more complicated models can be considered involving fewer restrictions. The limitations of panel data are usually related to the design and collection of such information: not just missing data (e.g., from non-response) but also measurement errors, attrition in the panel over time and selectivity problems (including issues such as the weighting of data that is sampled on the basis of a particular stratification of the population). Model estimation using unbalanced panels (where there are not T observations on all i individuals in the data set) is more complicated, but often necessary given the impacts of the problems just outlined.

This chapter begins with a brief overview of econometric techniques for use with panel data (see Baltagi, 2001 for an extensive review of the area; and Baltagi, Fomby and Hill, 2000 for issues related specifically to the use of non-stationary panel data). It then considers the various approaches that have become popular for testing for unit roots in panel data, before considering panel cointegration tests and estimating panel cointegration models.

PANEL DATA AND MODELLING TECHNIQUES

A simple two-variable model that uses panel data can be written as:

$$y_{it} = x'_{it}\beta + z'_{it}\gamma + e_{it} \tag{7.1}$$

with $i(=1,\dots,N)$denoting individuals, households, firms, countries, etc.; $t(=1,\dots,T)$ denoting time; y and x are the model variables with dimensions $(T \times 1)$ and $(T \times N)$, respectively; z_{it} is the deterministic component in the model and can take on several forms (see below); and e_{it} are assumed to be residuals with the standard properties IID(0, σ_e^2).

As can be seen from equation (7.1), when $N = 1$ and T is large the model reverts to the use of time series data, and when $T = 1$ and N is large the model uses only cross-sectional data. Some of the advantages of pooling cross-sectional and time series data have been noted above; within the context of non-stationary data and cointegration analysis there is another major advantage that can be derived from panel data. That is, adding the cross-sectional dimension to the time series dimension means that non-stationarity from the time series can be dealt with *and* combined with the increased data and power that the cross section brings. The latter acts as repeated draws from the same distribution, and thus while it is known that the standard Dickey–Fuller-type (DF) tests lack power in distinguishing the unit root null from stationary alternatives, using the cross-sectional dimension of panel data increases the power of unit root tests that are based on a single draw from the population under consideration. In empirical applications, where single-country augmented DF (ADF) tests for real exchange rates, nominal interest rates, inflation rates, and unemployment rates typically cannot reject the unit root hypothesis, panel tests usually do (e.g., Culver and Papell, 1997).[1] Moreover, and in direct contrast to standard DF-type tests, as N and T get large, panel test statistics and estimators converge to normally distributed random variables. This makes testing and inference simpler and results from the fact that panel estimators average across individuals, which leads to a stronger overall signal than that available from a pure time series estimator.

The standard textbook treatment of z_{it} in equation (7.1) is to limit it to a

[1] Levin and Lin (1992) found that the panel approach substantially increases power relative to single equation ADF tests in finite samples, based on Monte Carlo simulations. Rapach (2002) confirms this using his own Monte Carlo simulations.

simple individual effect, say α_i, that allows each household, individual, country, etc. to have a separate intercept in the regression model, thus allowing each individual to be heterogeneous (but note that the intercept is not allowed to change over time—the α_i therefore capture fixed effects). It treats observations for the same individual as having something specific in common such that they are more 'like' each other than observations from two or more different individuals. However, z_{it} can take on several forms, including zero, one, a simple time trend, the fixed effect α_i (as discussed) and a mixture of fixed effects and heterogeneous time trends. For example, we could replace z_{it} by any of the following alternatives:

$$\left.\begin{array}{ll}\text{(a)} & z_{it} = \delta_0 \\ \text{(b)} & z_{it} = \delta_0 + \delta_i t \\ \text{(c)} & z_{it} = \alpha_i \\ \text{(d)} & z_{it} = \nu_t \\ \text{(e)} & z_{it} = \alpha_i + \eta_i t\end{array}\right\} \tag{7.2}$$

The first two examples in (7.2) equate to a standard pooling of cross-sectional, time-series data (with a common intercept, or an intercept and time trend, in the model) such that there are observations on NT different individuals. In contrast (7.2c–7.2e) explicitly take into account the panel aspects of the data and allow for T observations on N individuals where it is assumed each individual is different in some (unobserved but nonetheless specific) way. That is, the last three alternatives in equation (7.2) allow for heterogeneity across individuals in terms of effects that do not vary with time (e.g., α_i—see Box 7.1 for more details on the standard treatment of this model), or shocks over time that affect all individuals equally (ν_t),[2] or lastly both fixed effects and individual effects that vary with time ($\alpha_i + \eta_i t$).

PANEL UNIT ROOT TESTS

Testing for unit roots in panel data is becoming more common, given both the development of testing procedures and their incorporation into econometric software packages. In this section the tests suggested by Levin and Lin (1992, 1993)—hereafter LL—and Im, Pesaran and Shin (1995, 1997)—hereafter IPS—are considered, together with more recent adjustments and extensions by Harris and Tzavalis (1999), Maddala and Wu (1999) and Breitung (2000). All these tests take non-stationarity (i.e., the presence of a unit root) as the null hypothesis and test against alternatives involving stationarity. The last test considered in the section is that proposed by Hadri (2000) for the null of stationarity against the alternative of unit roots in the panel data.

[2] Note that it is possible to consider a variant of equation (7.2c) and (7.2d) whereby $z_{it} = \alpha_i + \nu_t$.

Box 7.1 Random versus fixed effects panel model.

Econometric textbooks (e.g., Johnston and Dinardo, 1997; Green, 2000) discuss in detail how to estimate the panel model based on equations (7.1) and (7.2c). When α_i is uncorrelated with x_{it} we have a random effects (RE) model; and when α_i is correlated with x_{it} this is termed (rather confusingly) the fixed effects (FE) model. The RE model is applicable if the panel data comprise N individuals drawn randomly from a large population (e.g., the typical approach in household panel studies), such that the α_i (the individual specific constant terms) are randomly distributed across cross-sectional units. The FE model is more appropriate when focusing on a specific set of N firms (or N countries or households) that are not randomly selected from some large population. In the FE model, separate intercept terms α_i are estimated for each individual firm; hence, when N is large this can use up degrees of freedom very quickly.

Essentially then the difference between the FE and RE models centres on whether the α_i feature as part of the regressors (the FE model) or as part of the error term (the RE model) in equation (7.1)—although for each group of individuals i in the RE model there is but a single draw from the population that enters the regression model identically each period (specifically, $e_{it} = \alpha_i + \varepsilon_{it}$, where the ε_{it} are IID(0, σ_ε^2) capturing all other random effects on y_{it}).

The basic approach to unit root-testing is to consider a modified version of equation (7.1) involving only a single variable:

$$y_{it} = \rho_i y_{i,t-1} + z'_{it}\gamma + e_{it} \tag{7.3}$$

The LL (1992) tests assume that (i) e_{it} are IID(0, σ_e^2)—thus individual processes for each i are cross-sectionally independent and there is no serial correlation—and (ii) $\rho_i = \rho$ for all i.[3] The latter assumption imposes homogeneity by assuming that each individual-specific process is the same across all cross-sectional units of the panel. The first assumption ensures that there is no cointegration between pairs or groups of individuals in the cross sections.[4] This is a major assumption since in many instances (e.g., involving financial variables for different countries or exchange rates, as well as prices and output) it might be assumed (and indeed empirical evidence often shows) that markets are economically linked in terms of long-run equilibrium relationships. The consequence of assuming no cross-equation cointegration relationships has been

[3] Of course, if $\rho_i \neq \rho$ for all i, then incorrectly imposing this constraint will ensure that the first assumption is not correct as $\text{cov}(e_i, e_j) \neq 0$.

[4] Later we shall consider the IPS test that relaxes the assumption that $\rho_i = \rho$, but still imposes no cointegration since e_{it} are assumed to be IID(0, σ_e^2).

explored by Banerjee, Cockerill and Russell (2001); they found that the group of panel unit root tests considered here often over-reject the null of non-stationarity (i.e., these tests have poor size properties).[5,6]

There are various forms of the LL (1992) tests: the first (and simplest) sets $z_{it} = 0$, while tests 2–6 as presented by LL cover the alternatives set out in equation (7.2a–e). In all cases, the null is H_0: $\rho = 0$ against the alternative H_1: $\rho < 1$. Thus under the null all i series in the panel contain a unit root, while the alternative is that *all* individual series are stationary. Clearly, the alternative hypothesis is fairly restrictive. For the LL (1992) tests, where $z_{it} = 0$ or as set out in equation (7.2), Levin and Lin have shown that as $N \to \infty$ and $T \to \infty$ the underlying distribution of the t-statistic for testing the null is standard normally distributed $N(0,1)$, which makes statistical inferences about the value and significance of ρ straightforward (see Baltagi, 2001, eqn (12.4)).

There are various issues with the LL (1992) tests that have resulted in extensions or alternatives being suggested. LL (1993) developed testing procedures that take care of the problems of autocorrelation and heteroscedasticity that are apparent in the LL (1992) tests. Their maintained model comprised:

$$\Delta y_{it} = \rho^* y_{i,t-1} + \sum_{L=1}^{p_i} \theta_{iL} \Delta y_{i,t-L} + z'_{it}\gamma + u_{it} \tag{7.4}$$

where equation (7.3) is now transformed into a first-difference equivalent version (recall that $\Delta y_{it} = y_{it} - y_{i,t-1}$) such that the null is now H_0: $\rho^* = (\rho - 1) = 0$; thus the major change to the earlier LL (1992) test is that different lags are allowed across the i cross sections in the model. To implement this model, LL (1993) carry out separate ADF regressions for each individual in the panel, normalize for heteroscedasticity and compute pooled t-statistics for testing the null against the same alternative as in LL (1992) (viz., H_1: $\rho^* < 0$—all individual series are non-stationary). The test t-values are again asymptotically distributed under the standard normal distribution.

[5] In considering the LL, IPS and Maddala and Wu (1999) tests when cointegration is present, Banerjee et al. (2001) found that the LL tests did relatively better than the others in terms of its size properties. However, this was probably to do with the imposition of homogeneity ($\rho_i = \rho$) in the Monte Carlo experiments they undertook, which obviously favours the LL tests.

[6] The LL tests assume that e_{it} are IID(0, σ_e^2), hence $\text{cov}(e_{it}, e_{jt}) = 0$ for all $i \neq j$, so that as well as long-run cross-equational correlations being omitted (the case of cointegration between the i cross sections), short-run correlations are also omitted. O'Connell (1998) proposed using the seemingly unrelated regression (SUR) technique proposed by Zellner (1962) to account for short-run $\text{cov}(e_{it}, e_{jt}) \neq 0$ in the LL test where ($\rho_i = \rho$), while Taylor and Sarno (1998) suggest a similar SUR estimator when the ρ_i are free to vary across i. Both are argued to reduce the over-sizing of the usual LL and IPS tests, but they still do not account for over-sizing if cointegration is present in the data.

Table 7.1 Levin and Lin (1992, 1993) panel unit root tests.

Test name	Model	Hypothesis
LL_1	$\Delta y_{it} = \rho y_{i,t-1} + e_{it}$	H_0: $\rho = 0$; H_1: $\rho < 0$
LL_2	$\Delta y_{it} = \rho y_{i,t-1} + \delta_0 + e_{it}$	H_0: $\rho < 0$; H_1: $\rho < 0$
LL_3	$\Delta y_{it} = \rho y_{i,t-1} + \delta_0 + \delta_1 t + e_{it}$	H_0: $\rho = \delta = 0$; H_1: $\rho < 0$; $\delta \in R$
LL_4	$\Delta y_{it} = \rho y_{i,t-1} + \alpha_i + e_{it}$	H_0: $\rho = \alpha_i = 0$; H_1: $\rho < 0$; $\alpha_i \in R$ for all i
LL_5	$\Delta y_{it} = \rho y_{i,t-1} + v_t + e_{it}$	H_0: $\rho = 0$; H_1: $\rho < 0$
LL_6	$\Delta y_{it} = \rho y_{i,t-1} + \alpha_i + \eta_i t + e_{it}$	H_0: $\rho = \eta_i = 0$; H_1: $\rho < 0$; $\eta_i \in R$ for all i
LL_7	$\Delta y_{it} = \rho y_{i,t-1} + e_{it}$ with serial correlation	H_0: $\rho = 0$; H_1: $\rho < 0$
LL_8	$\Delta y_{it} = \rho y_{i,t-1} + \sum_{L=1}^{p_i} \theta_{iL} \Delta y_{i,t-L} + u_{it}$	H_0: $\rho = 0$; H_1: $\rho < 0$
LL_9	$\Delta y_{it} = \rho y_{i,t-1} + \sum_{L=1}^{p_i} \theta_{iL} \Delta y_{i,t-L} + \alpha_i + u_{it}$	H_0: $\rho = \alpha_i = 0$; H_1: $\rho < 0$; $\alpha_i \in R$ for all i
LL_10	$\Delta y_{it} = \rho y_{i,t-1} + \sum_{L=1}^{p_i} \theta_{iL} \Delta y_{i,t-L} + \alpha_i + \eta_i t + u_{it}$	H_0: $\rho = \eta_i = 0$; H_1: $\rho < 0$; $\eta_i \in R$ for all i

Three versions of the LL (1993) tests are considered here: first where $z_{it} = 0$ (denoted model 8 here, to be consistent with Chiang and Kao, 2002[7]), where $z_{it} = \alpha_i$ (model 9) and where $z_{it} = \alpha_i + \eta_i t$ (model 10). Table 7.1 summarizes the LL tests considered—all of which are available as a subroutine from Chiang and Kao, 2002, for estimation using the Gauss econometric package.

Harris and Tzavalis (1999)—hereafter HT—conducted Monte Carlo experiments to look at the properties of the LL tests when T (the time series component of the data set) is small. In particular, they looked at the power of the test to reject the null when it is false, finding that the assumption built into the LL tests that $T \to \infty$ yields a test with poorer power properties (especially when T is less than 50). Consequently, they suggested testing for panel unit roots based on the assumption that T is fixed, finding this had better power properties in small T samples. This is a particularly important issue when considering testing for unit roots using macro- or micro-panel data sets. In the latter, N tends to be large, but the time dimension T is often relatively short, suggesting that in such cases the HT tests are more appropriate. These are available for three models based on equation (7.3) with homogeneity imposed ($\rho_i = \rho$) and $z_{it} = \{0\}$, $z_{it} = \{\alpha_i\}$ or $z_{it} = \{(\alpha_i, t)'\}$. Labelling these as HT_1 to HT_3, the HT tests are equivalent to LL models LL_1, LL_4 and LL_6.

[7] Model 7 in Chiang and Kao (2002) is equivalent to equation (7.3) with $\rho_i = \rho$ and $z_{it} = 0$, but allowing for serial correlation.

Another issue with the LL tests is concerned with the methods used to estimate panel models with fixed effects (i.e., where $\alpha_i > 0$). Generally, if heterogeneity is allowed (α_i and/or η_i feature in the model), then the usual panel estimators based on the 'within-group' estimator (such as the least squares dummy variable model[8]) have been shown to suffer from a severe loss of power (Breitung, 2000). Thus Breitung suggests a test involving only a constant in the model (i.e., no fixed effects) and finds his UB test to be substantially more powerful than the LL tests (and fairly robust with respect to the presence of lags in the data-generating process—d.g.p.—underlying the true model).[9,10] The UB test will be included in the battery of panel unit root tests considered on p. 199 in Table 7.3.

As stated earlier, a major assumption of the LL tests is the imposition of homogeneity by setting $\rho_i = \rho$ in equation (7.3). The alternative hypothesis that is tested is therefore H_1: $\rho < 1$, which is that *all i* cross sections are stationary. Thus, IPS (1997) relax the homogeneity constraint by estimating equation (7.3) with ρ_i free to vary across the i individual series in the panel. They also allow for different lags for the i cross sections in the model (as do LL, 1993), using the following model:

$$\Delta y_{it} = \rho_i^* y_{i,t-1} + \sum_{L=1}^{p_i} \theta_{iL} \Delta y_{i,t-L} + z'_{it}\gamma + u_{it} \tag{7.5}$$

The null hypothesis (H_0: $\rho_i^* = 0$) is that each series in the panel contains a unit root for all i, and the alternative hypothesis (H_1: $\rho_i^* < 0$ for at least one i) is that at least one of the individual series in the panel is stationary. Essentially, the IPS test averages the ADF individual unit root test statistics that are obtained from estimating (7.5) for each i (allowing each series to have different lag lengths L, if necessary); that is:

$$\bar{t} = \frac{1}{N} \sum_{i=1}^{N} t_{\rho^*} \tag{7.6}$$

As $T \to \infty$ (for a fixed value of N) followed by $N \to \infty$ sequentially, IPS show that their test statistic (denoted IPS_97) for testing the null is standard normally distributed.[11] They also proposed an LM bar test (denoted IPS_LM)

[8] See Greene (2000, pp. 560–564) for a clear overview of this approach.

[9] The UB test does not include lagged dependent variables.

[10] The UB test is also found to be more powerful than the IPS tests (to be discussed next), since these are also based on the within-group estimator to account for fixed effects.

[11] Note that different distributions will be obtained depending on the mean and variance of the t_{ρ^*} series underlying the $\bar{t}$ statistic. Thus, IPS standardize their test statistic based on simulations of this mean and variance (with different values obtained depending on the lag length used in the ADF tests and the value of N). These simulated values are given in table 3 of the 2002 version of their paper, and they are used along with equation (7.6) to obtain the z-statistic as set out in equation (3.13) of IPS (2002) or similarly eqn (4.10) in their paper.

based on a lagrange multiplier test rather than t-statistics,[12] but essentially the issues are the same for both forms of the test. Note that, in principle, unbalanced panel data (with different values of T for different individual series i) can be handled by the test, and each individual series i can have different lags L. However, in practice, the critical values of the tests would need to be recomputed if either T or L differ across the i cross sections in the panel (IPS only calculate critical values for balanced data and homogeneous L).

The IPS test is a generalization of the LL tests in that it relaxes the form of the alternative hypothesis H_1. However, it suffers from many of the same problems discussed above with regard to the LL (1992, 1993) tests. Particularly important is the assumption that each i is cross-sectionally independent, implying no short- or long-run cross-equation correlations exist and thus no cointegration between pairs or groups of individuals in these cross sections. There is also the loss of power that results from the use of a 'within-group' estimator of the fixed effects—the LL and IPS tests both make correction for the bias that arises from using such estimators and Breitung (2000) shows that this can lead to significant under-rejection of the null when it is false. Lastly, the IPS test is in practice hard to implement for unbalanced data, which can limit its application (especially when using micro-based panel data sets where unbalanced panels are more prevalent).

The power of the LL and IPS tests have been analysed and compared in Karlsson and Lothgren (2000). When making comparisons an important factor was to recognize that an essential difference between the tests is that under the alternative hypothesis the IPS test needs only some of the series to be stationary, not all, while the LL test requires all to be stationary. The extent to which some of the i cross sections truly are stationary and some not impacts on the size and power of these tests when considering H_0 and H_1. Their main findings were: '... the power increases monotonically with: (1) an increased number N of the series in the panel; (2) an increased time-series dimension T in each individual series; and (3) an increased proportion ... of stationary series in the panel.' They also note that '... for large-T panels, there is a potential risk that the whole panel may erroneously be modelled as stationary ... due to the high power of the panel tests for small proportions of stationary series in the panel. For small-T panels, on the other hand, there is a potential risk that the whole panel may be erroneously modelled as non-stationary, due to the relatively low power of tests even for large proportions of stationary series in the panel.' In essence they warn the applied researcher from drawing inferences too quickly for different values of N and T.

The last test considered here based on the null of non-stationarity has been proposed by Maddala and Wu (1999). They advocate the use of a Fisher-type test that combines the significance levels for rejecting the null (the p-values)

[12] IPS advised the reader in their 1997 paper that the t-bar test is preferable to the LM test (the latter actually is omitted from the final version of the 1997 paper, which is forthcoming in the *Journal of Econometrics*).

obtained when estimating a unit root test (e.g., the ADF test) for each cross section i separately. That is:[13]

$$P = -2\sum_{i=1}^{N} \ln p_i \tag{7.7}$$

has a χ^2-distribution with $2N$ degrees of freedom. Thus, this procedure is similar to the IPS test that averages the ADF individual unit root test statistics obtained for each i, except that equation (7.7) combines the significance levels for rejecting the null of a unit root rather than the t-test values. The advantage of using (7.7) is that it is simple to calculate, does not require a balanced panel or impose the same lag lengths on each cross section i and it can be carried out for any unit root test statistic (not just the DF-type test). Maddala and Wu (1999) also found that this Fisher-type P-test is superior to the IPS test, which in turn is more powerful than the LL test.

All the previous tests are based on a null hypothesis that the individual series in the panel are jointly non-stationary, against alternatives where some or all of these series are stationary. Hadri (1999) has proposed a test of the null that the time series for each i are stationary around a deterministic trend, against the alternative hypothesis of a unit root in the panel data. His model assumes:

$$y_{it} = z'_{it}\gamma + r_{it} + \varepsilon_{it} \tag{7.8}$$

where $r_{it} = r_{i,t-1} + u_{it}$ and $u_{it} \sim \text{IID}(0, \sigma_u^2)$. Thus r_{it} is a simple random walk and ε_{it} is a stationary process. By repeated backward substitution it is possible to rewrite equation (7.8) as:

$$y_{it} = z'_{it}\gamma + e_{it} \tag{7.9}$$

where $e_{it} = \sum_{j=1}^{t} u_{ij} + \varepsilon_{it}$ is the accumulated sum for each cross section i of the past residuals u_{it}. Under the null hypothesis of stationarity the variance of e_{it} equals zero (the y_{it} do not drift, but rather are stationary around the deterministic component in equation (7.9)). An LM test can be computed that tests this null, which is distributed exactly[14] under the standard normal distribution as $T \to \infty$ followed by $N \to \infty$ sequentially.

To conclude the present discussion of panel unit root tests, annual data on (the log of) total factor productivity for 22 countries ($N = 22$), for the 1971–1990 period ($T = 20$), are used to perform the various tests outlined above. These data are taken from Chiang and Kao (2002), who use this series to illustrate their *NPT1.3* software package (written for Gauss).[15] Figure 7.1 plots each of the 22 cross-sectional series, while Table 7.2 reports the individual ADF tests for each country. In all cases a single lag was used when computing the various ADF tests (lag lengths were set based on their

[13] When N is large, Choi (1999) proposed a modified P-test: $P_m = [1/(2\sqrt{N})] \times \sum_{i=1}^{N}(-2\ln p_i - 2)$

[14] That is, no standardization is needed (as with the IPS_97 test) to obtain a statistic that is distributed asymptotically under the standard normal distribution.

[15] The data originate from Coe and Helpman (1995).

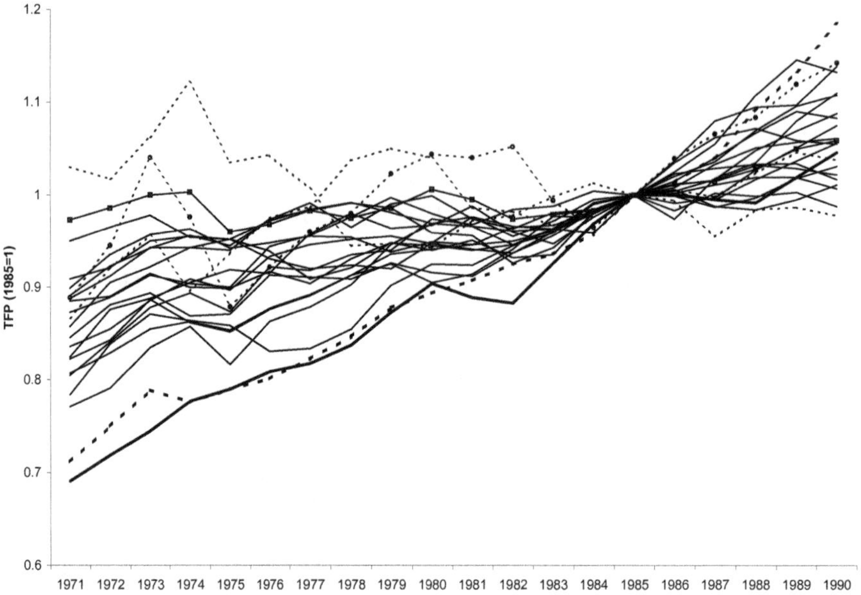

Figure 7.1. Total factor productivity (TFP) for 22 OECD countries, 1971–1990 (source: Chiang and Kao, 2002).

Table 7.2 ADF tests for non-stationarity for individual log TFP series (lag length = 1).

Country	t-statistic with constant and trend (τ_τ)	t-statistic with constant (τ_μ)
USA	−2.527	−0.992
Japan	−1.237	1.408
Germany	−2.709	−0.915
France	−2.566	0.270
Italy	−2.968	−1.257
UK	−2.971	−0.711
Canada	−2.658	−2.066
Australia	−3.108	−1.133
Austria	−1.831	−0.383
Belgium	−3.658	−1.189
Denmark	−3.681	−0.545
Finland	−3.687	0.045
Greece	−2.133	−1.828
Ireland	−1.505	−0.036
Israel	−1.437	0.689
Holland	−3.482	−1.652
New Zealand	−2.006	−1.630
Norway	−3.604	−1.138
Portugal	−3.823*	−1.660
Spain	−1.597	0.196
Sweden	−2.308	−1.259
Switzerland	−1.755	−0.532

5% critical values for $\tau_\tau = -3.692$ and for $\tau_\mu = -3.040$.
* Rejects at 5% significance level.

Table 7.3 Panel unit root tests for log TFP (where applicable lag length is set at 1).

Test name	Deterministic component (z_{it})	Test statistic*	Significance level for rejection
LL_1		−10.452	0.000
LL_2	δ_0	−5.997	0.000
LL_3	$\delta_0 + \delta_i t$	−3.975	0.000
LL_4	α_i	1.010	0.156
LL_5	ν_t	−6.178	0.000
LL_6	$\alpha_i + \eta_i t$	−2.414	0.008
LL_7		−10.662	0.000
LL_8		0.849	0.198
LL_9	α_i	7.401	0.000
LL_10	$\alpha_i + \eta_i t$	28.372	0.000
HT_1		−8.397	0.000
HT_2	α_i	2.337	0.010
HT_3	$\alpha_i + \eta_i t$	−15.963	0.000
UB test	δ_0	−3.271	0.000
IPS_97 (a)	α_i	3.903	0.000
IPS_97 (b)	$\alpha_i + \eta_i t$	−2.302	0.011
IPS_LM (a)	α_i	−2.387	0.008
IPS_LM (b)	$\alpha_i + \eta_i t$	−5.317	0.011
Fisher *P*-test (a)	$\delta_0 + \delta_i t$	66.264	0.000
Fisher *P*-test (b)	δ_0	17.040	0.999
Hadri test (a)	α_i	6.883	0.017
Hadri test (b)	$\alpha_i + \eta_i t$	6,975.451	0.000

* All tests are (asymptotically or exactly) distributed under the standard normal distribution, except the Fisher *P*-test, which is χ^2-distributed with $2N$ degrees of freedom.

significance in the ADF regression equation), and tests were undertaken both with and without a deterministic time trend included. Only once is the null of non-stationarity rejected for these individual country-based tests. In contrast, Table 7.3 presents the array of panel unit root tests discussed in this section. All tests were computed using *NPT 1.3*, except the Fisher-type *P*-test, which was computed manually using *TSP 4.5*.[16]

The results from the panel unit roots tests are ambiguous. Although most tests do reject the null of non-stationarity, the inclusion of fixed effects *vis-à-vis* fixed effects *and* heterogenous time effects clearly impacts on the ability to

[16] *TSP* provides the actual significance level for rejecting the null of non-stationarity (whereas *PcGive* does not provide this information automatically), and this is needed to compute the Fisher-type test. The data and program code used are available on the book's website. Note also that the IPS_97 test has also been coded for use with *TSP* and *STATA*. The code using the former is also available on the book's website. Using the *TSP* code provided somewhat different results than those reported in Table 7.3 for the IPS_97 test. Interested readers with access to *TSP* can run the program available on the book's website and note that, in the case of the constant and trend model, the *TSP* code does not reject the null, while *NPT 1.3* code produces results where the null is rejected at better than the 5% significance level.

reject the null (see, for example, the outcomes from the HT_2 and HT_3 tests). In particular, the Fisher P-test, which sums the significance levels for rejecting the null in each i cross section in the panel, rejects the null at better than the 0.1% significance level when a time trend is included in the test, but fails to reject when only a constant (i.e., drift) term is included in the underlying ADF model (cf. the results in Table 7.2). Moreover, the Hadri test based on the null of stationarity is clearly rejected, especially when individual time effects are included in the model. Thus, in the example used (where N and T are relatively small and where the series typically trend upward over time), panel unit root tests do not necessarily provide clear-cut results, although the evidence (excepting the Hadri test) is generally toward overall rejecting unit roots in the series, when individual tests generally fail to reject the null of non-stationarity.[17]

TESTING FOR COINTEGRATION IN PANELS

Testing for cointegration in panel data should have the same beneficial effects in terms of power that are present when testing for unit roots using panel data. That is, the low power of conventional tests (when $N = 1$, such as the Engle–Granger (EG) two-step approach), when applied to series of only moderate length, can be improved upon by pooling information across the i members of a panel.

In terms of extending testing beyond whether there are unit roots in panel data, the literature has two strands to it. Tests of (generally) the null of no cointegration between the variables in the panel, against the alternative of at least one cointegration relationship, have been developed in one strand; the other strand provides estimates of the cointegration vector itself. In this section we look at the tests for whether cointegration is present; while in the next section we consider the approaches that have been developed to provide estimates of the cointegration vector and thus inferences about the parameter estimates obtained. Typically, the literature in both directions has been limited to a single equation framework (in much the same way as the EG procedure pre-dates the multivariate framework developed by Johansen), although efforts are under way to extend testing and estimation using multivariate approaches.

Cointegration tests using a single equation approach include those developed by Kao (1999) and Pedroni (1995, 1999), where the null hypothesis is that there is no cointegration, and McKoskey and Kao (1998), who developed a residual-based test for the null of cointegration rather than the null of no cointegration in panels. Larsson, Lyhagen and Lothgren (2001) used a multi-equation framework to construct a panel test for cointegration rank in hetero-

[17] Note that, as in the case of unit root-testing in time series data where $N = 1$, the presence of a break in the panel series has serious consequences for the power of the test for unit roots. See Murray and Papell (2000) for a discussion and evidence.

geneous panels based on the average of the individual rank trace statistics developed by Johansen (1995a).

The tests proposed by Kao (1999) are DF- and ADF-type tests similar to the standard approach adopted in the EG two-step procedure (see Chapter 4). We start with the panel regression model as set out in equation (7.1):[18]

$$y_{it} = x'_{it}\beta + z'_{it}\gamma + e_{it} \tag{7.10}$$

where y and x are presumed to be non-stationary and:

$$\hat{e}_{it} = \rho\hat{e}_{i,t-1} + v_{it} \tag{7.11}$$

and where $\hat{e}_{it}(\equiv y_{it} - x'_{it}\hat{\beta} - z'_{it}\hat{\gamma})$ are the residuals from estimating equation (7.10). To test the null of no cointegration amounts to testing H_0: $\rho = 1$ in equation (7.11) against the alternative that y and x are cointegrated (i.e., H_1: $\rho < 1$). Kao developed four DF-type tests, with z_{it} in equation (7.10) limited to the fixed effects case (i.e., $z_{it} = \alpha_i$). Two of these tests assume strong exogeneity of the regressors and errors in (7.10) and are denoted DF_ρ and DF_t, while the other tests make (non-parametric) corrections for any endogenous relationships and are denoted DF^*_ρ and DF^*_t. All four tests include non-parametric corrections for any serial correlation, since equation (7.11) involves a single ordinary least squares (OLS) regression of $\hat{e}_{it}$ on only a single lagged value of $\hat{e}_{it}$. Alternatively, Kao also proposed a test that extends (7.11) to include lagged changes in the residuals, thus obtaining an ADF version of his test, and thus a version that parametrically tests for serial correlation as part of the estimation procedure. All the tests are asymptotically distributed under the standard normal distribution and are one-sided negatively tailed tests (i.e., reject the null if the test statistic is a large enough negative number). Note that all five versions of Kao's tests impose homogeneity in that the slope coefficient β is not allowed to vary across the i individual members of the panel.

This assumption of homogeneity has been relaxed by Pedroni (1995, 1999), who used the following model:

$$y_{it} = \alpha_i + \delta_t t + \beta_{1i}x_{1i,t} + \beta_{2i}x_{2i,t} + \cdots + \beta_{Ki}x_{Ki,t} + e_{it} \tag{7.12}$$

with tests for the null of no cointegration being based on the residuals $\hat{e}_{it}$ using:

$$\hat{e}_{it} = \rho_i\hat{e}_{i,t-1} + v_{it} \tag{7.13}$$

Since the α_i and the various β_i are allowed to vary across the i members of the panel, this approach allows for considerable short- and long-run heterogeneity—in effect the dynamics and fixed effects can differ across the individuals in the panel and the cointegration vector can also differ across members under the alternative hypothesis (although with regard to the latter point, see the discussion on the following page on alternative hypotheses and the form of the estimator used).

[18] Note that x_{it} can be expanded to K regressors, not just one.

The way the dynamics are taken into account to correct for serial correlation depends in Pedroni on the model that is used. First of all he constructs three non-parametric tests that 'correct' for serial correlation: (i) a non-parametric variance ratio statistic; (ii) a test analogous to the Phillips and Perron (PP) (1988) rho-statistic; and (iii) a test analogous to the PP t-statistic. He also constructs a fourth parametric test similar to the ADF-type test that allows the number of lags in the model to be estimated directly.[19]

In addition to different ways to correct for serial correlation, Pedroni considers different ways to estimate equation (7.12): estimators that are based on pooling along the within-dimension or estimators that pool along the between-dimension (see Greene, 2000, pp. 562–564 for a discussion). Pooling along the within-dimension amounts to effectively pooling ρ_i (in equation (7.13)) across the different i individuals in the panel such that $\rho_i = \rho$; the between-groups estimator (also referred to as the group-means estimator) is based on averaging the individual estimated values of $\hat{\rho}_i$ for each member i. Thus, using the within-groups approach, the test of the null of no cointegration H_0: $\rho_i = 1$ for all i is set against an alternative H_1: $\rho_i = \rho < 1$ for all i; whereas the group-means estimator is less restrictive in that it allows for potential heterogeneity across individual members of the panel since the alternative hypothesis is H_1: $\rho_i < 1$ for all i (it does not presume a common value for $\rho_i = \rho$ under the alternative hypothesis).

As well as being less restrictive (in terms of the alternative hypothesis being tested), Pedroni has found that the group-means estimators typically have lower small-sample size distortions than within-groups estimators (i.e., it tends to incorrectly reject the null hypothesis when it is true less often). Thus, in addition to the five tests outlined above, which are based on within-groups estimators, Pedroni (1995, 1999) has developed three panel cointegration statistics that are based on the group-means approach. The first is analogous to the PP rho-statistic, the second to the PP t-statistic and the last is analogous to the ADF-type t-statistic.[20]

In all seven tests, the null hypothesis is of no cointegration, with different alternative hypotheses (see Pedroni, 1999, table 1 for specific details and formulae). Endogeneity of the regressors is allowed as is considerable heterogeneity in the dynamics, fixed effects and the cointegration vectors for the i

[19] The issue about the best way to correct for serial correlation was discussed earlier when considering the PP-type tests (Chapter 4). Essentially, the PP tests are likely to be more robust to the problem of 'fat tails' in the data (i.e., severe outlier problems), although imposing parametric restrictions will add to the power of the test when these are valid. As to the size of the test, when T is relatively short compared with N, then parametric tests are often sensitive to the choice of lag used, whereas the non-parametric tests have problems with the size of the test if there are large negative MA components in the dynamics of the model (as is often the case with macro time series data).

[20] Note that Pedroni (1999) points out that his tests 4 and 7 are most closely analogous to the LL (1993) and the IPS (1997) unit root tests, respectively.

individuals in the panel, which contrasts with Kao's (1999) approach where homogeneity is imposed on the cointegration vectors and exogeneity of the regressors is needed for two of his tests. Pedroni (1995, 1999) also shows that his tests are distributed under the standard normal distribution as:

$$\frac{\chi_{N,T} - \mu\sqrt{N}}{\sqrt{\nu}} \quad \Rightarrow \quad N(0,1) \tag{7.14}$$

where $\chi_{N,T}$ is the standardized form for each of the seven statistics developed by Pedroni (see Pedroni, 1999, table 1), while μ and ν are the mean and variance of the underlying individual series used to compute the aggregate test statistics, and these are needed to adjust the seven test statistics to render them standard normal. The values of μ and ν depend on the number of regressors in the model and whether a constant and/or trend terms have been included in the regression model (7.12). These values (obtained by Monte Carlo simulation) are provided in Pedroni (1999, table 2). Note that under the alternative hypothesis the panel variance statistic (test 1) diverges to positive infinity and thus the right tail of the standard normal distribution needs to be used to reject the null hypothesis of no cointegration (large positive values imply rejection). For the other six tests these diverge to negative infinity, and large negative values imply that the null of no cointegration is rejected. Thus, the Pedroni (1995, 1999) statistics are one-sided tests under the standard normal distribution, and care must be taken to ensure that rejection of the null is not incorrectly applied using the wrong tail of the standard normal distribution.

To actually implement the Pedroni tests, there is a need to obtain the residuals from estimating equation (7.12)—see equation (7.13)—and then basically adjust for serial correlation and endogeneity, followed by applying the appropriate mean and variance adjustment terms (μ and ν) discussed above. Pedroni (1999) sets out the formulae for the test statistics in his table 1 and provides a step-by-step guide on pp. 659–662. Fortunately, these tests have been automated for more general use by the authors of the various tests. For example, *NPT 1.3* (Chiang and Kao, 2002) includes Pedroni's seven tests (for use with *Gauss*),[21] while Pedroni himself has written the relevant computer code for his tests for use with *RATS*.[22]

The issue of which test is most appropriate—or more particularly, whether to use a parametric or non-parametric or a within-groups or between-groups approach to testing the null of no cointegration—is not easy to decide. The between-groups estimator is less restrictive; non-parametric tests have particular strengths when the data have significant outliers. However, the latter tests have poor size properties (i.e., tend to over-reject the null when it is true) when the residual term (equation (7.13)) has large negative moving average (MA)

[21] At the time of writing, the *NPT 1.3* procedure wrongly computed the Pedroni (1995, 1999) tests. We discuss this on p. 205 when using this program.
[22] Pedroni's code can handle unbalanced data, unlike *NPT 1.3*.

components (a fairly common occurrence in macro time series data). Also, a parametric test (such as the ADF-type test) has greater power when modelling processes with AR errors, because the regression model captures the AR terms precisely. Thus, using various testing procedures is helpful when the underlying d.g.p.s are unknown.

The approach taken by McCoskey and Kao (1998) is to test the null of cointegration against the alternative of no cointegration. It is similar to the Hadri (1999) LM test discussed on p. 197 when considering panel unit roots. The model (allowing for heterogeneous intercepts) is:

$$y_{it} = \alpha_i + x'_{it}\beta_i + e_{it} \tag{7.15}$$

where

$$x_{it} = x_{i,t-1} + \varepsilon_{it} \tag{7.16}$$

$$e_{it} = \gamma_{it} + u_{it} \tag{7.17}$$

and

$$\gamma_{it} = \gamma_{i,t-1} + \theta u_{it} \tag{7.18}$$

where the u_{it} are $\text{IID}(0, \sigma_u^2)$.[23] Under the null of cointegration between y and x, $\theta = 0$ (the error term e_{it} in (7.15) has a constant variance). Hence, the null hypothesis is based on setting up such a test (H_0: $\theta = 0$). McCoskey and Kao (1999) proposed an LM test statistic that is asymptotically normally distributed, although dependent on complex mean and variance terms that are provided via Monte Carlo simulations and that depend on the number of regressors in the model and/or whether α_i is allowed to vary or set equal to zero. The McCoskey and Kao (1999) test has been incorporated into *NPT 1.3* for use with the *Gauss* econometric software package.

All the above panel cointegration tests are based on essentially univariate extensions of panel unit root tests, where the residuals from a first-step cointegration regression are then tested in the spirit of the two-step approach developed by Engle and Granger (1987). In contrast, Larsson et al. (2001) use a multivariate framework by developing a likelihood ratio panel test based on the average of the individual rank trace statistics developed by Johansen (1988, 1995a). Their LR bar test statistic is therefore very similar to the IPS (1997) t-bar statistic used to test for panel unit roots. Essentially, the trace statistics for each cross section i in the panel are computed, and the average is standardized using the mean and variance of the underlying trace statistics defining the model. These mean and variance terms are obtained via Monte Carlo simulations and depend on which test of the rank of the long-run matrix in the vector error correction model (VECM) is being considered

[23] Equation (7.15) needs to be estimated using an efficient procedure that allows for residual autocorrelation in a model involving cointegration. Non-parametric methods include the FMOLS estimator of Phillips and Hansen (1991); a parametric approach is to use a dynamic OLS estimator (e.g., Stock and Watson, 1993).

(table 1 in Larsson et al., 2001, provides the values of the means and variances to be used).

To illustrate the use of tests for cointegration in panels, we continue to use the data available in the *NPT 1.3* programme (Chiang and Kao, 2002), comprising a panel of 22 countries over 20 years with estimates of TFP, R&D spending and international R&D spending (see Coe and Helpman, 1995, for details). Table 7.4 presents the results relating to the various tests attributable to Kao (1999), Pedroni (1995, 1999) and McCoskey and Kao (1998). The latter test the null of cointegration, and this is firmly rejected, whereas the former tests have no cointegration as the null hypothesis. Of these tests, the Kao tests allowing for endogeneity generally reject the null in favour of cointegration (involving a homogeneous β for all i-countries in the cross section), while the Pedroni tests provide mixed results with only 5 of the 18 test statistics rejecting the null at the 5% level or better.[24] If it is believed that group-means parametric estimators should be preferred, then the null is rejected, although it should be noted that it is not uncommon for different tests to give mixed results when (as is likely) some of the series are cointegrated and some are not (see Table 7.5 for some evidence on this).

Finally, Table 7.5 reports the results from using the Larsson et al. (2001) procedure that computes the individual trace statistics for each cross section i in the panel and obtains the mean value (the panel trace statistic).[25] The procedure also simulates (based on 10,000 runs) the asymptotic critical value for each test and applies a small-sample correction to produce the Bartlett corrected critical value. Because there are only 20 time series observations for each cross section, it is not possible to include more than 6 countries maximum in each estimation (with 22 countries and two variables in the model, we would actually need 46 years of data to estimate the model with all countries included).[26] We also found that if all three variables (log TFP, log R&D and log foreign R&D) were included there were problems with singularity,[27] indicating that there is insufficient variability in the data set to estimate the full model. Hence, we dropped foreign R&D. The results in Table 7.5 indicate that the trace statistic exceeds the small-sample corrected

[24] We also tried using *NPT 1.3* for the Pedroni tests. However, at the time of writing it would appear that there are some limitations with the specification of the underlying OLS model used to generate the residuals that comprise step 1 of the Pedroni procedure. In effect it seems that the FE model is always used; thus we also estimated the panel OLS model incorporating a time trend. The overall results were very different from those reported in the text, with only the parametric panel t-test able to reject the null.

[25] We are indebted to Johan Lyhagen for providing us with a copy of his *Gauss* programme with which to undertake the estimations reported in the text.

[26] The requirement for T is $T \geq Np + 2$, where p is the number of regressors in the model.

[27] That is, let $\mathbf{z} = \{\log \text{TFP}, \log \text{R\&D}, \log \text{foreign R\&D}\}$; then $(\mathbf{z}'\mathbf{z})$ could not be inverted due to singularity of the $\mathbf{z}$ matrix.

Table 7.4 Panel cointegration tests for log TFP, log R&D (research and development) and log foreign R&D ($N = 22$; $T = 20$).

Test name	Deterministic component (z_{it})	Test statistic*	Significance level for rejection
Kao (1999) tests[a]			
DF_ρ	α_i	−0.117	0.453
DF_t	α_i	−0.420	0.337
DF_ρ^*	α_i	−5.450	0.000
DF_t^*	α_i	−2.249	0.012
ADF test	α_i	−2.366	0.009
Pedroni (1995, 1999) tests[b]			
Panel ν	α_i	−0.886	0.812
Panel ρ	α_i	1.243	0.893
Panel t (non-parametric)	α_i	−1.686	0.046
Panel t (parametric)	α_i	−3.167	0.008
Group ρ	α_i	2.992	0.999
Group t (non-parametric)	α_i	−0.708	0.239
Group t (parametric)	α_i	−2.853	0.002
Panel ν	$\alpha_i + \eta_i t$	−0.450	0.674
Panel ρ	$\alpha_i + \eta_i t$	1.133	0.871
Panel t (non-parametric)	$\alpha_i + \eta_i t$	−1.519	0.064
Panel t (parametric)	$\alpha_i + \eta_i t$	−2.577	0.005
Group ρ	$\alpha_i + \eta_i t$	2.685	0.996
Group t (non-parametric)	$\alpha_i + \eta_i t$	−0.532	0.297
Group t (parametric)	$\alpha_i + \eta_i t$	−1.720	0.043
McCoskey and Kao (1998) test[a]			
LM	α_i	3181.931	0.000

* All tests are (asymptotically) distributed under the standard normal distribution. The Kao tests are one-sided using the negative tail, as are all the Pedroni tests except the ν-tests, which are one-sided using the positive tail.

[a] Obtained using *NPT 1.3* (Chiang and Kao, 2002).

[b] Obtained using *RATS* code supplied by Peter Pedroni.

critical value when the USA, Japan, Germany and France are included in the model, but not when we replace France with the UK. Thus, cointegration is established for the former, but not the latter grouping of countries.

ESTIMATING PANEL COINTEGRATION MODELS

The last section outlined procedures for testing whether the variables in a panel data set are cointegrated. This section discusses the various (usually single equation) approaches for estimating a cointegration vector using panel data.

The various estimators available include within- and between-group fully

Table 7.5 Larsson et al. (2001) panel cointegration tests for log TFP and log R&D ($N = 4$; $T = 20$).

Countries included	Panel trace statistic	Asymptotic critical value	Bartlett corrected critical value
US, Japan, Germany, France	139.393	54.609	115.523
US, Japan, Germany, UK	73.400	54.609	115.523

modified OLS (FMOLS) and dynamic OLS (DOLS) estimators. FMOLS is a non-parametric approach to dealing with corrections for serial correlation, while DOLS is a parametric approach where lagged first-differenced terms are explicitly estimated (see Box 7.2). The advantages of parametric versus non-parametric approaches have already been discussed in the last section and depend on a number of judgements largely associated with the data (e.g., length of the time series, expectations of 'fat tails' and/or negative MA processes in the d.g.p.s).

Pedroni argues that the between-group estimators are preferable to the within-group estimators for a number of reasons. First, Pedroni (2000) found that the group-means FMOLS estimator (in contrast to other FMOLS estimators) has relatively minor size distortions in small samples. Second, within-dimension estimators test the null hypothesis H_0: $\beta_i = \beta_0$ for all i against the alternative H_1: $\beta_i = \beta_A \neq \beta_0$ where β_A is the same for all i. Group-means estimators have as an alternative hypothesis H_1: $\beta_i = \beta_0$, so that heterogeneity is allowed and all the i cross sections do not have imposed on them a common β_A value. Third, a related issue to the last one is that the point estimates of the cointegration vector have a more meaningful interpretation if the true cointegration vectors are heterogeneous across the i members of the panel. These point estimates are the mean value for the underlying i cointegration vectors, while the within-dimension estimator provides the sample mean of the underlying cointegration vectors.

As to whether FMOLS or DOLS is preferred, the evidence is conflicting: Kao and Chiang (2000) found that FMOLS may be more biased than DOLS (note that Kao and Chiang, 2000, only consider within-group estimators); in addition, Pedroni has undertaken unreported Monte Carlo simulations that find the group-means DOLS estimator has relatively small size distortions, but these were typically slightly higher than size distortions experienced using the group-means FMOLS estimator. The Pedroni experiments were based on a specification that included heterogeneous dynamics, and this may account for the slightly poorer performance of his group-means DOLS estimator.

Lastly, before considering an empirical example, some progress has recently been made toward developing a multivariate approach to panel

Box 7.2 Correction for endogeneity and serial correlation in FMOLS and DOLS models.[28]

Consider a simple two variable panel regression model:

$$y_{it} = \alpha_i + \beta_i x_{it} + u_{it} \tag{7.2.1}$$

A standard panel OLS estimator for the coefficient β_i is given by:

$$\hat{\beta}_{i,\text{OLS}} = \left(\sum_{i=1}^{N} \sum_{t=1}^{T} (x_{it} - \bar{x}_i)^2 \right)^{-1} \sum_{i=1}^{N} \sum_{t=1}^{T} (x_{it} - \bar{x}_i)(y_{it} - \bar{y}_i) \tag{7.2.2}$$

where $\bar{x}_i$ and $\bar{y}_i$ refer to the individual means for each i member of the cross section. As discussed in Pedroni (2000), this estimator is asymptotically biased and its distribution is dependent on nuisance parameters (regressors that do not belong to the true d.g.p.) associated with the dynamics underlying the processes determining x and y. Only if x is strictly exogenous and the dynamics are homogeneous across the i members of the panel is $\hat{\beta}_{i,\text{OLS}}$ unbiased.

To correct for endogeneity and serial correlation, Pedroni (2000) has suggested the group-means FMOLS estimator that incorporates the Phillips and Hansen (1990) semi-parametric correction to the OLS estimator to eliminate the bias due to the endogeneity of the regressors. He also adjusts for the heterogeneity that is present in the dynamics underlying x and y. Specifically, the FMOLS statistic is:

$$\hat{\beta}_{i,\text{FMOLS}} = N^{-1} \sum_{i=1}^{N} \left(\sum_{t=1}^{T} (x_{it} - \bar{x}_i)^2 \right)^{-1} \left(\sum_{t=1}^{T} (x_{it} - \bar{x}_i) y_{it}^{*} - T\hat{\gamma}_i \right) \tag{7.2.3}$$

where

$$y_{it}^{*} = (x_{it} - \bar{x}_i) - \frac{\hat{\Omega}_{21i}}{\hat{\Omega}_{22i}} \Delta x_{it} \tag{7.2.4}$$

$$\hat{\gamma}_i = \hat{\Gamma}_{21i} + \hat{\Omega}_{21i}^{0} - \frac{\hat{\Omega}_{21i}}{\hat{\Omega}_{22i}} (\hat{\Gamma}_{22i} - \hat{\Omega}_{22i}^{0}) \tag{7.2.5}$$

where the $\hat{\Omega}$ and $\hat{\Gamma}$ are covariances and sums of autocovariances obtained from the long-run covariance matrix for the model (7.2.1). Essentially, the difference between the OLS and FMOLS estimators (cf. (7.22) and (7.2.3)) is that the regressor x_{it} has been transformed in equation (7.2.4) by subtracting off the last term, which acts as an instrument for the endogeneity of the regressor. Similarly, the term $\hat{\gamma}_i$ (equation (7.2.5)) acts to correct for the effect of serial correlation due to the heterogeneous dynamics in the short-run processes determining x and y.

In contrast to the non-parametric FMOLS estimator, Pedroni (2001) has also constructed a between-dimension, group-means panel DOLS estimator that incorporates corrections for endogeneity and serial correlation

[28] The material in this box is heavily dependent on Pedroni (2000).

parametrically. This is done by modifying equation (7.2.1) to include lead and lag dynamics:

$$y_{it} = \alpha_i + \beta_i x_{it} + \sum_{j=-K_i}^{K_i} \gamma_{ik} \Delta x_{i,t-k} + e_{it} \tag{7.2.6}$$

where

$$\hat{\beta}_{i,\text{DOLS}} = \left[N^{-1} \sum_{i=1}^{N} \left(\sum_{t=1}^{T} z_{it} z_{it}' \right)^{-1} \left(\sum_{t=1}^{T} z_{it} \tilde{y}_{it} \right) \right]_1 \tag{7.2.7}$$

and z_{it} is the $2(K+1) \times 1$ vector of regressors $z_{it} = \{(x_{it} - \bar{x}_i), \Delta x_{it-K}, \ldots, \Delta x_{it+K}\}$; $\tilde{y}_{it} = y_{it} - \bar{y}_i$; the subscript 1 outside the brackets in (7.2.7) indicates that only the first element of the vector is taken to obtain the pooled slope coefficient.

cointegration estimation. Breitung (2002) has developed a two-step procedure that is based on estimating a VECM. In step 1, the short-run parameters of the model are allowed to vary across the i members of the cross section, while in step 2 the homogeneous long-run parameters[29] (the cointegration vectors[30]) are estimated from a pooled regression. He finds his approach results in lower small-sample bias than the FMOLS estimator suggested by Pedroni (2000) or the DOLS estimator suggested by Kao and Chiang (2000). The advantages of the multivariate approach also extend to allowing for the number of cointegration vectors that can be separately estimated to exceed 1.[31]

To illustrate the estimation of panel cointegration models, we again use the data from Chiang and Kao (2002), which was taken from Coe and Helpman (1995), comprising international TFP and R&D data. The group-means OLS, FMOLS and DOLS estimators developed by Pedroni (2000, 2001) are used to obtain the first block of results in Table 7.6.[32] Note that the current version of Pedroni's *Rats* program allows for fixed effects ($\alpha_i \neq 0$) and the imposition of common time dummies (the latter are different to common time trends, but these still impose homogeneity in this aspect across the i members of the panel, whereas heterogeneous time trends—not currently available—allow for a more general structure). When common time dummies are omitted, the results for all

[29] That is, the assumption that the $\boldsymbol{\beta}$ are the same across the members of the panel is imposed in the Breitung approach.

[30] Note that if the number of variables in the model k exceeds 2, then potentially more than one cointegration vector may exist and that, at the time of writing, Breitung has yet to extend his *Gauss* program to produce estimates of more than one cointegration vector when $k > 2$, although in principle this is possible and is planned in a future extension by Breitung.

[31] But see the last footnote for the current limitations on this approach.

[32] The *Rats* code for this is available from Pedroni (and on the book's website).

Table 7.6 Panel OLS, FMOLS, DOLS and VECM estimates of cointegration vectors involving log TFP, log R&D and log foreign R&D.

	$\hat{\beta}_1$	t-value	$\hat{\beta}_2$	t-value
(i) *Between-dimension estimator*				
Fixed effects and common time dummies				
OLS	0.05	0.40	−0.04	−0.11
FMOLS	0.05	1.74	−0.03	−0.42
DOLS	0.02	5.89	0.05	0.39
Fixed effects and no common time dummies				
OLS	0.31	3.86	−0.07	−0.79
FMOLS	0.31	16.73	−0.06	−3.18
DOLS	0.24	42.97	0.22	2.09
(ii) *Within-dimension estimator*				
Fixed effects and homogeneous covariance				
FMOLS	0.08	4.37	0.10	3.18
DOLS	0.10	4.14	0.05	1.32
Fixed effects and heterogeneous covariance				
DOLS	0.15	5.74	0.01	9.71
(iii) *VECM estimator*				
Fixed effects	0.03	3.74	0.01	1.24
Heterogeneous time trends	0.31	5.25	0.03	0.30

three group-means estimators suggest a much larger impact for domestic R&D on TFP (the elasticity ranges from 0.24 to 0.31). The spillover impact of foreign R&D is negative for the OLS and FMOLS estimators, but significantly positive for the DOLS estimator (and substantial when common time dummies are omitted). These results suggest that for this data set heterogeneity is important and omitting common time effects is probably the correct specification.

The within-groups estimators are those developed by Kao and Chiang (2000) and available in *NPT 1.3* (see Chiang and Kao, 2002). When homogeneous lagged dependent variables are imposed, the results suggest that the elasticity of domestic R&D on TFP is around 0.08–0.10, while spillover effects are positive although insignificant in the case of the DOLS result. If heterogeneity is allowed in the short-run dynamics of the model, then a larger domestic R&D effects is obtained together with a smaller (but highly significant) spillover effect.

Finally, the VECM estimator devised by Breitung (2002) produces results that are different, but still within the same range as the results obtained from the single equation approaches. If the VECM approach has lower small-sample bias, then the heterogeneous trends specification suggests that the elasticity of domestic R&D is similar to that obtained by the group-means estimators with no common time dummies, while spillover effects from foreign R&D are negligible. Further this suggests that the group-means estimator with heterogeneous time trends may be a useful future addition to the Pedroni approach.

CONCLUSION ON TESTING FOR UNIT ROOTS AND COINTEGRATION IN PANEL DATA

One of the major conclusions drawn in Chapter 3, when considering unit root-testing for time series data with dimension $N = 1$, was the poor size and power properties of such tests (i.e., the tendency to over-reject the null when it is true and under-reject the null when it is false, respectively). Basically, the problem stems from insufficient information in *finite* samples with which to distinguish between non-stationary and nearly non-stationary series. The major advantage of adding the cross-sectional dimension to the time series dimension means that non-stationarity from the time series can be dealt with *and* combined with the increased data and power that the cross section brings. The latter acts as repeated draws from the same distribution, and thus, while it is known that the standard DF-type tests lack power in distinguishing the unit root null from stationary alternatives, using the cross-sectional dimension of panel data increases the power of unit root tests that are based on a single draw from the population under consideration. Moreover, and in direct contrast to standard DF-type tests, as N and T get large, panel tests statistics and estimators converge to normally distributed random variables. This makes testing and inference simpler and results from the fact that panel estimators average across individuals leading to a stronger overall signal than that available from a pure time series estimator.

However, while there are increases in the power of testing for unit roots using panel data, there is still a need to be cautious when drawing any conclusions based on panel unit root tests. Since the panel comprising i cross sections may contain a mix of non-stationary and stationary series and given that several tests specify different forms of the alternative hypotheses (to the null of non-stationarity) in terms of whether all i cross sections are stationary or only some are stationary, inevitably there is the potential for a range of outcomes. Recall that Karlsson and Lothgren (2000) found that: '... for large-T panels, there is a potential risk that the whole panel may erroneously be modelled as stationary ... due to the high power of the panel tests for small proportions of stationary series in the panel. For small-T panels, on the other hand, there is a potential risk that the whole panel may be erroneously modelled as non-stationary, due to the relatively low power of tests even for large proportions of stationary series in the panel.' Certainly, the empirical examples provided in this chapter show that panel unit root-testing does not necessarily give clear outcomes.

Testing for cointegration in panel data should also have the same beneficial effects in terms of power that are present when testing for unit roots using panel data. That is, the low power of conventional tests (when $N = 1$, such as the EG two-step approach) when applied to series of only moderate length can be improved upon by pooling information across the i members of a panel. However, panel cointegration tests are still at a fairly early stage of development, mostly being based on a single equation approach. Moreover, tests for whether cointegration occurs are typically undertaken separately from estimating the cointegration vector, and there are issues over which estimator is to be preferred (the non-parametric versus parametric and/or estimators based on the within- or between-dimension approach). So while there are a number of tests and different estimators of the cointegration vector that are available, it is unlikely that unambiguous results will be obtained with panel data comprising moderate values of N and T. The empirical example used throughout this chapter (based on $N = 22$ and $T = 20$) showed this to be the case. Still, there are likely to be significant advances in panel data techniques in the near future, hopefully providing the applied economist with greater certainty as to whether (panel) data are non-stationary and/or contain cointegrated long-run relationships.

Important Terms and Concepts

Panel unit roots	Panel cointegration	FMOLS
DOLS	Group-means estimators	Within-group estimators

8
Modelling and Forecasting Financial Time Series

INTRODUCTION

The methods and techniques discussed in previous chapters of this book are as applicable to financial time series as they are to macroeconomic time series; however, the analysis of financial time series raises a number of additional issues that we have not yet covered in detail. For example, financial time series are often available at a higher frequency than macroeconomic time series and many high-frequency financial time series have been shown to exhibit the property of 'long-memory' (the presence of statistically significant correlations between observations that are a large distance apart). Another distinguishing feature of many financial time series is the time-varying volatility or 'heteroscedasticity' of the data. It is typically the case that time series data on the returns from investing in a financial asset contain periods of high volatility followed by periods of lower volatility (visually, there are clusters of extreme values in the returns series followed by periods in which such extreme values are not present). When discussing the volatility of time series, econometricians refer to the 'conditional variance' of the data, and the time-varying volatility typical of asset returns is otherwise known as 'conditional heteroscedasticity'. The concept of conditional heteroscedasticity was introduced to economists by Engle (1982), who proposed a model in which the conditional variance of a time series is a function of past shocks; the autoregressive conditional heteroscedastic (ARCH) model. The model provided a rigorous way of empirically investigating issues involving the volatility of economic variables. An example is Friedman's hypothesis that higher inflation is more volatile (cf. Friedman, 1977). Using data for the UK, Engle (1982) found that the ARCH model supported Friedman's hypothesis.[1]

[1] Engle (1983) applied the ARCH model to US inflation and the converse results emerged, although Cosimano and Jansen (1988) criticize this paper as they believe that Engle estimates a mis-specified model. The relationship between the level and variance of inflation has continued to interest applied econometricians (see, for example, Grier and Perry, 2000).

Although initial applications of the ARCH model involved time series on the rate of inflation, the model has since become particularly popular in financial econometrics. Referring to Engle's (1982) paper, Franses and McAleer (2002) write 'The ARCH paper had an enormous influence on both theoretical and applied econometrics, and was influential in the establishment of the discipline of Financial Econometrics' (p. 419). When applied to time series on the returns from investing in a financial asset, the concept of a conditional variance has a natural interpretation as the time-varying risk associated with that asset, and not only does the ARCH model allow for an estimate of the conditional variance of a time series to be obtained but it also enables forecasts of future values of the conditional variance to be computed. Obtaining an estimate of the risk associated with a share or a stock market index and being able to forecast that risk into the future is, for financial econometricians, an extremely attractive feature of a time series model.

Most of this chapter will be devoted to the topic of conditional heteroscedasticity. We also consider some forecasting issues. In time series analysis, finding the superior forecasting model is often an objective of the applied econometrician. While the evaluation of forecasts from competing models is traditionally done by directly comparing the mean squared error (MSE) of the forecasts, more recently tests to evaluate the statistical significance of differences in MSE and for comparing the informational content of forecasts have become popular. Some of these tests will be considered in this chapter. Throughout this chapter we use monthly data on Standard & Poor's (S&P) Composite index to illustrate the models and techniques discussed. All estimation is done using either *PcGive* or the *G@RCH* program of Laurent and Peters (2002a, b).[2]

[2] The current version of the *G@RCH* program is 2.3. Note that the conditional heteroscedasticity models referred to in this chapter could also be estimated using the volatility models package in *PcGive*. If this package is used instead of the *G@RCH* program, then the results will be similar, but not identical. The models are estimated by maximum likelihood involving numerical maximization of the likelihood function, and the exact algorithm used, in addition to details such as step length and convergence criteria, can lead to small differences in the final results. Note also that throughout this chapter, so that the results can be easily reproduced, when estimating ARCH and GARCH models we use the default starting values provided by the *G@RCH* program. It is possible in the *G@RCH* program and in *PcGive* to specify particular starting values when estimating by maximum likelihood and thus fine-tune the estimation of each model. It is also the case that throughout this chapter we present the estimated parameters, *t*-statistics and information criteria for the estimated models, but do not present detailed diagnostic tests. Both the *G@RCH* program and *PcGive* allow for numerous diagnostic tests and for detailed graphical analysis of the estimated models. We encourage readers to investigate these tests and model evaluation tools. Since many of them are similar to those already referred to in this text, for brevity they are omitted in our presentation of the results in this chapter.

ARCH AND GARCH

Up until now, when discussing the mean, variance and covariance (i.e., the moments) of a time series (as in Chapter 1), we have been referring to the long-run moments of the series. That is, the mean, variance and covariance as $t \to \infty$. In addition to the long-run unconditional moments of a time series we can also calculate the conditional moments (the mean, variance and covariance at time t conditional on the actual values taken by the series in previous periods). The ARCH model developed by Engle (1982) is a model that allows the conditional variance to be time-varying, while the unconditional variance is constant (a model with conditional heteroscedasticity, but unconditional homoscedasticity). Recall from Box 2.1 that if the mean, variance or covariance of a time series are time-varying, then the series is non-stationary. One might assume therefore that a series with conditional heteroscedasticity is non-stationary. Note, though, that when defining 'non-stationarity' we are actually referring to the long-run or unconditional moments of the series. A time series with conditional heteroscedasticity can still be stationary, as long as its unconditional moments are constant.

Distinguishing between the conditional and unconditional properties of a time series extends to its probability distribution. Typically, when using maximum likelihood to estimate econometric models, it is assumed that the series has a conditional normal distribution. However, a time series also has an unconditional probability distribution, and the unconditional distribution may not take the same form as the conditional distribution. In the case of an ARCH model, when a conditional normal distribution is assumed, it turns out that the unconditional distribution of the series will be non-normal, more specifically it will be leptokurtic (or have 'fat-tails').

Since the concept of autoregression is now familiar, the first-order autoregressive model (AR(1) model) will be used in an initial exposition of ARCH. Consider, first, the following conventional AR(1) model:

$$y_t = \rho y_{t-1} + u_t \tag{8.1}$$

where $t = 1, 2, \dots, T$, $u_t \sim \text{IID}(0, \sigma^2)$ and assume that $|\rho| < 1$. Thus, y_t is a stationary AR(1) process. If y_t is generated by (8.1), then as discussed in Chapter 1 the mean and variance (and covariance) of y_t are constant. Specifically, as shown in Chapter 1, the equations for the mean and variance of y_t are $E(y_t) = 0$ and $\text{var}(y_t) = \sigma^2/(1 - \rho^2)$, respectively. These are the unconditional mean and the unconditional variance of y_t. The conditional mean of y_t refers to the mean of y_t, conditional on information available at time $t - 1$. For brevity, define Ω_{t-1} to be the information set representing the information available at $t - 1$. Assuming y_t is generated by (8.1), the conditional mean of y_t is given by:

$$E(y_t \mid \Omega_{t-1}) = \rho y_{t-1} \tag{8.2}$$

and the conditional variance of y_t is given by:

$$\begin{aligned}\operatorname{var}(y_t \mid \Omega_{t-1}) &= E(u_t^2 \mid \Omega_{t-1}) \\ &= \sigma^2 \end{aligned} \tag{8.3}$$

In this case, clearly the conditional mean of y_t is time-varying, but the unconditional mean is not.

When defining ARCH, Engle (1982) proposed the following model for the error term u_t:

$$u_t = \varepsilon_t(\alpha_0 + \alpha_1 u_{t-1}^2)^{1/2} \tag{8.4}$$

where $\varepsilon_t \sim \text{IID}(0, 1)$ and we assume that $\alpha_0 > 0$ and $0 < \alpha_1 < 1$. The unconditional mean and variance of u_t are:

$$E(u_t) = 0 \tag{8.5}$$

$$\operatorname{var}(u_t) = \frac{\alpha_0}{(1 - \alpha_1)} \tag{8.6}$$

The conditional mean and variance of u_t are:

$$E(u_t \mid \Omega_{t-1}) = 0 \tag{8.7}$$

$$\begin{aligned}\operatorname{var}(u_t \mid \Omega_{t-1}) &= E(u_t^2 \mid \Omega_{t-1}) \\ &= \alpha_0 + \alpha_1 u_{t-1}^2 \end{aligned} \tag{8.8}$$

where Ω_{t-1} represents the relevant information set (more detail is given in Box 8.1). Hereafter we will refer to the conditional variance of u_t as h_t. In contrast to the unconditional variance of u_t given by (8.6), h_t given by (8.8) is *not* constant over time; it is a first-order autoregressive process (hence u_t is ARCH(1)). In the ARCH(1) model, the value of the conditional variance of this period is a function of the squared error term from the last period u_{t-1}^2. Note that it is necessary to place restrictions on α_0 and α_1: in particular, they must both be positive. If either of these parameters were negative, a negative conditional variance could be predicted from this model (which is not theoretically possible). If y_t is generated by (8.1), with u_t generated by (8.4), the conditional mean of y_t is given by:

$$E(y_t \mid \Omega_{t-1}) = \rho y_{t-1} \tag{8.9}$$

The conditional variance of y_t is given by:

$$\operatorname{var}(y_t \mid \Omega_{t-1}) = \alpha_0 + \alpha_1 u_{t-1}^2 \tag{8.10}$$

Thus, the conditional variance of y_t is also a function of the squared error term from the last period u_{t-1}^2. In terms of *specification*, ARCH directly affects the error terms u_t; however, the dependent variable y_t, generated from a linear model with an ARCH error term, is itself an ARCH process.

Box 8.1 Conditional and unconditional mean and variance of ARCH(1) process.

Assume the following model for u_t:

$$u_t = \varepsilon_t(\alpha_0 + \alpha_1 u_{t-1}^2)^{1/2} \tag{8.1.1}$$

where $\alpha_0 > 0$, $0 < \alpha_1 < 1$ and $\varepsilon_t \sim \text{IID}(0, 1)$. The unconditional mean of u_t is:

$$\begin{aligned} E(u_t) &= E(\varepsilon_t)E(\alpha_0 + \alpha_1 u_{t-1}^2)^{1/2} \\ &= 0 \quad \text{since } E(\varepsilon_t) = 0 \end{aligned} \tag{8.1.2}$$

The unconditional variance of u_t is:

$$\begin{aligned} E[\{u_t - E(u_t)\}^2] &= E(u_t^2) && \text{since } E(u_t) = 0 \\ &= E(\varepsilon_t^2)E(\alpha_0 + \alpha_1 u_{t-1}^2) \\ &= \alpha_0 + \alpha_1 E(u_{t-1}^2) && \text{since } E(\varepsilon_t^2) = 1 \\ &= \alpha_0/(1 - \alpha_1) && \text{since the line above can be rewritten as a geometric series} \end{aligned} \tag{8.1.3}$$

The conditional mean of u_t is:

$$\begin{aligned} E(u_t \mid \Omega_{t-1}) &= E(\varepsilon_t \mid \Omega_{t-1})(\alpha_0 + \alpha_1 u_{t-1}^2)^{1/2} \\ &= 0 \quad \text{since } E(\varepsilon_t \mid \Omega_{t-1}) = 0 \end{aligned} \tag{8.1.4}$$

The conditional variance of u_t is:

$$\begin{aligned} E(u_t^2 \mid \Omega_{t-1}) &= E(\varepsilon_t^2 \mid \Omega_{t-1})(\alpha_0 + \alpha_1 u_{t-1}^2) \\ &= \alpha_0 + \alpha_1 u_{t-1}^2 \quad \text{since } E(\varepsilon_t^2 \mid \Omega_{t-1}) = 1 \end{aligned} \tag{8.1.5}$$

In Figure 8.1(a), 100 simulated observations of an IID series ($\varepsilon_t \sim \text{IID}(0, 1)$) and an ARCH(1) series ($u_t = \varepsilon_t(\alpha_0 + \alpha_1 u_{t-1}^2)^{1/2}$, where $\alpha_0 = 1$, $\alpha_1 = 0.6$ and $\varepsilon_t \sim \text{IID}(0, 1)$) are plotted. It can be seen that the ARCH(1) series u_t has clusters of extreme values that are not in the IID series (see observations 30–35, for example). This is a direct consequence of the AR structure of the conditional variance. When the realized value of u_{t-1} is far from zero, h_t (the conditional variance of u_t) will tend to be large. Therefore extreme values of u_t are followed by other extreme values. In Figure 8.1(b), 100 simulated observations of an AR(1) series ($y_t = \rho y_{t-1} + u_t$, where $\rho = 0.9$ and $u_t \sim \text{IID}(0, 1)$) and an AR(1)–ARCH(1) series ($y_t = \rho y_{t-1} + u_t$, where $\rho = 0.9$ and $u_t = \varepsilon_t(\alpha_0 + \alpha_1 u_{t-1}^2)^{1/2}$ with $\alpha_0 = 1$, $\alpha_1 = 0.6$ and $\varepsilon_t \sim \text{IID}(0, 1)$) are plotted. In this case, due to the AR(1) parameter ρ being close to unity, it can be seen that both series in Figure 8.1(b) are smoother than those in Figure 8.1(a). However the AR(1)–ARCH(1) series is noticeably more volatile than

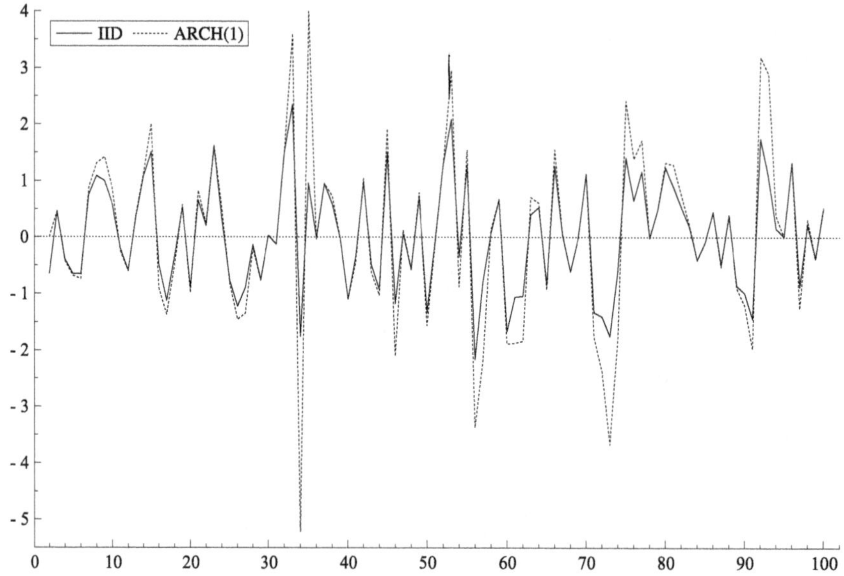

Figure 8.1(a). Simulated IID and ARCH(1) series.

the conditionally homoscedastic AR(1) series.[3] The clustering of extreme values and movement from calm to volatile periods of behaviour in these graphs is a particular feature of financial time series, hence the relevance of ARCH to financial econometricians.

The concept of ARCH can be extended to higher order ARCH processes and to other univariate times series models, bivariate and multivariate regression models and to systems of equations as well. For example, the AR(p)–ARCH(q) model can be written:

$$y_t = \delta + \sum_{i=1}^{p} \rho_i y_{t-i} + u_t \tag{8.11}$$

$$u_t = \varepsilon_t \left(\alpha_0 + \sum_{i=1}^{q} \alpha_i u_{t-i}^2 \right)^{1/2} \qquad \varepsilon_t \sim \text{IID}(0, 1) \tag{8.12}$$

The ARCH(q) multiple regression model can be written:

$$y_t = \beta_0 + \sum_{i=1}^{k} \beta_i x_{it} + u_t \tag{8.13}$$

$$u_t = \varepsilon_t \left(\alpha_0 + \sum_{i=1}^{q} \alpha_i u_{t-i}^2 \right)^{1/2} \qquad \varepsilon_t \sim \text{IID}(0, 1) \tag{8.14}$$

[3] The programs used to simulate these series are available in the *GiveWin* manual (p. 86).

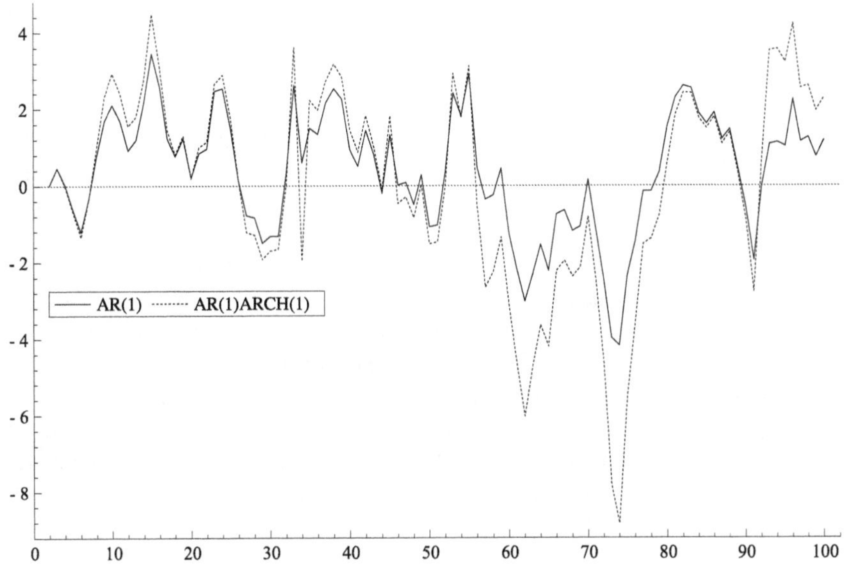

Figure 8.1(b). Simulated AR(1) and AR(1)–ARCH(1) series.

where the x_{it} are exogenous explanatory variables and/or lagged values of the dependent variable y_t. In financial time series analysis, if the series being modelled is an asset price one might also want to include dummy variables in the model for the conditional mean to capture particular features of the market such as 'day-of-the-week' effects. Assuming daily data this would involve replacing (8.13) with:

$$y_t = \sum_{i=1}^{k} \beta_i x_{it} + \sum_{l=1}^{5} \alpha_l D_{lt} + u_t \tag{8.15}$$

where $l = 1$ (Monday), 2 (Tuesday), 3 (Wednesday), 4 (Thursday), 5 (Friday) and D_{lt} is a 0/1 dummy variable. Note also that it is possible to include explanatory variables (and dummy variables) in the conditional variance. For example, we could replace (8.14) with:

$$u_t = \varepsilon_t \left(\sum_{i=1}^{q} \alpha_i u_{t-i}^2 + \sum_{r=1}^{s} \gamma_r x_{rt} + \sum_{l=1}^{5} \delta_l D_{lt} \right)^{1/2} \qquad \varepsilon_t \sim \mathrm{IID}(0, 1) \tag{8.16}$$

However, it is more common to restrict the inclusion of additional regressors to the conditional mean. Again, in practice it is necessary to place restrictions on the parameters of these ARCH models in order to ensure that the conditional variance is positive. Engle (1982) proves that if $\alpha_0 > 0$ and $\alpha_1, \alpha_2, \ldots, \alpha_q \geq 0$, qth-order ARCH models (excluding additional regressors in the conditional variance) satisfy certain regularity conditions, one of which is the non-negativity constraint. Generalizing the concept of ARCH models to systems of equations (referred to as multivariate ARCH models in the literature) seems like a natural extension of the original specification. This and other extensions of the ARCH model will be considered in more detail in subsequent sections of this chapter.

One of the difficulties when using the ARCH model is that often a large number of lagged squared error terms in the equation for the conditional variance are found to be significant on the basis of pre-testing. Furthermore we have already noted that to avoid problems associated with a negative conditional variance it is necessary to impose restrictions on the parameters in the model. Consequently in practice the estimation of ARCH models is not always straightforward. Bollerslev (1986) focuses on extending the ARCH model to allow for a more flexible lag structure. He introduces a conditional heteroscedasticity model that includes lags of the conditional variance $(h_{t-1}, h_{t-2}, \ldots, h_{t-p})$ as regressors in the model for the conditional variance (in addition to lags of the squared error term $u_{t-1}^2, u_{t-2}^2, \ldots, u_{t-q}^2$): the generalized ARCH (GARCH) model. Assume that y_t can be modelled as (8.13). In a GARCH(p, q) model, u_t is defined as:

$$u_t = \varepsilon_t \left(\alpha_0 + \sum_{i=1}^{q} \alpha_i u_{t-i}^2 + \sum_{j=1}^{p} \beta_j h_{t-j} \right)^{1/2} \tag{8.17}$$

where $\varepsilon_t \sim \text{NID}(0, 1)$; $p \geq 0$, $q > 0$; $\alpha_0 > 0$, $\alpha_i \geq 0$, $i = 1, \ldots, q$ and $\beta_j \geq 0$, $j = 1, 2, \ldots, p$.

It follows from manipulation of (8.17) that h_t (the conditional variance of u_t) is a function of lagged values of u_t^2 and lagged values of h_t:

$$h_t = \alpha_0 + \sum_{i=1}^{q} \alpha_i u_{t-i}^2 + \sum_{j=1}^{p} \beta_j h_{t-j} \tag{8.18}$$

Note that (8.17) nests both the ARCH(q) model $(p = 0)$ and a white-noise process $(p = q = 0)$.

Using the lag operator L $(Lu_t = u_{t-1})$, the conditional variance of the GARCH(p, q) process u_t can be written as:

$$h_t = \alpha_0 + \alpha(L)u_t^2 + \beta(L)h_t \tag{8.19}$$

where $\alpha(L) = \alpha_1 L + \alpha_2 L^2 + \cdots + \alpha_q L^q$ and $\beta(L) = \beta_1 L + \beta_2 L^2 + \cdots + \beta_p L^p$. Note that (8.19) can be rewritten as:[4]

$$\begin{aligned} h_t &= \alpha_0 [1 - \beta(L)]^{-1} + \alpha(L)[1 - \beta(L)]^{-1} u_t^2 \\ &= \alpha_0 \left(1 - \sum_{j=1}^{p} \beta_j \right)^{-1} + \sum_{i=1}^{\infty} \omega_i u_{t-i}^2 \end{aligned} \tag{8.20}$$

[4] This algebraic operation requires that all the roots of the polynomial $1 - \beta(L) = 0$ lie outside the unit circle.

where

$$\omega_i = \alpha_i + \sum_{l=1}^{n} \beta_l \omega_{i-l} \qquad i = 1, \ldots, q \tag{8.21}$$

and $n = \min\{p, i-1\}$. Therefore a GARCH(p, q) process has an infinite-dimensional ARCH representation. It follows logically that any stationary high-order ARCH model can be approximated as a GARCH model, and in practice it is usually the case that a GARCH(p, q) model with low values of p and q will provide a better fit to the data than an ARCH(q) model with a high value of q. The simplest GARCH model is the GARCH(1, 1) model for which the conditional variance is:

$$h_t = \alpha_0 + \alpha_1 u_{t-1}^2 + \beta_1 h_{t-1} \tag{8.22}$$

Bollerslev (1986) investigates the GARCH(1, 1) model in great detail and sets out the conditions required for the stationarity of h_t and the existence of higher moments. He also proves that the GARCH(p, q) process u_t is weakly stationary if and only if $\alpha(1) + \beta(1) < 1$.

MULTIVARIATE GARCH

If econometricians were interested in quantifying the relationship between the volatility of Standard & Poor's (S&P) Composite index returns and the FTSE 100 index returns, they might be tempted to include an estimate of the conditional variance of the FTSE returns as an explanatory variable in the equation for the conditional variance of the S&P Composite returns, or vice versa. Estimating a single equation ARCH or GARCH model would, however, be ignoring the possibility that there may be causality between the conditional variances in both directions and would not be truly exploiting the covariance between the series. A more effective way of capturing interactions between the volatility of N different time series is to estimate a multivariate GARCH model for the time series $\mathbf{y}_t = (y_{1t}, y_{2t}, \ldots, y_{Nt})'$. Here, the label 'multivariate GARCH' refers to a model for a multivariate time series $\mathbf{y}_t$ in which the conditional variances of the individual series and the conditional covariances between the series are estimated simultaneously (by maximum likelihood). The seminal paper on multivariate ARCH is by Engle, Granger and Kraft (1984), which introduced the bivariate ARCH model. A rigorous analysis of the theoretical properties of multivariate GARCH models, however, did not appear until Engle and Kroner (1995), which was based on the earlier working paper by Baba, Engle, Kraft and Kroner (1990).

In multivariate GARCH models, since $\mathbf{y}_t$ is a vector of dimension $(N \times 1)$, the conditional mean of $\mathbf{y}_t$ is an $(N \times 1)$ vector $\boldsymbol{\mu}_t$ and the conditional variance of $\mathbf{y}_t$ is an $(N \times N)$ matrix $\mathbf{H}_t$. The diagonal elements of $\mathbf{H}_t$ are the variance terms, and the off-diagonal elements of $\mathbf{H}_t$ are the covariance terms. There are numerous different representations of the multivariate GARCH model. The main representations are the VECH, diagonal, BEKK (after Baba, Engle, Kraft and Kroner) and constant correlation representations. These are discussed in more detail in Box 8.2. What Box 8.2 clearly reveals is that even for simple multivariate GARCH models such as the two-variable ($N = 2$) multivariate GARCH(1, 1) model, the number of parameters can be extremely large (21 parameters in the case of the VECH representation!). Estimating a large number of parameters is not in theory a problem as long as there is a large enough sample size. However, efficient estimation of the parameters in GARCH models is by maximum likelihood involving the numerical maximization of the likelihood function. Obtaining convergence of the typical optimization algorithms employed can in practice be very difficult when a large number of parameters are involved. Furthermore, as with the other GARCH models discussed so far, it is necessary to impose restrictions on the parameters of this model to ensure the non-negativity of the conditional variances of the individual series (this amounts to ensuring that $\mathbf{H}_t$ is positive-definite); in practice, this can be difficult to do. The diagonal representation improves on the VECH representation in the sense that there are fewer parameters to be estimated. The diagonal representation is based on the assumption that the individual conditional variances and conditional covariances are functions of only lagged values of themselves and lagged squared residuals. While in the case of $N = 2$ and $p = q = 1$, this representation reduces the number of parameters to be estimated from 21 to 9, it does so at the expense of losing information on certain interrelationships, such as the relationship between the individual conditional variances and the conditional covariances. Note also that it is still necessary to impose restrictions to ensure the positive-definiteness of $\mathbf{H}_t$.

The work of Engle and Kroner (1995) referred to above was a development of an earlier working paper by Baba et al. (1990). The BEKK representation of multivariate GARCH improves on both the VECH and diagonal representations, since $\mathbf{H}_t$ is almost guaranteed to be positive-definite. In the case of two variables ($N = 2$) and $p = q = 1$, the BEKK representation requires only 11 parameters to be estimated. It is more general than the diagonal representation as it allows for interaction effects that the diagonal representation does not. For example, as can be seen in Box 8.2, in the BEKK representation the individual conditional variances $h_{11,t-1}$ and $h_{22,t-1}$ affect the evolution of the covariance term $h_{12,t}$. Bollerslev (1990) employs the conditional correlation matrix $\mathbf{R}$ to derive a representation of the multivariate GARCH model that has become particularly popular in empirical work. In his $\mathbf{R}$ matrix, Bollerslev (1990) restricts the conditional correlations to be equal to the correlation coefficients between the variables, which are simply constants. Thus $\mathbf{R}$ is constant over time; hence the label 'constant correlation' representation. This representation has the advantage that $\mathbf{H}_t$ will be positive-definite if a plausible set of restrictions are met (given in Box 8.2).

The multivariate GARCH specification has been extended to the case of multivariate GARCH-M (see, for example, Grier and Perry, 2000, who use a

Box 8.2 Multivariate GARCH representations.

The VECH Representation

Applying the vech operator to a symmetric matrix stacks the lower triangular elements into a column. Since $\mathbf{H}_t$ is a symmetric matrix, in specifying the multivariate GARCH model we can employ the vech transformation of $\mathbf{H}_t$. Consider the following specification:

$$\text{vech}(\mathbf{H}_t) = \text{vech}(\mathbf{A}_0) + \sum_{i=1}^{q} \mathbf{A}_i \,\text{vech}(\boldsymbol{\varepsilon}_{t-i}\boldsymbol{\varepsilon}'_{t-i}) + \sum_{i=1}^{p} \mathbf{B}_i \,\text{vech}(\mathbf{H}_{t-i}) \quad (8.2.1)$$

where $\boldsymbol{\varepsilon}_t = (\varepsilon_{1t}, \ldots, \varepsilon_{Nt})'$ are the error terms associated with the conditional mean equations for y_{1t} to y_{Nt}, $\mathbf{A}_0$ is an $(N \times N)$ positive definite matrix of parameters and $\mathbf{A}_i$ and $\mathbf{B}_i$ are $[N(N+1)/2 \times N(N+1)/2]$ matrices of parameters. In the case of two variables $(N = 2)$ and $p = q = 1$, the multivariate GARCH representation given by (8.2.1) can be written out in full as:

$$\begin{bmatrix} h_{11,t} \\ h_{12,t} \\ h_{22,t} \end{bmatrix} = \begin{bmatrix} a_{11}^0 \\ a_{12}^0 \\ a_{22}^0 \end{bmatrix} + \begin{bmatrix} a_{11} & a_{12} & a_{13} \\ a_{21} & a_{22} & a_{23} \\ a_{31} & a_{32} & a_{33} \end{bmatrix} \begin{bmatrix} \varepsilon_{1,t-1}^2 \\ \varepsilon_{1,t-1}\varepsilon_{2,t-1} \\ \varepsilon_{2,t-1}^2 \end{bmatrix} + \begin{bmatrix} b_{11} & b_{12} & b_{13} \\ b_{21} & b_{22} & b_{23} \\ b_{32} & b_{32} & b_{33} \end{bmatrix} \begin{bmatrix} h_{11,t-1} \\ h_{12,t-1} \\ h_{22,t-1} \end{bmatrix} \quad (8.2.2)$$

where $h_{11,t}$ is the conditional variance of the error associated with y_{1t}, $h_{22,t}$ is the conditional variance of the error associated with y_{2t} and $h_{12,t}$ is the conditional covariance between the errors.

The Diagonal Representation

In the diagonal representation (due to Bollerslev, Engle and Woodridge, 1988) $\mathbf{A}_i$ and $\mathbf{B}_i$ in (8.2.1) are diagonal matrices. This assumption forces the individual conditional variances to have GARCH(p, q) forms and the covariances to have a GARCH(p, q) form. As an example, consider the diagonal representation of vech($\mathbf{H}_t$) in the case of two variables $(N = 2)$ and $p = q = 1$:

$$\begin{bmatrix} h_{11,t} \\ h_{12,t} \\ h_{22,t} \end{bmatrix} = \begin{bmatrix} a_{11}^0 \\ a_{12}^0 \\ a_{22}^0 \end{bmatrix} + \begin{bmatrix} a_{11} & 0 & 0 \\ 0 & a_{22} & 0 \\ 0 & 0 & a_{33} \end{bmatrix} \begin{bmatrix} \varepsilon_{1,t-1}^2 \\ \varepsilon_{1,t-1}\varepsilon_{2,t-1} \\ \varepsilon_{2,t-1}^2 \end{bmatrix}$$
$$+ \begin{bmatrix} b_{11} & 0 & 0 \\ 0 & b_{22} & 0 \\ 0 & 0 & b_{33} \end{bmatrix} \begin{bmatrix} h_{11,t-1} \\ h_{12,t-1} \\ h_{22,t-1} \end{bmatrix} \qquad (8.2.3)$$

The BEKK Representation

The BEKK representation (due to Baba et al., 1990) assumes the following model for $\mathbf{H}_t$:

$$\mathbf{H}_t = \mathbf{A}_0 + \sum_{i=1}^{q} \mathbf{A}_i^* \boldsymbol{\varepsilon}_{t-i} \boldsymbol{\varepsilon}_{t-i}' \mathbf{A}_i^{*\prime} + \sum_{i=1}^{p} \mathbf{B}_i^* \mathbf{H}_{t-i} \mathbf{B}_i^{*\prime} \qquad (8.2.4)$$

where $\mathbf{A}_i^*$ and $\mathbf{B}_i^*$ are $(N \times N)$ matrices of parameters and $\mathbf{A}_0$ is defined as before. Writing out (8.2.4) for $N = 2$ and $p = q = 1$ gives:

$$\begin{bmatrix} h_{11,t} & h_{12,t} \\ h_{12,t} & h_{22,t} \end{bmatrix} = \begin{bmatrix} a_{11}^0 & a_{12}^0 \\ a_{12}^0 & a_{22}^0 \end{bmatrix}$$
$$+ \begin{bmatrix} a_{11}^* & a_{12}^* \\ a_{21}^* & a_{22}^* \end{bmatrix} \begin{bmatrix} \varepsilon_{1,t-1}^2 & \varepsilon_{1,t-1}\varepsilon_{2,t-1} \\ \varepsilon_{1,t-1}\varepsilon_{2,t-1} & \varepsilon_{2,t-1}^2 \end{bmatrix} \begin{bmatrix} a_{11}^* & a_{21}^* \\ a_{12}^* & a_{22}^* \end{bmatrix}$$
$$+ \begin{bmatrix} b_{11}^* & b_{12}^* \\ b_{21}^* & b_{22}^* \end{bmatrix} \begin{bmatrix} h_{11,t-1} & h_{12,t-1} \\ h_{12,t-1} & h_{22,t-1} \end{bmatrix} \begin{bmatrix} b_{11}^* & b_{21}^* \\ b_{12}^* & b_{22}^* \end{bmatrix} \qquad (8.2.5)$$

The Constant Correlation Representation

Bollerslev (1990) defines $\mathbf{R}$ as:

$$\mathbf{R} = \begin{bmatrix} 1 & \cdots & \rho_{1N} \\ \vdots & \cdots & \vdots \\ \rho_{N1} & \cdots & 1 \end{bmatrix} \qquad (8.2.6)$$

where ρ_{ij} is the correlation coefficient measuring the correlation of variable i with variable j. He then defines the conditional variance matrix $\mathbf{H}_t$ as:

$$\mathbf{H}_t = \text{diag}\left(\sqrt{h_{11,t}}, \ldots, \sqrt{h_{NN,t}}\right) \mathbf{R}\, \text{diag}\left(\sqrt{h_{11,t}}, \ldots, \sqrt{h_{NN,t}}\right) \qquad (8.2.7)$$

where diag(·) denotes a diagonal matrix with the elements in (·) as the main diagonal. In the case of $N = 2$ and $p = q = 1$, $\mathbf{H}_t$ is:

$$\mathbf{H}_t = \begin{bmatrix} \sqrt{h_{11,t}} & 0 \\ 0 & \sqrt{h_{22,t}} \end{bmatrix} \begin{bmatrix} 1 & \rho_{12} \\ \rho_{21} & 1 \end{bmatrix} \begin{bmatrix} \sqrt{h_{11,t}} & 0 \\ 0 & \sqrt{h_{22,t}} \end{bmatrix} \tag{8.2.8}$$

where the individual variance terms $h_{11,t}$ and $h_{22,t}$ are taken to be individual GARCH processes with $p = q = 1$. In this representation, positive definiteness of $\mathbf{H}_t$ is assured if certain parameter restrictions are satisfied.

multivariate GARCH-M model to investigate Friedman's hypothesis regarding inflation volatility referred to in the introduction of this chapter). Other extensions of the original GARCH model (such as asymmetric GARCH models—p. 233) could also be applied to the multivariate case, although more recently there has been a greater focus on deriving simplified multivariate GARCH models that are easier to estimate and therefore of more use in practice. An example is the work of van der Weide (2002), who derives a simplified form that is nested in the BEKK representation and proposes an estimation method designed to avoid the usual convergence difficulties when estimating multivariate GARCH models. However, the complexity of multivariate GARCH models means they are still outside of the scope of most undergraduate econometrics courses, and the main econometrics software packages do not yet include automated or even semi-automated procedures for their estimation. In the rest of this chapter, therefore, we will focus only on single equation GARCH models.

ESTIMATION AND TESTING

When estimating the parameters of ARCH or GARCH models, even though ordinary least squares (OLS) estimation is consistent, maximum likelihood estimation is more efficient in the sense that the estimated parameters converge to their population counterparts at a faster rate.[5] For a simple ARCH(1) model, Engle (1982) actually calculates an expression for the gain in efficiency from using maximum likelihood compared with OLS. He shows that as the parameter on the lagged squared residual α_1 approaches unity, 'the gain in efficiency from using a maximum likelihood estimator may be very large' (p. 999).

[5] While we discuss the basics of maximum likelihood estimation of ARCH models in Box 8.3, for a more detailed discussion of maximum likelihood see Greene (2000, chs 4 and 9).

In Box 8.3 we outline the estimation procedure for the ARCH regression model:

$$\left.\begin{aligned} & y_t = \mathbf{x}_t\boldsymbol{\beta} + u_t && u_t = \varepsilon_t(\mathbf{z}_t\boldsymbol{\alpha})^{1/2} \\ & \mathbf{x}_t = (x_{1t}, x_{2t}, \dots, x_{pt}) && \mathbf{z}_t = (1, u_{t-1}^2, \dots, u_{t-q}^2) \\ & && \varepsilon_t \sim \text{NID}(0, 1) \end{aligned}\right\} \quad (8.23)$$

where $\boldsymbol{\beta}$ and $\boldsymbol{\alpha}$ are $(p \times 1)$ and $((q+1) \times 1)$ vectors of parameters.

Since the conditional distribution of u_t is normal, it follows that the conditional distribution of y_t will be normal with a conditional mean of $\mathbf{x}_t\boldsymbol{\beta}$ and a conditional variance of $h_t = \mathbf{z}_t\boldsymbol{\alpha}$. As with conventional time series models, the likelihood function for y_t can be obtained by multiplying the conditional probability density functions for each y_t together (the log-likelihood function is just the sum of the log-likelihood functions for each y_t). For the ARCH model, however, the first-order conditions for the maximum likelihood estimation of $\boldsymbol{\alpha}$ and $\boldsymbol{\beta}$ are non-linear, and closed-form solutions for these first-order conditions do not exist. An iterative OLS procedure (outlined in Box 8.3) or numerical optimization can be used to obtain the maximum likelihood estimators.

The form of the log-likelihood function for ARCH and GARCH models is of course dependent on the assumed distribution for ε_t and therefore the assumed conditional distribution of u_t and y_t. If conditional normality is assumed when estimating the model in Box 8.3, but in fact the correct distribution is non-normal, then the maximum likelihood estimates of $\boldsymbol{\alpha}$ and $\boldsymbol{\beta}$ will be inefficient and that inefficiency increases with the extent of the non-normality.[6] As we have already mentioned in this chapter, for the ARCH model with conditionally normal errors, the unconditional distribution is leptokurtic. Therefore the assumption of conditional normality is not as restrictive as it might first appear in that it allows for fat tails in the unconditional distribution. It is, however, possible to explicitly allow for non-normality in the conditional distribution as well as the unconditional distribution when estimating ARCH and GARCH models. For example, a Student-*t* distribution could be assumed when constructing the likelihood function—allowing for kurtosis.

In addition to kurtosis, a noticeable feature of financial time series is skewness. In the case of stock market prices, typically the distribution of returns is negatively skewed; large negative movements in stock markets are not usually matched by equally large positive movements. A distribution that

[6] See Engle and Gonzalez-Rivera (1991). When normality is assumed, but the true conditional distribution is non-normal, the maximum likelihood estimators are known as the *quasi-maximum likelihood* estimators. These estimators are shown to be consistent by Weiss (1986) and Bollerslev and Wooldridge (1992), but are inefficient.

Box 8.3 Estimating ARCH models.

Consider the following ARCH model:

$$y_t = \mathbf{x}_t\boldsymbol{\beta} + u_t \qquad u_t = \varepsilon_t(\mathbf{z}_t\boldsymbol{\alpha})^{1/2}$$

$$\mathbf{x}_t = (x_{1t}, x_{2t}, \ldots, x_{pt}) \qquad \mathbf{z}_t = (1, u_{t-1}^2, \ldots, u_{t-q}^2)$$

$$\boldsymbol{\alpha}' = (\alpha_0, \alpha_1, \ldots, \alpha_q) \qquad \boldsymbol{\beta}' = (\beta_1, \beta_2, \ldots, \beta_p)$$

$$\varepsilon_t \sim \text{NID}(0, 1) \qquad \boldsymbol{\alpha}'_{11} > 0 \quad \boldsymbol{\alpha}'_{1i} \geq 0 \quad 1 < i \leq q$$

The log-likelihood function for y_t assuming a sample of size T is:

$$l_t = -\frac{T}{2}\ln(2\pi) - \frac{1}{2}\sum_{t=1}^{T}\ln(h_t) - \frac{1}{2}\sum_{t=1}^{T}(u_t^2/h_t) \tag{8.3.1}$$

The first-order conditions for maximizing this function are non-linear and have no closed-form solutions. For example, the first-order condition for maximizing this function with respect to $\boldsymbol{\beta}$ is:

$$\frac{\partial l_t}{\partial \boldsymbol{\beta}} = \sum_{t=1}^{T}\left[\frac{u_t\mathbf{x}'_t}{h_t} + \frac{1}{2h_t}\frac{\partial h_t}{\partial \boldsymbol{\beta}}\left(\frac{u_t^2}{h_t} - 1\right)\right] = 0 \tag{8.3.2}$$

In order to obtain the asymptotically efficient estimates we can use an iterative approach that utilizes OLS and feasible generalized least squares (GLS). This approach can be set out as follows:

1. Estimate $\hat{\boldsymbol{\beta}}$ by OLS and obtain the residuals from the fitted model $\hat{u}_t$.
2. From these residuals estimate $\hat{\boldsymbol{\alpha}}$ (from an OLS regression of $\hat{u}_t^2$ on 1 and $\hat{u}_{t-1}^2, \ldots, \hat{u}_{t-q}^2$). Note that if we were to estimate an unrestricted model we might obtain negative values in the estimated parameter vector $\hat{\boldsymbol{\alpha}}$, yielding a fitted model from which a negative conditional variance could be predicted. In practice, therefore, it is necessary to estimate a restricted model to ensure that all elements of $\hat{\boldsymbol{\alpha}}$ are positive.
3. A new efficient estimate $\hat{\boldsymbol{\beta}}$ can be obtained by re-estimating using feasible GLS with the fitted values from step 2 as an estimate of h_t. A new set of residuals will be obtained.
4. Iterate steps 2 and 3 until the estimates converge.

More recently, rather than rely on an OLS/GLS iterative approach, econometricians tend to employ one of a number of numerical optimization algorithms that simultaneously search over $\boldsymbol{\alpha}$ and $\boldsymbol{\beta}$ in the likelihood function until the function is maximized. In the empirical examples throughout this chapter the parameters of all the conditional heteroscedasticity models are estimated simultaneously using this method.

allows for both kurtosis and skewness of the data is the skewed Student-t distribution proposed by Fernandez and Steel (1998).[7]

If ARCH is suspected in a series then it is sensible to pre-test the data. Engle (1982) proposes a Lagrange Multiplier (LM) test for ARCH. The first step is to estimate the conventional regression model for y_t by OLS:

$$y_t = \mathbf{x}_t \boldsymbol{\beta} + u_t \tag{8.24}$$

and obtain the fitted residuals $\hat{u}_t$. Then regress $\hat{u}_t^2$ on a constant and lags of $\hat{u}_t^2$:

$$\hat{u}_t^2 = \alpha_0 + \alpha_1 \hat{u}_{t-1}^2 + \alpha_2 \hat{u}_{t-2}^2 + \cdots + \alpha_q \hat{u}_{t-q}^2 + \nu_t \tag{8.25}$$

If ARCH is not present, the estimated parameters $\hat{\alpha}_1, \hat{\alpha}_2, \ldots, \hat{\alpha}_q$ should be statistically insignificant from zero. Engle (1982) recommends testing the null hypothesis H_0: $\alpha_1 = \alpha_2 = \cdots = \alpha_q = 0$ using the LM principle. In practice, an asymptotically equivalent test to the true LM statistic is usually employed. This test statistic is simply the sample size T multiplied by the R^2 for the regression involving the fitted OLS residuals and, under the null hypothesis, has a χ^2 distribution with q degrees of freedom. Bollerslev (1986) proposes the same kind of test for GARCH.

AN EMPIRICAL APPLICATION OF ARCH AND GARCH MODELS

In order to illustrate some of the concepts discussed so far, we continue with an application to monthly data on the S&P Composite index returns over the period 1954:1–2001:9. Lags of the consumer price index (CPI) inflation rate and the change in the three-month Treasury bill (T-bill) rate are used as regressors, in addition to lags of the returns.[8] We begin by modelling the returns series as a function of a constant, one lag of returns (Ret_1), one lag of the inflation rate (Inf_1) and one lag of the first-difference of the three-month T-bill rate (DT-bill_1). The results from a conventional regression model estimated by OLS using *PcGive* are given in Table 8.1. Both the inflation rate and the change in the T-bill rate are significant at the 5% level and the estimated parameters are negative; this is what we might expect.[9] The null hypothesis of normally dis-

[7] See Laurent and Peters (2002a, 2002b) for more information on the use of non-normal distributions when estimating GARCH models.

[8] The S&P Composite data are currently available on Robert Shiller's web page and comprise monthly data obtained via linear extrapolation from S&P's quarterly data. The returns series includes dividends and is calculated using the formula $R_t = (P_t + D_t - P_{t-1})/P_{t-1}$. The inflation series is calculated as the first-difference of the natural logarithm of the consumer price index taken from the Federal Reserve Bank of St Louis's database, and the T-bill series is the three-month T-bill rate also taken from the Federal Reserve Bank of St Louis's database. All data are converted into % amounts.

[9] Fama (1981) is the seminal article on the relationship between stock returns and macroeconomic variables.

Table 8.1 Conditional homoscedastic model for S&P Composite returns.

	Coefficient	Standard error	t-Value	t-Probability
Constant	1.177	0.210	5.60	0.000
Ret_1	0.208	0.041	5.07	0.000
Inf_1	−1.179	0.448	−2.63	0.019
DT-bill_1	−1.250	0.291	−4.29	0.000

ARCH(1) test: $F = (1, 565) = 6.947$ [0.009]**
ARCH(6) test: $F(6, 555) = 2.718$ [0.013]*

Normality test: $\chi^2_2 = 34.330$ [0.000]**

*Rejects null hypothesis at 5% level.
**Rejects null hypothesis at 1% level.

Table 8.2 ARCH(6) model for S&P Composite returns.

	Coefficient	Standard error	t-Value	t-Probability
Constant(M)	1.524	0.220	6.911	0.000
Ret_1(M)	0.222	0.047	4.743	0.000
Inf_1(M)	−1.012	0.559	−1.810	0.071
DT-bill_1(M)	−0.969	0.330	−2.934	0.004
Constant (V)	5.224	1.035	5.048	0.000
Alpha1(V)	0.115	0.058	1.985	0.048
Alpha2(V)	0.019	0.044	0.429	0.668
Alpha3(V)	0.135	0.072	1.876	0.061
Alpha4(V)	−0.002	0.034	−0.053	0.958
Alpha5(V)	0.140	0.083	1.682	0.093
Alpha6(V)	0.159	0.067	2.368	0.018

Information criteria:

Akaike	5.176	Shibata	5.176
Schwarz	5.260	Hannan–Quinn	5.209

tributed errors is strongly rejected by portmanteau tests, and in conventional regression models this would lead to a rejection of the estimated specification. However, non-normality is an inherent feature of the errors from regression models for financial data, and here, as in all cases henceforth, robust standard errors are calculated. The F version of the LM test for ARCH indicates the presence of conditional heteroscedasticity—both the tests for ARCH(1) and ARCH(6) yield rejections at the 5% significance level. Consequently we estimated the same model for the conditional mean, but this time allowing for ARCH(6) (thus we estimated the model given by (8.23) assuming $q = 6$). The results obtained using the *G@RCH* program are presented in Table 8.2, where an M denotes the conditional mean equation and a V denotes the conditional

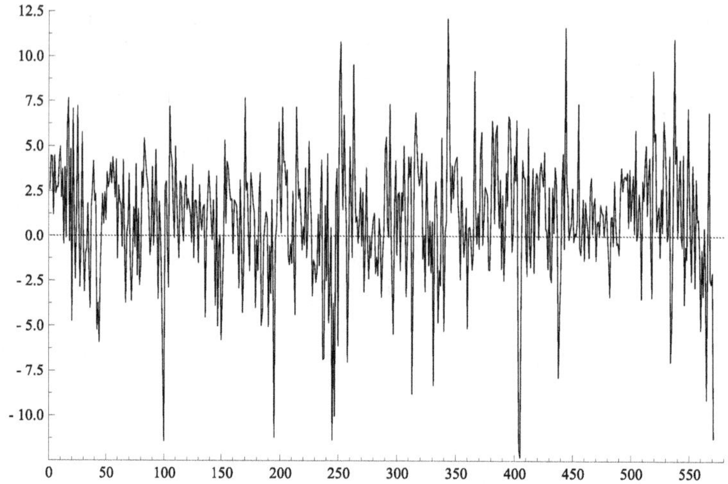

Figure 8.2(a). S&P Composite returns.

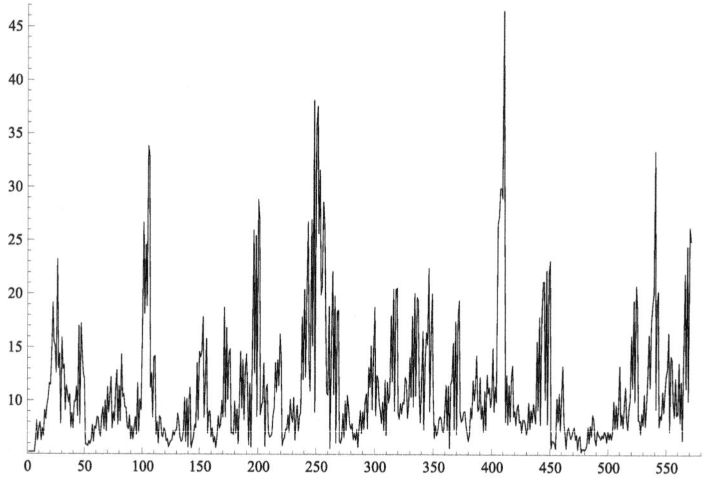

Figure 8.2(b). Estimated conditional variance of S&P Composite returns from ARCH(6) model.

variance. As expected, given the results of the tests for ARCH(1) and ARCH(6), the parameters on the first and sixth lag in the equation for the conditional variance are significant. Note however that the estimated value of α_4 (Alpha4(V)) is negative. This is because we did not impose the non-negativity constraint when estimating this model. Imposing this constraint gives virtually identical results, with the only difference being that Alpha4(V) = 0. Graphs of the raw data and the estimated conditional variance obtained from the ARCH(6) model are given in Figures 8.2(a) and 8.2(b), respectively. The conditional heteroscedasticity of the S&P Composite returns is clearly visible in

Table 8.3 GARCH(1, 1) model for S&P Composite returns.

	Coefficient	Standard error	t-Value	t-Probability
Constant(M)	1.567	0.223	7.070	0.000
Ret_1(M)	0.183	0.046	3.958	0.000
Inf_1(M)	−1.492	0.496	−3.008	0.003
DT-bill_1(M)	−1.231	0.323	−3.815	0.000
Constant(V)	1.206	0.553	2.181	0.030
Beta1(V)	0.780	0.069	11.23	0.000
Alpha1(V)	0.114	0.041	2.798	0.005

Information criteria:

Akaike	5.183	Shibata	5.182
Schwarz	5.236	Hannan–Quinn	5.203

both graphs. Note that the spike in the conditional variance around observation 400 corresponds to the crash of October 1987.

Continuing with our S&P Composite data set, we estimated a GARCH(1, 1) model using the *G@RCH* program (the equation for the conditional mean is (8.13) and includes the same variables as in the ARCH(6) model, with the equation for the error term being (8.17) with $p = q = 1$). The results are given in Table 8.3. The parameters on inf_1 and DT-bill_1 maintain their negative signs, and the estimated parameters in the equation for the conditional variance are highly significant. Furthermore the sum of the alpha and beta parameters is quite close to unity, indicating that the persistence of the conditional variance of the S&P Composite returns is high. The information criteria computed (Akaike, Shibata, Schwarz and Hannan–Quinn) allow the fit of competing models to be compared while penalizing for additional variables (the aim is to minimize the criteria). On the basis of the Schwarz criteria, which is often the preferred method of comparing fitted models in applied time series analysis, the GARCH(1, 1) specification would be preferred to the ARCH(6) specification (although, overall, two of the criteria support the ARCH(6) model and two support the GARCH(1, 1) model).

The *G@RCH* program allows for a non-normal conditional distribution to be specified when estimating ARCH and GARCH models by maximum likelihood. The alternatives available include the Student-t, the generalized error distribution and skewed Student-t distributions. We re-estimated the GARCH(1, 1) model for our S&P Composite data for each of these alternative distributions. Measuring the fit of the models using the Schwarz criteria, the statistically preferred GARCH model is the skewed Student-t version. The results for this estimated model are given in Table 8.4. The asymmetry and tail parameters of the conditional distribution are estimated along with the other parameters in the model by the maximum likelihood procedure. On the basis of their t-statistics, these estimated parameters are both statistically significant and have their expected signs, indicating that this model is picking

Table 8.4 Skewed Student-t distribution GARCH(1, 1) model for S&P Composite returns.

	Coefficient	Standard error	t-Value	t-Probability
Constant(M)	1.351	0.225	6.011	0.000
Ret_1(M)	0.181	0.042	4.301	0.000
Inf_1(M)	−1.015	0.499	−2.036	0.042
DT-bill_1(M)	−1.125	0.302	−3.724	0.000
Constant(V)	1.065	0.567	1.879	0.061
Beta1(V)	0.825	0.067	12.23	0.000
Alpha1(V)	0.079	0.036	2.206	0.028
Asymmetry	−0.135	0.064	−2.123	0.034
Tail	6.776	1.896	3.574	0.000

Information criteria:

Akaike	5.147	Shibata	5.147
Schwarz	5.216	Hannan-Quinn	5.174

up the fat-tailed and negatively skewed features of the data. The information criteria reported in Table 8.4 are *all* below those reported in Tables 8.2 and 8.3, indicating that on the basis of the information criteria calculated this specification is preferred.

ARCH-M

When modelling the returns from investing in a risky asset one might expect that the variance of those returns would add significantly to the explanation of the behaviour of the conditional mean, since risk-averse investors require higher returns to invest in riskier assets. Engle, Lilien and Robins (1987) consider the following time series model for the excess return on a long-term bond relative to a one period T-bill rate:

$$y_t = \mu_t + \varepsilon_t \tag{8.26}$$

$$h_t = \alpha_0 + \sum_{i=1}^{q} \alpha_i \varepsilon_{t-i}^2 \tag{8.27}$$

$$\mu_t = \beta + \delta h_t^{1/2} \tag{8.28}$$

where y_t is the excess return from holding the long-term bond, μ_t is the risk premium for investing in a long-term bond, ε_t is the difference between the *ex ante* and *ex post* rate of return and h_t is the conditional variance of ε_t. Thus the expected return (the conditional mean) is a linear function of the conditional standard deviation (in Engle et al., 1987, the conditional standard deviation is used in the model for the conditional mean, but the conditional variance could also be used). Over periods in which the bond return is volatile, risk-averse

Table 8.5 GARCH-M(1, 1) model for S&P Composite returns.

	Coefficient	Standard error	*t*-Value	*t*-Probability
Constant(M)	0.935	0.440	2.13	0.034
Ret_1(M)	0.183	0.045	4.05	0.000
Inf_1(M)	−1.368	0.582	−2.35	0.019
DT-bill_1(M)	−1.149	0.379	−3.03	0.003
h_t(M)	0.041	0.039	1.05	0.296
Constant(V)	1.103	0.505	2.19	0.029
Beta_1(V)	0.786	0.068	11.6	0.000
Alpha_1(V)	0.118	0.054	2.19	0.029

agents will switch to less risky assets driving the risk premium upward. Therefore a positive relationship between h_t and y_t would be expected, and indeed this is what Engle et al. (1987) find, with an estimated value for δ of 0.687. This model is called the ARCH in mean, or ARCH-M model, reflecting the presence of conditional variance in the conditional mean. Similarly, one can estimate a GARCH-M model. Using the volatility models package in *PcGive* to estimate a GARCH-M(1,1) model for the S&P Composite returns yields the results in Table 8.5 (the conditional variance term in the conditional mean equation is represented by h_t in the table).[10] In this case, the conditional variance is not statistically significant in the equation for the conditional mean.

ASYMMETRIC GARCH MODELS

A feature of many financial time series that is not captured by ARCH and GARCH models is the 'asymmetry effect', also known as the 'leverage effect'.[11] In the context of financial time series analysis the asymmetry effect refers to the characteristic of time series on asset prices that an unexpected drop tends to increase volatility more than an unexpected increase of the same magnitude (or, that 'bad news' tends to increase volatility more than 'good news'). The notion of an asymmetry effect has its origins in the work of Black (1976), French, Schwert and Stambaugh (1987), Nelson (1991) and Schwert (1990). ARCH and GARCH models do not capture this effect since the lagged error terms are squared in the equations for the conditional variance, and therefore a positive error has the same impact on the conditional variance as a negative error.

[10] Note that the *G@RCH* program does not currently allow for the estimation of GARCH-M models.

[11] The title 'leverage effect' is used because it is thought that the operating leverage of companies is responsible for the asymmetric behaviour of their share prices in response to 'good' and 'bad' news (see Nelson, 1991, fn. 3 for further details).

A model specifically designed to capture the asymmetry effect is the exponential GARCH (EGARCH) model proposed by Nelson (1991). In an EGARCH model the natural logarithm of the condition variance is allowed to vary over time as a function of the lagged error terms (rather than lagged squared errors). The EGARCH(p, q) model for the conditional variance can be written:

$$\ln(h_t) = \omega + [1 - \beta(L)]^{-1}[1 + \alpha(L)]f(u_{t-1}/h_{t-1}^{1/2}) \tag{8.29}$$

where

$$f(u_{t-1}/h_{t-1}^{1/2}) = \theta u_{t-1} + \gamma(|u_{t-1}/h_{t-1}^{1/2}| - E|u_{t-1}/h_{t-1}^{1/2}|) \tag{8.30}$$

and $\alpha(L)$ and $\beta(L)$ are q- and p-order lag polynomials, respectively; $\alpha(L) = \alpha_1 L + \alpha_2 L^2 + \cdots + \alpha_q L^q$, $\beta(L) = \beta_1 L + \beta_2 L^2 + \cdots + \beta_p L^p$. Rearranging (8.29) makes it easier to see the link with the conventional GARCH model. For example, setting p and q equal to 1 and rearranging (8.29), we can write the EGARCH(1, 1) model as:

$$\ln(h_t) = \delta + (1 + \alpha_1 L)f(u_{t-1}/h_{t-1}^{1/2}) + \beta_1 \ln h_{t-1} \tag{8.31}$$

which looks similar to the GARCH(1, 1) model (see equation (8.22)). However, by making the natural log of the conditional variance the dependent variable, in an EGARCH model the conditional variance is always positive even if the parameter values are negative, thus eliminating the need for parameter restrictions to impose non-negativity (recall that a problem with ARCH and GARCH models is that parameter restrictions are required to ensure a positive conditional variance).

The function $f(u_{t-1}/h_{t-1}^{1/2})$ in the EGARCH model allows for the asymmetry effect. In particular the term multiplied by the parameter θ allows the *sign* of the errors to affect the conditional variance, while the term multiplied by γ allows for a separate *size* effect.[12] If the asymmetry effect is present, then $\theta < 0$, while if $\theta = 0$ there is no asymmetry effect. Testing is based on the t-statistic for testing $\theta = 0$. Convergence difficulties are not uncommon when estimating EGARCH models, and this is indeed the case when we attempt to estimate an EGARCH(1, 1) model for our S&P Composite returns using the *G@RCH* program. An EGARCH(1, 0) model with one lag of returns in the conditional mean equation is easier to estimate for this data set, and the results from estimating this model assuming a skewed Student-t distribution when specifying the likelihood function are given in Table 8.6 (note that if we use (8.29) as our model for the conditional variance, in the EGARCH(1, 0) model, while there are no alpha parameters since $q = 0$, the model still allows for an asymmetry effect as the function $f(u_{t-1}/h_{t-1}^{1/2})$ is still present). As expected, for this data set the estimated value of θ is negative and significant, indicating the

[12] Determining the degree of persistence of shocks to GARCH processes can be quite difficult, and this is commented on by Nelson (1991). The notion of persistence and conditions for stationarity are easier to formalize within the EGARCH model (see Nelson, 1991, theorem 2.1).

Table 8.6 EGARCH(1, 0) model for S&P Composite returns.

	Coefficient	Standard error	t-Value	t-Probability
Constant(M)	1.032	0.068	15.19	0.000
Ret_1(M)	0.251	0.023	10.75	0.000
Constant(V)	2.217	0.123	18.05	0.000
Beta1(V)	0.764	0.076	10.10	0.000
Theta(V)	−0.200	0.068	−2.939	0.003
Gamma(V)	0.167	0.072	2.324	0.021
Asymmetry	−0.115	0.060	−1.921	0.075
Tail	8.379	2.866	2.923	0.004

Information criteria:

Akaike	5.150	Shibata	5.150
Schwarz	5.211	Hannan–Quinn	5.174

presence of the asymmetry effect. Engle and Ng (1993) introduced a graphical representation of the asymmetry effect known as the 'news impact curve'. The news impact curve is a graph of u_{t-1} against h_t holding constant the information at $t-2$ and earlier. In practice fitted values are used to graph the curve. If there is asymmetry in the series, then either the slope of the two sides of the news impact curve will differ and/or the centre of the curve will be located at a point where $u_{t-1} > 0$ (the GARCH(1, 1) model has a news impact curve that is centred on $u_{t-1} = 0$ and the slopes of each side of the curve are equal).[13]

An *ex post* analysis of parameter significance could be used to assess whether asymmetry is a significant feature of the data being examined; however, it is also possible to pre-test for asymmetry having estimated a symmetric GARCH model. Engle and Ng (1993) propose three tests: the sign bias test (SBT), the negative sign bias test (NSBT) and the positive sign bias test (PSBT). The logic of the tests is to see whether having estimated a particular GARCH model, an asymmetry dummy variable is significant in predicting the squared residuals. The tests are of the null hypothesis that the null model is correctly specified (i.e., there is no remaining asymmetry). They assume that the model under the alternative hypothesis is:

$$\ln(h_t) = \ln(h_{0t}(\boldsymbol{\delta}_0'\mathbf{z}_{0t})) + \boldsymbol{\delta}_a'\mathbf{z}_{at} \tag{8.32}$$

where $h_{0t}(\boldsymbol{\delta}_0'\mathbf{z}_{0t})$ is the volatility model under the null and $\boldsymbol{\delta}_a$ is the vector of parameters corresponding to the additional explanatory variables $\mathbf{z}_{at}$ that

[13] See Engle and Ng (1993) for further details on the functional forms of the news impact curve for different ARCH and GARCH specifications.

Table 8.7 SBTs based on the news impact curve (GARCH versus EGARCH).

	Test	Probability
Sign bias t-test	0.984	0.325
Negative size bias t-test	1.188	0.235
Positive size bias t-test	0.499	0.618
Joint test for the three effects	9.988	0.019

capture asymmetric effects. The three tests can be individually computed from the following regressions:

$$v_t^2 = a + bS_{t-1}^- + \boldsymbol{\beta}'\mathbf{z}_{0t}^* + e_t \tag{8.33}$$

$$v_t^2 = a + bS_{t-1}^- u_{t-1} + \boldsymbol{\beta}'\mathbf{z}_{0t}^* + e_t \tag{8.34}$$

$$v_t^2 = a + bS_{t-1}^+ u_{t-1} + \boldsymbol{\beta}'\mathbf{z}_{0t}^* + e_t \tag{8.35}$$

where u_t is the error term under the null, S_{t-1}^- is a dummy variable that takes the value of one when $u_{t-1} < 0$ and zero otherwise (vice versa for S_{t-1}^+), $v_t^2 = u_t^2/h_{0t}^{1/2}$ where h_{0t} is the conditional variance under the null and $\mathbf{z}_{0t}^* \equiv h_{0t}^{-1}\,\partial h_t/\partial \boldsymbol{\delta}_0$. The SBT is the t-statistic for testing H_0: $b = 0$ in (8.33), the NSBT is the t-statistic for testing H_0: $b = 0$ in (8.34) and the PSBT is the t-statistic for testing H_0: $b = 0$ in (8.35). These tests can also be carried out jointly using the following specification:

$$v_t^2 = a + b_1 S_{t-1}^- + b_2 S_{t-1}^- u_{t-1} + b_3 S_{t-1}^+ u_{t-1} + \boldsymbol{\beta}'\mathbf{z}_{0t}^* + e_t \tag{8.36}$$

The LM test of the joint null hypothesis H_0: $b_1 = b_2 = b_3 = 0$ has a χ_3^2 distribution. The results from applying the SBT, NSBT, PSBT and the joint test to the residuals from the GARCH(1, 1) model for the S&P Composite returns reported in Table 8.4, computed using the *G@RCH* program, are given in Table 8.7 and illustrate that for this data set there is evidence against the null of symmetry from the joint test for the three effects, but not from the individual size bias tests. These contradictions are somewhat surprising, although, as Engle and Ng (1993) note, the joint test is more powerful than the individual tests.

While the EGARCH model allows the sign of the errors to affect the conditional variance, it does so using a fundamentally different specification from the original GARCH framework: one in which the dependent variable is the natural logarithm of the conditional variance. The asymmetry effect can also be captured simply by modifying the original GARCH specification using a dummy variable. Glosten, Jagannathan and Runkle (1993) (hereafter GJR) introduced the following model for h_t:

$$h_t = \alpha_0 + \alpha_1 u_{t-1}^2 + \gamma_1 u_{t-1}^2 I_{t-1} + \beta_1 h_{t-1} \tag{8.37}$$

Table 8.8 GJR-GARCH(1, 1) model for S&P Composite returns.

	Coefficient	Standard error	t-Value	t-Probability
Constant(M)	1.307	0.211	6.178	0.000
Ret_1(M)	0.220	0.040	5.546	0.000
Inf_1(M)	−0.892	0.405	−2.203	0.028
DT-bill_1(M)	−1.073	0.308	−3.482	0.001
Constant(V)	2.512	0.885	2.839	0.005
Beta1(V)	0.708	0.082	8.568	0.000
Alpha1(V)	−0.089	0.049	−1.822	0.069
Gamma1(V)	0.281	0.094	2.998	0.003
Asymmetry	−0.115	0.063	−1.822	0.069
Tail	8.558	3.032	2.822	0.005

Information criteria:

Akaike	5.131	Shibata	5.131
Schwarz	5.208	Hannan–Quinn	5.161

where $I_{t-1} = 1$ if $u_{t-1} > 0$ and $I_{t-1} = 0$ otherwise. In (8.37) the ARCH parameter in the conditional variance switches between $\alpha_1 + \gamma_1$ and α_1 depending on whether the previous period's error term is positive or negative. The results from estimating a GJR-GARCH(1, 1) model for the S&P Composite data are given in Table 8.8 (the skewed Student-t distribution is assumed when estimating this model). When using the *G@RCH* program to estimate a GJR model, I_{t-1} by default is defined the opposite way around to the definition given above. That is, $I_{t-1} = 1$ if $u_{t-1} < 0$ and $I_{t-1} = 0$ otherwise, and therefore for evidence of an asymmetry effect we are looking for the estimated values of γ_1 to be greater than zero. The estimated gamma parameter given in Table 8.8 is indeed positive and is highly significant, indicating that negative shocks increase the volatility of the S&P Composite returns by more than positive shocks of the same magnitude. On the basis of all the information criteria computed, the GJR-GARCH(1, 1) model provides a better fit to the data than the conventional ARCH and GARCH specifications estimated, and the information criteria indicate that the GJR-GARCH(1, 1) model is preferred to the EGARCH(0, 1) model reported in Table 8.6.

Choosing between the various asymmetric specifications could be done on the basis of conventional measures of model fit and/or by assessing parameter significance. Alternatively, a useful development of the GARCH specification would be one that nests the various asymmetric specifications and therefore allows the data to determine the true form of asymmetry. Such a general model was proposed by Ding, Granger and Engle (1993) and is known as the asymmetric power ARCH model, or APARCH model. In this model, the equation for the conditional variance has the following form:

$$h_t^{\delta/2} = \alpha_0 + \sum_{i=1}^{q} \alpha_i(|u_{t-i}| - \gamma_i u_{t-i}| - \gamma_i u_{t-i})^{\delta} + \sum_{j=1}^{p} \beta_j h_{t-j}^{\delta/2} \tag{8.38}$$

where $\delta > 0$ and $-1 < \gamma_i < 1$. Clearly, if $\delta = 2$, $\gamma_i = 0$ and $\beta_j = 0$, then we have the conventional ARCH model; while if $\delta = 2$, $\gamma_i = 0$, then we have a conventional GARCH model. However, allowing either δ and/or γ_i to vary permits a number of different specifications including a threshold GARCH model for the conditional standard deviation ($\delta = 1$) (which is another asymmetric specification proposed by Zakonian, 1994), a version of the GJR model ($\delta = 2$), and a non-linear ARCH model ($\gamma_i = 0$, $\beta_j = 0$) (cf. Higgins and Bera, 1992). Finally, note that all the asymmetric and non-linear specifications mentioned can be estimated including the conditional variance in the conditional mean.

INTEGRATED AND FRACTIONALLY INTEGRATED GARCH MODELS

So far we have assumed that the error term u_t and its conditional variance h_t are stationary processes (recall, in the GARCH(p, q) model u_t is weakly stationary if and only if $\alpha(1) + \beta(1) < 1$). The stationarity of the conditional variance h_t also depends on the values of the α and β parameters. For example, in the GARCH(p, q) model (see the representation given by (8.17)), if $\sum_{i=1}^{q} \alpha_i + \sum_{j=1}^{p} \beta_j < 1$, then a shock to h_t decays over time. When $\sum_{i=1}^{q} \alpha_i + \sum_{j=1}^{p} \beta_j = 1$, then h_t behaves like a unit root process in that shocks to h_t do not decay.[14] For this reason the GARCH(p, q) model subject to the restriction $\sum_{i=1}^{q} \alpha_i + \sum_{j=1}^{p} \beta_j = 1$ is known as an integrated GARCH(p, q) model (i.e. IGARCH(p, q)). If we estimate an IGARCH(1, 1) model for the S&P Composite returns (assuming a skewed Student-t distribution), we might expect the estimated parameters in the model to be similar in value to those in Table 8.4, given that in the unrestricted GARCH(1, 1) model the sum of the alpha and beta parameters is quite close to unity. Estimating an IGARCH(1, 1) model for the S&P Composite returns using the *G@RCH* program yields the results given in Table 8.9. This confirms that the values of the estimated parameters are indeed similar to those in Table 8.4.

Throughout this book we have focused on modelling time series primarily in levels or in first-differences. With financial time series, however, sometimes a fractional difference of the series is necessary. The concept of *fractional integration* was proposed by Granger and Joyeux (1980) and Hosking (1981). In the first-order case, the time series y_t is said to be fractionally integrated if the fractional difference of y_t is a stationary process:

$$(1 - L)^d y_t = \varepsilon_t \qquad \varepsilon_t \sim \text{IID}(0, 1) \tag{8.39}$$

If $d = 0$, then y_t is a white-noise stationary process and so its autocorrelations are all equal to zero, whereas if $d = 1$, y_t contains a unit root at the zero frequency as defined in Chapter 3 and its autocorrelations remain at unity.

[14] The terminology IGARCH was introduced by Engle and Bollerslev (1986).

Table 8.9 IGARCH(1, 1) model for S&P Composite returns.[15]

	Coefficient	Standard error	t-Value	t-Probability
Constant(M)	1.317	0.223	5.896	0.000
Ret_1(M)	0.177	0.043	4.150	0.000
Inf_1(M)	−1.062	0.510	−2.084	0.038
DT-bill_1(M)	−1.138	0.328	−3.466	0.001
Constant(V)	0.341	0.204	1.668	0.096
Beta1(V)	0.869	NA	NA	NA
Alpha1(V)	0.131	0.045	2.926	0.004
Asymmetry	−0.147	0.066	−2.242	0.025
Tail	5.597	1.528	3.663	0.000

Information criteria:

Akaike	5.157	Shibata	5.156
Schwarz	5.218	Hannan–Quinn	5.181

However, for non-integer values of d $(0 < d < 1)$, the autocorrelations of y_t will decline very slowly to zero (more specifically the decay has a hyperbolic pattern). The main feature of a fractionally integrated process that distinguishes it from other time series processes is the very slow decay of its autocorrelations. For this reason, a fractional integrated series is often referred to as having 'long-memory'. The autocorrelations can be calculated as $\rho_k = \Gamma k^{2d-1}$, where Γ is the ratio of two gamma functions and the actual speed of decay depends on the value of d. Note that y_t is weakly stationary for $d < 0.5$, but non-stationary for $d \geq 0.5$. Using the ARIMA terminology, a natural extension of the ARIMA(p, d, q) model is a fractionally integrated version—the ARFIMA(p, d, q) model:

$$\phi(L)(1 - L)^d y_t = \theta(L)\varepsilon_t \tag{8.40}$$

where $\phi(L)$ and $\theta(L)$ are p- and q-order lag polynomials, respectively (cf. equation (1.17)). In a study of the S&P Composite index using daily data, Ding et al. (1993) found that the squared index is a fractionally integrated process.

While these initial studies of fractional integration focused on modelling the conditional mean of a time series, Bailey, Bollerslev and Mikkelsen (1996) applied the concept of fractional integration to the conditional variance of a time series, proposing the fractionally integrated GARCH model (FIGARCH). The concept of fractional integration has also been applied to the EGARCH model (the FIEARCH model of Bollerslev and Mikkelsen, 1996) and APARCH model (the FIAPARCH model of Tse, 1998). The *G@RCH* program allows for these variants to be estimated. In practice, the

[15] In the IGARCH model the beta parameter is restricted ($\hat{\alpha}_1 + \hat{\beta}_1 = 1$), and therefore standard errors are not estimated.

concept of long memory has been shown to be most relevant when analysing high-frequency financial data (such as daily data). Since our data on the S&P Composite index returns are monthly, when we estimate a FIGARCH(1, 1) model it is not surprising that, on the basis of its t-statistic, the estimated value of the fractional differencing parameter for the conditional variance is insignificant from zero, indicating that the conditional variance of the monthly S&P Composite index returns does not possess the property of long memory.

CONDITIONAL HETEROSCEDASTICITY, UNIT ROOTS AND COINTEGRATION

Much of this book has focused on issues relating to non-stationary time series and cointegration analysis. An assumption of many of the time series models and tests discussed in previous chapters is that the error terms are zero mean, homoscedastic, independently and identically distributed random variables. For example, the tabulated critical values for the Dickey–Fuller (DF) tests (see Table 3.1) are computed under this assumption. Since conditional heteroscedasticity is a common feature of many financial time series and since there are many instances in which econometricians may want to test for a unit root in financial time series or test for cointegrating relationships involving financial time series, the performance of unit root and cointegration tests in the presence of conditional heteroscedasticity is an important issue. It has been shown that, asymptotically, DF tests are robust to the presence of conditional heteroscedasticity, such as ARCH and GARCH. This has been proved by a number of authors including Pantula (1986, 1988) and Phillips and Perron (1988) (although Kim and Schmidt, 1993, note a number of gaps in the theoretical support for this argument). Consequently, in applied studies it is rarely the case that conditional heteroscedasticity is considered to be a problem when testing for unit roots or cointegration.[16] However, a number of studies of the effects of conditional heteroscedasticity on the finite sample performance of unit root and cointegration tests have shown that for sample sizes up to 1,000 observations in length, ignoring the presence of conditional heteroscedasticity can have a sig-

[16] For example, Huang, Yang and Hu (2000) apply unit root and cointegration analysis in their study of the comovement of Japanese and Chinese stock markets with the US stock market. They investigate the presence of a unit root in stock market indices using the ADF and other conventional unit root tests, and then go on to test for cointegration between various indices using the conventional EG approach. Nasseh and Strauss (2000) investigate cointegration between stock market indices and macroeconomic variables using conventional methods. They employ the Johansen methodology to test for cointegrating rank in a vector error correction model, including stock market indices and macroeconomic variables, such as industrial production and short-term and long-term interest rates. Neither of these studies consider the impact of conditional heteroscedasticity on their results.

nificant impact on both the size and power of the tests. Since in applied econometrics small sample sizes are often used, particularly when only quarterly or annual data are available, it is important for practitioners to be aware of the impact that conditional heteroscedasticity can have on the results of unit root and cointegration tests.

An early analysis of the effects of conditional heteroscedasticity on unit root tests is the work of Kim and Schmidt (1993), who investigate the finite sample performance of DF tests in the presence of GARCH and find that serious size distortions can occur if the data display certain GARCH characteristics. Kim and Schmidt (1993) focus on the performance of the DF test when the error terms are a GARCH(1, 1) process. They restrict their analysis to the stationary, but degenerate the GARCH(1, 1) process ('degenerate' means the constant in the GARCH model is equal to zero) and the IGARCH(1, 1) process. They find that for the kinds of sample sizes typical in applied econometrics, the DF test is over-sized (it rejects too frequently in their simulation analysis). From these results we can conclude that despite the asymptotic robustness of DF-type tests, in practice, if one is using such tests to investigate the order of integration of financial time series, in which the series are possibly ARCH or GARCH processes, it is important to recognize the increased probability of spurious rejections.

Despite the evidence of Kim and Schmidt (1993), in applied work on testing for unit roots and cointegration in financial time series it is still extremely rare that potential difficulties caused by the presence of conditional heteroscedasticity are considered. More recently, however, there has been a renewed interest in the properties of unit root tests in the presence of ARCH and GARCH (see, for example, Ling and Li, 1997, 1998; Seo, 1999; Boswijk, 2001). In particular, these authors focus on conventional models for non-stationary time series, such as the augmented DF (ADF) specification, but they assume the error terms are ARCH or GARCH processes and that estimation of all the parameters in the models is by maximum likelihood. For example, Seo (1999) considers the following model:

$$\Delta y_t = \beta y_{t-1} + \sum_{i=1}^{k-1} \gamma_i \Delta y_{t-i} + u_t \tag{8.41}$$

where $E(u_t|\Omega_{t-1}) = 0$, $E(u_t^2|\Omega_{t-1}) = h_t$ (Ω_{t-1} represents the relevant information set) and:

$$\phi(L)h_t = \omega + \zeta(L)u_{t-1}^2 \tag{8.42}$$

where $\phi(L) = 1 - \phi_1 L - \cdots - \phi_q L^q$ and $\zeta(L) = \zeta_1 + \zeta_2 L + \cdots + \zeta_p L^{p-1}$. Seo (1999) proposes estimating the AR and GARCH parameters of (8.41) and (8.42) jointly by maximum likelihood and then using the t-statistic in the jointly estimated model for testing an AR root of unity. That is, the null hypothesis of non-stationarity is H_0: $\beta = 0$ and the alternative is H_1: $\beta < 0$; Seo (1999) finds that the asymptotic distribution of this unit root test is *not* the same as the conventional DF distribution, but is actually a mixture of the conventional DF distribution and the standard normal distribution, with the weighting of this mixture depending on the size of the GARCH effect in the data.[17] As the GARCH effect increases, the power of the t-statistic for testing the null hypothesis of a unit root calculated when the AR and GARCH parameters are estimated jointly, and using the critical values tabulated in Seo (1999), increases relative to the conventional ADF test. Seo (1999) conducts Monte Carlo simulation experiments, comparing the power of the tests, and finds that in some quite realistic instances the power of the conventional ADF test is less than half that of the test derived from the jointly estimated model. Applying this test to monthly time series on the NYSE monthly stock price index, Seo (1999) finds that the null hypothesis of a unit root cannot be rejected and the GARCH parameters are statistically significant.

Another recent analysis of conditional heteroscedasticity and unit root tests is the work of Boswijk (2001). Recall that Kim and Schmidt (1993) investigate the finite sample performance of unit root tests in the presence of GARCH, but they rely on Monte Carlo evidence in their analysis and do not derive the asymptotic distributions of the test statistics considered. Boswijk (2001) compares the finite sample and asymptotic properties of the likelihood ratio statistic with those of the DF statistic when the error terms are a GARCH process. He considers the following GARCH(1, 1) version of the DF specification:

$$\Delta y_t = \gamma(y_{t-1} - \mu) + \varepsilon_t \tag{8.43}$$

$$\varepsilon_t = h_t^{1/2}\eta_t \tag{8.44}$$

$$h_t = \omega + \alpha\varepsilon_{t-1}^2 + \beta h_{t-1} \tag{8.45}$$

$$\eta_t \sim \text{NID}(0, 1) \tag{8.46}$$

Under the null hypothesis H_0: $\gamma = 0$, y_t is a unit root process with GARCH errors, and under the alternative hypothesis H_1: $\gamma < 0$, y_t is a stationary process with GARCH errors. The GARCH parameters ω, α and β are all assumed to be greater than zero, as is conventional in GARCH models. Boswijk (2001) focuses on two particular cases: (i) $\alpha + \beta < 1$ and (ii) $\alpha + \beta = 1 + \lambda/T$, where $\alpha = \zeta/\sqrt{2T}$, ζ is a scalar, λ is a scalar such that $\lambda < \zeta^2/2$ and T is the sample size. In the first case the conditional variance is stationary, but in the second case the conditional variance is 'near-integrated' (because λ/T will be a small value, $\alpha + \beta$ will be close to 1). Boswijk (2001) compares the power of the likelihood ratio statistic for testing H_0: $\gamma = 0$ against H_1: $\gamma < 0$ (which involves estimating all the parameters of the model) with the conventional DF F-statistic (involving OLS estimation and therefore ignoring the presence of conditional heteroscedasticity), and finds that for certain parameter values

[17] Recall from discussion of Table 3.1 that the DF distribution sits to the left of the usual Student-t distribution, making it 'harder' to reject the null of non-stationarity.

there are notable power gains to be had by using the likelihood ratio statistic rather than the DF test (thus, Boswijk's results support those of Seo, 1999).[18]

The work of Seo (1999) and Boswijk (2001) is important, because for a long time the literature on unit root-testing has tended to somewhat ignore the issue of conditional heteroscedasticity; however, perhaps of more interest to financial econometricians is the performance of tests for cointegration in the presence of conditional heteroscedasticity. For many financial time series there is often very strong theoretical support for the unit root hypothesis (viz., the efficient market hypothesis—EMH) or, conversely, the hypothesis of stationarity (EMH implies returns should be stationary).[19] However, many results on cointegration involving financial time series are finely balanced. For example, it is rarely the case that cointegration of financial time series with macroeconomic time series is strongly supported. Often in empirical work investigating such relationships, rejections of the null hypothesis of no cointegration using the Engle–Granger (EG) approach or Johansen approach are at borderline significance levels. Furthermore, the empirical support for cointegration between financial time series is often mixed, with some authors finding a cointegrating relationship and other authors using almost identical methods finding no evidence of cointegration. It seems possible that borderline and mixed empirical support for cointegrating relationships involving financial time series could be a consequence of the effects of conditional heteroscedasticity on the finite sample performance of the test statistics being used. Certainly, the empirical application of Boswijk (2001) on the term structure of interest rates would suggest that practitioners investigating cointegrating relationships involving financial time series should seriously consider the impact that conditional heteroscedasticity may be having on their results. The seminal empirical work on the term structure of interest rates employing the cointegration methodology is the work of Campbell and Shiller (1987). These authors show that if short-term and long-term nominal interest rates are both

[18] A particularly interesting feature of the work by Boswijk (2001) is the procedure he employs to obtain p-values for the test. The limiting distribution of the likelihood ratio statistic for testing H_0: $\gamma = 0$ in (8.43) depends on a nuisance parameter in a complicated fashion. The exact dependence is unknown, but can be approximated. However, these difficulties mean that obtaining critical values, or p-values for the test statistic, is not straightforward. Monte Carlo simulation is one method that could be used to obtain p-values, but Boswijk (2001) employs an approximation procedure proposed by Boswijk and Doornik (1999). The latter show that the asymptotic distributions of certain tests based on non-Gaussian log-likelihood functions can be approximated by a gamma distribution. While use of this approximation procedure is not yet widely established in empirical studies, we believe it is likely to become so in the future.

[19] In an 'efficient' market natural log of the asset price at time $t(p_t)$ reacts instantaneously to new information (ε_t), thus p_t follows a random walk $(p_t = p_{t-1} + \varepsilon_t)$ (i.e., p_t contains a unit root). Defining returns as the first-difference of p_t, if p_t follows a random walk and assuming that ε_t is stationary, it follows that returns are stationary.

integrated of order one $I(1)$, these series should be cointegrated with a cointegrating vector of unity, yielding a stationary term spread. Alternatively, the term structure, defined as the long-term rate minus the short-term rate, should be a stationary process. Boswijk (2001) investigates the presence of a unit root in the term structure of interest rates in the Netherlands. He finds from a conventional ADF test that the null hypothesis of no cointegration cannot be rejected. However, applying a likelihood ratio test that takes account of GARCH, Boswijk (2001) finds that the null hypothesis of no cointegration can be rejected.

Since this work is still in its infancy, there are few theoretical results on the implications of conditional heteroscedasticity for cointegration analysis. Some work has been done on the performance of the Johansen trace test for cointegrating rank in VAR models. See, for example, Rahbek, Hansen and Dennis (2002), who consider the following conventional VAR specification for testing cointegrating rank:

$$\Delta\mathbf{Y}_t = \mathbf{\Pi}\mathbf{Y}_{t-1} + \sum_{i=1}^{k-1}\mathbf{\Gamma}_i\Delta\mathbf{Y}_{t-i} + \mathbf{E}_t \tag{8.47}$$

Typically, it would be assumed that $\mathbf{E}_t \sim \text{IID}(\mathbf{0}, \mathbf{\Omega})$. However, Rahbek et al. (2002) consider testing for cointegrating rank when the errors $\mathbf{E}_t$ follow a BEKK-ARCH process. The details of the theoretical work in Rahbek et al. (2002) are beyond the scope of this book; however, on the basis of this work it appears that cointegration rank-testing in VAR models, based on the usual procedures, seems to be asymptotically valid in the presence of multivariate conditional heteroscedasticity. Of course the question remains: Are the finite sample properties of multivariate cointegration procedures affected in the same way as finite sample properties of unit roots tests? The complexity of multivariate GARCH models means that investigating such an issue using Monte Carlo methods would be extremely computer-intensive. Certainly, it would not be surprising if the finite sample properties of tests for cointegration are affected by the presence of conditional heteroscedasticity in a similar way to unit root tests.

FORECASTING WITH GARCH MODELS

While much of the published work on GARCH appears to be concerned with extending the original specifications in order to capture particular features of financial data such as asymmetry, there are many practical applications of GARCH models and many of these are concerned with forecasting. Even with the growth in popularity of non-linear forecasting models, such as nearest-neighbour non-parametric forecasting and locally weighted regression-forecasting, GARCH models remain a popular forecasting model when dealing with financial time series.[20] Meade (2002) compares forecasts of high-frequency exchange rate data made from a linear AR-GARCH model with forecasts made using non-linear techniques and finds that the AR-GARCH forecasts are not improved upon by the non-linear methods he considers. Of course, the results in Meade's (2002) paper are specific to a particular data set, and moreover his 'good' forecasting results are for conditional mean forecasts (the forecasts of the series itself are referred to as 'conditional mean forecasts' or 'forecasts of the conditional mean'). As we have already mentioned in this chapter, GARCH models allow forecasts of the conditional variance of a time series in addition to forecasts of the conditional mean to be computed. While computing forecasts of the conditional variance of a time series is straightforward to do using GARCH models (more detail is given on p. 247), there is still debate on how best to evaluate forecasts of the conditional variance. When evaluating the accuracy of a particular model for computing conditional mean forecasts, it is traditional to estimate the model using a subsample of the full sample of data and then compare the forecasts with the observed future values of the series using a standard measure of forecast accuracy, such as forecast MSE. However, when forecasting the conditional variance of a time series, such as stock returns, the observed values of the conditional variance of the series are not available for comparison, even if sample observations are held back when estimating the GARCH model. Consequently, it is traditional to use the squared values of the data as a proxy for the observed values of the conditional variance of the series. The forecasts of the conditional variance can then be compared with this proxy and the forecasts can be evaluated in the same way as forecasts of the series itself. The problem with this approach (discussed in detail by Anderson and Bollerslev, 1998) is that the squared values of the series are sometimes a very poor proxy of the conditional variance. As a result, many applied studies have reported that the GARCH model produces poor forecasts of the conditional variance (see, for example, Cumby, Figlewski and Hasbrouck, 1993; Jorion, 1995; Figlewski, 1997). Anderson and Bollerslev (1998) focus on evaluating the forecasts of the conditional variance of a returns series using alternative measures to the squared returns as a proxy for observed values of the conditional variance. Their analysis shows that in fact the GARCH model is capable of producing very accurate forecasts of the conditional variance of a time series. We consider forecasting both the conditional mean and conditional variance of our returns series; however, since we are merely illustrating the application of the GARCH model, we take the traditional route of employing the squared values of the S&P Composite returns series as a proxy for the observed conditional variance of the series. This should be borne in mind

[20] See Fernandez-Rodriguez, Sosvilla-Rivero and Andrada-Felix (1999) for an empirical application of the nearest neighbour approach to forecasting exchange rates. See Diebold and Nason (1990), Meese and Rose (1990) and LeBaron (1992) for empirical applications of the locally weighted regression approach in forecasting exchange rates.

when interpreting our evaluation measures for the conditional variance forecasts.

We discussed in Chapter 1 that to calculate the *optimal* h-steps ahead forecast of y_t, the forecast function obtained by taking the conditional expectation of y_{T+h} (where T is the sample size) is used. So, for example, in the case of the AR(1) model:

$$y_t = \delta + \rho y_{t-1} + \varepsilon_t \tag{8.48}$$

where $\varepsilon \sim \text{IID}(0, \sigma^2)$, the optimal h-step ahead forecast is:

$$E(y_{T+h} \,|\, \Omega_T) = \delta + \rho y_{T+h-1} \tag{8.49}$$

where Ω_T is the relevant information set. Therefore the optimal one-step ahead forecast of y_t is simply $\delta + \rho y_T$. While the forecasting functions for the conditional variances of ARCH and GARCH models are less well documented than the forecast functions for conventional ARIMA models (see Granger and Newbold, 1986, ch. 5, for detailed information on the latter), the methodology used to obtain the optimal forecast of the conditional variance of a time series from a GARCH model is the same as that used to obtain the optimal forecast of the conditional mean. For further details on the forecast function for the conditional variance of a GARCH(p, q) process see Box 8.4.

The *G@RCH* program enables forecasts of the conditional variance of a time series to be computed in addition to forecasts of the conditional mean. To illustrate, we utilize this program to forecast our S&P Composite returns series and its conditional variance using three different GARCH models: a GARCH(0, 1) model assuming a conditional normal distribution, a GARCH(1, 1) model and an IGARCH(1, 1) model, both assuming a conditional skewed Student-t distribution. In each case the same variables are used in the conditional mean: one lag of the returns (Ret_1), one lag of inflation (Inf_1) and one lag of the change in the three-month T-bill rate (DT-bill_1). Each model is estimated using the data for the period 1954:1–2000:9 and forecasts of the conditional mean and the conditional variance of the returns are computed from these estimated models for the period 2000:10–2001:9. The fitted models obtained are given in Table 8.10.

The *G@RCH* program also produces graphs of the forecasts of the conditional mean (with approximate 95% confidence bands) and conditional variance of the series (plotted in Figures 8.3(a)–8.3(c)) and some standard measures of forecast accuracy derived from the forecast errors; specifically, the MSE, median squared error (MedSE), mean error (ME), mean absolute error (MAE) and root mean squared error (RMSE). These are given in Table 8.11. Before looking at these, it is clear from Figures 8.3(a)–8.3(c) that the conditional mean forecasts obtained from these models are very similar. This is not surprising since the same variables are used in each model to describe the behaviour of the conditional mean. The graphs of the conditional variance forecasts vary considerably: the forecast of the conditional variance from the GARCH(0, 1) model approaches a constant value within a few steps, the

Box 8.4 Forecasting the conditional variance.

Consider the equation for the conditional variance in a GARCH(p, q) model:

$$h_t = \alpha_0 + \sum_{i=1}^{q} \alpha_i u_{t-i}^2 + \sum_{j=1}^{p} \beta_j h_{t-j} \tag{8.4.1}$$

Taking conditional expectations and assuming a sample size of T and for convenience that the parameters in the forecast functions are known, the forecast function for the optimal h-step ahead forecast of the conditional variance can be written:

$$E(h_{T+h} \mid \Omega_T) = \alpha_0 + \sum_{i=1}^{q} \alpha_i E(u_{T+h-i}^2 \mid \Omega_T) + \sum_{j=1}^{p} \beta_j E(h_{T+h-j} \mid \Omega_T) \tag{8.4.2}$$

where Ω_T is the relevant information set, $E(u_{T+i}^2 \mid \Omega_T) = E(h_{T+i} \mid \Omega_T)$ for $i > 0$, $E(u_{T+i}^2 \mid \Omega_T) = u_{T+i}^2$ and $E(h_{T+i} \mid \Omega_T) = h_{T+i}$ for $i \leq 0$, and for $i > 1$, $E(h_{T+i} \mid \Omega_T)$ is computed recursively. Thus the one-step ahead forecast of h_T is given by:

$$E(h_{T+1} \mid \Omega_T) = \alpha_0 + \alpha_1 u_T^2 + \beta_1 h_T \tag{8.4.3}$$

Forecasts of the conditional variance for GARCH-M models can be obtained in a similar way. Clearly, the forecast functions for some of the extensions of the original GARCH specification will be more difficult to derive. For example, in the GJR-GARCH model recall that the conditional variance is given by:

$$h_t = \alpha_0 + \alpha_1 u_{t-1}^2 + \gamma_1 u_{t-1}^2 I_{t-1} + \beta_1 h_{t-1} \tag{8.4.4}$$

where $I_{t-1} = 1$ if $u_{t-1} > 0$ and $I_{t-1} = 0$ otherwise. Unless $\gamma_1 = 0$, forecasts of the indicator function I_{t-1} need to be computed. The sign of u_{t-1} and therefore the forecasts of I_{t-1} will depend on the assumed distribution for ε_t.[21]

forecast of the conditional variance from the IGARCH(1, 1) model is a positively sloped straight line. On the basis of the measures of forecast accuracy given in Table 8.11, the IGARCH model produces the most accurate forecasts of the conditional mean and the conditional variance.[22]

[21] See Laurent and Peters (2002a, 2002b) for further details.

[22] A popular measure for evaluating forecasts of the conditional variance of a time series is the Mincer–Zarnowitz regression, proposed by Mincer and Zarnowitz (1969). This involves regressing the proxy for the observed future volatility on the forecast volatility and conducting hypothesis tests on the parameters of this model. In addition, the R^2 for this model can be used as a general test of predictability. We do not discuss this particular measure in detail, but similar regression-based methods for evaluating forecasts are considered in the next section.

Table 8.10 Fitted models for S&P Composite returns.[23]

y_t = Ret, y_{t-1} = Ret_1, x_{1t-1} = Inf_1, x_{2t-1} = DT-bill_1.
(t-statistics are in parentheses)

AR(1)-GARCH(0, 1):

$$y_t = \underset{(7.842)}{1.724} + \underset{(3.112)}{0.152}y_{t-1} - \underset{(-3.539)}{1.692}\,x_{1t-1} - \underset{(-4.845)}{1.429}\,x_{2t-1} + \hat{u}_t$$

$$\hat{h}_t = \underset{(12.69)}{8.619} + \underset{(2.430)}{0.148}\hat{u}_{t-1}^2$$

AR(1)-GARCH(1, 1):

$$y_t = \underset{(6.470)}{1.433} + \underset{(3.979)}{0.169}y_{t-1} - \underset{(-2.156)}{1.064}\,x_{1t-1} - \underset{(-3.830)}{1.156}\,x_{2t-1} + \hat{u}_t$$

$$\hat{h}_t = \underset{(1.836)}{1.181} + \underset{(2.048)}{0.075}\hat{u}_{t-1}^2 + \underset{(10.320)}{0.811}\,\hat{h}_{t-1}$$

AR(1)-IGARCH(1, 1):

$$y_t = \underset{(6.231)}{1.372} + \underset{(3.791)}{0.165}y_{t-1} - \underset{(-2.154)}{1.095}\,x_{1t-1} - \underset{(-3.523)}{1.163}\,x_{2t-1} + \hat{u}_t$$

$$\hat{h}_t = \underset{(1.638)}{0.348} + \underset{(2.910)}{0.136}\hat{u}_{t-1}^2 + \underset{(\mathrm{NA})}{0.864}\hat{h}_{t-1}$$

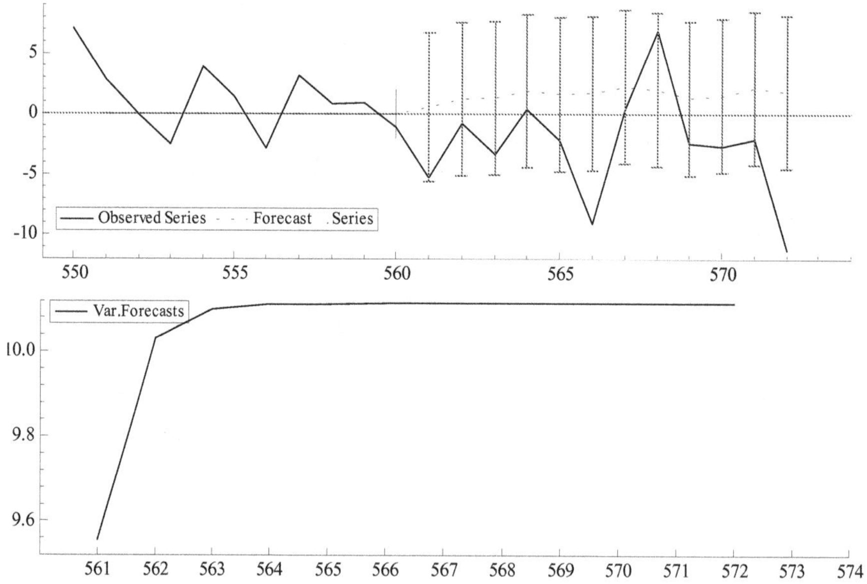

Figure 8.3(a). Forecasts of S&P Composite returns from GARCH(0, 1) model.

[23] Standard errors are not calculated for the estimated beta parameter in the IGARCH model.

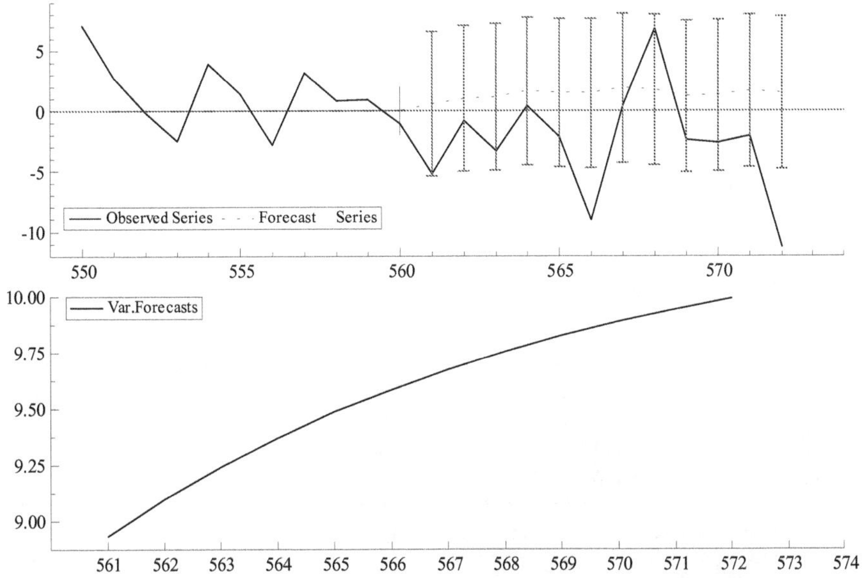

Figure 8.3(b). Forecasts of S&P Composite returns from GARCH(1, 1) model.

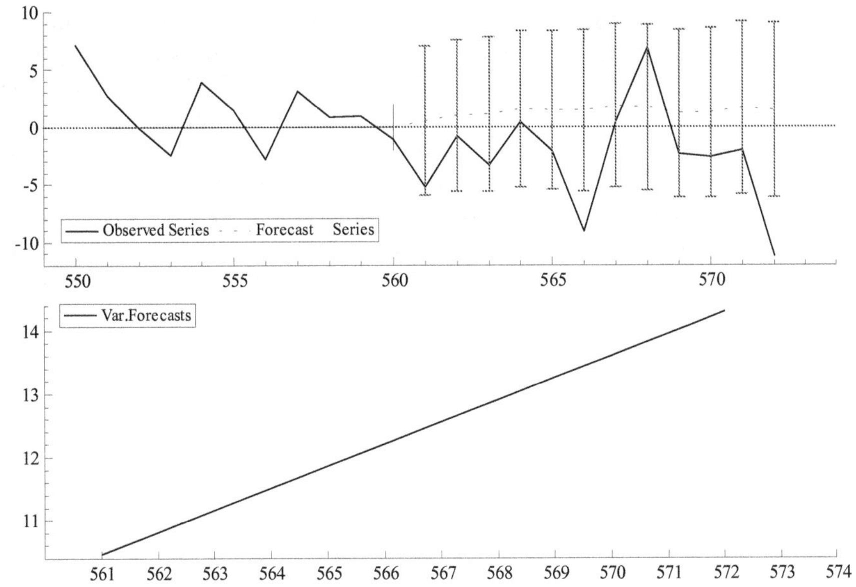

Figure 8.3(c). Forecasts of S&P Composite returns from IGARCH(1, 1) model.

Table 8.11 Forecast evaluation measures for forecasts from GARCH(p, q) models for S&P Composite returns.

	AR(1)-GARCH(0, 1)	AR(1)-GARCH(1, 1)	AR(1)-IGARCH(1, 1)
Conditional mean forecasts			
MSE	36.647	34.959	34.448
MedSE	17.663	15.069	14.604
ME	−4.223	−4.010	−3.945
MAE	5.031	4.862	4.808
RNSE	6.054	5.913	5.869
Conditional variance forecasts			
MSE	2,541.129	2,555.720	2,403.565
MedSE	89.489	83.504	94.956
ME	23.061	23.555	20.738
MAE	27.474	27.587	27.035
RMSE	50.410	50.554	49.026

Note that the scale of the forecast errors is affected by the way the data has been scaled (in this case % amounts are used). When comparing the forecast errors from different studies it is of crucial importance that in each study the data has been scaled in the same way.

FURTHER METHODS FOR FORECAST EVALUATION

If one forecasting model has a lower MSE than a competing model for the same times series, it does not necessarily mean that it is a superior forecasting specification, since the difference between the MSEs may be statistically insignificant from zero. Rather than just compare the MSE of forecasts from different forecasting models, it is also important to *test* for whether any reductions in MSE are statistically significant. Diebold and Mariano (1995) developed a test of equal forecast accuracy. Having generated n, h-steps-ahead forecasts from two different forecasting models, the forecaster has two sets of forecast errors e_{1t} and e_{2t}, where $t = 1, 2, \ldots, n$. Using MSE as a measure of forecast quality, the hypothesis of equal forecast accuracy can be represented as $E[d_t] = 0$, where $d_t = e_{1t}^2 - e_{2t}^2$ and E is the expectations operator. The mean of the difference between the MSEs $\bar{d} = n^{-1} \sum_{t=1}^{n} d_t$ has an approximate asymptotic variance of:

$$V(\bar{d}) \approx n^{-1} \left[\gamma_0 + 2 \sum_{k=1}^{h-1} \gamma_k \right] \tag{8.50}$$

where γ_k is the kth autocovariance of d_t, which can be estimated as:

$$\hat{\gamma}_k = n^{-1} \sum_{t=k+1}^{n} (d_t - \bar{d})(d_{t-k} - \bar{d}) \tag{8.51}$$

The Diebold and Mariano (1995) statistic for testing the null hypothesis of equal forecast accuracy is $S_1 = [\hat{V}(\bar{d})]^{-1/2} \bar{d}$ and under the null hypothesis S_1

has an asymptotic standard normal distribution. Diebold and Mariano (1995) show, through Monte Carlo simulation experiments, that the performance of this test statistic is good, even for small samples and when forecast errors are autocorrelated and have non-normal distributions. However, they do find that their test is over-sized for small numbers of forecast observations and forecasts of two-steps ahead or greater.

Testing the equality of forecast errors is a topic also investigated by Harvey, Leybourne and Newbold (1997). In particular they consider modifying Diebold and Mariano's (1995) test in order to improve its finite sample performance. Their main modification involves using an approximately unbiased estimator of the variance of $\bar{d}$.[24] Incorporating this into the Diebold and Mariano (1995) test statistic gives a modified statistic:

$$S_1^* = \left[\frac{n+1-2h+n^{-1}h(h-1)}{n}\right]^{1/2} S_1 \tag{8.52}$$

where S_1 is the original Diebold and Mariano statistic. Harvey et al. (1997) propose comparing their modified statistic with Student's t critical values rather than with those of the standard normal distribution. They compare the finite sample performance of S_1^* with S_1 using Monte Carlo simulation methods and confirm that the original Diebold and Mariano statistic S_1 is over-sized in a number of instances and that this problem gets worse as the forecast horizon increases. The modified statistic S_1^* is found to perform much better at all forecast horizons and if the forecast errors are autocorrelated or have non-normal distributions.

Comparing MSE or testing for significant differences in MSE is not the only means of forecast comparison and evaluation. Harvey, Leybourne and Newbold (HLN) (1998) argue:

> ... the discovery that an analyst's preferred forecasts are better, or even 'significantly better', than those from some possibly naive competitor ought not to induce complacency. A more stringent requirement would be that the competing forecasts embody no useful information absent in the preferred forecasts. (p. 254)

The notion of 'forecast encompassing' refers to whether or not the forecasts from a competing model, say model 2, contain information missing from the forecasts from the original model—model 1. If they do not, then the forecasts from model 2 are said to be 'encompassed' by the forecasts from model 1. Research on testing whether forecasts from one model encompass those of another applies to one-step ahead forecasts and can be traced back to Granger and Newbold (1973), who applied the concept of 'conditional efficiency' to forecasts. A forecast is 'conditionally efficient' if the variance of the forecast error from a combination of that forecast and a competing forecast is

[24] The estimator used by Diebold and Mariano (1995) is consistent but biased.

equal to or greater than the variance of the original forecast error. Therefore a forecast that is conditionally efficient 'encompasses' the competing forecast.

Let y_{1t} and y_{2t} be one-step ahead forecasts from two different models. Assume there are n of these forecasts and that e_{1t} and e_{2t} are the two sets of forecast errors. One of the first tests of forecast encompassing proposed is that of Chong and Hendry (1986) (who were the first to use the term 'encompassing' to describe conditionally efficient forecasts). They propose a test that involves regressing the forecast error from the original model (model 1) on the forecast from the competing model (model 2):

$$e_{1t} = \alpha y_{2t} + \varepsilon_t \tag{8.53}$$

If the forecasts from model 1 encompass those of model 2, then $\alpha = 0$. Therefore to test the null hypothesis that forecasts from model 1 encompass those of model 2, the t-statistic for testing $\alpha = 0$ can be used. Under the null hypothesis this t-statistic has an asymptotic normal distribution. Ericsson (1992) suggests testing the null hypothesis of forecast encompassing by regressing the forecast error from model 1 on the difference in the forecast errors from model 1 and model 2:

$$e_{1t} = \gamma(e_{1t} - e_{2t}) + \varepsilon_t \tag{8.54}$$

If $\gamma = 0$, the forecasts from model 2 carry information that is not in the forecasts from model 1, and so the forecasts from model 1 do not encompass those from model 2. If $\gamma = 0$, the forecasts from model 2 contain no additional information compared with the forecasts from model 1 and so are encompassed. Therefore to test the null hypothesis of forecast encompassing the t-statistic for testing the null hypothesis $\gamma = 0$ can be used, which also has an asymptotic standard normal distribution.

Harvey et al. (1998) have shown that conventional tests of forecast encompassing can be over-sized in the presence of non-normal forecast errors. They develop an alternative test of the null hypothesis of forecast encompassing using the methodology of the tests for equal forecast accuracy discussed in Diebold and Mariano (1995) and Harvey et al. (1997). More specifically, their test is based on the fact that if the forecasts from model 1 encompass the forecasts from model 2, then the covariance between e_{1t} and $e_{1t} - e_{2t}$ will be negative or zero. The alternative hypothesis is that the forecasts from model 1 do not encompass those from model 2, in which case the covariance between e_{1t} and $e_{1t} - e_{2t}$ will be positive. Exploiting this to test the null hypothesis of forecast encompassing, Harvey et al. (1998) propose the following test statistic:

$$\text{HLN} = \frac{\bar{c}}{\sqrt{\text{var}(\bar{c})}} \tag{8.55}$$

where $c_t = e_{1t}(e_{1t} - e_{2t})$ and $\bar{c} = n^{-1}\sum_{t=1}^{n} c_t$. Under the null hypothesis of forecast encompassing, the HLN statistic has an asymptotic standard normal distribution.

Clark and McCracken (2000, 2001) consider the case that, under the null hypothesis of forecast encompassing, model 2 nests model 1. They show that when the forecasts being evaluated are computed from linear models that are nested and a recursive or rolling forecasting scheme is being used, the asymptotic distributions of the conventional tests of forecast encompassing have non-normal distributions. Clark and McCracken (2000, 2001) derive the true asymptotic distributions of a number of encompassing tests for various forecasting schemes when the forecasts are made from nested models and provide asymptotic critical values. Note that for the fixed forecasting scheme, the established tests of forecast encompassing are asymptotically standard normal, even when the forecasts are made from nested models. The forecasting scheme used for the examples in this chapter is fixed: the parameters of the model are estimated using a fixed number of sample observations and the forecasts are computed from that model without updating.[25]

Clark and McCracken (CM) (2001) argue that the denominator used in the HLN test statistic may adversely affect the small-sample properties of the test. They propose a modified HLN statistic that, they argue, has improved finite sample performance:

$$\mathrm{CM} = n\frac{\bar{c}}{\mathrm{MSE}_2} \tag{8.56}$$

where MSE_2 is the mean squared error for the forecasts from model 2. Like the HLN test, this test uses information on the covariance between e_{1t} and $e_{1t} - e_{2t}$, but here MSE_2 replaces the standard deviation of $\bar{c}$ as a scaling factor. For a fixed forecasting scheme (and nested forecasting models), unlike the established tests for encompassing, the CM test does not have an asymptotic standard normal distribution. In particular, the critical values depend on the number of additional variables in the competing model compared with the original model and the ratio of the number of forecasts to the number of in-sample observations. Detailed critical values for the CM test when a fixed forecasting scheme is used are given in Clark and McCracken (2000, appendix table 5).

In order to illustrate these methods we apply a selection to forecasts of the S&P Composite returns, computed from GARCH models (although the tests are applicable to forecasts from any type of econometric model). Rather than investigate exactly the same sample of data as in the previous examples in this chapter, here we use a slightly shorter sample 1959:4–2001:9. This enables us to augment the model with some additional explanatory variables, as well as the inflation and interest rate data used earlier. These additional variables were only available from 1959:4 onward.

A number of studies have focused on predicting stock market returns using macroeconomic variables (see, for example, Pesaran and Timmermann, 1995,

[25] See Clark and McCracken (2001) for a specific definition of a recursive forecast scheme and Clark and McCracken (2000) for a definition of a rolling forecasting scheme.

Table 8.12 AR(1)-GARCH(1, 1) benchmark model.

	Coefficient	Standard error	t-Value	t-Probability
Constant(M)	0.866	0.210	4.123	0.000
Ret_1(M)	0.215	0.047	4.536	0.000
Constant(V)	1.791	1.050	1.707	0.089
Beta1(V)	0.787	0.101	7.763	0.000
Alpha1(V)	0.063	0.037	1.686	0.093
Asymmetry	−0.130	0.075	−1.739	0.083
Tail	5.452	1.525	3.574	0.000

Information criteria:

Akaike	5.230	Shibata	5.229
Schwarz	5.300	Hannan–Quinn	5.257

2000, and Bossaerts and Hillion, 1999). The types of variables typically used are the inflation rate, interest rate, output and money supply variables. We employ lags of the following macroeconomic variables in GARCH models to forecast the S&P Composite returns: the inflation rate (inf), the change in the three-month T-bill rate (DT-bill), the growth rate of M1 (M1gr), the growth rate of industrial production (Indgr) and the growth rate of the rate of return on long-term Government bonds (D10yr). We use the data from 1959:4–1992:6 for the purposes of estimation, with the observations for the period 1992:7–2001:9 held back for the purposes of forecast comparison.

First, we estimated a AR(1)-GARCH(1, 1) model for the S&P Composite returns as a benchmark specification, assuming a skewed Student-t distribution when specifying the likelihood function. The estimated parameters are given in Table 8.12. Next we estimated a GARCH(1, 1) model, but this time including two lags of the five macroeconomic variables in the conditional mean plus an AR(1) term. The results are given in Table 8.13. Only the first lag of the T-bill and money supply variables are significant at the 10% level and while, on the basis of the Akaike information criteria, this model is an improvement on the benchmark model, the Schwarz criteria indicates the opposite. Finally, we estimated a GARCH(1, 1) model including only the significant T-bill and money supply variables in the conditional mean. The results are given in Table 8.14. Compared with the results in Table 8.12, on the basis of the information criteria computed, this model is preferred to the benchmark model.

All three fitted models were used to compute one-step ahead forecasts of the conditional mean and conditional variance of the series over the period 1992:7–2001:9 (thus in each case 110 one-step ahead forecasts were computed). In Table 8.15, for the benchmark model and for the GARCH(1, 1) model including two lags of the five macroeconomic variables in the conditional mean, we report MSE along with some of the tests of equal forecast accuracy and forecast encompassing. The following labels are used in the table:

Table 8.13 GARCH(1, 1) model with two lags of five macro-variables in the conditional mean.

	Coefficient	Standard error	*t*-Value	*t*-Probability
Constant(M)	1.074	0.392	2.740	0.006
Ret_1(M)	0.172	0.052	3.327	0.001
DT-bill_1(M)	−0.837	0.420	−1.990	0.047
Inf_1(M)	−0.727	0.620	−1.172	0.242
M1gr_1(M)	−0.697	0.395	−1.766	0.078
Indgr_1(M)	−0.013	0.190	−0.069	0.945
D10yr-bill_1(M)	−1.163	0.731	−1.591	0.112
DT-bill_2(M)	−0.508	0.389	−1.303	0.193
Inf_2(M)	0.631	0.573	1.100	0.272
M1gr_2(M)	0.573	0.392	1.464	0.144
Indgr_2(M)	−0.213	0.189	−1.126	0.261
D10yr-bill_2(M)	0.569	0.729	0.780	0.436
Constant(V)	1.647	1.025	1.607	0.109
Beta1(V)	0.797	0.108	7.430	0.000
Alpha1(V)	0.054	0.038	1.421	0.156
Asymmetry	−0.125	0.073	−1.708	0.089
Tail	5.351	1.580	3.386	0.001

Information criteria:

Akaike	5.214	Shibata	5.210
Schwarz	5.384	Hannan–Quinn	5.281

- Diebold and Mariano (1995) test: DM.
- Modified Diebold and Mariano test proposed by Harvey et al. (1997): MDM.
- Ericsson (1992) encompassing test: ER.
- Harvey et al. (1998) encompassing test: HLN.

For the conditional mean forecasts the model that contains macroeconomic variables in the conditional mean has a higher MSE than the benchmark specification, suggesting that the macroeconomic variables contain no useful information for forecasting returns and that in fact their inclusion leads to inferior forecasts. However, the null hypothesis of equal forecast accuracy is not rejected by the DM or MDM tests—so neither model is deemed significantly better than the other. On the basis of MSE, the model that includes macroeconomic variables in the conditional mean appears to be the superior forecasting model for the conditional variance since its MSE is lowest. Again, however, the null hypothesis of equal forecast accuracy and the null hypothesis of forecast encompassing are not rejected by any of the tests, so this improvement is not deemed statistically significant.

Table 8.14 GARCH(1, 1) model with significant lags of five macro-variables in the conditional mean.

	Coefficient	Standard error	t-Value	t-Probability
Constant(M)	1.179	0.267	4.400	0.000
Ret_1(M)	0.202	0.048	4.245	0.000
DT-bill_1(M)	−1.141	0.311	−3.667	0.000
M1gr_1(M)	−0.613	0.365	−1.678	0.094
Constant(V)	1.612	1.044	1.544	0.125
Beta1(V)	0.813	0.102	7.956	0.000
Alpha1(V)	0.045	0.034	1.345	0.179
Assymmetry	−0.152	0.071	−2.138	0.033
Tail	5.278	1.470	3.590	0.000

Information criteris:

Akaike	5.201	Shibata	5.200
Schwarz	5.291	Hannan–Quinn	5.237

Table 8.15 Forecasting results for GARCH(1, 1) no macro versus GARCH(1, 1) with two lags of five macro-variables in the conditional mean.

	Conditional mean forecasts	Conditional variance forecasts
MSE no macro	10.346	456.770
MSE macro	10.809	455.470
DM	−1.173	0.856
MDM	−1.168	0.852
ER	−0.974	0.192
HLN	−0.480	1.051

In Table 8.16 we report results that compare forecasts from the benchmark model with forecasts from the GARCH(1, 1) model including the two significant macroeconomic variables in the conditional mean. In this case, on the basis of MSE, the model that includes macroeconomic variables appears to be the preferred forecasting specification for the conditional mean, since it has the lowest MSE. Note, however, that despite the inclusion of two macroeconomic variables leading to a lower MSE, the DM and MDM tests indicate that this reduction is not statistically significant and the ER and HLN tests do not reject the null of forecast encompassing. For this reason we should be cautious of concluding that the inclusion of these macroeconomic variables leads to a superior forecasting model. For forecasts of the conditional variance, the model that includes macroeconomic variables leads to a higher MSE than the benchmark specification and there are no rejections from any of the tests.

Table 8.16 Conditional mean forcasting results for GARCH(1, 1) no macro versus GARCH(1, 1) with significant lags of five macro-variables in the conditional mean.

	Conditional mean forecasts	Conditional variance forecasts
MSE no macro	10.346	456.77
MSE macro	10.260	457.29
DM	0.332	−0.254
MDM	0.331	−0.253
ER	1.269	−0.027
HLN	0.911	−0.109

CONCLUSIONS ON MODELLING AND FORECASTING FINANCIAL TIME SERIES

The application of econometric techniques to financial time series raises a number of additional issues not focused on elsewhere in this book. The most important of these is the concept of ARCH. This chapter has outlined the development of the original ARCH model through to more recent integrated and asymmetric specifications. Not all developments of the original ARCH model have proved to be as popular in the applied literature as the extension to capture asymmetry. For example, many of the early multivariate GARCH specifications proposed are not very useful in practice, as they require the estimation of large numbers of parameters, even in the case of very small systems of equations. Future developments in this area are likely to involve simplifying the original multivariate forms proposed to enable easier estimation. In this chapter we have also commented on research investigating the effects of conditional heteroscedasticity on unit root and cointegration tests. Many applied econometric analyses involving tests for unit roots in financial time series or tests for cointegrating relationships between variables including financial time series have largely ignored the issue of conditional heteroscedasticity. This is sometimes justified by referring to earlier theoretical work that proves that the DF test is asymptotically robust to the presence of ARCH. However, a small but growing body of literature is developing that is concerned with the performance of unit root and cointegration tests in the presence of conditional heteroscedastcity. Among other things, these studies reveal that ignoring the presence of ARCH and GARCH can lead to serious distortions to the size and power of conventional unit root tests. While there is still a lot to be done in terms of the theoretical work in this area, we perceive this issue to be an important one for future research. The final part of this chapter has focused on forecasting and forecast evaluation. The forecasting literature is itself a huge body of work and includes excellent higher level texts by Granger and Newbold (1986), Clements and Hendry (1998) and Clements and Hendry (1999). In this chapter we have discussed forecasting the conditional mean and conditional variance of a time series and the evaluation of forecasts using tests of equal forecast accuracy and forecast encompassing.

Important Terms and Concepts

Conditional mean	Conditional variance	Volatility
ARCH	GARCH	ARCH-M
EGARCH	GJR-GARCH	IGARCH
FIGARCH	Forecasting	MSE
Forecast evaluation	Forecast encompassing	

Appendix
Cointegration Analysis Using the Johansen Technique: A Practitioner's Guide to *PcGive 10.1*

This appendix provides a basic introduction on how to implement the Johansen technique using the *PcGive 10.1* econometric program (see Doornik and Hendry, 2001 for full details). Using the same data set as underlies much of the analysis in Chapters 5 and 6, we show the user how to work through Chapter 5 up to the point of undertaking joint tests involving restrictions on $\boldsymbol{\alpha}$ and $\boldsymbol{\beta}$.

This latest version of *PcGive* brings together the old *PcGive* (single equation) and *PcFiml* (multivariate) stand-alone routines into a single integrated software program (that in fact is much more than the sum of the previous versions, since it is built on the *Ox* programming language and allows various bolt-on *Ox* programs to be added—such as dynamic panel data analysis (DPD), time series models and generalized autoregressive conditional heteroscedastic (GARCH) models—see Chapter 8). It is very flexible to operate, providing drop-down menus and (for the present analysis) an extensive range of modelling features for $I(1)$ and $I(0)$ systems (and limited analysis of the $I(2)$ system).[1] Cointegration facilities are embedded in an overall modelling strategy leading through to structural vector autoregression (VAR) modelling.

After the data have been read-in to *GiveWin*[2] (the data management and graphing platform that underpins *PcGive* and the other programs that can operate in what has been termed the *Oxmetrics* suite of programs), it is first necessary to (i) start the *PcGive* module, (ii) select 'Multiple-equation Dynamic Modelling' and then (iii) 'Formulate' a model. This allows the user to define the model in (log) levels, fix which deterministic variables should enter the cointegration space, determine the lag length of the VAR and decide whether

[1] *PcGive* also allows users to run batch jobs where previous jobs can be edited and rerun.
[2] The program accepts data files based on spreadsheets and unformatted files.

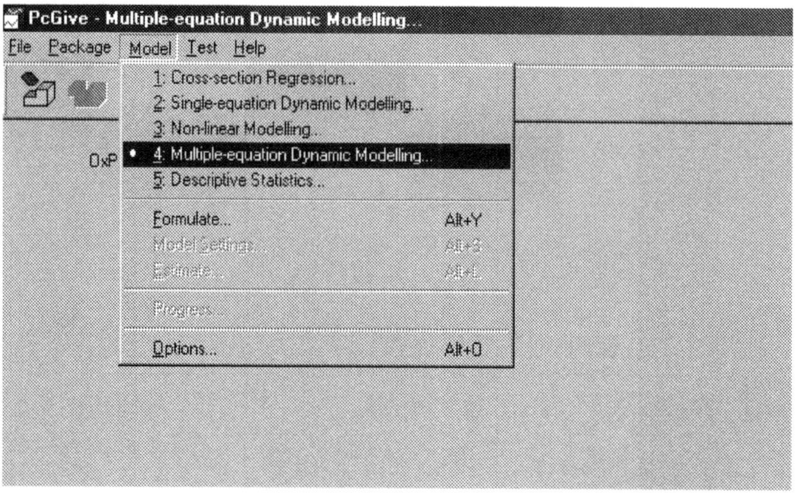

Figure A.1. Formulating a model in *PcGive 10.1*: Step (1) choosing the correct model option.

I(0) variables, particularly dummies, need to be specified to enter the model in the short-run dynamics but not in the cointegration spaces (see Figures A.1 and A.2).

When the 'Formulate' option is chosen, the right-hand area under 'Database' shows the variables available for modelling. Introducing dummies and transformations of existing variables can be undertaken using the 'Calculator' or 'Algebra Editor' under 'Tools' in *GiveWin*, and these new variables when created will also appear in the 'Database'. In this instance, we will model the demand for real money (rm) as a function of real output (y), inflation (dp) and the interest rate (rstar), with all the variables already transformed into log levels. The lag length (k) is set equal to 4 (see lower right-hand option in Figure A.2); if we want to use an information criterion (IC) to set the lag length, then k can be set at different values, and when the model is estimated it will produce the Akaike, Hannan–Quinn and Schwarz IC for use in determining which model is appropriate.[3] (However, it is also necessary to ensure that the model passes diagnostic tests with regard to the properties of the residuals of the equations in the model—see below—and therefore use of an IC needs to be done carefully.)

Each variable to be included is highlighted in the 'Database' (either one at a time, allowing the user to determine the order in which these variables enter, or all variables can be simultaneously highlighted). This will bring up an '≪Add' option, and, once this is clicked on, then the model selected appears on the left-hand side under 'Model'. The 'Y' next to each variable indicates

[3] Make sure you have this option turned on as it is not the default. To do this in *PcGive*, choose 'Model', then 'Options', 'Additional output' and put a cross in the information criterion box.

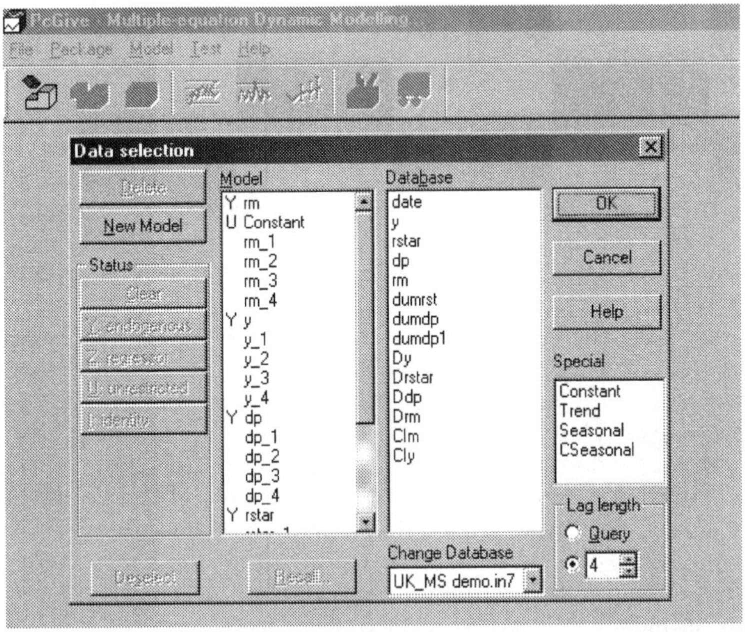

Figure A.2. Formulating a model in *PcGive 10.1*: Step (2) choosing the 'Formulate' option.

that it is endogenous and therefore will be modelled, a 'U' indicates the variable (e.g., the Constant, which enters automatically) is unrestricted and will only enter the short-run part of the vector error correction model (VECM), and the variables with '_k' next to them denote the lags of the variable (e.g., rm_{t-1}).

We also need to enter some dummies into the short-run model to take account of 'outliers' in the data (of course we identify these only after estimating the model, checking its adequacy, and then creating deterministic dummies to try to overcome problems; however, we shall assume we have already done this,[4]

[4] In practice, if the model diagnostics—see Figure A.3—indicates, say, a problem of non-normality in the equation determining a variable, plot the residuals using the graphing procedures (select, in *PcGive*, 'Test' and 'Graphic analysis' and then choose 'Residuals' by putting a cross in the relevant box). Visually locate outliers in terms of when they occur, then again under 'Test' choose 'Store residuals in database', click on residuals and accept the default names (or choose others) and store these residuals in the spreadsheet. Then go to the 'Window' drop-down option in *GiveWin* and select the database, locate the residuals just stored, locate the outlier residuals by scrolling down the spreadsheet (using the information gleaned from the graphical analysis) and then decide how you will 'dummy out' the outlier (probably just by creating a dummy variable using the 'Calculator' option in *GiveWin*, with the dummy being 0 before and after the outlier date and 1 for the actual date of the outlier).

or that *ex ante* we know such impacts have occurred and need to be included). Hence, highlight these (dumrst, dumdp, dumdp1), set the lag length option at the bottom right-hand side of the window to 0 and then click on '≪Add'. Scroll down the 'Model' window, and you will see that these dummies have 'Y' next to them, which indicates they will be modelled as additional variables. Since we only want them to enter unrestrictedly in the short-run model, select/highlight the dummies and then in the 'Status' options on the left-hand side (the buttons under 'Status' become available once a variable in the model is highlighted) click on 'Unrestricted', so that each dummy now has a 'U' next to it in the model.

Finally, on the right-hand side of the 'Data selection' window is a box headed 'Special'. These are the deterministic components that can be selected and added to the model. In this instance, we select 'CSeasonal' (centred seasonal dummies), as the data are seasonally unadjusted, and add the seasonal dummies to the model. They automatically enter as unrestricted. Note that if the time 'Trend' is added, it will not have a 'U' next to it in the model, indicating it is restricted to enter the cointegration space (Model 4 in Chapter 5—see equation (5.6)). If we wanted to select Model 2 then we would not enter the time trend (delete it from the model if it is already included), but would instead click on 'Constant' in the 'Model' box and click on 'Clear' under the 'Status' options. Removing the unrestricted status of the constant will restrict it to enter the cointegration space. Thus, we can select Models 2–4, one at a time, and then decide which deterministic components should enter Π, following the Pantula principle (see Chapter 5).

Having entered the model required, click OK, bringing up the 'Model settings' window, accept the default of 'Unrestricted system' (by clicking OK again) and accept ordinary least squares (OLS) as the estimation method (again by clicking OK). The results of estimating the model will be available in *GiveWin* (the 'Results' window—accessed by clicking on the *GiveWin* toolbar on your Windows status bar). Return to the *PcGive* window (click on its toolbar), choose the 'Test' option to activate the drop-down options, and click on 'Test summary'. This produces the output in *GiveWin* as shown in Figure A.3. The model passes the various tests equation by equation and by using system-wide tests.

Several iterations of the above steps are likely to be needed in practice to obtain the lag length (k) for the VAR, which deterministic components should enter the model (i.e., any dummies or other $I(0)$ variables that are needed in the short-run part of the VECM to ensure the model passes the diagnostic tests on the residuals) and which deterministic components should enter the cointegration space (i.e., should the constant or trend be restricted to be included in Π). To carry out the last part presumes you have already tested for the rank of Π, so we turn to this next.

To undertake cointegration analysis of the $I(1)$ system in *PcGive*, choose 'Test', then 'Dynamic Analysis and Cointegration tests' and check the '$I(1)$

```
rm              : Portmanteau(11): 11.2164
y               : Portmanteau(11): 6.76376
dp              : Portmanteau(11): 3.66633
rstar           : Portmanteau(11): 11.6639
rm              : AR 1-5 test:      F(5,73)    =    1.4131 [0.2297]
y               : AR 1-5 test:      F(5,73)    =    1.8569 [0.1125]
dp              : AR 1-5 test:      F(5,73)    =    1.0269 [0.4083]
rstar           : AR 1-5 test:      F(5,73)    =    1.8359 [0.1164]
rm              : Normality test:   Chi^2(2)   =    2.8297 [0.2430]
y               : Normality test:   Chi^2(2)   =    5.0521 [0.0800]
dp              : Normality test:   Chi^2(2)   =    4.6973 [0.0955]
rstar           : Normality test:   Chi^2(2)   =    2.7019 [0.2590]
rm              : ARCH 1-4 test:    F(4,70)    =    1.5882 [0.1871]
y               : ARCH 1-4 test:    F(4,70)    =    1.1669 [0.3329]
dp              : ARCH 1-4 test:    F(4,70)    =    1.1133 [0.3573]
rstar           : ARCH 1-4 test:    F(4,70)    =   0.68023 [0.6080]
rm              : hetero test:      F(35,42)   =   0.38980 [0.9974]
y               : hetero test:      F(35,42)   =   0.72070 [0.8385]
dp              : hetero test:      F(35,42)   =   0.67314 [0.8838]
rstar           : hetero test:      F(35,42)   =   0.88183 [0.6463]

Vector Portmanteau(11): 148.108
Vector AR 1-5 test:      F(80,219)=   1.0155 [0.4555]
Vector Normality test:   Chi^2(8)  =  15.358 [0.0525]
Vector hetero test:      F(350,346)=  0.47850 [1.0000]
Not enough observations for hetero-X test
```

Figure A.3. Estimating the unrestricted VAR in *PcGive 10.1*: model diagnostics.

cointegration analysis' box.[5] The results are produced in Figure A.4,[6] providing the eigenvalues of the system (and log-likelihoods for each cointegration rank), standard reduced rank test statistics *and* those adjusted for degrees of freedom (plus the significance levels for rejecting the various null hypotheses) and full-rank estimates of $\boldsymbol{\alpha}$, $\boldsymbol{\beta}$ and $\boldsymbol{\Pi}$ (the $\boldsymbol{\beta}$ are automatically normalized along the principal diagonal). Graphical analysis of the $\boldsymbol{\beta}$-vectors (unadjusted and adjusted for short-run dynamics) are available to provide a visual test of which vectors are stationary,[7] and graphs of the recursive eigenvalues associated with each eigenvector can be plotted to consider the stability of the cointegration vectors.[8]

[5] Note that the default output only produces the trace test. To obtain the λ-max test as well as the default (and tests adjusted for degrees of freedom), in *PcGive* choose 'Model', then 'Options', 'Further options' and put a cross in the box for cointegration test with Max test.

[6] Note that these differ from Box 5.5 and Table 5.5, since the latter are based on a model without the outlier dummies included in the unrestricted short-run model.

[7] The companion matrix that helps to verify the number of unit roots at or close to unity, corresponding to the $I(1)$ common trends, is available when choosing the 'Dynamic analysis' option in the 'Test' model menu in *PcGive*.

[8] Note that, to obtain recursive options, the 'recursive estimation' option needs to be selected when choosing OLS at the 'Estimation Model' window when formulating the model for estimation.

```
I(1) cointegration analysis, 1964 (2) to 1989 (2)
       eigenvalue      loglik for rank
                        1235.302   0
          0.57076       1278.012   1
          0.11102       1283.955   2
          0.063096      1287.246   3
          0.0020654     1287.350   4

rank Trace test [ Prob]   Max test  [ Prob]    Trace test [T-nm]    Max test [T-nm]
  0      104.10 [0.000]**    85.42 [0.000]**       87.61 [0.000]**     71.89 [0.000]**
  1       18.68 [0.527]      11.89 [0.571]         15.72 [0.737]       10.00 [0.747]
  2        6.79 [0.608]       6.58 [0.547]          5.72 [0.731]        5.54 [0.676]
  3        0.21 [0.648]       0.21 [0.648]          0.18 [0.675]        0.18 [0.675]

Asymptotic p-values based on: Unrestricted constant
Unrestricted variables:
[0] = Constant
[1] = CSeasonal
[2] = CSeasonal_1
[3] = CSeasonal_2
[4] = dumrst
[5] = dumdp
[6] = dumdp1
Number of lags used in the analysis: 4

beta (scaled on diagonal; cointegrating vectors in columns)
rm             1.0000         15.719      -0.046843          1.6502
y             -1.0337         1.0000       0.064882        -0.13051
dp             6.4188        -207.49         1.0000          8.6574
rstar          6.7976         131.02      -0.039555          1.0000

alpha
rm           -0.18373     0.00073499      0.0012372     -0.0010530
y          -0.0081691     -0.0010447       -0.16551    -0.00080063
dp           0.022631     0.00023031      -0.042258      0.0010822
rstar       0.0046324     -0.0011461     -0.0022919      0.0018533

long-run matrix, rank 4
                   rm              y             dp           rstar
rm           -0.17397        0.19088        -1.3397         -1.1537
y           -0.018159     -0.0032342     -0.0081182        -0.18666
dp           0.030017      -0.026047       0.064590         0.18677
rstar       -0.010218     -0.0063252        0.28129        -0.11673
```

Figure A.4. $I(1)$ cointegration analysis in *PcGive 10.1*.

After deciding on the value of $r \leq n$, it is necessary to select a reduced rank system. In *PcGive*, under 'Model', choose 'Model settings' (not 'Formulate'), select the option 'Cointegrated VAR' and in the window that appears set the cointegration rank (here we change '3' to '1', as the test statistics indicate that $r = 1$). Leave the 'No additional restrictions' option unchanged as the default, click OK in this window and the next, and the output (an estimate of the new value of $\mathbf{\Pi}$ together with the reduced-form cointegration vectors) will be written to the results window in *GiveWin*.

Finally, we test for restrictions on $\boldsymbol{\alpha}$ and $\boldsymbol{\beta}$ (recall that these should usually be conducted together). To illustrate the issue, the model estimated in Chapter 6

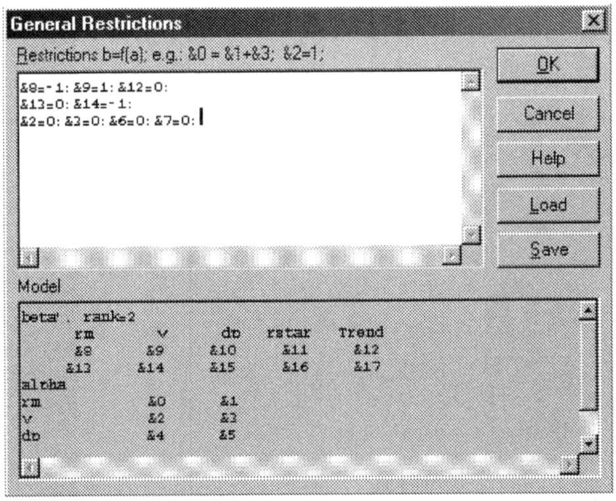

Figure A.5. Testing restrictions on $\boldsymbol{\alpha}$ and $\boldsymbol{\beta}$ using 'General Restrictions' in *PcGive 10.1.*

is chosen (instead of the one above) with a time trend restricted into the cointegration space and $r = 2$. Thus, we test the following restrictions:

$$\boldsymbol{\beta}' = \begin{bmatrix} -1 & 1 & * & * & 0 \\ 0 & -1 & * & * & * \end{bmatrix}$$

$$\boldsymbol{\alpha}' = \begin{bmatrix} * & 0 & * & 0 \\ * & 0 & * & 0 \end{bmatrix}$$

using the option 'General restrictions'. To do this in *PcGive*, under 'Model', choose 'Model settings', select the option 'Cointegrated VAR' and in the window that appears set the cointegration rank (here we change '3' to '2', since we have chosen $r = 2$). Click the 'General restrictions' option, type the relevant restrictions into the window (note that in the 'Model' the parameters are identified by '&' and a number—see Figure A.5), click OK in this window (and the next) and the results will be written into *GiveWin* (Figure A.6—see also the top half of Box 6.1).

CONCLUSION

For the applied economist wishing to estimate cointegration relations and then to test for linear restrictions, *PcGive 10.1* is a flexible option. But there are others. Harris (1995) compared three of the most popular options available in the 1990s (Microfit *3.0*, *Cats* (*in Rats*) and *PcFiml*—the latter the predecessor to the current *PcGive*). The *Cats* program[9] has seen little development since its

[9] *Cointegration Analysis of Times Series (Cats in Rats)*, version 1.0, by Henrik Hansen and Katrina Juselius, distributed by Estima.

```
Cointegrated VAR (4) in:
[0] = rm
[1] = y
[2] = dp
[3] = rstar
Unrestricted variables:
[0] = dumrst
[1] = dumdp
[2] = dumdp1
[3] = Constant
[4] = CSeasonal
[5] = CSeasonal_1
[6] = CSeasonal_2
Restricted variables:
[0] = Trend
Number of lags used in the analysis: 4

General cointegration restrictions:
&8=-1;&9=1;&12=0;
&13=0;&14=-1;
&2=0;&3=0;&6=0;&7=0;

beta
rm          -1.0000       0.00000
y            1.0000       -1.0000
dp          -6.5414        2.8091
rstar       -6.6572       -1.1360
Trend       0.00000     0.0066731

Standard errors of beta
rm          0.00000       0.00000
y           0.00000       0.00000
dp          0.88785       0.46671
rstar       0.33893       0.19346
Trend       0.00000    0.00020557

alpha
rm          0.17900      0.083003
y           0.00000       0.00000
dp        -0.011637      -0.15246
rstar       0.00000       0.00000

Standard errors of alpha
rm         0.018588      0.074038
y           0.00000       0.00000
dp        0.0078017      0.031076
rstar       0.00000       0.00000

log-likelihood            1290.6274    -T/2log|Omega|          1863.87857
no. of observations             101    no. of parameters               85
rank of long-run matrix           2    no. long-run restrictions        5
beta is identified
AIC                        -35.2253    SC                        -33.0245
HQ                         -34.3344    FPE                    1.08703e-015

LR test of restrictions: Chi^2(5) =   3.6020 [0.6080]
```

Figure A6. Output from testing restrictions on α and β using 'General restrictions' in *PcGive 10.1*.

inception (although there is an $I(2)$ version available as a free download for users of the standard $I(1)$ version of *Cats*). *Microfit 4.0*[10] offers a modelling strategy based closely on the approach used in, for example, Garratt, Lee, Pesaran and Shin (1999), whereby the user moves toward estimating the conditional $I(1)$ model with exogenous variables. All three packages have their strengths and limitations (in comparison with each other), and therefore it is likely that different users will have different views on which they prefer.

[10] *Microfit 4.0, An Interactive Econometric Analysis*, developed by Hashem Pesaran and Bahram Pesaran and distributed by Oxford University Press.

Statistical Appendix

Table A.0 Seasonally unadjusted data for UK money demand model, 1963q1–1989q2 (for sources see Hendry and Ericsson, 1991, and Ericsson, Hendry and Tran, 1992). These data are available in various formats on the website for the book (together with other data sets used).

y_t	m_t	p_t	R
11.242 49	8.923 458	−2.199 126	0.043 125
11.309 40	8.950 517	−2.181 253	0.043 542
11.314 34	8.963 848	−2.182 139	0.042 083
11.350 35	9.016 422	−2.164 564	0.043 542
11.321 81	8.992 091	−2.168 929	0.048 958
11.364 70	9.002 809	−2.148 149	0.050 000
11.364 34	9.023 770	−2.143 021	0.050 746
11.399 99	9.048 013	−2.129 472	0.067 300
11.343 51	9.021 326	−2.119 431	0.075 200
11.381 89	9.035 228	−2.107 018	0.067 900
11.391 72	9.046 821	−2.099 644	0.065 033
11.412 49	9.085 797	−2.087 474	0.062 933
11.377 48	9.075 036	−2.081 844	0.062 317
11.401 92	9.070 388	−2.066 723	0.063 350
11.413 33	9.080 431	−2.059 639	0.074 800
11.422 55	9.085 287	−2.046 394	0.073 021
11.406 22	9.076 195	−2.047 943	0.063 646
11.437 89	9.092 274	−2.039 452	0.056 458
11.444 67	9.132 717	−2.034 851	0.055 833
11.461 16	9.158 758	−2.027 229	0.072 708
11.455 02	9.130 891	−2.009 915	0.080 104
11.464 72	9.148 518	−1.991 431	0.082 500
11.493 27	9.161 006	−1.977 607	0.076 771
11.522 63	9.198 470	−1.965 399	0.074 375
11.457 67	9.146 482	−1.954 749	0.084 896
11.494 81	9.128 208	−1.944 911	0.092 500

(continued)

Table A.0 (*cont.*)

y_t	m_t	p_t	R
11.507 90	9.143 239	−1.933 784	0.096 042
11.541 01	9.201 653	−1.918 684	0.089 688
11.469 55	9.166 428	−1.899 122	0.091 042
11.525 54	9.206 182	−1.877 971	0.080 417
11.537 34	9.226 312	−1.857 899	0.075 104
11.579 53	9.290 941	−1.840 110	0.071 979
11.501 49	9.296 736	−1.819 542	0.075 104
11.554 21	9.311 079	−1.795 767	0.065 208
11.574 29	9.348 906	−1.775 492	0.058 021
11.607 88	9.397 040	−1.761 424	0.047 917
11.544 71	9.409 320	−1.746 404	0.049 583
11.590 17	9.453 241	−1.733 302	0.056 875
11.587 17	9.470 233	−1.707 602	0.077 500
11.663 26	9.529 387	−1.689 022	0.080 833
11.656 99	9.503 455	−1.665 479	0.100 833
11.669 42	9.569 498	−1.653 912	0.089 167
11.686 61	9.547 008	−1.611 941	0.127 292
11.707 70	9.579 166	−1.566 857	0.147 500
11.633 17	9.538 432	−1.520 512	0.155 625
11.669 11	9.569 498	−1.461 880	1.133 125
11.692 54	9.594 829	−1.413 460	0.127 708
11.706 73	9.681 674	−1.366 492	0.126 042
11.631 86	9.681 403	−1.300 851	0.113 750
11.641 89	9.712 169	−1.243 060	0.097 708
11.657 36	9.765 979	−1.196 666	0.106 042
11.691 41	9.808 451	−1.162 831	0.114 688
11.658 29	9.824 644	−1.125 546	0.093 021
11.674 24	9.849 699	−1.090 049	0.109 375
11.704 58	9.900 239	−1.058 142	0.117 187
11.740 65	9.913 141	−1.019 154	0.151 250
11.676 40	9.917 179	−1.979 763	0.114 167
11.691 82	9.958 089	−0.947 265	0.078 958
11.710 70	10.037 76	−0.926 593	0.067 396
11.747 62	10.110 13	−1.914 542	0.061 458
11.710 93	10.137 03	−0.885 761	0.065 937
11.733 70	10.156 54	−0.862 276	0.090 937
11.751 59	10.208 35	−1.839 561	0.096 667
11.769 09	10.259 91	−0.813 960	0.118 229
11.725 91	10.260 62	−0.787 678	0.129 167
11.783 56	10.274 70	−0.752 473	0.126 875
11.789 88	10.312 69	−0.701 381	0.141 979
11.809 06	10.344 01	−0.662 424	0.162 396
11.765 07	10.317 78	−0.618 782	0.182 083
11.739 93	10.339 32	−0.574 298	0.172 500
11.758 40	10.339 73	−0.542 832	0.158 750

y_t	m_t	p_t	R
11.754 20	10.382 59	−0.517 011	0.153 540
11.711 60	10.395 13	−0.500 051	0.131 042
11.713 80	10.434 79	−0.469 844	0.124 687
11.761 78	10.450 85	−1.448 007	0.148 229
11.772 59	10.490 02	−0.429 092	0.157 188
11.743 81	10.486 37	−0.415 667	0.140 417
11.743 04	10.512 63	−0.392 746	0.133 854
11.766 09	10.540 57	−0.379 944	0.111 667
11.788 41	10.597 51	−0.368 314	0.100 417
11.777 79	10.62838	−0.349 416	0.112 708
11.772 29	10.655 73	−0.340 520	0.100 208
11.817 89	10.663 50	−0.328 087	0.098 333
11.840 90	10.704 14	−0.318 278	0.092 917
11.820 17	10.744 47	−0.306 661	0.092 083
11.805 00	10.789 32	−0.286 749	0.093 750
11.836 75	10.816 89	−0.274 042	0.110 457
11.887 24	10.850 48	−0.257 217	0.096 065
11.859 27	10.886 75	−0.236 862	0.114 193
11.846 22	10.932 18	−0.227 403	0.084 310
11.875 96	10.976 92	−0.228 156	0.053 998
11.910 71	11.017 94	−0.222 518	0.042 187
11.887 05	11.069 63	−0.220 771	0.037 409
11.895 37	11.132 70	−0.219 899	0.026 567
11.929 95	11.202 43	−0.216 665	0.030 419
11.968 28	11.221 17	−0.195 650	0.038 817
11.928 37	11.279 37	−0.185 848	0.029 188
11.934 45	11.350 25	−0.171 382	0.027 763
12.001 55	11.392 63	−0.165 111	0.036 876
12.024 24	11.428 10	−0.155 835	0.026 459
11.999 32	11.469 98	−0.150 707	0.029 792
12.009 75	11.521 71	−0.130 678	0.029 166
12.048 89	11.552 02	−0.114 850	0.049 266
12.082 53	11.562 16	−0.101 147	0.050 708
12.046 65	11.598 19	−0.084 796	0.046 375
12.046 74	11.647 30	−0.061 237	0.054 700

Table A.1 Empirical cumulative distribution of $\hat{\tau}$ for $\rho = 1$ (see Table 3.2).

Sample size T	Probability of a smaller value							
	0.01	0.025	0.05	0.10	0.90	0.95	0.975	0.99
$\hat{\tau}$								
25	−2.66	−2.26	−1.95	−1.60	0.92	1.33	1.70	2.16
50	−2.62	−2.25	−1.95	−1.61	0.91	1.31	1.66	2.08
100	−2.60	−2.24	−1.95	−1.61	0.90	1.29	1.64	2.03
250	−2.58	−2.23	−1.95	−1.62	0.89	1.29	1.63	2.01
500	−2.58	−2.23	−1.95	−1.62	0.89	1.28	1.62	2.00
∞	−2.58	−2.23	−1.95	−1.62	0.89	1.28	1.62	2.00
$\hat{\tau}_\mu$								
25	−3.75	−3.33	−3.00	−2.63	−0.37	0.00	0.34	0.72
50	−3.58	−3.22	−2.93	−2.60	−0.40	−0.03	0.29	0.66
100	−3.51	−3.17	−2.89	−2.58	−0.42	−0.05	0.26	0.63
250	−3.46	−3.14	−2.88	−2.57	−0.42	−0.06	0.24	0.62
500	−3.44	−3.13	−2.87	−2.57	−0.43	−0.07	0.24	0.61
∞	−3.43	−3.12	−2.86	−2.57	−0.44	−0.07	0.23	0.60
$\hat{\tau}_T$								
25	−4.38	−3.95	−3.60	−3.24	−1.14	−0.80	−0.50	−0.15
50	−4.15	−3.80	−3.50	−3.18	−1.19	−0.87	−0.58	−0.24
100	−4.04	−3.73	−3.45	−3.15	−1.22	−0.90	−0.62	−0.28
250	−3.99	−3.69	−3.43	−3.13	−1.23	−0.92	−0.64	−0.31
500	−3.98	−3.68	−3.42	−3.13	−1.24	−0.93	−0.65	−0.32
∞	−3.96	−3.66	−3.41	−3.12	−1.25	−0.94	−0.66	−0.33

Standard errors (SEs) of the estimates vary, but most are less than 0.02.
Source: Fuller (1976), reprinted by permission of John Wiley & Sons.

Table A.2 Empirical distribution of Φ_3 (see Table 3.2).

Sample size T	Probability of a smaller value							
	0.01	0.025	0.05	0.10	0.90	0.95	0.975	0.99
25	0.74	0.90	1.08	1.33	5.91	7.24	8.65	10.61
50	0.76	0.93	1.11	1.37	5.61	6.73	7.81	9.31
100	0.76	0.94	1.12	1.38	5.47	6.49	7.44	8.73
250	0.76	0.94	1.13	1.39	5.39	6.34	7.25	8.43
500	0.76	0.94	1.13	1.39	5.36	6.30	7.20	8.34
∞	0.77	0.94	1.13	1.39	5.34	6.25	7.16	8.27
SE	0.004	0.004	0.003	0.004	0.015	0.020	0.032	0.058

Source: Dickey and Fuller (1981), reprinted by permission of the Econometric Society.

Table A.3 Empirical distribution of Φ_1 (see Table 3.2).

Sample size T	Probability of a smaller value							
	0.01	0.025	0.05	0.10	0.90	0.95	0.975	0.99
25	0.29	0.38	0.49	0.65	4.12	5.18	6.30	7.88
50	0.29	0.39	0.50	0.66	3.94	4.86	5.80	7.06
100	0.29	0.39	0.50	0.67	3.86	4.71	5.57	6.70
250	0.30	0.39	0.51	0.67	3.81	4.63	5.45	6.52
500	0.30	0.39	0.51	0.67	3.79	4.61	5.41	6.47
∞	0.30	0.40	0.51	0.67	3.78	4.59	5.38	6.43
SE	0.002	0.002	0.002	0.002	0.01	0.02	0.03	0.05

Source: Dickey and Fuller (1981), reprinted by permission of the Econometric Society.

Table A.4 Additive and innovative outlier tests for unit root: critical values (see Table 3.4).

Model	Percentiles			
	0.01	0.025	0.05	0.10
Crash model	−5.34	−5.02	−4.80	−4.58
Slowdown model	−5.57	−5.30	−5.08	−4.82

Source: Tables 4.2–4.5 in Perron (1994), reprinted by permission of Macmillan.

Table A.5 Critical values for seasonal unit root tests (see Table 3.5).

Model[a]	Years	π_1				π_2				$\pi_3 \cap \pi_4$				$\pi_2 \cap \pi_3 \cap \pi_4$				$\pi_1 \cap \pi_2 \cap \pi_3 \cap \pi_4$			
		0.01	0.025	0.05	0.10	0.01	0.025	0.05	0.10	0.10	0.05	0.025	0.01	0.10	0.05	0.025	0.01	0.10	0.05	0.025	0.01
nc, nd, nt	10	−2.52	−2.15	−1.86	−1.55	−2.55	−2.18	−1.89	−1.55	2.44	3.21	3.99	5.09	2.26	2.89	3.52	4.33	2.17	2.69	3.22	3.90
	20	−2.51	−2.19	−1.90	−1.56	−2.55	−2.19	−1.90	−1.57	2.41	3.15	3.90	4.91	2.23	2.77	3.35	4.14	2.10	2.58	3.01	3.66
	30	−2.58	−2.22	−1.93	−1.60	−2.54	−2.23	−1.92	−1.59	2.38	3.06	3.75	4.69	2.20	2.74	3.26	3.91	2.10	2.55	2.98	3.55
	40	−2.54	−2.21	−1.91	−1.59	−2.53	−2.20	−1.93	−1.61	2.39	3.11	3.86	4.85	2.22	2.78	3.33	4.05	2.09	2.55	3.02	3.58
c, nd, nt	10	−3.43	−3.09	−2.79	−2.47	−2.52	−2.16	−1.86	−1.54	2.35	3.06	3.80	4.95	2.17	2.77	3.39	4.20	2.89	3.48	4.10	4.87
	20	−3.46	−3.11	−2.83	−2.52	−2.53	−2.19	−1.89	−1.57	2.37	3.09	3.81	4.83	2.18	2.71	3.29	4.04	2.83	3.40	3.95	4.65
	30	−3.45	−3.12	−2.84	−2.54	−2.53	−2.22	−1.91	−1.59	2.35	3.01	3.71	4.61	2.18	2.72	3.22	3.87	2.83	3.35	3.85	4.54
	40	−3.42	−3.13	−2.85	−2.55	−2.53	−2.20	−1.93	−1.61	2.37	3.08	3.82	4.83	2.20	2.76	3.31	4.01	2.83	3.36	3.87	4.52
c, nd, t	10	−4.02	−3.65	−3.34	−3.03	−2.49	−2.13	−1.85	−1.53	2.25	2.94	3.69	4.70	2.09	2.66	3.23	4.03	3.66	4.32	5.05	6.02
	20	−3.99	−3.66	−3.38	−3.07	−2.52	−2.18	−1.88	−1.56	2.32	3.04	3.73	4.70	2.14	2.67	3.23	3.96	3.58	4.20	4.77	5.57
	30	−3.98	−3.67	−3.41	−3.11	−2.52	−2.21	−1.91	−1.59	2.30	2.98	3.65	4.57	2.16	2.69	3.19	3.85	3.58	4.17	4.69	5.37
	40	−3.98	−3.67	−3.40	−3.11	−2.53	−2.19	−1.93	−1.61	2.35	3.05	3.79	4.76	2.18	2.74	3.29	3.96	3.59	4.19	4.73	5.44
c, d, nt	10	−3.42	−3.06	−2.77	−2.44	−3.40	−3.07	−2.77	−2.45	5.44	6.63	7.80	9.32	5.21	6.15	7.18	8.49	5.06	6.00	6.90	8.03
	20	−3.43	−3.09	−2.81	−2.51	−3.40	−3.07	−2.80	−2.51	5.47	6.62	7.65	8.94	5.12	6.04	6.88	7.93	4.94	5.70	6.42	7.42
	30	−3.43	−3.10	−2.83	−2.53	−3.41	−3.10	−2.82	−2.53	5.62	6.70	7.72	8.97	5.18	6.02	6.84	7.91	4.93	5.67	6.35	7.25
	40	−3.41	−3.11	−2.84	−2.54	−3.41	−3.09	−2.83	−2.53	5.52	6.57	7.57	8.79	5.09	5.95	6.73	7.63	4.86	5.56	6.23	7.07
c, d, t	10	−4.02	−3.64	−3.34	−3.02	−3.40	−3.06	−2.77	−2.45	5.38	6.56	7.77	9.30	5.15	6.12	7.10	8.41	5.84	6.92	7.83	9.18
	20	−3.97	−3.66	−3.37	−3.06	−3.41	−3.08	−2.81	−2.51	5.44	6.57	7.58	8.86	5.10	6.03	6.84	7.86	5.64	6.47	7.26	8.26
	30	−3.96	−3.65	−3.40	−3.09	−3.40	−3.10	−2.83	−2.53	5.59	6.66	7.67	8.91	5.16	6.01	6.82	7.85	5.65	6.41	7.16	8.12
	40	−3.96	−3.65	−3.39	−3.10	−3.41	−3.10	−2.82	−2.53	5.48	6.55	7.54	8.79	5.09	5.93	6.71	7.62	5.55	6.31	7.01	7.93

[a] The auxiliary regression can contain constants (c), no constants (nc), seasonal dummies (d), no seasonal dummies (nd), trends (t) and no trends (nt). The DGP is $(1 - B^S)y_t = \varepsilon_t$, with $\varepsilon_t \sim N(0, 1)$ (based on Monte Carlo replications).

Source: Franses and Hobijn (1997), reprinted by permission of Taylor & Francis.

Table A.6 Response surfaces for critical values of cointegration tests (see Table 4.1).

n	Model	Point (%)	ϕ_∞	SE	ϕ_1	ϕ_2
1	No constant, no trend	1	−2.5658	(0.0023)	−1.960	−10.04
		5	−1.9393	(0.0008)	−0.398	0.0
		10	−1.6156	(0.0007)	−0.181	0.0
1	Constant, no trend	1	−3.4336	(0.0024)	−5.999	−29.25
		5	−2.8621	(0.0011)	−2.738	−8.36
		10	−2.5671	(0.0009)	−1.438	−4.48
1	Constant + Trend	1	−3.9638	(0.0019)	−8.353	−47.44
		5	−3.4126	(0.0012)	-4.039	−17.83
		10	−3.1279	(0.0009)	−2.418	−7.58
2	Constant, no trend	1	−3.9001	(0.0022)	−10.534	−30.03
		5	−3.3377	(0.0012)	−5.967	−8.98
		10	−3.0462	(0.0009)	−4.069	−5.73
2	Constant + Trend	1	-4.3266	(0.0022)	−15.531	−34.03
		5	−3.7809	(0.0013)	−9.421	−15.06
		10	−3.4959	(0.0009)	−7.203	−4.01
3	Constant, no trend	1	−4.2981	(0.0023)	−13.790	−46.37
		5	−3.7429	(0.0012)	−8.352	−13.41
		10	−3.4518	(0.0010)	−6.241	−2.79
3	Constant + Trend	1	−4.6676	(0.0022)	−18.492	−49.35
		5	−4.1193	(0.0011)	−12.024	−13.13
		10	−3.8344	(0.0009)	−9.188	−4.85
4	Constant, no trend	1	−4.6493	(0.0023)	−17.188	−59.20
		5	−4.1000	(0.0012)	−10.745	−21.57
		10	−3.8110	(0.0009)	−8.317	−5.19
4	Constant + Trend	1	−4.9695	(0.0021)	−22.504	−50.22
		5	−4.4294	(0.0012)	−14.501	−19.54
		10	−4.1474	(0.0010)	−11.165	−9.88
5	Constant, no trend	1	−4.9587	(0.0026)	−22.140	−37.29
		5	−4.4185	(0.0013)	−13.641	−21.16
		10	−4.1327	(0.0009)	−10.638	−5.48
5	Constant + Trend	1	−5.2497	(0.0024)	−26.606	−49.56
		5	−4.7154	(0.0013)	−17.432	−16.50
		10	−4.4345	(0.0010)	−13.654	−5.77
6	Constant, no trend	1	−5.2400	(0.0029)	−26.278	−41.65
		5	−4.7048	(0.0018)	−17.120	−11.17
		10	−4.4242	(0.0010)	−13.347	0.0
6	Constant + Trend	1	−5.5127	(0.0033)	−30.735	−52.50
		5	−4.9767	(0.0017)	−20.883	−9.05
		10	−4.6999	(0.0011)	−16.445	0.0

Source: MacKinnon (1991), reprinted by permission of Oxford University Press.

Table A.7 Approximate asymptotic critical values for cointegration model with a break (see equation (4.12)).

No. of regressors	Level	0.01	0.025	0.05	0.10	0.975
$m = 1$	ADF*, Z_t^*					
	C	−5.13	−4.83	−4.61	−4.34	−2.25
	C/T	−5.45	−5.21	−4.99	−4.72	−2.72
	C/S	−5.47	−5.19	−4.95	−4.68	−2.55
	Z_α^*					
	C	−50.07	−45.01	−40.48	−36.19	−10.63
	C/T	−57.28	−52.09	−47.96	−43.22	−15.90
	C/S	−57.17	−51.32	−47.04	−41.85	−13.15
$m = 2$	ADF*, Z_t^*					
	C	−5.44	−5.16	−4.92	−4.69	−2.61
	C/T	−5.80	−5.51	−5.29	−5.03	−3.01
	C/S	−5.97	−5.73	−5.50	−5.23	−3.12
	Z_α^*					
	C	−57.01	−51.41	−46.98	−42.49	−14.27
	C/T	−64.77	−58.57	−53.92	−48.94	−19.19
	C/S	−68.21	−63.28	−58.33	−52.85	−19.72
$m = 3$	ADF*, Z_t^*					
	C	−5.77	−5.50	−5.28	−5.02	−2.96
	C/T	−6.05	−5.79	−5.57	−5.33	−3.33
	C/S	−6.51	−6.23	−6.00	−5.75	−3.65
	Z_α^*					
	C	−63.64	−57.96	−53.58	−48.65	−18.20
	C/T	−70.27	−64.26	−59.76	−54.94	−22.72
	C/S	−80.15	−73.91	−68.94	−63.42	−26.64
$m = 4$	ADF*, Z_t^*					
	C	−6.05	−5.80	−5.56	−5.31	−3.26
	C/T	−6.36	−6.07	−5.83	−5.59	−3.59
	C/S	−6.92	−6.64	−6.41	−6.17	−4.12
	Z_α^*					
	C	−70.18	−64.41	−59.40	−54.38	−22.04
	C/T	−76.95	−70.56	−65.44	−60.12	−26.46
	C/S	−90.35	−84.00	−78.52	−72.56	−33.69

These critical values (c.v.s) are based on the response surface:

$$\text{c.v.} = \psi_0 + \psi_1 n^{-1} + \text{Error}$$

where c.v. is the critical value obtained from 10,000 replications at sample size $n = 50$, 100, 150, 200, 250, 300. The asymptotic c.v. is the ordinary least squares (OLS) estimate of ψ_0. Z_α^*, Z_t^* and ADF* refer to the Phillips Z_α, Z_t and the augmented Dickey–Fuller (ADF) test statistics. The symbols C, C/T and C/S refer to models (i)–(iii) underlying equation (4.12)—see text for details. *Source*: Gregory and Hansen (1996, table 1), reprinted by permission of Elsevier Science SA, Lausanne, Switzerland (publishers of the *Journal of Econometrics*).

Table A.8 Critical values of the (t-ratio) ECM test (different number of regressors).

	T	0.01	0.05	0.10	0.25
A (with constant)					
($k = 1$)	25	−4.12	−3.35	−2.95	−2.36
	50	−3.94	−3.28	−2.93	−2.38
	100	−3.92	−3.27	−2.94	−2.40
	500	−3.82	−3.23	−2.90	−2.40
	5,000	−3.78	−3.19	−2.89	−2.41
(2)	25	−4.53	−3.64	−3.24	−2.60
	50	−4.29	−3.57	−3.20	−2.63
	100	−4.22	−3.56	−3.22	−2.67
	500	−4.11	−3.50	−3.19	−2.66
	5,000	−4.06	−3.48	−3.19	−2.65
(3)	25	−4.92	−3.91	−3.46	−2.76
	50	−4.59	−3.82	−3.45	−2.84
	100	−4.49	−3.82	−3.47	−2.90
	500	−4.47	−3.77	−3.45	−2.90
	5,000	−4.46	−3.74	−3.42	−2.89
(4)	25	−5.27	−4.18	−3.68	−2.90
	50	−4.85	−4.05	−3.64	−3.03
	100	−4.71	−4.03	−3.67	−3.10
	500	−4.62	−3.99	−3.67	−3.11
	5,000	−4.57	−3.97	−3.66	−3.10
(5)	25	−5.53	−4.46	−3.82	−2.99
	50	−5.04	−4.43	−3.82	−3.18
	100	−4.92	−4.30	−3.85	−3.28
	500	−4.81	−4.39	−3.86	−3.32
	5,000	−4.70	−4.27	−3.82	−3.29

(*continued*)

Table A.8 (*cont.*)

	T	0.01	0.05	0.10	0.25
B (with constant and trend)					
($k = 1$)	25	−4.77	−3.89	−3.48	−2.88
	50	−4.48	−3.78	−3.44	−2.92
	100	−4.35	−3.75	−3.43	−2.91
	500	−4.30	−3.71	−3.41	−2.91
	5,000	−4.27	−3.69	−3.39	−2.89
(2)	25	−5.12	−4.18	−3.72	−3.04
	50	−4.76	−4.04	−3.66	−3.09
	100	−4.60	−3.98	−3.66	−3.11
	500	−4.54	−3.94	−3.64	−3.11
	5,000	−4.51	−3.91	−3.62	−3.10
(3)	25	−5.42	−4.39	−3.89	−3.16
	50	−5.04	−4.25	−3.86	−3.25
	100	−4.86	−4.19	−3.86	−3.30
	500	−4.76	−4.15	−3.84	−3.31
	5,000	−4.72	−4.12	−3.82	−3.29
(4)	25	−5.79	−4.56	−4.04	−3.26
	50	−5.21	−4.43	−4.03	−3.39
	100	−5.07	−4.38	−4.02	−3.46
	500	−4.93	−4.34	−4.02	−3.47
	5,000	−4.89	−4.30	−4.00	−3.45
(5)	25	−6.18	−4.76	−4.16	−3.31
	50	−5.37	−4.60	−4.19	−3.53
	100	−5.24	−4.55	−4.19	−3.66
	500	−5.15	−4.54	−4.20	−3.69
	5,000	−5.11	−4.52	−4.18	−3.67

Source: Banerjee, Dolado and Mestre (1998, table 1), reprinted by permission of the *Journal of Time Series Forecasting*.

Table A.9 Critical values for the t and F statistics on π_3 and π_4 (see Table 4.3).

Cointegrated regressors with determinants	T	t_{π_3}				t_{π_4}						$F_{\pi_3 \cap \pi_4}$				
		0.01	0.025	0.05	0.01	0.01	0.025	0.05	0.95	0.975	0.99	0.50	0.90	0.95	0.975	0.99
—	48	−4.04	−3.66	−3.34	−3.00	−2.99	−2.46	−2.05	2.05	2.42	2.90	2.59	6.01	7.46	8.81	10.80
	100	−3.94	−3.59	−3.30	−3.00	−3.01	−2.54	−2.12	2.10	2.50	2.94	2.61	5.91	7.21	8.63	10.24
	136	−3.90	−3.57	−3.28	−2.98	−3.01	−2.53	−2.15	2.13	2.51	2.92	2.60	5.83	7.11	8.39	10.14
	200	−3.89	−3.56	−3.29	−2.98	−3.04	−2.56	−2.13	2.13	2.52	2.99	2.63	5.84	7.11	8.35	10.10
I	48	−3.96	−3.57	−3.27	−2.93	−2.93	−2.44	−2.03	2.12	2.54	2.96	2.59	5.96	7.35	8.77	10.51
	100	−3.86	−3.54	−3.27	−2.95	−2.95	−2.49	−2.08	2.12	2.52	2.95	2.59	5.83	7.10	8.42	10.15
	136	−3.84	−3.54	−3.26	−2.96	−2.99	−2.52	−2.10	2.14	2.52	2.98	2.60	5.83	7.13	8.40	10.09
	200	−3.86	−3.52	−3.26	−2.96	−2.95	−2.53	−2.13	2.15	2.55	3.00	2.61	5.79	7.01	8.26	10.02
I, SD	48	−4.87	−4.49	−4.18	−3.84	−2.97	−2.48	−2.07	2.08	2.47	2.95	4.71	9.00	10.65	12.18	14.11
	100	−4.77	−4.40	−4.12	−3.81	−3.02	−2.56	−2.14	2.10	2.50	2.98	4.70	8.66	10.12	11.48	13.26
	136	−4.77	−4.42	−4.14	−3.81	−2.99	−2.55	−2.14	2.13	2.50	2.97	4.71	8.57	9.99	11.41	13.25
	200	−4.76	−4.40	−4.12	−3.81	−2.96	−2.52	−2.13	2.12	2.52	2.97	4.71	8.57	9.99	11.41	13.25

Source: Engle, Granger, Hylleberg and Lee (1993, table A.1), reprinted by permission of Elsevier Science SA, Lausanne, Switzerland (publishers of the *Journal of Econometrics*).

Table A.10 Critical values of the cointegration rank test statistics: model 2 in text (see equation (5.1)).

$n - r \backslash k^a$	λ_{trace}						λ_{max}					
	0	1	2	3	4	5	0	1	2	3	4	5
0.05												
12	341.2	365.1	389.4	413.6	437.1	461.5	75.51	78.57	81.74	84.82	87.90	91.11
11	291.7	314.2	336.4	358.7	381.0	403.4	69.76	73.11	76.02	79.23	82.36	85.20
10	245.7	265.9	287.0	307.2	327.8	348.5	64.11	66.85	70.17	73.47	76.20	79.28
9	204.0	223.8	242.3	260.8	279.5	297.9	57.95	61.34	64.47	67.77	70.86	73.65
8	166.1	182.7	199.7	216.6	232.8	249.3	52.06	55.26	58.21	61.59	64.40	67.45
7	132.5	148.0	163.1	178.0	192.5	206.5	46.47	49.57	52.87	55.81	58.85	61.74
6	102.6	116.3	128.9	141.7	154.4	167.0	40.53	43.76	46.90	49.97	52.88	55.65
5	75.98	86.58	97.57	108.6	119.8	130.8	34.40	37.48	40.57	43.62	46.77	49.80
4	53.48	62.75	72.15	81.25	90.60	99.37	28.27	31.48	34.69	37.83	40.19	43.58
3	34.87	42.40	49.43	56.28	63.10	69.72	22.04	25.54	28.49	31.56	34.15	37.19
2	20.18	25.23	30.46	35.46	39.94	44.56	15.87	18.88	21.92	24.97	27.82	30.50
1	9.16	12.45	15.27	17.80	20.63	23.02	9.16	12.45	15.27	17.80	20.63	23.02
0.10												
12	332.0	356.4	380.3	403.8	427.3	450.6	72.09	75.35	78.55	81.40	84.36	87.24
11	284.2	305.4	328.1	350.1	371.6	393.4	66.47	69.48	72.75	75.71	78.68	81.72
10	238.3	259.0	279.0	299.3	319.2	338.9	60.66	63.77	66.78	69.98	72.86	75.88
9	197.7	216.4	234.7	253.0	271.4	289.3	54.91	58.17	61.21	64.27	67.35	70.32
8	160.3	176.4	192.9	209.2	226.1	241.8	49.04	52.23	55.38	58.31	61.28	64.24
7	127.2	142.2	157.0	171.5	185.7	199.5	43.44	46.59	49.67	52.67	55.61	58.57
6	97.87	110.5	123.5	136.0	148.3	160.6	37.65	40.93	44.05	47.09	49.85	52.67
5	71.81	82.17	92.93	103.6	114.4	125.2	31.73	34.99	37.81	40.86	43.80	46.87
4	49.95	59.07	67.83	76.69	85.34	93.92	25.80	29.01	32.00	35.08	38.03	40.84
3	31.93	39.12	45.89	52.71	59.23	65.69	19.86	22.98	26.08	28.83	31.73	34.56
2	17.88	22.76	27.58	32.38	36.84	41.33	13.81	16.74	19.67	22.54	25.27	27.87
1	7.53	10.50	13.21	15.68	18.24	20.57	7.53	10.50	13.21	15.68	18.24	20.57

[a] Number of exogenous $I(1)$ variables in the model.

Source: Pesaran et al. (2000, table 6b); reproduced by permission of Elsevier Science SA, Lausanne, Switzerland (publishers of the *Journal of Econometrics*).

Table A.11 Critical values of the cointegration rank test statistics: model 3 in text (see equation (5.1)).

$n-r\backslash k$[a]	λ_{trace}						λ_{max}					
	0	1	2	3	4	5	0	1	2	3	4	5
0.05												
12	328.5	352.4	376.5	400.8	424.3	448.8	74.62	77.72	80.87	83.93	87.13	90.23
11	279.8	302.2	324.4	347.7	369.5	391.5	68.91	72.31	75.22	78.42	81.56	84.41
10	235.0	255.5	276.5	297.2	317.4	337.7	63.32	65.98	69.40	72.56	75.48	78.58
9	194.4	214.4	232.7	251.6	270.4	288.6	57.20	60.66	63.68	67.04	70.20	72.98
8	157.8	174.2	191.6	208.3	224.8	241.2	51.15	54.44	57.54	60.80	63.54	66.61
7	124.6	140.5	155.9	170.7	185.6	199.8	45.53	48.91	52.22	55.04	58.05	61.03
6	95.87	109.6	122.8	135.4	148.4	160.9	39.83	42.95	46.09	49.10	52.06	54.84
5	70.49	81.45	92.42	103.7	114.6	125.9	33.64	36.80	39.85	42.92	45.98	49.02
4	48.88	58.63	68.06	77.21	86.42	95.14	27.42	30.71	33.87	37.08	39.99	42.68
3	31.54	38.93	46.44	53.41	60.19	66.94	21.12	24.59	27.75	30.74	33.63	36.38
2	17.86	23.32	28.42	33.35	38.15	42.73	14.88	18.06	21.07	24.22	26.94	29.79
1	8.07	11.47	14.35	16.90	19.73	22.19	8.07	11.47	14.35	16.90	19.73	22.19
0.10												
12	319.6	343.5	367.5	391.1	415.0	438.0	71.36	74.61	77.65	80.60	83.55	86.49
11	272.7	294.1	316.9	338.8	360.1	381.8	65.63	68.80	71.95	75.02	77.86	80.86
10	227.7	248.3	268.5	288.8	309.1	328.9	59.85	63.00	65.97	69.13	72.08	74.91
9	187.9	207.1	225.3	243.7	262.1	280.2	54.10	57.56	60.49	63.59	66.59	69.53
8	152.0	168.4	184.8	201.3	217.7	233.6	48.23	51.47	54.54	57.55	60.46	63.40
7	119.7	134.9	149.7	164.2	178.3	192.3	42.70	45.74	48.96	51.93	54.68	57.85
6	91.40	104.4	117.3	130.0	142.1	154.6	36.84	40.21	43.25	46.30	49.06	51.90
5	66.23	76.95	87.93	98.45	109.3	120.4	31.02	34.10	37.15	40.02	42.95	45.97
4	45.70	54.84	63.57	72.69	81.40	89.90	24.99	28.27	31.30	34.30	37.21	39.99
3	28.78	35.88	42.67	49.56	56.08	62.65	19.02	22.15	25.21	28.11	30.85	33.67
2	15.75	20.75	25.63	30.37	35.06	39.59	12.98	15.98	18.78	21.67	24.37	27.05
1	6.50	9.53	12.27	14.76	17.39	19.63	6.50	9.53	12.27	14.76	17.39	19.63

[a] Number of exogenous $I(1)$ variables in the model.

Source: Pesaran et al. (2000, table 6b); reproduced by permission of Elsevier Science SA, Lausanne, Switzerland (publishers of the *Journal of Econometrics*).

Table A.12 Critical values of the cointegration rank test statistics: model 4 in text (see equation (5.1)).

$n-r\backslash k^a$	λ_{trace}						λ_{max}					
	0	1	2	3	4	5	0	1	2	3	4	5
0.05												
12	364.8	389.2	413.5	437.3	460.7	484.3	78.42	81.85	84.73	87.82	90.74	93.75
11	314.1	335.5	358.0	380.5	402.3	423.7	72.50	75.77	78.97	81.99	85.08	87.98
10	265.8	286.8	307.0	327.7	347.9	367.8	67.05	70.20	73.82	76.15	78.87	81.89
9	222.6	242.4	260.4	279.3	297.3	315.6	61.27	64.53	67.67	70.71	73.62	76.51
8	183.0	199.1	215.8	232.9	249.2	265.3	55.14	58.08	61.22	64.42	67.45	70.48
7	147.3	163.0	177.8	192.8	207.1	221.4	49.32	52.62	55.83	59.01	62.00	64.61
6	115.9	128.8	141.7	154.3	166.9	179.6	43.61	46.97	50.10	53.08	55.83	58.78
5	87.17	97.83	108.9	120.0	130.6	141.2	37.86	40.89	43.72	46.84	49.76	52.63
4	63.00	72.10	81.20	90.02	99.11	107.6	31.79	34.70	37.85	40.98	43.75	46.66
3	42.34	49.36	56.43	63.54	69.84	76.82	25.42	28.72	31.68	34.65	37.44	40.12
2	25.77	30.77	35.37	40.37	45.10	49.52	19.22	22.16	24.88	27.80	30.55	33.26
1	12.39	15.44	18.08	20.47	23.17	25.70	12.39	15.44	18.08	20.47	23.17	25.70
0.10												
12	355.9	379.8	403.3	426.8	450.3	473.6	75.02	78.09	81.31	84.34	87.34	90.08
11	305.8	327.1	349.2	371.0	392.4	414.1	69.45	72.72	75.59	78.45	81.52	84.23
10	258.0	278.9	298.9	319.2	338.7	358.9	63.60	66.78	69.90	72.94	75.64	78.53
9	215.9	235.1	253.2	271.2	289.5	306.9	58.09	61.42	64.28	67.43	70.30	73.07
8	176.9	192.8	209.1	225.5	241.7	257.5	52.08	55.25	58.18	61.19	63.99	67.02
7	141.8	157.0	171.6	185.9	199.9	214.0	46.54	49.70	52.69	55.51	58.58	61.37
6	110.6	123.3	136.2	148.4	160.9	173.0	40.76	44.01	47.08	49.78	52.73	55.62
5	82.88	93.13	103.7	114.7	125.1	135.8	35.04	37.92	40.94	43.92	46.74	49.59
4	59.16	68.04	76.68	85.59	93.98	102.5	29.13	32.12	35.04	38.04	41.01	43.66
3	39.34	46.00	52.71	59.39	65.90	72.33	27.10	26.10	29.00	31.89	34.66	37.28
2	23.08	27.96	32.51	37.07	41.57	46.10	17.18	19.79	22.53	25.28	27.86	30.54
1	10.55	13.31	15.82	18.19	20.73	23.11	10.55	13.31	15.82	18.19	20.73	23.11

[a] Number of exogenous $I(1)$ variables in the model.

Source: Pesaran et al. (2000, table 6b); reproduced by permission of Elsevier Science SA, Lausanne, Switzerland (publishers of the *Journal of Econometrics*).

Table A.13 Sample size is 25; the data-generating process (d.g.p.) contains no trend and the constant term $\boldsymbol{\mu}$ is unrestricted.

Dim	50%	80%	90%	95%	97.5%	99%	Mean	Var
(a) Maximal eigenvalue								
1	2.43	4.93	6.70	8.29	9.91	12.09	3.06	7.36
2	7.86	11.38	13.70	15.75	17.88	20.51	8.54	14.76
3	13.80	18.16	20.90	23.26	25.66	28.57	14.46	22.80
4	20.36	25.56	28.56	31.66	34.47	37.61	21.07	32.97
(b) Trace								
1	2.43	4.93	6.70	8.29	9.91	12.09	3.06	7.36
2	9.78	13.99	16.56	18.90	21.26	23.70	10.45	20.64
3	21.79	27.69	31.22	34.37	37.44	40.98	22.54	42.57
4	39.32	47.10	51.59	55.92	59.60	64.33	40.09	77.08

Source: Franses (1994, table A.1); reproduced by permission of Elsevier Science SA, Lausanne, Switzerland (publishers of the *Journal of Econometrics*).

Table A.14 Sample size is 25; the d.g.p. contains no trend and the constant term μ is restricted by $\boldsymbol{\mu} = \boldsymbol{\alpha\beta}_0$.

Dim	50%	80%	90%	95%	97.5%	99%	Mean	Var
(a) Maximal eigenvalue								
1	3.55	6.01	7.72	9.35	10.97	12.09	4.14	7.08
2	8.82	12.15	14.40	16.51	18.36	20.56	9.36	14.33
3	14.56	18.89	21.56	23.90	26.21	29.44	15.24	22.84
4	21.01	26.15	29.26	32.18	34.74	38.12	21.69	32.79
(b) Trace								
1	3.55	6.01	7.72	9.35	10.97	12.90	4.14	7.08
2	11.95	16.09	18.63	20.96	22.78	25.71	12.55	20.81
3	25.01	31.01	34.44	37.85	40.56	44.60	25.74	44.16
4	43.40	51.38	55.78	59.98	63.51	67.74	44.20	78.19

Source: Franses (1994, table A.2); reproduced by permission of Elsevier Science SA, Lausanne, Switzerland (publishers of the *Journal of Econometrics*).

Table A.15 Sample size is 50, the d.g.p. contains no trend and the constant term $\boldsymbol{\mu}$ is unrestricted.

Dim	50%	80%	90%	95%	97.5%	99%	Mean	Var
(a) Maximal eigenvalue								
1	2.44	4.89	6.40	8.09	9.54	11.39	3.02	6.73
2	7.71	11.09	13.15	15.18	16.98	19.18	8.30	13.42
3	13.34	17.44	19.94	22.29	24.31	26.98	13.92	20.61
4	19.00	23.78	26.63	29.15	31.93	35.20	19.64	28.05
(b) Trace								
1	2.44	4.89	6.40	8.09	9.54	11.39	3.02	6.73
2	9.51	13.57	16.06	18.25	20.13	22.81	10.18	19.02
3	21.07	26.78	30.07	32.94	35.59	39.10	21.75	38.87
4	36.86	44.10	48.25	51.98	55.88	59.94	37.59	65.89

Source: Franses (1994, table A.3); reproduced by permission of Elsevier Science SA, Lausanne, Switzerland (publishers of the *Journal of Econometrics*).

Table A.16 Sample size is 50, the d.g.p. contains no trend and the constant term μ is restricted by $\boldsymbol{\mu} = \boldsymbol{\alpha\beta}_0$.

Dim	50%	80%	90%	9.5%	97.5%	99%	Mean	Var
(a) Maximal eigenvalue								
1	3.49	5.91	7.59	9.22	10.93	13.06	4.10	7.05
2	8.58	12.05	14.05	15.99	17.92	20.60	9.19	13.94
3	13.99	18.01	20.57	23.01	25.24	27.95	14.59	20.88
4	19.63	24.44	27.23	29.79	32.47	35.33	20.32	27.78
(b) Trace								
1	3.49	5.91	7.59	9.22	10.93	13.06	4.10	7.05
2	11.74	15.79	18.25	20.61	22.85	25.49	12.32	20.40
3	24.16	29.91	33.08	36.33	39.28	45.58	24.79	40.81
4	40.88	48.44	52.71	56.62	60.00	64.29	41.73	69.24

Source: Franses (1994, table A.4); reproduced by permission of Elsevier Science SA, Lausanne, Switzerland (publishers of the *Journal of Econometrics*).

References

Anderson, T.G. and T. Bollerslev (1998) Answering the skeptics: Yes, standard volatility models do provide accurate forecasts, *International Economic Review*, **39**, 885–905.

Baba, Y., R.F. Engle, D.F. Kraft and K.F. Kroner (1990) Multivariate Simultaneous Generalized ARCH, *Mimeo*, University of California at San Diego, Department of Economics.

Bailey, R.T., T. Bollerslev and H.O. Mikkelsen (1996) Fractionally integrated generalised autoregressive conditional heteroskedasticity, *Journal of Econometrics*, **74**, 3–30.

Baltagi, B.H. (2001) *Econometric Analysis of Panel Data*, John Wiley & Sons, Chichester, UK.

Baltagi, B.H., T.B. Fomby and R.C. Hill (eds) (2000) Nonstationary panels, panel cointegration, and dynamic panels, *Advances in Econometrics*, Vol. 15, Elsevier Science, Amsterdam.

Banerjee, A., D.F. Hendry and G.W. Smith (1986) Exploring equilibrium relationships in econometrics through static models: Some Monte Carlo evidence, *Oxford Bulletin of Economics and Statistics*, **52**, 95–104.

Banerjee, A., J.J. Dolado and R. Mestre (1998) Error-correction mechanism tests for cointegration in a single-equation framework, *Journal of Time Series Analysis*, **19**, 267–284.

Banerjee, A., R.L. Lumsdaine and J.H. Stock (1992) Recursive and sequential tests of the unit-root and trend-break hypotheses: Theory and international evidence, *Journal of Business & Economic Statistics*, **10**, 271–287.

Banerjee, A., J.J. Dolado, J.W. Galbraith and D.F. Hendry (1993) *Co-integration, Error-Correction, and the Econometric Analysis of Non-Stationary Data*, Advanced Texts in Econometrics, Oxford University Press, Oxford, UK.

Banerjee, A., L. Cockerill and B. Russell (2001) An I(2) analysis of inflation and the markup, *Journal of Applied Econometrics*, **16**, 221–240.

Baumol, W.J. (1952) The transactions demand for cash: An inventory theoretic approach, *Quarterly Journal of Economics*, **66**, 545–556.

Ben-David, D., R.L. Lumsdaine and D.H. Papell (2001) Unit roots, postwar slowdowns and long-run growth: evidence from two structural break, *Mimeo*.

Black, F. (1976) Studies in stock price volatility changes, *Proceedings of the 1976 Business Meeting of the Business and Economics Section, American Statistical Association*, 177–181.

Blough, S.R. (1992) The relationship between power and level for generic unit root tests in finite samples, *Journal of Applied Econometrics*, **7**, 295–308.

Bollerslev, T. (1986) Generalized autoregressive conditional heteroscedasticity, *Journal of Econometrics*, **31**, 307–327.

Bollerslev, T. (1990) Modeling the coherence in short-run nominal exchange rates: a multivariate generalized ARCH approach, *Review of Economics and Statistics*, **72**, 498–505.

Bollerslev, T. and H.O. Mikkelsen (1996) Modeling and pricing long-memory in stock market volatility, *Journal of Econometrics*, **73**, 151–184.

Bollerslev, T. and J.M. Wooldridge (1992) Quasi-maximum likelihood estimation and inference in dynamic models with time-varying covariances, *Econometric Reviews*, **11**, 143–172.

Bollerslev, T., R.F. Engle and J.M. Wooldridge (1988) A capital asset pricing model with time varying covariances, *Journal of Political Economy*, **96**, 116–131.

Bossaerts, P. and P. Hillion (1999) Implementing statistical criteria to select return forecasting models: what do we learn? *Review of Financial Studies*, **12**, 315–342.

Boswijk, H.P. (2001) Testing for a unit root with near-integrated volatility, Tinbergen Institute Discussion Paper, 01-077. Tinbergen Institute, The Netherlands.

Boswijk, H.P. and J.A. Doornik (1999) Distribution approximations for cointegration tests with stationary exogenous regressors, Tinbergen Institute Discussion Paper, 99-012. Tinbergen Institute, The Netherlands.

Boswijk, H.P. and P.H Franses (1995) Periodic cointegration: representation and inference, *Review of Economics and Statistics*, **77**, 436–454.

Boswijk, H.P. and P.H Franses (1996) Unit roots in periodic autoregressions, *Journal of Time Series Analysis*, **17**, 221–245.

Boswijk, H.P., P.H. Franses and N. Haldrup (1997) Multiple unit roots in periodic autoregression, *Journal of Econometrics*, **80**, 167–193.

Box, G.E.P. and G.M. Jenkins (1970) *Time Series Analysis, Forecasting and Control*, Holden Day, San Francisco.

Breitung, J. (2000) The local power of some unit root tests for panel data, in B.H. Baltagi, T.B. Fomby, and R.C. Hill (eds) *Nonstationary Panels, Panel Cointegration, and Dynamic Panels, Advances in Econometrics*, Vol. 15, Elsevier Science, Amsterdam.

Breitung, J. (2002) A parametric approach to the estimation of cointegration vectors in panel data, *Mimeo*.

Campbell, J.Y. and P. Perron (1991) Pitfalls and Opportunities: What macroeconomists should know about unit roots, in O.J. Blanchard and S. Fischer (eds) *NBER Economics Annual 1991*, MIT Press, Cambridge, MA.

Campbell, J.Y. and R.J. Shiller (1987). Cointegration and tests of present value models. *Journal of Political Economy*, **95**, 1062–1088.

Carrion-i-Silvestre, J.L., A. Sanso-i-Rossello and M.A. Ortuno (2001) Unit root and stationarity tests wedding, *Economics Letters*, **70**, 1–8.

Cheung, Y.-W. and K.S. Lai (1993) Finite-sample sizes of Johansen's likelihood ratio tests for cointegration, *Oxford Bulletin of Economics and Statistics*, **55**, 313–328.

Chiang, M-H. and C. Kao (2002) *Nonstationary Panel Time Series Using NPT 1.3*, A user guide, Center for Policy Research, Syracuse University, New York.

Choi, I. (1999) Unit root tests for panel data, Department of Economics Working Paper, Kookmin University, Korea.

Chong, Y.Y. and D.F. Hendry (1986) Econometrics evaluation of linear macroeconomic models, *Review of Economic Studies*, **53**, 671–690.

Clark, T.E. and M.E. McCracken (2000) Not-for-publication appendix to 'Tests of equal forecast accuracy and encompassing for nested models'. Manuscript, Federal Reserve Bank of Kansas City (currently available from www.kc.frb.org).

Clark, T.E. and M.E. McCracken (2001) Tests of equal forecast accuracy and encompassing for nested models, *Journal of Econometrics*, **105**, 85–110.

Clemente, J., A. Montanes and M. Reyes (1998) Testing for a unit root in variables with a double change in the mean, *Economics Letters*, **59**, 175–182.

Clements, M.P. and G.E. Mizon (1991) Empirical analysis of macroeconomic time series: VAR and structural models, *European Economic Review*, **35**, 887–932.

Clements, M. and D.F. Hendry (1998) *Forecasting Economic Time Series*, Cambridge University Press, Cambridge, UK.

Clements, M. and D.F. Hendry (1999) *Forecasting Non-stationary Economic Time Series*, Zeuthen Lecture Book Series, MIT Press, Cambridge, MA.

Coe, D.T. and E. Helpman (1995) International R&D spillovers, *European Economic Review*, **39**, 859–887.

Cosimano, T.F. and D.W. Jansen (1988) Estimates of the variance of U.S. inflation based upon the ARCH model: comment, *Journal of Money, Credit and Banking*, **20**, 409–421.

Culver, S.E and D.H. Papell (1997) Is there a unit root in the inflation rate? Evidence from sequential break and panel data model, *Journal of Applied Econometrics*, **12**, 435–444.

Cumby, R.S., S. Figlewski and J. Hasbrouck, (1993) Forecasting volatility and correlations with EGARCH models, *Journal of Derivatives*, Winter, 51–63.

Da Silva Lopes, A.C.B. (2001) *The Order of Integration for Quarterly Macroeconomic Time Series: A Simple Testing Strategy*, Instituto Superior de Economia e Gestão, Lisbon.

Davidson, J. (1998) Structural relations, cointegration and identification: Some simple results and their application, *Journal of Econometrics*, **87**, 87–113.

Davidson, R. and J.G. MacKinnon (1993) *Estimation and Inference in Econometrics*, Oxford University Press, Oxford, UK.

DeJong, D.N., J.C. Nankervis and N.E. Savin (1992) Integration versus trend stationarity in time series, *Econometrica*, **60**, 423–433.

Dickey, D.A. (1976) Estimation and hypothesis testing for nonstationary time series, Ph.D. dissertation, Iowa State University, IA.

Dickey, D.A. and W.A. Fuller (1979) Distribution of the estimators for autoregressive time series with a unit root, *Journal of the American Statistical Association*, **74**, 427–431.

Dickey, D.A. and W.A. Fuller (1981) Likelihood ratio statistics for autoregressive time series with a unit root, *Econometrica*, **49**, 1057–1072.

Dickey, D.A. and S.G. Pantula (1987) Determining the order of differencing in autoregressive processes, *Journal of Business and Economic Statistics*, **15**, 455–461.

Diebold, F.X. and R.S. Mariano (1995) Comparing predictive accuracy, *Journal of Business and Economic Statistics*, **13**, 253–263.

Diebold, F.X. and J.A. Nason (1990) Nonparametric exchange rate prediction, *Journal of International Economics*, **28**, 315–332.

Ding, Z., C.W.J. Granger and R.F. Engle (1993) A long memory property of stock market returns and a new model, *Journal of Empirical Finance*, **1**, 83–106.

Doornik, J.A. (1999) Approximations to the asymptotic distributions of cointegration tests, in M. McAleer and L. Oxley (eds), *Practical Issues in Cointegration Analysis*, Blackwell, Oxford.

Doornik, J. and H. Hansen (1993) *A Practical Test of Multivariate Normality*, Nuffield College, University of Oxford, Oxford, UK.

Doornik, J. and D.F. Hendry (1994) *PcFiml Version 8: Interactive Econometric Modelling of Dynamic Systems*, Institute of Economics and Statistics, University of Oxford, Oxford, UK.

Doornik, J. and D.F. Hendry (2001) *Modelling Dynamic Systems Using PcGive*, Timberlake Consultants, London.

Elliott, G., T.J. Rothenberg, and J.H. Stock (1996) Efficient tests for an autoregressive unit root, *Econometrica*, **64**, 813–836.

Enders, W. and C.W.J. Granger (1998) Unit root tests and asymmetric adjustment with an example using the term structure of interest rates, *Journal of Business and Economic Statistics*, **16**, 304–311.

Enders, W. and P.L. Siklos (2001) Cointegration and threshold adjustment, *Journal of Business and Economic Statistics*, **19**, 166–177.

Engle, R.F. (1982) Autoregressive conditional heteroscedasticity with estimates of the variance of United Kingdom inflation, *Econometrica*, **50**, 987–1007.

Engle, R.F. (1983) Estimates of the variance of U.S. inflation based on the ARCH model, *Journal of Money, Credit and Banking*, **15**, 286–301.

Engle, R.F. and T. Bollerslev (1986) Modeling the persistence of conditional variances, *Econometric Reviews*, **5**, 1–50.

Engle, R.F. and G. Gonzalez-Rivera (1991) Semiparametric ARCH model, *Journal of Business and Economic Statistics*, **9**, 345–360.

Engle, R.F. and C.W.J. Granger (1987) Cointegration and error correction: Representation, estimation and testing, *Econometrica*, **55**, 251–276.

Engle, R.F., C.W.J. Granger and D. Kraft (1984) Combining competing forecasts of inflation using a bivariate ARCH Model, *Journal of Economic Dynamics and Control*, **8**, 151–165.

Engle, R.F., Hendry, D.F. and J.-F. Richard (1983) Exogeneity, *Econometrica*, **51**, 277–304.

Engle, R.F. and D.F. Hendry (1993) Testing super exogeneity and invariance in regression models, *Journal of Econometrics*, **56**, 119–139.

Engle, R.F. and Kroner, K.F. (1995) Multivariate simultaneous generalized ARCH, *Econometric Theory*, **11**, 122–150.

Engle, R.F. and Ng, V.K. (1993) Measuring and testing the impact of news on volatility, *Journal of Finance*, **48**, 1749–1778.

Engle, R.F. and B.S. Yoo (1991) Cointegrated economic time series: An overview with new results, in R.F. Engle and C.W.J. Granger (eds) *Long-Run Economic Relationships*, pp. 237–266, Oxford University Press, Oxford, UK.

Engle, R.F., D.M. Lilien and R.P. Robins (1987) Estimating time-varying risk premia in the term structure: The ARCH-M model, *Econometrica*, **55**, 391–407.

Engle, R.F., C.W.J. Granger, S. Hylleberg and H.S. Lee (1993) Seasonal cointegration: The Japanese Consumption Function, *Journal of Econometrics*, **55**, 275–298.

Ermini, L. and D. Chang (1996) Testing the joint hypothesis of rationality and neutrality under seasonal cointegration, *Journal of Econometrics*, **74**, 363–386.

Ericsson, N.R. (1992) Parameter constancy, mean squared forecast errors, and measuring forecast performance: An exposition, extensions, and illustration, *Journal of Policy Modeling*, **14**, 465–495.

Ericsson, N.R., D.F. Hendry and H.-A. Tran (1992) *Cointegration, Seasonality, Encompassing, and the Demand for Money in the United Kingdom*, Discussion Paper, Board of Governors of the Federal Reserve System, Washington, DC.

Fama, E.F. (1981) Stock returns, real activity, inflation and money, *American Economic Review*, **71**, 545–565.

Favero, C.A. (2001) *Applied Macroeconometrics*, Oxford University Press, Oxford, UK.

Fernandez, C. and M. Steel (1998) On Bayesian modelling of fat tails and skewness, *Journal of the American Statistical Association*, **93**, 359–371.

Fernandez-Rodriguez, F., S. Sosvilla-Rivero and J. Andrada-Felix (1999) Exchange rate forecasts with simultaneous nearest neighbour methods: evidence from the EMS, *International Journal of Forecasting*, **15**, 383–392.

Figlewski, S. (1997) Forecasting volatility, *Financial Markets, Institutions and Instruments*, **6**, 1–88.

Fischer, A.M. (1993) Weak exogeneity and dynamic stability in cointegrated VARs, *Economic Letters*, **43**, 167–170.

Franses, P.H. (1993) A method to select between periodic cointegration and seasonal cointegration, *Economic Letters*, **41**, 7–10.

Franses, P.H. (1994) A Multivariate Approach to modeling univariate seasonal time series, *Journal of Econometrics*, **63**, 133–151.

Franses, P-H. and B. Hobijn (1997) Critical values for unit root tests in seasonal time series, *Journal of Applied Statistics*, **24**, 25–47.

Franses, P-H. and R. Kunst (1998) On the role of seasonal intercepts in seasonal cointegration, *Oxford Bulletin of Economics and Statistics*, **61**, 409–433.

Franses, P-H. and R.M. Kunst (1999) On the role of seasonal intercepts in seasonal cointegration, *Oxford Bulletin of Economics and Statistics*, **61**(3), 409–433.

Franses, P-H. and M. McAleer (1998) Testing for unit roots and nonlinear data transformations, *Journal of Time Series Analysis*, **19**, 147–164.

Franses, P-H. and M. McAleer (1999) Cointegration analysis of seasonal time series, in M. McAleer and L. Oxley (eds), *Practical Issues in Cointegration Analysis*, Blackwell, Oxford, UK.

Franses, P.H. and M. McAleer (2002) Financial volatility: An introduction, *Journal of Applied Econometrics*, **17**, 419–424.

Franses, P-H. and T.J. Vogelsang (1998) On seasonal cycles, unit roots, and mean shifts, *Review of Economics and Statistics*, **80**, 231–240.

Franses, P-H. and A.M.R. Taylor (2000) Determining the order of differencing in seasonal time series processes, *Econometrics Journal*, **3**, 250–264.

French, K., Schwert, G.W. and R. Stambaugh (1987) Expected stock returns and volatility, *Journal of Financial Economics*, **19**, 3–29.

Friedman, M. (1977) Nobel lecture: inflation and unemployment, *Journal of Political Economy*, **85**, 451–472.

Friedman, M. and A.J. Schwartz (1982) *Monetary Trends in the United States and the United Kingdom: Their Relation to Income, Prices, and Interest Rates, 1867–1975*, University of Chicago Press, Chicago.

Fuller, W.A. (1976) *Introduction to Statistical Time Series*, John Wiley & Sons, New York.

Gabriel, V.J., Z. Psaradakis and M. Sola (2002) A simple method of testing for cointegration subject to multiple regime shifts, *Economics Letters*, **76**, 213–221.

Garratt, A., K. Lee, M.H. Pesaran and Y. Shin (1999) A structural cointegrating VAR approach to macroeconomic modelling, *Mimeo*.

Garratt, A., K. Lee, M.H. Pesaran and Y. Shin (2001) A long run structural macroeconometric model of the UK, *Mimeo*.

Ghysels, E. and D.R. Osborn (2001) *The Econometric Analysis of Seasonal Time Series*, Cambridge University Press, Cambridge, UK.

Ghysels, E. and P. Perron (1993) The effect of seasonal adjustment filters on tests for a unit root, *Journal of Econometrics*, **55**, 57–98.

Ghysels, E., H.S. Lee and J. Noh (1994) Testing for unit roots in seasonal time series, *Journal of Econometrics*, **62**, 415–442.

Ghysels, E., A. Hall and H.S. Lee (1996) On periodic structures and testing for seasonal unit roots, *Journal of the American Statistical Association*, **91**, 1551–1559.

GiveWin (2001) *GiveWin: An Interface to Empirical Modelling*, Timberlake Consultants, London.

Glosten, L.R., R. Jagannathan and D.E. Runkle (1993) On the relation between the expected value and the volatility of the nominal excess return on stocks, *Journal of Finance*, **48**, 1779–1801.

Gonzalo, J. and T-H. Lee (1998) Pitfalls in testing for long run relationships, *Journal of Econometrics*, **86**, 129–154.

Granger, C.W.J. and R. Joyeux (1980) An introduction to long-memory time series models and fractional differencing, *Journal of Time Series Analysis*, **1**, 15–29.

Granger, C.W.J. and P. Newbold (1973) Some comments on the evaluation of economic forecasts, *Applied Economics*, **5**, 35–47.

Granger, C.W.J. and P. Newbold (1986) *Forecasting Economic Time Series*, 2nd edn, Academic Press, New York.

Greene, W.H. (2000) *Econometric Analysis*, 4th edn, Prentice Hall International, London.

Greenslade, J.V., S.G. Hall and S.G.B. Henry (2002) On the identification of cointegrated systems in small samples: A modelling strategy with an application to UK wages and prices, *Journal of Economic Dynamics and Control*, **26**, 1517–1537.

Gregory, A.W. and B.E. Hansen (1996) Residual-based tests for cointegration in models with regime shifts, *Journal of Econometrics*, **70**, 99–126.

Grier, K.B. and M.J. Perry (2000) The effects of real and nominal uncertainty on inflation and output growth: Some GARCH-M evidence, *Journal of Applied Econometrics*, **15**, 45–58.

Hadri, K. (1999) Testing the null hypothesis of stationarity against the alternative of a unit root in panel data with serially correlated errors, Manuscript, Department of Economics and Accounting, University of Liverpool, Liverpool.

Hadri, K. (2000) Testing for stationarity in heterogenous panel data, *Econometrics Journal*, **3**, 148–161.

Haldrup, N. (1994) The asymptotics of single-equation cointegration regressions with I(1) and I(2) Variables, *Journal of Econometrics*, **63**, 153–181.

Hansen, B.E. (1992) Efficient estimation and testing of cointegrating vectors in the presence of deterministic trends, *Journal of Econometrics*, **53**, 87–121.

Hansen, H. and K. Juselius (1994) *Manual to Cointegration Analysis of Time Series CATS in RATS*, Institute of Economics, University of Copenhagen, Copenhagen.

Harris, R.I.D. (1985) Interrelated demand for factors of production in the UK engineering industry, 1968–1981, *Economic Journal*, **95**, 1049–1068 (reprinted in G. Galeazzi and D.S. Hamermesh (eds) (1993) *Dynamic Labor Demand and Adjustment Costs*, Edward Elgar, Aldershot, UK).

Harris, R.I.D. (1992a) Testing for unit roots using the augmented Dickey–Fuller test: Some issues relating to the size, power and the lag structure of the test, *Economic Letters*, **38**, 381–386.

Harris, R.I.D. (1992b) Small sample testing for unit roots, *Oxford Bulletin of Economics and Statistics*, **54**, 615–625.

Harris, R.I.D. (1995) *Using Cointegration Analysis in Econometric Modelling*, Prentice Hall/Harvester Wheatsheaf, Hemel Hempstead, UK.

Harris, R.I.D. and G. Judge (1998) Small sample testing for cointegration using the bootstrap approach, *Economics Letters*, **58**, 31–37.

Harris, R.D.F. and E. Tzavalis (1999) Inference for unit roots in dynamic panels where the time dimension is fixed, *Journal of Econometrics*, **91**, 201–226.

Harvey, A.C. (1990) *The Econometric Analysis of Time Series*, 2nd edn, Philip Allan, Oxford, UK.

Harvey, D.I., S.J. Leybourne and P. Newbold (1997) Testing the equality of prediction mean squared errors, *International Journal of Forecasting*, **13**, 281–291.

Harvey, D.I., S.J. Leybourne and P. Newbold (1998) Tests for forecast encompassing, *Journal of Business and Economic Statistics*, **16**, 254–259.

Harvey, D.I., S.J. Leybourne and P. Newbold (2001) Innovation outlier unit root tests with an endogenously determined break in level, *Oxford Bulletin of Economics and Statistics*, **63**, 559–575.

Harvey, D.I., S.J. Leybourne and P. Newbold (2002) Seasonal unit root tests with seasonal mean shifts, *Economics Letters*, **76**, 295–302.

Hendry, D.F. (1995) *Dynamic Econometrics*, Oxford University Press, Oxford, UK.

Hendry, D.F. and M.P. Clements (2002) Economic forecasting: Some lessons from recent research, *Mimeo*.

Hendry, D.F. and J.A. Doornik (1994) Modelling linear dynamic econometric systems, *Scottish Journal of Political Economy*, **41**, 1–33.

Hendry, D.F. and N.R. Ericsson (1991) Modelling the demand for narrow money in the United Kingdom and the United States, *European Economic Review*, **35**, 833–881.

Hendry, D.F., and G.E. Mizon (1993) Evaluating dynamic econometric models by encompassing the VAR, in P.C.P. Phillips (ed.), *Models, Methods, and Applications of Econometrics*, Basil Blackwell, Oxford, UK.

Hendry, D.F., A.R. Pagan, and J.D. Sargan (1984) Dynamic specification, in Z. Griliches and M.D. Intriligator (eds) *Handbook of Econometrics*, Vol. II, North-Holland, Amsterdam.

Higgins, M.L. and A.K. Bera (1992) A class of nonlinear ARCH models, *International Economic Review*, **33**, 137–158.

Hosking, J.R.M. (1981) Fractional differencing, *Biometrika*, **68**, 165–176.

Huang, B-N., C-W. Yang and J.W-S. Hu (2000) Causality and cointegration of stock markets among the United States, Japan, and the South China Growth Triangle, *International Review of Financial Analysis*, **9**, 281–297.

Hylleberg, S., Engle, R.F., C.W.J Granger, and B.S. Yoo (1990) Seasonal integration and co-integration, *Journal of Econometrics*, **44**, 215–228.

Im, K.S., M.H. Pesaran and Y. Shin (1995, 1997) Testing for unit roots in heterogeneous panels, *Journal of Econometrics* (forthcoming).

Inder, B. (1993) Estimating long-run relationships in economics: A comparison of different approaches, *Journal of Econometrics*, **57**, 53–68.

Inoue, A. (1999) Tests of cointegrating rank with a trend-break, *Journal of Econometrics*, **90**, 215–237.

Johansen, S. (1988) Statistical analysis of cointegration vectors, *Journal of Economic Dynamics and Control*, **12**, 231–254.

Johansen, S. (1991) *A Statistical Analysis of Cointegration for I(2) Variables*, University of Copenhagen, Copenhagen.

Johansen, S. (1992a) Cointegration in partial systems and the efficiency of single equations analysis, *Journal of Econometrics*, **52**, 389–402.

Johansen, S. (1992b) Determination of cointegration rank in the presence of a linear trend, *Oxford Bulletin of Economics and Statistics*, **54**, 383–397.

Johansen, S. (1992c) *Identifying Restrictions of Linear Equations, Institute of Mathematical Statistics*, University of Copenhagen, Copenhagen.

Johansen, S. (1992d) Testing weak exogeneity and the order of cointegration in UK money demand, *Journal of Policy Modeling*, **14**, 313–334.

Johansen, S. (1995a) *Likelihood-based Inference in Cointegrated Vector Autoregressive Models*, Oxford University Press, Oxford, UK.

Johansen, S. (1995b) A statistical analysis of I(2) variables, *Econometric Theory*, **11**, 25–59.

Johansen, S. (2002a) A small sample correction for the test of cointegration rank in the vector autoregressive model, *Econometrica*, **70**, 1929–1961.

Johansen, S. (2002b) A small sample correction for tests of hypotheses on the cointegrating vectors, *Journal of Econometrics*, **111**, 195–221.

Johansen, S. and K. Juselius (1992) Testing structural hypotheses in a multivariate cointegration analysis of the PPP and the UIP for UK, *Journal of Econometrics*, **53**, 211–244.

Johansen, S. and K. Juselius (1994) Identification of the long-run and the short-run structure: An application to the ISLM model, *Journal of Econometrics*, **63**, 7–36.

Johansen, S. and B. Nielsen (1993) Asymptotics for cointegration rank tests in the presence of intervention dummies. *Manual for the Simulation Program DisCo*, Institute of Mathematical Statistics, University of Copenhagen, Copenhagen.

Johansen, S., R. Mosconi and B. Nielsen (2000) Cointegration analysis in the presence of structural breaks in the deterministic trend, *Econometrics Journal*, **3**, 216–249.

Johnston, J. (1984) *Econometric Methods*, 3rd edn, McGraw-Hill International, London.

Johnston, J. and J. Dinardo (1997) *Econometric Methods*, 4th edn, McGraw-Hill International, New York.

Jorion, P. (1995) Predicting volatility in the foreign exchange market, *Journal of Finance*, **50**, 507–528.

Juselius, K. (1995) Do purchasing power parity and uncovered interest rate parity hold in the long-run? – An example of likelihood inference in a multivariate times-series model, *Journal of Econometrics*, **69**, 211–240.

Kahn, J.A. and M. Ogaki (1992) A consistent test for the null of stationarity against the alternative of a unit root, *Economic Letters*, **39**, 7–11.

Kao, C. (1999) Spurious regression and residual-based tests for cointegration in panel data, *Journal of Econometrics*, **90**, 1–44.

Kao, C. and M.H. Chiang (2000) On the estimation and inference of a cointegrated regression in panel data, in B.H. Baltagi, T.B. Fomby and R.C. Hill (eds), *Nonstationary Panels, Panel Cointegration, and Dynamic Panels, Advances in Econometrics*, Vol. 15, Elsevier Science, Amsterdam.

Karlsson, S. and M. Lothgren (2000) On the power and interpretation of panel unit root tests, *Economics Letters*, **66**, 249–255.

Kim, K. and P. Schmidt (1993) Unit root tests with conditional heteroscedasticity, *Journal of Econometrics*, **59**, 287–300.

Kiviet, J. and G.D.A. Phillips (1992) Exact similar tests for unit roots and cointegration, *Oxford Bulletin of Economics and Statistics*, **54**, 349–367.

Kleibergen, F. and H.K. van Dijk (1994) Direct cointegration testing in error correction models, *Journal of Econometrics*, **63**, 61–103.

Kremers, J.J.M., N.R. Ericsson and J. Dolado (1992) The power of co-integration tests, *Oxford Bulletin of Economics and Statistics*, **54**, 325–348.

Kwiatkowski, D., P.C.B. Phillips, P. Schmidt and Y. Shin (1992) Testing the null of stationarity against the alternative of a unit root, *Journal of Econometrics*, **54**, 159–178.

Laidler, D.E.W. (1984) The 'buffer stock' notion in monetary economics, *Economic Journal*, **94**(suppl.), 17–94.

Larsson, R., J. Lyhagen and M. Lothgren (2001) Likelihood-based cointegration tests in heterogeneous panels, *Econometrics Journal*, **4**, 109–142.

Laurent, S. and J-P. Peters (2002a) G@RCH 2.2: an Ox package for estimating and forecasting various ARCH models, *Journal of Economic Surveys*, 16, 447–485.

Laurent, S. and J-P. Peters (2002b) A tutorial for G@RCH 2.3, a complete *Ox* package for estimating and forecasting ARCH models, *Mimeo*, Department of Economics, University of Liège, Liège, Belgium and Department of Quantitative Economics, University of Amsterdam, Amsterdam.

LeBaron, D.A. (1992) Forecast improvements using a volatility index, *Journal of Applied Economics*, **7**, 137–149.

Lee, H.S. (1992) Maximum likelihood inference on cointegration and seasonal cointegration, *Journal of Econometrics*, **54**, 1–47.

Lee, H.S. and P. Siklos (1995) A note on the critical values for the maximum likelihood (seasonal) cointegration tests, *Economics Letters*, **49**, 137–145.

Lee, H.S. and P. Siklos (1997) The role of seasonality in time series: Reinterpreting money-output causality in US data, *International Journal of Forecasting*, **13**, 301–391.

Levin, A. and C.F. Lin (1992) *Unit Root Test in Panel Data: Asymptotic and Finite Sample Properties*, Discussion Paper #92-93, University of California at San Diego.

Levin, A. and C.F. Lin (1993) *Unit Root Test in Panel Data: New Results*, Discussion Paper #93-56, University of California at San Diego.

Levtchenkova, S., A. Pagan, and J. Robertson (1999) Shocking stories, in M. McAleer and L. Oxley (eds), *Practical Issues in Cointegration Analysis*, Blackwell, Oxford, UK.

Lin, J.-L. and R.S. Tsay (1996) Cointegration constraints and forecasting: An empirical examination, *Journal of Applied Econometrics*, **11**, 519–538.

Ling, S. and W.K. Li (1997) *Estimating and Testing for Unit Root Processes with GARCH(1, 1) Errors*, Technical Report 140, Department of Statistics and Actuarial Science, The University of Hong Kong.

Ling, S. and W.K. Li (1998) Limiting distributions of maximum likelihood estimators for unstable autoregressive moving-average time series with general autoregressive heteroskedastic errors, *Annals of Statistics*, **26**, 84–125.

Lucas, R.E. (1976) Econometric policy evaluation: A critique, in K. Brunner and A. Meltzer (eds), *The Phillips Curve and Labor Markets*, Vol. 1 of Carnegie-Rochester Conferences on Public Policy, North-Holland, Amsterdam.

Lutkepohl, H. and P. Saikkonen (1999) Order selection in testing for the cointegration rank of a VAR process, in R.F. Engle and H. White (eds), *Cointegration, Causality, and Forecasting*, Oxford University Press, Oxford, UK.

Lutkepohl, H., P. Saikkonen and C. Trenkler (2001) Maximum eigenvalue versus trace tests for the cointegrating rank of a VAR process, *Econometrics Journal*, **4**, 287–310.

MacKinnon, J. (1991) Critical values for co-integration tests, in R.F. Engle and C.W.J. Granger (eds), *Long-Run Economic Relationships*, pp. 267–276, Oxford University Press, Oxford, UK.

Maddala, G.S. and I-M. Kim (1998) *Unit Roots, Cointegration, and Structural Change*, Cambridge University Press, Cambridge, UK.

Maddala, G.S. and S. Wu (1999) A comparative study of unit root tests with panel data and a new simple test, *Oxford Bulletin of Economics and Statistics*, **61**, 631–652.

McCoskey, Suzanne K. (2002) Convergence in Sub-Saharan Africa: A nonstationary panel data approach, *Applied Economics*, **34**, 819–829.

McCoskey, S. and C. Kao (1998) A residual-based test of the null of cointegration in panel data, *Econometric Reviews*, **17**, 57–84.

Meade, N. (2002) A comparison of the accuracy of short term foreign exchange forecasting methods, *International Journal of Forecasting*, **18**, 67–83.

Meese, R.A. and A.K. Rose (1990) Non-linear, non-parametric, non-essential exchange rate estimation, *American Economic Review*, **80**, 192–196.

Mincer, J. and V. Zarnowitz, (1969) The evaluation of economic forecasts, in J. Mincer (ed.), *Economic Forecasts and Expectations*, National Bureaus of Economic Research, New York.

Murray, C.J. and D.H. Papell (2000) Testing for unit roots in panels in the presence of structural change with an application to OECD unemployment, in B.H. Baltagi, T.B. Fomby and R.C. Hill (eds), *Nonstationary Panels, Panel Cointegration, and Dynamic Panels, Advances in Econometrics*, Vol. 15, Elsevier Science, Amsterdam.

Muscatelli, V.A. and S. Hurn (1991). Cointegration and dynamic time series models, *Journal of Economic Surveys*, **6**, 1–43.

Nankervis, J.C. and N.E. Savin (1985) Testing the autoregressive parameter with the *t*-statistic, *Journal of Econometrics*, **27**, 143–161.

Nasseh, A. and J. Strauss (2000) Stock prices and domestic and international macroeconomic activity: A cointegration approach, *The Quarterly Review of Economics and Finance*, **40**, 229–245.

Nelson, C.R. (1972) The prediction performance of the FRB-MIT-PENN model of the U.S. Economy, *American Economic Review*, **62**, 902–917.

Nelson, D. (1991) Conditional heteroscedasticity in asset returns: A new approach, *Econometrica*, **59**, 347–370.

Ng, S. and P. Perron (1995) Unit root tests in ARMA models with data dependent methods for the truncation lag, *Journal of the American Statistical Association*, **90**, 268–281.

Ng, S. and P. Perron (2001) Lag length selection and the construction of unit root test with good size and power, *Econometrica*, **69**, 1519–1554.

O'Connell, P.G.J. (1998) The overevaluation of purchasing power parity. *Journal of International Econmics*, **44**, 1–19.

Ohtani, K. (2002) Exact critical values of unit root tests with drift and trend, *Applied Economics Letters*, **9**, 137–145.

Osborn, D.R. (1990) A survey of seasonality in UK macroeconomic variables, *International Journal of Forecasting*, **6**, 327–336.

Osborn, D.R., A.P.L. Chui, J.P. Smith and C.R. Birchenhall (1988) Seasonality and the order of integration for consumption, *Oxford Bulletin of Economics and Statistics*, **50**, 361–377.

Osterwald-Lenum, M. (1992) A note with quantiles of the asymptotic distribution of the ML cointegration rank test statistics, *Oxford Bulletin of Economics and Statistics*, **54**, 461–472.

Pantula, S.G. (1986) Comment on modelling the persistence of conditional variances, *Econometric Reviews*, **5**, 71–74.

Pantula, S.G. (1988) Estimation of autoregressive models with ARCH errors, *Sankhya*, **B50**, 119–138.

Paruolo, P. (1996) On the determination of integration indices in I(2) systems, *Journal of Econometrics*, **72**, 313–356.

Pedroni, P. (1995) *Panel Cointegration: Asymptotic and Finite Sample Properties of Pooled Time Series Tests, with an Application to the PPP Hypothesis*, Indiana University Working Papers in Economics, No. 95-013 (June), Indiana University, Indianapolis, IN.

Pedroni, P. (1999) Critical values for cointegration tests in heterogeneous panels with multiple regressors, *Oxford Bulletin of Economics and Statistics*, **61**, 653–678.

Pedroni, P. (2000) Fully modified OLS for heterogeneous cointegrated panels, in B.H. Baltagi, T.B. Fomby and R.C. Hill (eds), *Nonstationary Panels, Panel Cointegration, and Dynamic Panels, Advances in Econometrics*, Vol. 15, Elsevier Science, Amsterdam.

Pedroni, P. (2001) Purchasing power parity tests in cointegrated panels, *Review of Economics and Statistics*, **83**, 727–731.

Perron, P. (1988) Trends and random walks in macroeconomic time series: Further evidence from a new approach, *Journal of Economic Dynamics and Control*, **12**, 297–332.

Perron, P. (1989) The Great Crash, the Oil Shock and the unit root hypothesis, *Econometrica*, **57**, 1361–1402.

Perron, P. (1990) Testing for a unit root in a time series with a changing mean, *Journal of Business and Economic Statistics*, **8**, 153–162.

Perron, P. (1994) Trend, unit root and structural change in macroeconomic time series, in B. Bhaskara Rao (ed.), *Cointegration for the Applied Economist*, Macmillan Press, Basingstoke, UK.

Perron, P. and S. Ng (1996) Useful modifications to some unit root tests with dependent errors and their local asymptotic properties, *Review of Economic Studies*, **63**, 435–463.

Pesaran, M.H. and Y. Shin (1998) Generalized impulse response analysis in linear multivariate models, *Economics Letters*, **58**, 17–29.

Pesaran M.H. and A.G. Timmermann (1995) Predictability of stock returns: Robustness and economic significance, *Journal of Finance*, **50**, 1201–1228.

Pesaran M.H. and A.G. Timmermann (2000) A recursive modeling approach to predicting UK stock returns, *Economic Journal*, **110**, 159–191.

Pesaran, M.H., Y. Shin and R.J. Smith (2000) Structural analysis of vector error correction models with exogenous I(1) variables, *Journal of Econometrics*, **97**, 293–343.

Phillips, P.C.B. (1987) Time series regression with a unit root, *Econometrica*, **55**, 277–301.

Phillips, P.C.B. and S.N. Durlauf (1986) Multiple time series regression with integrated processes, *Review of Economic Studies*, **53**, 473–495.

Phillips, P.C.B. and P. Perron (1988) Testing for a unit root in times series regression, *Biometrica*, **75**, 335–446.

Phillips, P.C.B. and B.E. Hansen (1990) Statistical inference in instrumental variables regression with $I(1)$ processes, *Review of Economic Studies*, **57**, 99–125.

Podivinsky, J.M. (1992) Small sample properties of tests of linear restrictions on cointegrating vectors and their weights, *Economic Letters*, **39**, 13–18.

Psaradakis, Z (1994) A Comparison of tests of linear hypotheses in cointegrated vector autoregressive models, *Economic Letters*, **45**, 137–144.

Quintos, C.E. (1997) Stability tests in error correction models, *Journal of Econometrics*, **82**, 289–315.

Rahbek, A. Hansen, E. and J.G. Dennis (2002) ARCH innovations and their impact on cointegration rank testing, *Mimeo*, Department of Statistics and Operations Research, University of Copenhagen, Copenhagen.

Rapach, D.E. (2002) Are real GDP levels nonstationary? Evidence from panel data tests, *Southern Economic Journal*, **68**(3), 473–495.

Reimers, H.-E (1992) Comparisons of tests for multivariate cointegration, *Statistical Papers*, **33**, 335–359.

Said, S.E. and D.A. Dickey (1984) Testing for unit roots in autoregressive-moving average models of unknown order, *Biometrika*, **71**, 599–607.

Sargan, J.D. (1964) Wages and prices in the United Kingdom: A study in econometric methodology, in P.E. Hart, G. Mills and J.K. Whitaker (eds), *Econometric Analysis for National Economic Planning*, pp. 25–63, Butterworth, London.

Sargan, J.D. and A. Bhargava (1983) Testing residuals from least squares regression for being generated by the Gaussian random walk, *Econometrica*, **51**, 153–174.

Schwert, G.W. (1989) Tests for unit roots: A Monte Carlo investigation, *Journal of Business and Economic Statistics*, **7**, 147–159.

Schwert, G.W. (1990) Stock volatility and the crash of '87, *Review of Financial Studies*, **3**, 77–102.

Seo, B. (1999) Distribution theory for unit root tests with conditional heteroscedasticity, *Journal of Econometrics*, **91**, 113–144.

Sims, C. (1980) Macroeconomics and reality, *Econometrica*, **48**, 1–48.

Smith, J. and J. Otero (1997) Structural breaks and seasonal integration, *Economic Letters*, **56**, 13–19.

Smith, R.J. and A.M.R. Taylor (2001) Recursive and rolling regression-based tests of the seasonal unit root hypothesis, *Journal of Econometrics*, **105**, 309–336.

Stock, J.H. (1987) Asymptotic properties of least-squares estimators of co-integrating vectors, *Econometrica*, **55**, 1035–1056.

Stock, J. and M. Watson (1993) A simple estimator of cointegrating vectors in higher order integrated systems, *Econometrica*, **61**, 783–820.

Taylor, M.P. and L. Sarno (1998) The behavior of real exchange rates during the post-Bretton Woods period. *Journal of International Economics*, **46**, 281–312.

Thomas, R.L. (1993) *Introductory Econometrics: Theory and Applications*, Longman, London.

Tobin, J. (1956) The interest-elasticity of transactions demand for cash, *Review of Economics and Statistics*, **38**, 241–247.

Tobin, J. (1958) Liquidity preference as behavior towards risk, *Review of Economic Studies*, **25**, 65–86.

Tse, T.Y. (1998) The conditional heteroscedasticity of the yen–dollar exchange rate, *Journal of Applied Econometrics*, **193**, 49–55.

Urbain, J.-P. (1992) On weak exogeneity in error correction models, *Oxford Bulletin of Economics and Statistics*, **54**, 187–207.

van der Weide, R. (2002) GO-GARCH: A multivariate generalized orthogonal GARCH model, *Journal of Applied Econometrics*, **17**, 549–564.

Weber, C.E. (2001) F-tests for lag length selection in augmented Dickey–Fuller regressions: some Monte Carlo evidence, *Applied Economics Letters*, **8**, 455–458.

Weiss, A. (1986) Asymtotic theory for ARCH models: Estimation and testing, *Econometric Theory*, **2**, 107–131.

West, K.D. (1988) Asymptotic normality, when regressors have a unit root, *Econometrica*, **56**, 1397–1418.

Wickens, M.R. and A.R. Pagan (1989) A survey of some recent econometric methods, *Economic Journal*, **99**, 962–1025.

Zakonian, J-M. (1994) Threshold heteroskedastic models, *Journal of Economic Dynamics and Control*, **15**, 931–955.

Zellner, A. (1962) An efficient method of estimating seemingly unrelated regressions and tests for aggregation bias. *Journal of the American Statistical Association*, **57**, 348–368.

Zivot, E. and D.W.K. Andrews (1992) Further evidence on Great Crash, the oil price shock and the unit root hypothesis, *Journal of Business and Economic Statistics*, **10**, 251–270.

Index